Everyday Family Suppers 2007

459 Family-Pleasing Choices for Easy, Heartwarming Weeknight Dishes

Welcome to *Everyday Family Suppers 2007*, a handy, one-stop source for the mouthwatering meals your gang adores. With this colorful kitchen helper, whipping up a delicious, home-made dinner has never been easier…no matter how busy your family's schedule becomes.

Direct from Pillsbury, America's most-trusted Test Kitchen, each chapter in this new line of cookbooks is chock-full of the comforting favorites your family enjoys most. Best of all, the recipes are timed right for workweek preparation and call for ingredients you likely have on hand.

Consider any of the effortless beef, chicken, pork or seafood entrees found here. Each is loaded with home-style flair and weeknight ease. Surprise your family with main courses such as Speedy Meat Loaf (p. 133), Barbecued Chicken Pizza (p. 176) or Maple-Glazed Pork Chops (p. 213).

Turn to the chapter "Stovetop Specialties" (p. 276) for skillet dishes that come together in a pinch, or see "Meal-in-One Wonders" (p. 34) featuring casseroles, stir-fries and other one-dish mainstays that keep menu planning to a mini-mum. You'll also enjoy "All-Time Favorites" (p. 4) for classics such as Beef Stew (p. 33), Easy Mac 'n Cheese (p. 17) and other surefire family pleasers.

Creating a soup-and-sandwich dinner is a snap with the 51 ideas that begin on page 70. And if you're looking for a simple side dish, see page 244 for dozens of easy options.

What meal would be complete without a satisfying finale? With "Swift Sweets & Snacks" (p. 310), you'll find 44 desserts perfect for everyday meals. Banana Roll-Ups (p. 317), Toaster Apple Sundaes (p. 321) and S'mores Nachos (p. 334) are sure to get thumbs-up reviews.

TIME-SAVING STRATEGIES

Today's cooks know that deciding what to make can sometimes take just as long as preparing it. To help, we've highlighted four types of week-night dishes that appear in this book:

* super fast: These recipes are perfect for busy work nights because they are table-ready in less than 30 minutes. Scattered throughout the book, the 194 lifesavers are dishes you will turn to time and again.

* slow cooked: Nothing's better than coming home to a sensational dinner that simmered to perfection all day. Let the welcoming aroma of a savory meal greet you at the door by taking advantage of our many slow-cooked recipes.

* plan ahead: Casseroles, marinated meats and baked goodies sometimes require extra moments in the oven or refrigerator. Low in hands-on work but high in flavor, these items are ideal for assem-bling early in the day or the night before.

Bake-Off® Contest Winners: Not only do these all-time favorites come from family cooks, but they have been deemed the best of the best in a Pillsbury Bake-Off® Contest.

You'll also find "Prep" and "Ready to Serve" timelines with many of the recipes. These guides help you choose the dish that best fits your schedule. In addition, two indexes make finding the perfect recipe a breeze. Helpful hints offer-ing ideas for menu options and ingredient substi-tutions are sprinkled throughout the book, too.

In fact, this brand-new line of cookbooks promises to make mealtime as easy as can be…even on your busiest nights. With *Everyday Family Suppers 2007*, you'll discover how simple it is to spend less time in the kitchen and more time creating mem-ories at the dinner table with your loved ones.

Everyday Family Suppers 2007

Our recipes have been tested in the Pillsbury Kitchens and meet our standards of easy preparation, reliability and great taste.

PUBLISHED BY
Taste of Home Books
Reiman Media Group, Inc.
5400 S. 60th St., Greendale WI 53129
www.reimanpub.com

This edition published by arrangement with Wiley Publishing, Inc.

Printed in U.S.A.

International Standard Book Number (10): 0-89821-582-X
International Standard Book Number (13): 978-0-89821-582-3
International Standard Serial Number: 1935-5157

CREDITS
General Mills, Inc.
PUBLISHER, COOKBOOKS & MAGAZINES: Sheila Burke
EDITOR, PILLSBURY COOKBOOKS: Sharon Secor
RECIPE DEVELOPMENT AND TESTING: Pillsbury Test Kitchens
PHOTOGRAPHY: General Mills Photo Studios and Image Center

Reiman Media Group, Inc.
PRESIDENT: Barbara Newton
EDITOR IN CHIEF: Catherine Cassidy
CREATIVE DIRECTOR: Ardyth Cope
VICE PRESIDENT/BOOKS: Heidi Reuter Lloyd
SENIOR BOOK EDITOR: Mark Hagen
ART DIRECTOR: Gretchen Trautman
LAYOUT DESIGNERS: Catherine Fletcher, Nancy Novak
PROOFREADER: Linne Bruskewitz
INDEXER: Jean Steiner
FOUNDER: Roy Reiman

For more great recipes, visit Pillsbury.com.

FRONT COVER PHOTOGRAPH:
Pizza Skillet Hot Dish, p. 121

BACK COVER PHOTOGRAPHS:
Black Forest Cherry Cake, p. 317
Easy Pork Chop Suey, p. 5
Skillet Turkey and Dressing, p. 51

contents

family-favorite beef stew ✳ p. 54

roast beef panini ✳ p. 90

italian sausage lasagna ✳ p. 194

toaster apple sundaes ✳ p. 321

all-time favorites

easy pork chop suey ✳ p. 7

grandma's chicken noodle soup ✳ p. 20

family heroes ✳ p. 24

penne with cheesy tomato-sausage sauce ✳ p. 29

do-ahead lasagna logs ✳ p. 23

ALL-TIME FAVORITES ✳ 5

tomato-olive-pesto pizza

READY TO SERVE: 20 MINUTES
SERVINGS: 4

∗ super fast

1 can (10-oz.) refrigerated pizza crust

⅓ cup purchased pesto

4 Italian plum tomatoes, thinly sliced

1 can (2¼-oz.) sliced ripe olives, drained

¼ cup finely chopped red onion

6 oz. shredded Italian cheese blend (1½ cups)

1. Heat oven to 425°F. Spray cookie sheet with nonstick cooking spray. Unroll dough; place on sprayed cookie sheet. Starting at center, press out dough with hands to form 13x9-inch rectangle.

2. Spread pesto evenly over dough. Top with tomatoes, olives, onion and cheese.

3. Bake at 425°F for 10 to 12 minutes or until crust is deep golden brown and cheese is melted.

Nutrition Information Per Serving: Calories 460 • Total Fat 25g • Saturated Fat 10g • Cholesterol 35mg • Sodium 1120mg • Total Carbohydrate 40g • Dietary Fiber 2g • Sugars 7g • Protein 19g. **Dietary Exchanges:** 2½ Starch • 1½ High-Fat Meat • 2½ Fat OR 2½ Carbohydrate • 1½ High-Fat Meat • 2½ Fat.

6 ∗ Pillsbury Everyday Family Suppers

easy pork chop suey

PREP TIME: 15 MINUTES
READY TO SERVE: 7 HOURS 30 MINUTES
SERVINGS: 5

* slow cooked

1 lb. boneless pork shoulder, cut into ¾-inch cubes

1 small onion, cut into ¼-inch wedges

1 can (5-oz.) sliced bamboo shoots, drained

½ cup purchased teriyaki baste and glaze

1 teaspoon grated gingerroot

1 package (1-lb.) frozen broccoli, carrots and water chestnuts, thawed, drained

2 cups uncooked instant white rice

2 cups water

1. In 4- to 6-quart slow cooker, combine pork, onion, bamboo shoots, teriyaki baste and glaze and gingerroot; mix well.

2. Cover; cook on Low setting for 5 to 7 hours.

3. About 15 minutes before serving, stir vegetables into pork mixture. Increase heat setting to High; cover and cook an additional 10 to 15 minutes or until the vegetables are tender.

4. Meanwhile, cook rice in 2 cups water as directed on package. Serve pork mixture over rice.

Nutrition Information Per Serving: Calories 430 • Total Fat 14g • Saturated Fat 5g • Cholesterol 55mg • Sodium 1180mg • Total Carbohydrate 54g • Dietary Fiber 3g • Sugars 16g • Protein 21g. **Dietary Exchanges:** 2½ Starch • 1 Fruit • 1 Vegetable • 2 Lean Meat • 1 Fat OR 3½ Carbohydrate • 1 Vegetable • 2 Lean Meat • 1 Fat.

skillet sweet-and-sour chicken

READY TO SERVE: 20 MINUTES
SERVINGS: 3

✳ **super fast**

- 1 package (12-oz.) frozen breaded cooked chicken nuggets
- 1½ cups uncooked instant white rice
- 1½ cups water
- 1 bag (1-lb. 5-oz.) frozen stir-fry vegetables with tangy sweet-and-sour sauce meal starter
- ¼ cup cashews or peanuts, if desired

1. Cook chicken nuggets as directed on package.

2. Cook rice in water as directed on package.

3. Meanwhile, in 10-inch skillet, combine frozen vegetables, contents of pineapple pouch and frozen sauce from packet; mix well. Cover; cook over medium-high heat for 7 to 10 minutes or until vegetables are crisp-tender, stirring frequently.

4. Add cooked chicken; stir until well coated. Serve over cooked rice; sprinkle with cashews.

Nutrition Information Per Serving: Calories 680 • Total Fat 19g • Saturated Fat 4g • Cholesterol 20mg • Sodium 1350mg • Total Carbohydrate 108g • Dietary Fiber 7g • Sugars 29g • Protein 19g. **Dietary Exchanges:** 3½ Starch • ½ High-Fat Meat • 2½ Fat • 3 Other Carbohydrate.

fiesta spaghetti

READY TO SERVE: 30 MINUTES
SERVINGS: 8
MICHELE C. SANTOS ✳ AUSTIN, TEXAS

- 16 oz. uncooked spaghetti
- 2 tablespoons olive oil
- ½ cup chopped onion
- 1 medium red bell pepper, chopped
- 1 lb. lean ground beef
- ⅓ cup sugar
- 1 package (1.25-oz.) taco seasoning mix
- 1 can (28-oz.) crushed tomatoes, undrained
- 1 can (8-oz.) tomato sauce
- 1 can (11-oz.) whole kernel corn with red and green peppers, drained
- 1 jar (4.5-oz.) sliced mushrooms, drained

  Grated Parmesan cheese, if desired

1. Cook spaghetti to desired doneness as directed on package. Drain; cover to keep warm.

2. Meanwhile, heat oil in 12-inch nonstick skillet over medium heat until hot. Add onion and bell pepper; cook 3 to 4 minutes or until tender, stirring occasionally. Remove from skillet. Add ground beef to same skillet; cook until thoroughly cooked, stirring frequently. Drain.

3. Add onion and bell pepper to ground beef; mix well. Add sugar, taco seasoning mix, tomatoes, tomato sauce, corn and mushrooms; mix well. Bring to a boil. Reduce heat to low; simmer 5 minutes, stirring occasionally. Serve over spaghetti. Sprinkle with cheese.

Nutrition Information Per Serving: Calories 490 • Total Fat 13g • Sodium 1050mg • Total Carbohydrate 72g • Protein 22g.

EASY ENTREE FROM TONIGHT'S EXTRAS

It's a snap to whip up a no-fuss meal by taking advantage of any leftover sauce from Fiesta Spaghetti. Simply warm the extra sauce in a microwave-safe bowl on Low until it's heated through. Spread the sauce over the cut side of English muffins, bagels or slices of French bread. Top with a sprinkling of shredded cheese and set under your oven's broiler until the cheese is melted. The individual pizzas are a surefire success everyone will enjoy!

summer pork kabobs

READY TO SERVE: 30 MINUTES
SERVINGS: 4

- **4** boneless pork loin chops, ¾-inch thick (1 lb.)
- **½** teaspoon seasoned salt or dried pork seasoning
- **2** small zucchini, cut into 12 (1-inch) pieces
- **8** medium mushrooms
- **1** medium red bell pepper, cut into 12 pieces
- **½** cup apricot preserves
- **1** tablespoon cider vinegar

1. Heat gas or charcoal grill. Sprinkle pork chops with seasoned salt; cut each chop into 4 pieces. Alternately thread pork pieces, zucchini, mushrooms and bell pepper equally onto each of 4 (12- to 14-inch) metal skewers. In small bowl, mix preserves and vinegar.

2. When grill is heated, place kabobs on gas grill over medium heat or on charcoal grill over medium coals. Brush kabobs with preserves mixture; cover grill. Cook 5 to 7 minutes. Turn kabobs; brush with preserves mixture. Cook covered 5 to 7 minutes longer or until pork is no longer pink in center.

Nutrition Information Per Serving: Calories 310 • Total Fat 9g • Saturated Fat 3g • Trans Fat 0g • Cholesterol 70mg • Sodium 230mg • Total Carbohydrate 33g • Dietary Fiber 2g • Sugars 22g • Protein 26g. **Dietary Exchanges:** 2 Other Carbohydrate • 1 Vegetable • 3½ Lean Meat.

easy chicken cacciatore

PREP TIME: 25 MINUTES
READY TO SERVE: 8 HOURS 25 MINUTES
SERVINGS: 4

* slow cooked

- 4 bone-in chicken thighs, skin removed
- 4 chicken drumsticks, skin removed
- 1 can (15-oz.) Italian-style tomato sauce
- 1 jar (4.5-oz.) whole mushrooms, drained
- 1 teaspoon dried oregano leaves
- 1 small onion, sliced
- 1 small green bell pepper, cut into 1-inch pieces
- 2 garlic cloves, minced
- ¼ cup water
- 2 tablespoons all-purpose flour

1. In 3¼- to 4-quart slow cooker, combine all ingredients except water and flour; stir gently to mix.

2. Cover; cook on Low setting for 6 to 8 hours.

3. About 15 minutes before serving, with slotted spoon, remove chicken and vegetables from slow cooker; place in serving bowl. Cover to keep warm.

4. In small bowl, blend water and flour until smooth. Stir into liquid in slow cooker. Increase heat setting to High; cover and cook an additional 5 to 10 minutes or until thickened. Stir well; spoon mixture over chicken.

Nutrition Information Per Serving: Calories 340 • Total Fat 17g • Saturated Fat 4g • Cholesterol 105mg • Sodium 690mg • Total Carbohydrate 14g • Dietary Fiber 3g • Sugars 8g • Protein 32g. Dietary Exchanges: ½ Starch • 1 Vegetable • 4 Lean Meat • 1 Fat OR ½ Carbohydrate • 1 Vegetable • 4 Lean Meat • 1 Fat.

fiesta quesadillas

READY TO SERVE: 15 MINUTES
SERVINGS: 6

✻ super fast

1 can (11-oz.) whole kernel corn with red and green peppers, drained

1 can (16-oz.) fat-free refried beans

6 flour tortillas (8 to 10 inch)

1 cup shredded Colby-Monterey Jack cheese blend (4 oz.)

1. Heat gas or charcoal grill. In medium bowl, mix corn and refried beans. Spread mixture evenly onto 3 tortillas. Top with remaining tortillas.

2. When grill is heated, place filled tortillas on gas grill over low heat or on charcoal grill over low coals; cover grill. Cook 5 minutes. With pancake turner, carefully turn tortillas; sprinkle with cheese. Cook 3 to 5 minutes longer or until cheese is melted. Cut into wedges to serve.

Nutrition Information Per Serving: Calories 300 • Total Fat 9g • Saturated Fat 4.5g • Trans Fat 0.5g • Cholesterol 20mg • Sodium 590mg • Total Carbohydrate 45g • Dietary Fiber 6g • Sugars 2g • Protein 13g. Dietary Exchanges: 3 Starch • $\frac{1}{2}$ Very Lean Meat • 1 Fat.

easy beef stroganoff

READY TO SERVE: 30 MINUTES
SERVINGS: 4

8 oz. uncooked wide egg noodles (4 cups)

1 lb. lean ground beef

$\frac{1}{2}$ cup finely chopped onion

2 tablespoons all-purpose flour

$\frac{1}{2}$ cup water

1 can (4-oz.) mushroom pieces and stems, drained

1 cup light sour cream

1. Cook noodles to desired doneness as directed on the package. Drain; cover to keep warm.

2. Meanwhile, in large skillet, brown ground beef and onion until beef is thoroughly cooked, stirring frequently. Drain. Stir in flour. Add water and mushrooms; cook, stirring constantly, until mixture thickens.

3. Reduce heat; stir in sour cream. If desired, add salt and pepper to taste. Serve over noodles.

Nutrition Information Per Serving: Calories 530 • Total Fat 21g • Saturated Fat 9g • Cholesterol 145mg • Sodium 310mg • Total Carbohydrate 54g • Dietary Fiber 3g • Sugars 7g • Protein 31g. Dietary Exchanges: $3\frac{1}{2}$ Starch • 3 Lean Meat • 2 Fat OR $3\frac{1}{2}$ Carbohydrate • 3 Lean Meat • 2 Fat.

speedy tortilla soup

READY TO SERVE: 20 MINUTES
SERVINGS: 4

✻ super fast

2 cans (14.5-oz. each) low-sodium chicken broth

4 medium tomatoes, chopped (2 cups)

$\frac{1}{4}$ cup chopped green chiles (from 4.5-oz. can)

16 baked tortilla chips

1 cup shredded reduced-fat Cheddar-Monterey Jack cheese blend (4 oz.)

Fresh cilantro leaves, if desired

1. In 2-quart saucepan, heat broth to boiling over high heat. Stir in tomatoes and chiles. Return to boiling. Reduce heat to medium-low; cover and simmer 6 to 8 minutes.

2. For each serving, place 4 tortilla chips in individual soup bowl. Top each with $\frac{1}{4}$ cup cheese and hot broth mixture. If desired, garnish with fresh cilantro.

Nutrition Information Per Serving: Calories 160 • Total Fat 8g • Saturated Fat 4.5g • Trans Fat 0g • Cholesterol 20mg • Sodium 490mg • Total Carbohydrate 12g • Dietary Fiber 2g • Sugars 2g • Protein 12g. Dietary Exchanges: $\frac{1}{2}$ Starch • 1 Vegetable • 1 Medium-Fat Meat • $\frac{1}{2}$ Fat.

slow-and-easy barbecued ribs

PREP TIME: 10 MINUTES
READY TO SERVE: 10 HOURS 40 MINUTES
SERVINGS: 6

* slow cooked

2 lb. boneless country-style pork loin ribs

1 medium onion, sliced

1 garlic clove, minced

²/₃ cup barbecue sauce

¹/₃ cup plum jam

1. Spray 4- to 6-quart slow cooker with nonstick cooking spray. Place pork ribs, onion and garlic in sprayed slow cooker.

2. Cover; cook on Low setting for 8 to 10 hours.

3. About 35 minutes before serving, drain and discard juices from slow cooker; wipe edge of cooker clean. In measuring cup, combine barbecue sauce and jam; mix well. Pour or spoon mixture over ribs, coating evenly.

4. Increase heat setting to High; cover and cook an additional 25 to 30 minutes or until ribs are glazed. Serve ribs with sauce.

Nutrition Information Per Serving: Calories 440 • Total Fat 29g • Saturated Fat 11g • Cholesterol 105mg • Sodium 290mg • Total Carbohydrate 18g • Dietary Fiber 1g • Sugars 10g • Protein 27g. **Dietary** Exchanges: 1 Fruit • 4 Medium-Fat Meat • 1¹/₂ Fat OR 1 Carbohydrate • 4 Medium-Fat Meat • 1¹/₂ Fat.

tomato dill soup

READY TO SERVE: 25 MINUTES
SERVINGS: 4

* super fast

2 cans (10.75-oz. each) condensed tomato soup

¹/₂ to 1 cup nonfat plain yogurt

³/₄ cup water

¹/₂ cup half-and-half

1 teaspoon dried dill

1. In medium saucepan, combine all ingredients.

2. Cook over medium heat, stirring occasionally, until thoroughly heated. (Do not boil because it may curdle.)

Nutrition Information Per Serving: Calories 170 • Total Fat 6g • Saturated Fat 3g • Cholesterol 10mg • Sodium 940mg • Total Carbohydrate 26g • Dietary Fiber 1g • Sugars 12g • Protein 5g. **Dietary** Exchanges: ¹/₂ Starch • 1 Fat.

chick-n-broccoli pot pies

SERVINGS: 10 POT PIES

LINDA L. WOOD ✳ INDIANAPOLIS, INDIANA

1 can (12-oz.) refrigerated flaky biscuits

⅔ cup shredded Cheddar or American cheese

⅔ cup crisp rice cereal

1 package (9-oz.) frozen cut broccoli, thawed

1 cup cubed cooked chicken or turkey

1 can (10¾-oz.) reduced-sodium condensed cream of chicken or mushroom soup

⅓ cup slivered or sliced almonds

1. Heat oven to 375°F. Separate dough into 10 biscuits. Place 1 biscuit in each of 10 ungreased muffin cups; firmly press in bottom and up sides, forming ½-inch rim over edge of muffin cup. Spoon about 1 tablespoon each of cheese and cereal into each biscuit-lined cup. Press mixture into bottom of each cup.

2. Cut large pieces of broccoli in half. In large bowl, combine broccoli, chicken and soup; mix well. Spoon about ⅓ cup of chicken mixture over cereal. Cups will be full. Sprinkle with almonds.

3. Bake at 375°F for 20 to 25 minutes or until edges of biscuits are deep golden brown.

Nutrition Information Per Serving: Calories 220 • Total Fat 11g • Sodium 600mg • Total Carbohydrate 20g • Protein 10g.

peppers olé

SERVINGS: 8

SUSAN KAKUK ✳ PLYMOUTH, MINNESOTA

peppers
- 4 large green bell peppers, halved, seeded
- 2 tablespoons water

filling
- 2 cups cooked rice
- 4 oz. (1 cup) shredded sharp Cheddar cheese
- ½ cup dairy sour cream
- 1 can (15-oz.) spicy chili beans, undrained
- 1 can (11-oz.) whole kernel corn with red and green peppers, drained

garnish
- ½ cup picante salsa
- 8 tortilla chips
- Fresh cilantro, if desired

1. Place peppers and water in ungreased 9x13-inch (3-quart) microwave-safe dish or divide peppers and water between two 8-inch (1½-quart) microwave-safe dishes. Cover with microwave-safe plastic wrap; microwave on High for 2 minutes. Drain.

2. In medium bowl, combine all filling ingredients. Spoon heaping ½ cup of filling into each pepper half. Cover; microwave 9x13-inch dish on High for 15 to 16 minutes or until peppers are tender. (Microwave each 8-inch dish for 6 to 8 minutes.) Top each pepper with 1 tablespoon of salsa, a tortilla chip and cilantro.

Nutrition Information Per Serving: Calories 270 • Total Fat 10g • Sodium 570mg • Total Carbohydrate 37g • Protein 10g.

CONVENTIONAL WISDOM

You can prepare the colorful peppers in a conventional oven if you'd like. Simply heat the oven to 350°F and combine the filling ingredients as directed in the recipe. Spoon a heaping ½ cup of filling into each pepper half, and set the peppers in an ungreased 13x9-inch (3-quart) baking dish or pan. Omit the water called for in the recipe. Cover the pan with foil; bake at 350°F for 50 minutes or until the peppers are tender. Garnish as directed.

herbed alfredo sauce over linguine

READY TO SERVE: 30 MINUTES
SERVINGS: 5

- 2 packages (9-oz. each) refrigerated linguine or 12 oz. uncooked linguine
- 2 teaspoons butter or margarine
- 1 teaspoon olive oil
- 3 large garlic cloves, minced
- ½ cup finely chopped red bell pepper
- ⅓ cup sliced green onions
- ⅓ cup chopped fresh parsley or 3 teaspoons dried parsley flakes
- ¼ cup all-purpose flour
- 2 cans (12-oz. each) evaporated low-fat 2% milk
- 1 teaspoon dried basil leaves
- ½ teaspoon dried oregano leaves
- ½ teaspoon salt
- ⅓ cup grated Parmesan cheese

1. Cook linguine in Dutch oven as directed on package. Drain; return to Dutch oven and cover to keep warm.

2. Meanwhile, in large nonstick skillet, melt butter with oil over medium heat. Add garlic; cook and stir 1 minute. Add bell pepper, onions, parsley and flour; cook and stir 1 minute.

3. Gradually stir in milk until well blended. Bring to a boil, stirring constantly. Cook 6 to 10 minutes or until sauce is bubbly and thickened, stirring frequently.

4. Remove skillet from heat. Stir in basil, oregano and salt. Pour sauce over linguine; toss gently to coat. Sprinkle with cheese.

Nutrition Information Per Serving: Calories 390 • Total Fat 11g • Saturated Fat 6g • Cholesterol 35mg • Sodium 690mg • Total Carbohydrate 53g • Dietary Fiber 2g • Sugars 19g • Protein 20g. **Dietary Exchanges:** 2½ Starch • 1 Low-Fat Milk • ½ Lean Meat • 1 Fat • 3½ Carbohydrate Choices.

vegetable minestrone soup

* slow cooked

2 medium carrots, cut into ½-inch slices (1 cup)

1 medium stalk celery, coarsely chopped (½ cup)

1 medium onion, halved cross-wise, cut into thin wedges

1 garlic clove, minced

2 cans (14-oz. each) chicken broth

1 can (19-oz.) cannellini beans, drained, rinsed

1 can (15.5- or 15-oz.) kidney beans, drained, rinsed

1 can (14.5-oz.) Italian-style stewed tomatoes, undrained, cut up

½ teaspoon salt

⅛ teaspoon pepper

1 cup frozen cut leaf spinach, thawed

3 oz. uncooked spaghetti, broken into thirds (¾ cup)

1. In 3¼- to 4-quart slow cooker, combine all ingredients; mix well.

2. Cover; cook on Low setting for 5 to 6 hours.

3. About 20 minutes before serving, stir thawed spinach and spaghetti into soup. Increase heat setting to High; cover and cook an additional 15 to 20 minutes or until spaghetti is tender.

Nutrition Information Per Serving: Calories 420 • Total Fat 19g • Saturated Fat 7g • Cholesterol 40mg • Sodium 1540mg • Total Carbohydrate 47g • Dietary Fiber 10g • Sugars 21g • Protein 16g. **Dietary Exchanges:** 2 Starch • 1 Fruit • 1½ High-Fat Meat • 1 Fat OR 3 Carbohydrate • 1½ High-Fat Meat • 1 Fat.

ADD FLAIR IN A FLASH

For an attractive touch that also adds a boost of terrific flavor, garnish individual bowls of the Vegetable Minestrone Soup with a little shredded Parmesan cheese, chopped fresh parsley or even swirls of store-bought basil pesto.

Regardless of what soup you're serving, you can jazz it up with a sprinkling of chopped nuts, sliced green onions, crumbled bacon or crunchy croutons. Some folks even float a few sunflower kernels or toasted sesame seeds over their favorite chill-chaser.

so-easy sloppy joes

* slow cooked

3 lb. lean ground beef

1 cup chopped onions

1 cup chopped celery

½ cup chopped green bell pepper

1 bottle (12-oz.) chili sauce

1 can (6-oz.) tomato paste

2 to 3 tablespoons brown sugar

2 tablespoons Worcestershire sauce

¼ teaspoon pepper

16 sandwich buns, split

1. In large skillet, cook ground beef, onions, celery and bell pepper until beef is thoroughly cooked, stirring frequently. Drain.

2. In 3½- to 4-quart slow cooker, combine ground beef mixture and all remaining ingredients except buns; mix well.

3. Cover; cook on Low setting for 3 to 5 hours, stirring occasionally. Spoon beef mixture into buns.

Nutrition Information Per Serving: Calories 335 • Total Fat 14g • Saturated Fat 5g • Cholesterol 50mg • Sodium 690mg • Total Carbohydrate 34g • Dietary Fiber 2g • Sugars 14g • Protein 20g. **Dietary Exchanges:** 2 Starch • 1 Vegetable • 2 Medium-Fat Meat OR 2 Carbohydrate • 1 Vegetable • 2 Medium-Fat Meat.

easy mac 'n cheese

READY TO SERVE: 25 MINUTES
SERVINGS: 2

* super fast

1 can (14-oz.) fat-free chicken broth with ⅓ less sodium

1½ cups uncooked elbow macaroni (6 oz.)

1 box (10-oz.) frozen broccoli in cheese-flavored sauce in a pouch

¾ cup shredded Cheddar cheese (3 oz.)

2 tablespoons grated Parmesan cheese

1. Pour broth into saucepan. Heat broth to boiling over medium-high heat.

2. While the chicken broth is heating, measure out the macaroni. When the broth starts bubbling, toss the macaroni into the saucepan. Return to boil. Cook macaroni for 10 minutes, stirring occasionally, until pasta is tender. Do not drain off the broth.

3. While the macaroni is cooking, microwave the broccoli as directed on the box.

4. When the pasta is done, add the broccoli with the cheese sauce to the saucepan. Gently mix in the Cheddar cheese.

5. Divide macaroni mixture between two plates. Top each with equal amounts of Parmesan cheese.

Nutrition Information Per Serving: Calories 630 • Total Fat 23g • Sodium 1450mg • Total Carbohydrate 77g • Sugars 9g • Protein 31g. **Dietary Exchanges:** 5 Starch • 1 Vegetable • 2 High-Fat Meat • 1 Fat.

foot-long pizza

foot-long pizza

READY TO SERVE: 30 MINUTES
SERVINGS: 4

1   loaf French bread (12 inch), cut in half lengthwise

¼   cup garlic-and-herb spreadable cheese (from 4- to 6.5-oz. container)

1   cup thinly sliced mushrooms

1   cup thin strips red, green or yellow bell pepper

½   cup julienne-cut zucchini (2x¼x¼-inch)

⅓   cup sliced ripe olives

Olive oil flavor or regular cooking spray

1   teaspoon Italian seasoning

1   cup shredded reduced-fat mozzarella cheese (4 oz.)

1. Heat oven to 450°F. Line 15x10-inch pan with sides with foil. Place bread halves, cut side up, in pan.

2. Spread spreadable cheese evenly over each bread half. Arrange mushrooms, bell pepper, zucchini and olives evenly over top. Spray gently with cooking spray. Sprinkle with Italian seasoning.

3. Bake 15 minutes or just until vegetables begin to brown. Remove from oven; reduce oven temperature to 425°F. Sprinkle cheese over pizza.

4. Return to oven; bake at 425°F 5 minutes longer or until cheese is melted. Cut each bread half in half crosswise.

Nutrition Information Per Serving: Calories 300 • Total Fat 13g • Saturated Fat 7g • Trans Fat 0.5g • Cholesterol 25mg • Sodium 690mg • Total Carbohydrate 33g • Dietary Fiber 3g • Sugars 2g • Protein 14g. Dietary Exchanges: 2 Starch • 1 High-Fat Meat • 1 Fat.

skillet shepherd's pie

READY TO SERVE: 40 MINUTES
SERVINGS: 4

1   lb. lean ground turkey

1   cup coarsely chopped carrots

1   cup coarsely chopped celery

1   medium onion, chopped (½ cup)

1   can (10.75-oz.) reduced-fat and reduced-sodium cream of mushroom soup

¼   cup beef broth

1⅓   cups water

½   cup fat-free sour cream

1⅓   cups plain mashed potato mix (dry)

2   tablespoons chopped fresh parsley or 2 teaspoons dried parsley flakes

1. In 10-inch nonstick skillet, cook ground turkey, carrots, celery and onion over medium-high heat, stirring frequently, until turkey is no longer pink. If necessary, drain.

2. Stir in soup and broth. Reduce heat to low; cover and simmer 15 minutes, stirring occasionally.

3. Meanwhile, in 2-quart saucepan, heat water to boiling. Remove from heat. Stir in sour cream and mashed potato mix until desired consistency. Stir in parsley.

4. Spoon large dollops of potato mixture over turkey mixture in skillet. Cover; cook about 5 minutes or until potatoes are thoroughly heated.

Nutrition Information Per Serving: Calories 470 • Total Fat 8g • Saturated Fat 2g • Trans Fat 0g • Cholesterol 80mg • Sodium 410mg • Total Carbohydrate 71g • Dietary Fiber 7g • Sugars 6g • Protein 32g. Dietary Exchanges: 3½ Starch • 1 Other Carbohydrate • 3 Very Lean Meat • 1 Fat.

SMART SUBSTITUTIONS

Skillet Shepherd's Pie calls for 1 pound of lean ground turkey, but feel free to use extra-lean ground beef if that's what you have on hand. In fact, you can swap out the chopped carrot and celery in the recipe, too, if you have some leftovers in the refrigerator you'd like to use up. For instance, cooked corn, sliced mushrooms, diced peppers and even vegetable medleys make tasty additions to the versatile main course.

Don't forget the herbs! If there is an herb or seasoning that your family is particularly fond of, be sure to add a dash or two to the potato mixture when you are stirring in the parsley.

grandma's chicken noodle soup

PREP TIME: 40 MINUTES
READY TO SERVE: 7 HOURS 40 MINUTES
SERVINGS: 6

✳ slow cooked

¾ lb. boneless skinless chicken thighs, cut into 1-inch pieces

2 medium stalks celery (with leaves), sliced (1¼ cups)

1 large carrot, chopped (¾ cup)

½ cup chopped onion

1 can (14.5-oz.) diced tomatoes, undrained

1 can (14-oz.) chicken broth

1 teaspoon dried thyme leaves

1 package (10-oz.) frozen sweet peas

1 cup frozen home-style egg noodles (from 12-oz. pkg.)

1. Spray large skillet with nonstick cooking spray. Heat over medium heat until hot. Add chicken; cook 5 minutes or until browned, stirring frequently.

2. In 3½- to 4-quart slow cooker, combine chicken and all remaining ingredients except peas and noodles; mix well.

3. Cover; cook on Low setting for 6½ to 7 hours.

4. About 10 minutes before serving, stir peas and noodles into soup. Cover; cook on Low setting for 10 minutes or until noodles are tender.

Nutrition Information Per Serving: Calories 215 • Total Fat 7g • Saturated Fat 2g • Cholesterol 45mg • Sodium 1260mg • Total Carbohydrate 20g • Dietary Fiber 4g • Sugars 5g • Protein 22g. **Dietary Exchanges:** 1 Starch • 1 Vegetable • 2 Very Lean Meat • 1 Fat OR 1 Carbohydrate • 1 Vegetable • 2 Very Lean Meat • 1 Fat.

herbed mac 'n cheese

READY TO SERVE: 25 MINUTES
SERVINGS: 4

✳ super fast

12 oz. (about 5 cups) rigatoni (pasta tubes with ridges), ziti (long tubular pasta) or large elbow macaroni

2 tablespoons all-purpose flour

1 tablespoon spicy brown mustard

1½ teaspoons dried basil leaves

¼ teaspoon garlic powder

1½ cups skim milk

6 oz. shredded reduced-fat Cheddar cheese (1½ cups)

1 tablespoon grated Parmesan cheese

1. Cook rigatoni to desired doneness as directed on package.

2. Meanwhile, in large nonstick saucepan, combine flour, mustard, basil and garlic powder. Gradually stir in milk with wire whisk. Cook and stir over medium-high heat for about 4 minutes or until bubbly and thickened. Reduce heat to low; stir in Cheddar and Parmesan cheeses until melted.

3. Drain rigatoni. Stir into cheese sauce until well mixed.

Nutrition Information Per Serving: Calories 500 • Total Fat 10g • Saturated 5g • Cholesterol 35mg • Sodium 510mg • Total Carbohydrate 73g • Dietary Fiber 2g • Sugars 8g • Protein 29g. **Dietary Exchanges:** 5 Starch • 1½ Medium-Fat Meat OR 5 Carbohydrate • 1½ Medium-Fat Meat.

grandma's chicken noodle soup

do-ahead lasagna logs

do-ahead lasagna logs

* plan ahead

- 8 uncooked lasagna noodles
- 1 egg
- 1 container (12-oz.) low-fat cottage cheese
- 1 cup shredded mozzarella cheese (4 oz.)
- ¼ cup grated Parmesan cheese
- ½ teaspoon dried basil leaves
- 2 cups purchased tomato pasta sauce

BEEF-UP DINNER

If your family prefers meat sauce with their Italian fare, brown some ground beef and stir it into the tomato pasta sauce before pouring the sauce over the lasagna rolls.

You can round out the menu with a simple green salad, breadsticks or a loaf of garlic bread and cups of lemon sherbert for dessert.

1. Fill saucepan half full with water. Heat the water over medium-high heat until it is boiling.

2. Set lasagna noodles in boiling water. Return to a boil, stirring occasionally.

3. Meanwhile, crack egg into a medium bowl. Beat lightly. Stir in cottage cheese, mozzarella cheese, and Parmesan cheese. Add basil leaves.

4. Drain noodles when they reach desired consistency.

5. Spread each noodle equally with the cheese mixture. Leave some space at the short end of the noodle. Roll up the noodles tightly toward the unfilled end.

6. Wrap each lasagna log with plastic wrap. Put the logs in the refrigerator or freezer until thoroughly chilled.

7. To cook one lasagna log, take the log out the refrigerator or freezer and remove the plastic wrap. Put it with the seam side down in a microwavable bowl. Cover the bowl with waxed paper.

8. If you refrigerated your lasagna roll, microwave it on High for 1 to 2 minutes or until the cheese starts to melt at the end. Carefully remove the waxed paper. Pour ¼ cup pasta sauce and over the lasagna roll. Microwave on High another 20 to 30 seconds or until it is heated through. If you froze your lasagna roll, microwave it on Low for 1 to 2 minutes first until it is thawed out, then reheat per the above directions.

Nutrition Information Per Serving: Calories 240 • Total Fat 7g • Sodium 620mg • Total Carbohydrate 29g • Sugars 7g • Protein 15g. Dietary Exchanges: 2 Starch • 1 Very Lean Meat • 1 Fat.

beans 'n wieners

* slow cooked

- 1 lb. wieners, cut into fourths
- 3 cans (16-oz. each) pork and beans in tomato sauce
- ½ cup ketchup
- ¼ cup finely chopped onion
- ¼ cup molasses
- 2 teaspoons prepared mustard

1. In 3¼- to 4-quart slow cooker, combine all ingredients; mix well.

2. Cover; cook on Low setting for 5 to 6 hours.

Nutrition Information Per Serving: Calories 420 • Total Fat 19g • Saturated Fat 7g • Cholesterol 40mg • Sodium 1540mg • Total Carbohydrate 47g • Dietary Fiber 10g • Sugars 21g • Protein 16g. Dietary Exchanges: 2 Starch • 1 Fruit • 1½ High-Fat Meat • 1 Fat OR 3 Carbohydrate • 1½ High-Fat Meat • 1 Fat.

family heroes

READY TO SERVE: 10 MINUTES
SERVINGS: 4 SANDWICHES

* super fast

- ¼ cup Thousand Island salad dressing
- 4 hoagie buns, split
- 4 large lettuce leaves
- ¾ lb. sliced cooked turkey
- 8 thin slices tomato (1 large)
- ¼ lb. sliced hard salami
- 1 small cucumber, thinly sliced
- 4 slices American cheese, halved

1. Spread salad dressing evenly on cut sides of buns.

2. Layer bottom halves of buns with lettuce, turkey, tomato, salami, cucumber and cheese. Cover with top halves of buns.

Nutrition Information Per Serving: Calories 690 • Total Fat 31g • Saturated Fat 11g • Cholesterol 110mg • Sodium 1610mg • Total Carbohydrate 57g • Dietary Fiber 4g • Sugars 7g • Protein 46g. Dietary Exchanges: 3½ Starch • 5 Lean Meat • 2½ Fat • ½ Other Carbohydrate.

chili dogs

READY TO SERVE: 20 MINUTES
SERVINGS: 6

* super fast

- 6 hot dogs
- 1 can (15-oz.) spicy chili beans, undrained
- 6 hot dog buns, split
- ¼ cup chopped onion, if desired
- 3 slices (¾-oz. each) American cheese, each cut into 4 strips

1. Heat grill. When ready to grill, place hot dogs on gas grill over medium heat or on charcoal grill 4 to 6 inches from medium-high coals. Cook 5 to 6 minutes or until thoroughly heated, turning frequently.

2. Meanwhile, heat beans in small saucepan over medium heat until hot.

3. Place buns, cut side down, on grill; cook 30 to 60 seconds or until lightly toasted.

4. Place hot dogs in buns. Top each with about ¾ cup beans, onion and 2 cheese strips. If desired, place sandwiches on grill; cover grill and heat until cheese is melted.

Nutrition Information Per Serving: Calories 370 • Total Fat 19g • Saturated Fat 8g • Cholesterol 35mg • Sodium 1170mg • Total Carbohydrate 35g • Dietary Fiber 4g • Sugars 7g • Protein 14g. Dietary Exchanges: 2½ Starch • 1 High-Fat Meat • 2 Fat OR 2½ Carbohydrate • 1 High-Fat Meat • 2 Fat.

home-style chicken and gravy

READY TO SERVE: 25 MINUTES
SERVINGS: 6

* super fast

- 6 boneless skinless chicken breast halves
- ½ teaspoon seasoned salt
- ¾ teaspoon paprika
- ¾ teaspoon garlic-pepper blend
- 1 jar (12-oz.) chicken gravy
- 2 tablespoons fat-free half-and-half or milk
- 1 tablespoon Worcestershire sauce

1. Heat 10-inch nonstick skillet over medium-high heat until hot. Sprinkle chicken with seasoned salt, paprika and garlic-pepper blend; add to skillet. Cook 4 to 6 minutes or until brown on both sides.

2. In medium bowl, combine gravy, half-and-half and Worcestershire sauce; mix well. Pour gravy mixture over chicken. Cover; simmer over medium-low heat for 10 to 15 minutes or until juice of chicken is no longer pink when center of thickest part is cut.

Nutrition Information Per Serving: Calories 180 • Total Fat 6g • Saturated Fat 2g • Cholesterol 75mg • Sodium 580mg • Total Carbohydrate 4g • Dietary Fiber 0g • Sugars 0g • Protein 28g. Dietary Exchanges: ½ Starch • 4 Very Lean Meat • ½ Fat.

family heroes

knife and fork meatball sandwiches

READY TO SERVE: 25 MINUTES
SERVINGS: 6

✳ super fast

¾ lb. extra-lean (at least 90%) ground beef

1 box (9-oz.) frozen spinach in a pouch, thawed, squeezed and patted dry with paper towels

1 slice whole wheat bread, torn into small pieces

½ teaspoon onion powder

1 teaspoon Italian seasoning or 1/2 teaspoon dried oregano leaves

1 egg or 2 egg whites

2 cups reduced-fat tomato pasta sauce

1 loaf (8-oz.) French or Italian bread

½ cup shredded mozzarella cheese (2 oz.)

2 tablespoons grated Parmesan cheese

1. Heat oven to 425°F. Line 15x10x1-inch pan with foil, extending foil over short sides of pan.

2. In medium bowl, mix ground beef, spinach, bread crumbs, onion powder, Italian seasoning and egg. Press mixture into 8x6-inch rectangle in pan. Cut rectangle into 36 pieces; do not separate.

3. Bake 10 to 15 minutes or until centers of meatballs are firm and no longer pink and juice is clear. Drain; pat beef with paper towels to remove moisture. With sharp knife, cut into 36 meatballs.

4. Meanwhile, in 3-quart saucepan, heat pasta sauce. Add meatballs; stir to coat.

5. Cut loaf of bread lengthwise but not through one long side; cut loaf into 6 sections. Place opened sections on individual plates. Spoon 6 meatballs with sauce onto each bread section. Sprinkle with mozzarella and Parmesan cheeses. Serve immediately.

Nutrition Information Per Serving: Calories 340 • Total Fat 12g • Saturated Fat 4.5g • Trans Fat 0.5g • Cholesterol 80mg • Sodium 800mg • Total Carbohydrate 39g • Dietary Fiber 3g • Sugars 7g • Protein 21g. Dietary Exchanges: 2 Starch • ½ Other Carbohydrate • 2 Medium-Fat Meat • 1 Fat.

classic pizza

READY TO SERVE: 35 MINUTES
SERVINGS: 8

- 1 can (13.8-oz.) refrigerated pizza crust
- ½ lb. bulk light turkey and pork sausage
- 1 can (14.5-oz.) stewed tomatoes, drained
- ½ teaspoon dried oregano leaves
- ⅛ teaspoon crushed red pepper
- 1 clove garlic, minced
- 2 tablespoons grated Parmesan cheese
- 2 cups shredded mozzarella cheese (8 oz.)

1. Heat oven to 425°F. Spray 13x9-inch pan with cooking spray. Unroll dough; place in pan. Starting at center, press out dough in bottom and ½ inch up sides of the pan to form the crust.

2. Bake 7 minutes. Meanwhile, in 8-inch skillet, cook sausage over medium-high heat, stirring frequently, until no longer pink. Remove sausage from skillet; drain on paper towels.

3. In same skillet, mix tomatoes, oregano, red pepper and garlic; cook over medium-high heat until bubbly. Reduce heat to medium-low; simmer uncovered 5 to 8 minutes, stirring occasionally, to blend flavors.

4. Spread tomato mixture over partially baked crust. Sprinkle sausage evenly over tomato mixture. Top with Parmesan and mozzarella cheeses.

5. Return to oven; bake 10 to 12 minutes longer or until cheese is melted and crust is golden brown. Cut into squares.

Nutrition Information Per Serving: Calories 300 • Total Fat 13g • Saturated Fat 6g • Trans Fat 0g • Cholesterol 35mg • Sodium 850mg • Total Carbohydrate 29g • Dietary Fiber 1g • Sugars 6g • Protein 17g. Dietary Exchanges: 2 Starch • 1½ Medium-Fat Meat • ½ Fat.

tuna salad sandwiches

READY TO SERVE: 15 MINUTES
SERVINGS: 4

* super fast

- 2 tablespoons fat-free plain yogurt
- 2 tablespoons reduced-fat mayonnaise or salad dressing
- 1 can (8-oz.) pineapple tidbits in juice, drained
- 1 can (6-oz.) white tuna in water, drained, flaked
- ¼ cup finely chopped green bell pepper
- ¼ cup coarsely chopped water chestnuts
- ½ teaspoon lemon-pepper seasoning
- 2 tablespoons sunflower nuts
- 4 kaiser rolls, split

1. In medium bowl, mix yogurt and mayonnaise until well blended. Stir in remaining ingredients except rolls.

2. Fill each roll with about ½ cup tuna mixture.

Nutrition Information Per Serving: Calories 280 • Total Fat 7g • Saturated Fat 1g • Trans Fat 0.5g • Cholesterol 15mg • Sodium 500mg • Total Carbohydrate 38g • Dietary Fiber 3g • Sugars 9g • Protein 17g. Dietary Exchanges: 2 Starch • ½ Other Carbohydrate • 1½ Very Lean Meat • 1 Fat.

GRAB-AND-GO DELIGHTS

Don't let a busy schedule detour your plans to prepare homemade tastes for your family. Keep the following in mind when you have got to run and hunger comes calling:

* Speedy Stackers. Make sandwiches a standby when on-the-go dinners are a must. For instance, you can quickly wrap Tuna Salad Sandwiches securely with foil or plastic wrap before you and your gang head out the door.

* Wrap it up! Wrap you favorite deli meats and cheeses in flour tortillas. The handheld greats are both versatile and simple to assemble. Paired with a piece of fruit and a juice box, a quick wrap makes a simple meal solution.

* Smooth moves. Blend together a thick and refreshing smoothie the next time you have to eat on the run. Combine milk with yogurt, ice cubes and some berries or fruit for a fast treat.

penne with cheesy tomato-sausage sauce

country breaded pork chops

READY TO SERVE: 35 MINUTES
SERVINGS: 4

½ cup corn flake crumbs
1 tablespoon Dijon mustard
2 teaspoons orange juice
¼ teaspoon dried thyme leaves
4 boneless pork loin chops,
¾-inch thick (1 lb.)

1. Heat oven to 425°F. Line cookie sheet with foil; spray foil lightly with cooking spray. In shallow dish, place corn flake crumbs. In small bowl, mix mustard, orange juice and thyme.

2. Brush 1 side of each pork chop with mustard mixture. Place 1 chop, mustard side down, in crumbs; brush remaining side of chop with mustard mixture. Turn chop to coat both sides well with crumbs. Place on cookie sheet. Repeat with remaining chops.

3. Bake 20 to 25 minutes or until pork is no longer pink and thermometer inserted in center of pork reads 160°F.

Nutrition Information Per Serving: Calories 200 • Total Fat 9g • Saturated Fat 3g • Trans Fat 0g • Cholesterol 70mg • Sodium 190mg • Total Carbohydrate 7g • Dietary Fiber 0g • Sugars 0g • Protein 25g. Dietary Exchanges: ½ Starch • 3 Lean Meat.

penne with cheesy tomato-sausage sauce

READY TO SERVE: 25 MINUTES
SERVINGS: 4

∗ super fast

2⅔ cups uncooked penne pasta
(8 oz.)
½ lb. bulk Italian pork sausage
1 container (15-oz.) refrigerated tomato pasta sauce
¼ cup thinly sliced fresh basil
2 oz. mozzarella cheese, diced (½ cup)
¼ cup shredded Parmesan cheese (1 oz.)

1. Cook penne as directed on package. Drain; cover to keep warm.

2. Meanwhile, in 3-quart saucepan, cook sausage until no longer pink, stirring frequently. Drain; return to saucepan. Add pasta sauce; bring to a boil. Reduce heat to medium-low. Stir in basil and mozzarella cheese. Cook 1 to 2 minutes or until cheese is slightly melted, stirring occasionally.

3. Serve sauce mixture over cooked penne. Sprinkle with Parmesan cheese.

Nutrition Information Per Serving: Calories 500 • Total Fat 19g • Saturated Fat 6g • Cholesterol 45mg • Sodium 1010mg • Total Carbohydrate 59g • Fiber 4g • Sugars 12g • Protein 23g. Dietary Exchanges: 3 Starch • 2 High-Fat Meat.

chicken chow mein

READY TO SERVE: 30 MINUTES
SERVINGS: 4

⅔ cup uncooked regular long-grain white rice
1⅓ cups water
1½ cups cubed cooked chicken
1 cup sliced celery
1 can (14½-oz.) ready-to-serve chicken broth
2 tablespoons cornstarch
2 tablespoons soy sauce
1 can (14-oz.) chow mein vegetables, drained
1 jar (2.5-oz.) sliced mushrooms, drained

1. Cook rice in water as directed on package.

2. Meanwhile, in large saucepan, combine all remaining ingredients; mix well. Bring to a boil, stirring constantly. Reduce heat; simmer 15 minutes, stirring frequently.

3. Serve chicken mixture over rice.

Nutrition Information Per Serving: Calories 250 • Total Fat 5g • Saturated Fat 1g • Cholesterol 45mg • Sodium 1220mg • Total Carbohydrate 31g • Dietary Fiber 2g • Sugars 1g • Protein 21g. Dietary Exchanges: 1½ Starch • 1 Vegetable • 2 Lean Meat OR 1½ Carbohydrate • 1 Vegetable • 2 Lean Meat.

juicy burgers

READY TO SERVE: 20 MINUTES
SERVINGS: 4

* super fast

1   egg

1   lb. lean (at least 80%) ground beef

¼   cup Italian-style dry bread crumbs

¼   cup milk

1   teaspoon dried instant minced onion

½   teaspoon salt

⅛   teaspoon pepper

4   burger buns, split

1. Heat gas or charcoal grill. In large bowl, beat egg. Stir in all remaining ingredients except buns until well mixed. Shape mixture into 4 (½-inch-thick) patties.

2. When grill is heated, place patties on gas grill over medium heat or on charcoal grill 4 to 6 inches from medium coals. Cook covered 11 to 13 minutes or until meat thermometer inserted in center of patties reads 160°F, turning once.

3. If desired, to toast buns, during last minute of cooking time, place buns, cut sides down, on grill. Serve patties in toasted buns with desired condiments.

Nutrition Information Per Serving: Calories 400 • Total Fat 20g • Saturated Fat 8g • Cholesterol 120mg • Sodium 670mg • Total Carbohydrate 28g • Dietary Fiber 1g • Sugars 7g • Protein 27g. Dietary Exchanges: 2 Starch • 3 Medium-Fat Meat • 1 Fat.

lemon-chicken primavera

READY TO SERVE: 25 MINUTES
SERVINGS: 6

* super fast

1   package (12-oz.) uncooked fettuccine

1   tablespoon olive oil

2   garlic cloves, minced or ¼ teaspoon garlic powder

1   package (9-oz.) frozen grilled cooked chicken breast strips

1   lb. fresh asparagus spears, trimmed, cut into 1½-inch pieces

1½   cups baby-cut carrots, quartered lengthwise

1   teaspoon lemon-pepper seasoning

2   cups chicken broth

2   tablespoons cornstarch

2   tablespoons chopped fresh *or* 1½ teaspoons dried basil

2   teaspoons grated lemon peel

⅓   cup shredded Parmesan cheese (1⅓ oz.)

1. In 3- to 4-quart saucepan, cook fettuccine as directed on package. Drain; return to saucepan. Cover to keep warm.

2. Meanwhile, in 10-inch skillet, heat oil over medium-high heat until hot. Add garlic; cook and stir 30 to 60 seconds or until softened. Add chicken, asparagus, carrots and lemon-pepper seasoning. Reserve ¼ cup of the broth; stir remaining broth into chicken mixture. Bring to a boil. Reduce heat to medium; cover and cook 5 minutes or until vegetables are crisp-tender, stirring occasionally.

3. In small bowl, mix reserved ¼ cup broth and cornstarch until smooth. Add to skillet; cook and stir until thickened. Stir in basil and lemon peel.

4. Pour chicken mixture over cooked fettuccine in saucepan; toss to coat. Sprinkle individual servings with cheese.

Nutrition Information Per Serving: Calories 450 • Total Fat 12g • Saturated Fat 3g • Cholesterol 105mg • Sodium 1120mg • Total Carbohydrate 54g • Dietary Fiber 3g • Sugars 3g • Protein 31g. Dietary Exchanges: 3½ Starch • 3 Very Lean Meat • 2 Fat.

juicy burgers

favorite salisbury steak

READY TO SERVE: 30 MINUTES
SERVINGS: 6

patties

- 1 lb. extra-lean ground beef
- ½ cup unseasoned dry bread crumbs
- ½ cup milk
- 1 egg white
- ¼ cup finely chopped onion
- 1 teaspoon Worcestershire sauce
- ¼ teaspoon salt
- ¼ teaspoon pepper

gravy

- ¾ cup beef broth
- ¼ cup dry red wine or beef broth
- 1 tablespoon cornstarch
- ¼ teaspoon dried thyme leaves
- 1 jar (2.5-oz.) sliced mushrooms, drained

1. In medium bowl, combine all patty ingredients; mix gently. (Mixture will be moist.) Shape into 6 oval patties, about ¾-inch thick.

2. Spray large nonstick skillet with nonstick cooking spray. Heat over medium heat until hot. Add patties; cook 3 minutes on each side or until browned. Remove patties from skillet; drain, if necessary.

3. In small bowl, combine broth, wine, cornstarch and thyme; blend well. Pour into same skillet. Cook over low heat until mixture boils and thickens, stirring constantly. Stir in mushrooms. Return patties to skillet. Cover; simmer about 15 minutes or until patties are no longer pink in center.

Nutrition Information Per Serving: Calories 200 • Total Fat 10g • Saturated Fat 4g • Cholesterol 50mg • Sodium 390mg • Total Carbohydrate 10g • Dietary Fiber 1g • Sugars 2g • Protein 18g. **Dietary Exchanges:** ½ Starch • 2 Medium-Fat Meat OR ½ Carbohydrate • 2 Medium-Fat Meat.

swiss spinach strudel

SERVINGS: 5

DEVON P. DELANEY ✷ PRINCETON, NEW JERSEY

1 egg

½ cup chive and onion light cream cheese spread (from 8-oz. container)

1 package (9-oz.) frozen spinach in a pouch, thawed, squeezed to drain

4 oz. (1 cup) shredded Swiss cheese

¼ teaspoon salt

¼ teaspoon pepper

⅛ to ¼ teaspoon nutmeg

⅛ teaspoon hot pepper sauce

1 can (8-oz.) refrigerated reduced-fat or regular crescent dinner rolls

¼ cup sliced almonds

Olive oil, nonstick cooking spray or regular cooking spray

2 tablespoons Italian-style dry bread crumbs

1. Heat oven to 400°F. Beat egg in large bowl. Add cream cheese spread; blend well. Add spinach, Swiss cheese, salt, pepper, nutmeg and hot pepper sauce; mix well.

2. Unroll dough onto ungreased cookie sheet. Press to form 12x8-inch rectangle; firmly press perforations to seal. Spoon and spread spinach mixture lengthwise on half of dough. Sprinkle with almonds. Fold untopped half of dough over filling; press edges and ends to seal. Spray top of dough with cooking spray. Sprinkle with bread crumbs.

3. Bake at 400°F for 18 to 24 minutes or until deep golden brown. Cool 5 minutes. Cut into crosswise slices.

Nutrition Information Per Serving: Calories 360 • Total Carbohydrate 27g • Total Fat 21g • Sodium 820mg • Protein 16g.

TIME TO BEAT THE CLOCK

To quickly thaw the pouch of frozen spinach called for in Swiss Spinach Strudel, cut a small slit in the center of the pouch. Microwave the pouch on High for 2 to 3 minutes or until the spinach is thawed. Carefully remove the spinach from the pouch. Squeeze it dry with paper towels or by setting it in a colander and pressing the liquid out with the back of a serving spoon.

---

beef stew

READY TO SERVE: 30 MINUTES

SERVINGS: 5

¾ lb. boneless beef top sirloin steak, cut into ½-inch cubes

1 small onion, chopped

3 cups frozen southern-style hash brown potatoes (from 32-oz. pkg.)

1½ cups thinly sliced carrots

1 cup thinly sliced celery

1 jar (4.5-oz.) sliced mushrooms, drained

1 envelope dry beef-mushroom soup mix

¼ teaspoon dried thyme leaves, crushed

¼ teaspoon pepper

3½ cups water

1. Heat nonstick Dutch oven or large saucepan over medium-high heat until hot. Add beef and onion; cook 5 minutes or until beef is browned.

2. Stir in potatoes, carrots, celery and mushrooms; cook and stir 2 minutes. Add soup mix, thyme, pepper and water; mix well. Bring to a boil. Reduce heat; simmer 15 minutes or until vegetables are tender. If desired, serve sprinkled with chopped fresh parsley.

Nutrition Information Per Serving: Calories 240 • Total Fat 4g • Saturated 1g • Cholesterol 35mg • Sodium 550mg • Total Carbohydrate 34g • Dietary Fiber 4g • Sugars 4g • Protein 17g. **Dietary Exchanges:** 2 Starch • 1 Vegetable • 1 Lean Meat OR 2 Carbohydrate • 1 Vegetable • 1 Lean Meat.

meal-in-one wonders

baja chicken salad with taco vinaigrette * p. 37

one-pot turkey dinner * p. 38

chicken-vegetable salad * p. 48

hamburger hash skillet supper * p. 53

family-favorite beef stew ✳ p. 54

baja chicken salad
with taco vinaigrette

turkey stuffing casserole

PREP TIME: 15 MINUTES
READY TO SERVE: 35 MINUTES
SERVINGS: 6

2 cups water

1 package (8-oz.) one-step chicken-flavor stuffing mix

¾ lb. turkey tenderloin, cut into ½-inch cubes

2 packages (10-oz. each) frozen peas and carrots, thawed

1 can (10¾-oz.) condensed 98% fat-free cream of chicken soup with 30% less sodium

1 container (8-oz.) nonfat sour cream

1 jar (4½-oz.) sliced mushrooms, drained

⅔ cup skim milk

1. Heat oven to 450°F. Spray 13x9-inch (3-quart) baking dish with nonstick cooking spray.

2. In medium saucepan, bring water to a boil. Stir in stuffing mix. Remove from heat; cover and let stand 5 minutes.

3. Meanwhile, in large nonstick skillet, cook turkey over medium-high heat until no longer pink. Add peas and carrots, soup, sour cream, mushrooms and milk; mix well. Heat until bubbly.

4. Spoon ⅔ of stuffing evenly into sprayed dish. Top with turkey mixture and remaining ⅓ of stuffing.

5. Bake at 450°F for 10 to 15 minutes or until bubbly and browned. Let stand 5 minutes before serving.

Nutrition Information Per Serving: Calories 340 • Total Fat 6g • Saturated 1g • Cholesterol 40mg • Sodium 1080mg • Total Carbohydrate 47g • Dietary Fiber 5g • Sugars 12g • Protein 25g. Dietary Exchanges: 3 Starch • 1 Vegetable • 2 Very Lean Meat OR 3 Carbohydrate • 1 Vegetable • 2 Very Lean Meat.

baja chicken salad with taco vinaigrette

SERVINGS: 6

PAT HARMONM ✳ BADEN, PENNSYLVANIA

1 package (1.25-oz.) taco seasoning mix

1 tablespoon brown sugar

½ cup oil

½ cup cider vinegar

4 boneless skinless chicken breast halves, cut into 1-inch pieces

1 to 2 tablespoons oil

1 package (10-oz.) mixed salad greens or baby greens

1 cup grape tomatoes, halved

½ cup sliced red onion

2⅔ oz. shredded Cheddar-Monterey Jack cheese blend (⅔ cup)

⅓ cup dairy sour cream

1 avocado, pitted, peeled and sliced

3 tablespoons sliced ripe olives

Blue tortilla chips

1. In medium bowl, combine taco seasoning mix, brown sugar, ½ cup oil and vinegar; mix well. Place chicken in shallow medium bowl. Pour ½ cup seasoning mixture over chicken. Reserve remaining mixture for dressing.

2. Heat 1 to 2 tablespoons oil in medium nonstick skillet over medium-high heat until hot. With slotted spoon, remove chicken from seasoning mixture; add to skillet. Cook 5 minutes or until no longer pink in center, stirring frequently. Discard remaining used seasoning mixture.

3. In large bowl, combine mixed greens, tomatoes and onion. Add reserved seasoning mixture; toss to coat. Arrange salad mixture on serving platter. Top with chicken, cheese, sour cream, avocado and olives. Arrange tortilla chips around salad.

Nutrition Information Per Serving: Calories 460 • Total Fat 34g • Sodium 740mg • Total Carbohydrate 15g • Protein 23g.

TOMATO TURNABOUT

When buying ingredients for the hearty salad, remember that grape tomatoes are nothing more than baby Roma tomatoes. They are slightly sweeter than the popular cherry variety and complement the other items in the salad nicely. If you can't find grape tomatoes however, feel free to use cherry tomatoes instead. You can also chop a cup of whatever tomatoes you have on hand, tossing the pieces into the flavorful entree.

one-pot turkey dinner

PREP TIME: 15 MINUTES
READY TO SERVE: 8 HOURS 15 MINUTES
SERVINGS: 6

✳ slow cooked

- 3 medium dark-orange sweet potatoes, peeled, cut into 2-inch pieces
- 3 bone-in turkey thighs (about 2¼ lb.), skin removed
- 1 jar (12-oz.) turkey gravy
- 2 tablespoons all-purpose flour
- 1 teaspoon dried parsley flakes
- ½ teaspoon dried rosemary leaves, crushed
- ⅛ teaspoon pepper
- 1 package (10-oz.) frozen cut green beans

1. Place sweet potatoes in 4- to 5-quart slow cooker. Top with turkey thighs. In small bowl, combine all remaining ingredients except beans; mix until smooth. Pour over turkey.

2. Cover; cook on High setting for 1 hour. Reduce heat setting to Low; cook 5 hours.

3. One to 2 hours before serving, stir beans into turkey mixture. Cover; cook on Low setting for an additional 1 to 2 hours.

4. With slotted spoon, remove turkey and vegetables from slow cooker; place on serving platter. Remove turkey meat from bones and cut into pieces; discard bones. Stir sauce. Serve turkey and vegetables with sauce.

Nutrition Information Per Serving: Calories 340 • Total Fat 9g • Saturated Fat 3g • Cholesterol 155mg • Sodium 460mg • Total Carbohydrate 26g • Dietary Fiber 4g • Sugars 13g • Protein 43g. Dietary Exchanges: 1½ Starch • 1 Vegetable • 5 Very Lean Meat • ½ Fat OR 2 Carbohydrate • 1 Vegetable • 5 Very Lean Meat • ½ Fat.

biscuit-topped fiesta supper

PREP TIME: 25 MINUTES
READY TO SERVE: 45 MINUTES
SERVINGS: 5

meat mixture
- 1 lb. ground beef
- ½ cup chopped onion
- ¾ cup picante sauce
- 1 can (11-oz.) vacuum-packed whole kernel corn with red and green peppers, drained
- 1 can (8-oz.) tomato sauce
- 1 teaspoon sugar
- ½ teaspoon garlic powder
- ½ teaspoon chili powder
- ⅛ teaspoon pepper
- 4 oz. shredded Cheddar cheese (1 cup)

biscuit topping
- 2 tablespoons yellow cornmeal
- ½ teaspoon paprika
- ⅛ teaspoon garlic powder
- 1 can (12-oz.) refrigerated flaky biscuits
- 1 tablespoon margarine or butter, melted

1. Heat oven to 375°F. In large ovenproof skillet, brown ground beef and onion until thoroughly cooked. Drain. Stir in picante sauce, corn, tomato sauce, sugar, garlic powder, chili powder and pepper. Bring to a boil. Reduce heat to low; simmer, uncovered, 10 to 15 minutes or until most of liquid is absorbed.

2. Meanwhile, in small bowl, combine cornmeal, paprika and garlic powder; mix well.

3. Separate dough into 10 biscuits. Cut each biscuit in half. Arrange biscuits around outer edge of hot beef mixture. Brush biscuits with margarine; sprinkle with cornmeal mixture. Sprinkle cheese in center of ground beef mixture.

4. Bake at 375°F for 15 to 20 minutes or until biscuits are golden brown.

Nutrition Information Per Serving: Calories 610 • Total Fat 33g • Saturated 12g • Cholesterol 80mg • Sodium 1800mg • Total Carbohydrate 50g • Dietary Fiber 4g • Sugars 11g • Protein 27g. Dietary Exchanges: 3½ Starch • 2½ High-Fat Meat • 2 Fat OR 3½ Carbohydrate • 2½ High-Fat Meat • 2 Fat.

MAKE IT A LIGHT BITE

Featuring golden biscuits and a hearty filling, Biscuit-Topped Fiesta Supper is a meaty sensation that your family is bound to request time and again.

If you'd like to lighten it up a bit, try replacing the ground beef the recipe calls for with ground turkey. Your gang likely won't even notice the difference, and you'll be cutting back on fat.

Vegetarian beef crumbles are another option when trimming down your family favorites. Available in plain and seasoned varieties, packages of the meat-free crumbles are usually available in the freezer aisle or meat section of most grocery stores. Try them the next time you make spaghetti sauce, sloppy joe mix or tacos.

one-pot turkey dinner

skillet canadian bacon and potatoes

READY TO SERVE: 30 MINUTES
SERVINGS: 4

- 3½ cups water
- 2 teaspoons margarine or butter
- 1 package (7.8-oz.) creamy scalloped potato mix
- 1¼ cups milk
- ½ lb. Canadian bacon or cooked ham slices, cut into strips
- 1 package (9-oz.) frozen sugar snap peas in a pouch, thawed, drained

1. In large nonstick skillet, combine water and margarine. Bring to a boil over medium-high heat. Stir in potato slices, reserving sauce mix packet; return to a boil. Boil 15 minutes.

2. Do not drain potatoes. Stir in contents of sauce mix packet from potatoes, milk, Canadian bacon and peas. Reduce heat to medium; cook an additional 4 to 5 minutes or until sauce is slightly thickened, stirring occasionally. If desired, add pepper to taste.

Nutrition Information Per Serving: Calories 390 • Total Fat 10g • Saturated Fat 3g • Cholesterol 35mg • Sodium 1720mg • Total Carbohydrate 54g • Dietary Fiber 5g • Sugars 11g • Protein 20g. Dietary Exchanges: 2½ Starch • 1 Fruit • 1 Vegetable • 1½ Very Lean Meat • 1½ Fat OR 3½ Carbohydrate • 1 Vegetable • 1½ Very Lean Meat • 1½ Fat.

easy pork chow mein

PREP TIME: 20 MINUTES
SERVINGS: 4

* super fast

- 4 cups hot cooked instant rice (cooked as directed on package, omitting margarine and salt)
- ½ cup purchased stir-fry sauce with ginger and garlic
- ⅓ cup water
- 2 teaspoons cornstarch
- 1 package (16-oz.) fresh cut stir-fry vegetables (6 cups)
- ½ lb. pork tenderloin, cut into ½-inch cubes
- 2 tablespoons chow mein noodles, if desired

1. While rice is cooking, in small bowl, combine stir-fry sauce, water and cornstarch; blend well. Set aside.

2. In large saucepan, bring 6 cups water to a boil. Add vegetables; cook 1 minute or until green vegetables brighten. Drain.

3. Spray large nonstick wok or skillet with nonstick cooking spray. Heat over medium-high heat until hot. Add pork; cook and stir about 2 minutes or until pork is browned.

4. Stir in vegetables and cornstarch mixture. Reduce heat to medium-low; cover and cook 3 minutes or until vegetables are crisp-tender and sauce has thickened, stirring frequently. Serve over rice; top with chow mein noodles.

Nutrition Information Per Serving: Calories 330 • Total Fat 3g • Saturated 1g • Cholesterol 35mg • Sodium 1140mg • Total Carbohydrate 58g • Dietary Fiber 4g • Sugars 2g • Protein 18g. Dietary Exchanges: 3 Starch • 2 Vegetable • 1 Lean Meat OR 3 Carbohydrate • 2 Vegetable • 1 Lean Meat.

spicy broccoli beef stir-fry

PREP TIME: 25 MINUTES
SERVINGS: 4

* super fast

- 8 oz. uncooked vermicelli

sauce
- ½ cup orange juice
- 1 tablespoon cornstarch
- 2 tablespoons soy sauce
- 2 teaspoons sugar
- ¾ teaspoon Chinese five-spice powder
- ⅛ to ¼ teaspoon crushed red pepper flakes

stir-fry
- ¾ lb. boneless beef sirloin steak, thinly sliced
- 1 medium onion, cut into 16 wedges
- 1 garlic clove, minced
- 3 cups fresh broccoli florets (about 6 oz.)
- 1 small red bell pepper, cut into thin strips (about 1 cup)

1. Cook vermicelli to desired doneness as directed on package.

2. Meanwhile, in small bowl, combine all of the sauce ingredients; mix until well blended. Set aside.

3. Spray large nonstick skillet or wok with nonstick cooking spray. Heat over medium-high heat until hot. Add beef, onion and garlic; cook and stir 3 to 5 minutes or until beef is no longer pink and onion is crisp-tender.

4. Add broccoli and bell pepper. Cover; cook 2 to 4 minutes or until vegetables are crisp-tender, stirring occasionally. Add sauce; cook and stir 2 to 3 minutes or until bubbly and thickened.

5. Drain vermicelli. Serve beef mixture over vermicelli.

Nutrition Information Per Serving: Calories 380 • Total Fat 5g • Saturated Fat 2g • Cholesterol 45mg • Sodium 570mg • Total Carbohydrate 57g • Dietary Fiber 4g • Sugars 10g • Protein 26g. Dietary Exchanges: 3 Starch • 1 Vegetable • 2 Lean Meat OR 3 Carbohydrate • 1 Vegetable • 2 Lean Meat.

NO NEED TO CHOP 'TIL YOU DROP

Precut vegetables that are found in the refrigerated produce section let you skip the most time-consuming step of stir-frying: the chopping! These fresh medleys may include broccoli, celery, cauliflower, snow pea pods, red bell pepper and/or carrots. A package of frozen stir-fry vegetables is another smart option.

Other handy items that round out stir-fries include canned baby corn, water chestnuts, straw mushrooms or bamboo shoots, canned bean sprouts and even cubes of tofu. In the Asian foods section of most supermarkets, you'll also find bottles of stir-fry sauce, chow mein noodles, rice noodles, plum sauce and more.

veggie salisbury steak

READY TO SERVE: 20 MINUTES
SERVINGS: 4

✳ super fast

4 ground beef patties
(4-oz. each)

½ teaspoon peppered
seasoned salt

1 cup frozen mixed vegetables
(from 1-lb. bag)

1 medium onion, chopped
(½ cup)

2 tablespoons ketchup

1 tablespoon Worcestershire
sauce

1 jar (4.5-oz.) sliced
mushrooms, drained

1 jar (12-oz.) beef gravy

1. Heat 12-inch nonstick skillet over medium-high heat until hot. Add beef patties; sprinkle with peppered seasoned salt. Cook 3 to 5 minutes or until brown on both sides, turning once.

2. In medium bowl, combine all remaining ingredients; mix well. Add to skillet; bring to a boil. Reduce heat to medium-low; cover and simmer 10 to 12 minutes or until meat thermometer inserted in center of patties reads 160°F and vegetables are tender, stirring and turning patties once or twice.

Nutrition Information Per Serving: Calories 340 • Total Fat 20g • Saturated Fat 8g • Cholesterol 70mg • Sodium 990mg • Total Carbohydrate 16g • Dietary Fiber 3g • Sugars 6g • Protein 24g. Dietary Exchanges: 1 Starch • 3 Medium-Fat Meat • 1 Fat.

chicken nugget caesar salad

READY TO SERVE: 20 MINUTES
SERVINGS: 4

✳ super fast

1 package (10-oz.) frozen
breaded chicken breast
chunks

4 cups torn romaine lettuce

1 cup halved cherry tomatoes

5 oz. mozzarella cheese, cut
into small cubes (1 cup)

½ cup Caesar salad dressing

1. Cook chicken breast chunks as directed on package.

2. Meanwhile, in large bowl, combine lettuce, tomatoes and cheese. If desired, cut warm chicken chunks in half. Add chicken and salad dressing to salad; toss to coat. Serve immediately.

Nutrition Information Per Serving: Calories 410 • Total Fat 29g • Saturated Fat 9g • Cholesterol 55mg • Sodium 970mg • Total Carbohydrate 15g • Dietary Fiber 1g • Sugars 3g • Protein 22g. Dietary Exchanges: ½ Starch • 1 Vegetable • 2½ Medium-Fat Meat • 3½ Fat.

sloppy joe casserole

PREP TIME: 15 MINUTES
READY TO SERVE: 35 MINUTES
SERVINGS: 4

1 lb. lean ground beef

½ cup sliced green onions

1 can (15½-oz.) sloppy joe
sandwich sauce

1 can (11-oz.) vacuum-packed
whole kernel corn with red
and green peppers,
undrained

1 can (6-oz.) refrigerated
buttermilk flaky biscuits

1. Heat oven to 375°F. In large skillet, brown ground beef with green onions until beef is thoroughly cooked. Drain. Stir in sandwich sauce and corn. Cook 2 to 3 minutes or until thoroughly heated, stirring occasionally. Spoon mixture into ungreased 1- to 1½-quart casserole.

2. Separate dough into 5 biscuits; cut each in half. Arrange, cut side down, around outside edge of hot mixture with sides of biscuits touching.

3. Bake at 375°F for 15 to 20 minutes or until biscuits are deep golden brown.

Nutrition Information Per Serving: Calories 480 • Total Fat 21g • Saturated Fat 8g • Cholesterol 70mg • Sodium 1620mg • Total Carbohydrate 45g • Dietary Fiber 4g • Sugars 19g • Protein 27g. Dietary Exchanges: 2 Starch • 1 Fruit • 3 Lean Meat • 2 Fat OR 3 Carbohydrate • 3 Lean Meat • 2 Fat.

veggie salisbury steak

chicken, mushroom and asparagus stir-fry

chicken, mushroom and asparagus stir-fry

READY TO SERVE: 20 MINUTES
SERVINGS: 4

* super fast

1 cup uncooked instant white rice

1 cup water

2 tablespoons vegetable oil

1 lb. chicken breast strips for stir-frying

1 lb. fresh asparagus spears, trimmed, cut into 2-inch pieces

1 medium onion, cut into ½-inch wedges

1 package (8-oz.) sliced fresh mushrooms (3 cups)

¼ cup water

½ cup stir-fry sauce

¼ cup oyster sauce

1. Cook rice in 1 cup water as directed on package.

2. Meanwhile, heat 1 tablespoon of the oil in wok or 10-inch skillet over medium-high heat until hot. Add chicken strips; cook and stir 5 to 6 minutes or until no longer pink in center. Remove chicken from wok; place on plate.

3. Add remaining tablespoon oil to wok. Add asparagus and onion; cook and stir 3 minutes. Add mushrooms; cook and stir an additional 3 minutes.

4. Add reserved chicken, ¼ cup water, the stir-fry sauce and oyster sauce; cover and steam 2 to 3 minutes or until asparagus is tender and chicken is hot.

Nutrition Information Per Serving: Calories 460 • Total Fat 11g • Saturated Fat 2g • Cholesterol 70mg • Sodium 1890mg • Total Carbohydrate 55g • Dietary Fiber 2g • Sugars 9g • Protein 35g. Dietary Exchanges: 3 Starch • 1 Vegetable • 3½ Very Lean Meat • 2 Fat.

cheesy broccoli loaf

SERVINGS: 4

BECKY YEOMAN * NEW BRAUNFELS, TEXAS

2 cups frozen cut broccoli (from 1-lb. pkg.)

1 package (12-oz.) bulk sage-flavored pork sausage

1 can (11-oz.) refrigerated French loaf

4 oz. shredded mozzarella cheese (1 cup)

4 oz. shredded Cheddar cheese (1 cup)

1. Heat oven to 350°F. Cook broccoli as directed on package. Drain. Cook sausage in medium skillet over medium-high heat until thoroughly cooked, stirring frequently. Drain.

2. Unroll dough onto ungreased cookie sheet. Press to form 14x12-inch rectangle. Spoon sausage down center of dough. Top with broccoli and cheeses. Fold long sides of dough over filling meeting in center; press edges and ends to seal.

3. Bake at 350°F for 20 to 30 minutes or until golden brown. Cut into crosswise slices.

Nutrition Information Per Serving: Calories 540 • Total Fat 29g • Sodium 1320mg • Total Carbohydrate 38g • Protein 30g.

creamy scalloped potatoes and ham supper

READY TO SERVE: 30 MINUTES
SERVINGS: 4

3½ cups water

1 package (7.8-oz.) sour cream and chives potato mix

1 cup milk

2 cups cubed cooked ham

2 cups frozen mixed vegetables, thawed

1 teaspoon prepared mustard

1. Bring water to a boil in large saucepan over high heat. Stir in potato slices, reserving sauce mix packet. Boil 15 minutes.

2. Stir in milk, contents of sauce mix packet from potatoes, ham, vegetables and mustard. Reduce heat to medium; cook and stir 4 to 5 minutes or until mixture is thoroughly heated and sauce is of desired consistency, stirring frequently.

Nutrition Information Per Serving: Calories 380 • Total Fat 9g • Saturated Fat 4g • Cholesterol 45mg • Sodium 1950mg • Total Carbohydrate 53g • Dietary Fiber 4g • Sugars 6g • Protein 21g. Dietary Exchanges: 3 Starch • 1 Vegetable • 1½ Lean Meat • ½ Fat OR 3 Carbohydrate • 1 Vegetable • 1½ Lean Meat • ½ Fat.

garlic and herb shrimp and pasta supper

READY TO SERVE: 20 MINUTES
SERVINGS: 2

✻ **super fast**

4 oz. (1 cup) uncooked small shell pasta

1 cup frozen sweet peas

4 to 5 oz. shelled deveined cooked shrimp

1 container (5-oz.) light garlic and herbs soft spreadable cheese

1 jar (2.5-oz.) sliced mushrooms, drained

2 tablespoons milk

1. In large saucepan, cook pasta to desired doneness as directed on package, adding peas during last 2 minutes of cooking time. Drain; return to saucepan.

2. Add shrimp, cheese, mushrooms and milk; cook over low heat for 1 to 2 minutes or until cheese is melted and mixture is hot, stirring constantly.

Nutrition Information Per Serving: Calories 510 • Total Fat 13g • Saturated Fat 7g • Cholesterol 165mg • Sodium 900mg • Total Carbohydrate 60g • Dietary Fiber 5g • Sugars 7g • Protein 38g. Dietary Exchanges: 4 Starch • 4 Very Lean Meat • 1 Fat OR 4 Carbohydrate • 4 Very Lean Meat • 1 Fat.

skillet spanish beef 'n rice

READY TO SERVE: 20 MINUTES
SERVINGS: 4

✻ **super fast**

³⁄₄ lb. extra-lean (at least 90%) ground beef

½ medium green bell pepper, chopped (½ cup)

1 medium zucchini, quartered lengthwise, sliced (2 cups)

1 can (8 oz.) tomato sauce

1 cup water

½ teaspoon salt

½ teaspoon dried oregano leaves

½ teaspoon chili powder

1½ cups uncooked instant white rice

1. In 10-inch nonstick skillet, cook ground beef over medium-high heat for 5 to 7 minutes or until thoroughly cooked, stirring frequently. Drain.

2. Stir in bell pepper, zucchini, tomato sauce, water, salt, oregano and chili powder. Bring to a boil. Cover; cook over low heat for 2 to 3 minutes or until vegetables are tender.

3. Stir in rice. Cover; cook over low heat for 5 to 8 minutes or until liquid is absorbed. Fluff with fork before serving.

Nutrition Information Per Serving: Calories 320 • Total Fat 11g • Saturated Fat 4g • Cholesterol 55mg • Sodium 660mg • Total Carbohydrate 36g • Dietary Fiber 2g • Sugars 4g • Protein 20g. Dietary Exchanges: 2 Starch • 1 Vegetable • 2 Medium-Fat Meat.

creole-style skillet dinner

PREP TIME: 20 MINUTES
SERVINGS: 4

✻ **super fast**

1 medium onion

½ medium green bell pepper, chopped

½ lb. 97% fat-free smoked turkey kielbasa, quartered lengthwise, sliced

1 can (14½-oz.) diced tomatoes with olive oil, garlic and herbs, undrained

1 cup water

1½ cups uncooked instant rice

1. Spray large nonstick skillet with nonstick cooking spray. Heat over medium-high heat until hot. Add onion and bell-pepper; cover and cook until vegetables are crisp-tender, stirring once.

2. Add kielbasa, tomatoes and water; mix well. Bring to a boil. Stir in rice; return to a boil. Cook over low heat for about 5 minutes or until rice is tender. Fluff with a fork before serving. If desired, serve with hot pepper sauce.

Nutrition Information Per Serving: Calories 240 • Total Fat 3g • Saturated Fat 1g • Cholesterol 15mg • Sodium 1140mg • Total Carbohydrate 39g • Dietary Fiber 2g • Sugars 8g • Protein 14g. Dietary Exchanges: 1½ Starch • ½ Fruit • 2 Vegetable • 1 Lean Meat OR 2 Carbohydrate • 2 Vegetable • 1 Lean Meat.

garlic and herb shrimp and pasta supper

chicken-vegetable salad

READY TO SERVE: 30 MINUTES
SERVINGS: 5

1½ cups uncooked rotini pasta (4 oz.)

4 boneless skinless chicken breasts (about 1 lb.)

½ cup reduced-calorie Caesar dressing with ⅓ less fat

1 medium zucchini, cut lengthwise into ½-inch-thick slices

1 medium red bell pepper, halved, seeded

½ small eggplant, peeled, cut into ½-inch-thick slices

4 cups chopped romaine

1. Heat gas or charcoal grill. Cook pasta as directed on package. Drain; rinse with cold water to cool. Drain well.

2. Meanwhile, brush chicken with 1 tablespoon of the dressing (if desired, sprinkle chicken with salt and pepper).

3. When grill is heated, place chicken, zucchini, bell pepper (skin side down) and eggplant on gas grill over medium heat or on charcoal grill over medium coals; cover grill. Cook 10 to 13 minutes, turning once, until juice of chicken is no longer pink when center of thickest part is cut (170°F) and vegetables are tender.

4. Cut chicken and vegetables into bite-size pieces; place in large bowl. Gently stir in cooked pasta and lettuce. Pour remaining dressing over salad; toss gently to coat.

Nutrition Information Per Serving: Calories 250 • Total Fat 5g • Saturated Fat 1g • Trans Fat 0g • Cholesterol 60mg • Sodium 410mg • Total Carbohydrate 29g • Dietary Fiber 4g • Sugars 7g • Protein 26g. Dietary Exchanges: 1 Starch • ½ Other Carbohydrate • 1 Vegetable • 3 Very Lean Meat • ½ Fat.

A GRILLED GREAT FOR THE WHOLE GANG!

Chicken-Vegetable Salad is a great choice for family cooks who don't have time to fuss in the kitchen. Not only does the entire dish come together on the grill, but it's a delicious meal-in-one that appeals to all tastes.

Serve the salad with refreshing glasses of iced tea and bake up some cornbread twists or purchase whole grain rolls from the bakery for an even heartier meal.

And for a dinner finale that won't take a bite out of your busy, weeknight schedule, scoop some vanilla ice cream or frozen yogurt into individual serving bowls.

easy taco casserole

PREP TIME: 30 MINUTES
READY TO SERVE: 55 MINUTES
SERVINGS: 6

1 lb. ground beef

¾ cup chopped onions

1 package (1¼-oz.) taco seasoning mix with 40% less sodium

¾ cup water

1 can (16-oz.) refried beans

1 jar (8-oz.) taco sauce

2½ cups crushed tortilla chips

7 oz. shredded Cheddar cheese (1¾ cups)

1½ cups shredded lettuce

½ cup chopped tomatoes

1. Heat oven to 400°F. In medium skillet, cook ground beef and onions over medium-high heat until beef is thoroughly cooked. Drain. Stir in taco seasoning mix and water; simmer 10 minutes.

2. In medium bowl, combine refried beans and taco sauce. In ungreased 8-inch square (2-quart) baking dish, layer ½ the bean mixture, ½ the beef mixture, 2 cups tortilla chips and 1 cup of the cheese. Top with remaining bean mixture and beef mixture.

3. Bake at 400°F for 25 minutes. Remove from oven. Top with remaining tortilla chips and cheese. Return to oven; bake an additional 3 to 5 minutes or until cheese is melted. Serve with lettuce and tomatoes.

Nutrition Information Per Serving: Calories 500 • Total fat 28g • Saturated Fat 12g • Cholesterol 80mg • Sodium 1280 mg • Total Carbohydrate 36g • Dietary Fiber 6g • Sugars 3g • Protein 26g. Dietary Exchanges: 2½ Starch • 2½ Medium-Fat Meat • 3 Fat OR 2½ Carbohydrate • 2½ Medium-Fat Meat • 3 Fat.

broccoli-rice quiche

PREP TIME: 15 MINUTES
READY TO SERVE: 50 MINUTES
SERVINGS: 6

1½ cups milk

3 eggs

1 tablespoon Dijon mustard

¼ cup finely chopped onion

3 oz. shredded Swiss cheese (¾ cup)

1 jar (2 oz.) diced pimientos, drained

1½ cups chopped fresh broccoli

¾ cup uncooked instant brown or white rice

1. Heat oven to 350°F. Spray 9-inch pie pan with nonstick cooking spray. In large saucepan, heat milk until very hot but not boiling.

2. Meanwhile, in a small bowl, beat eggs and mustard until well blended. Add onion, cheese and pimientos; mix well.

3. Stir broccoli and rice into hot milk. Slowly add egg mixture, stirring constantly. Pour into sprayed pan.

4. Bake at 350°F for 30 to 35 minutes or until knife inserted in center comes out clean. Let stand for 5 minutes before serving.

Nutrition Information Per Serving: Calories 170 • Total Fat 8g • Saturated 4g • Cholesterol 125mg • Sodium 170mg • Total Carbohydrate 14g • Dietary Fiber 1g • Sugars 4g • Protein 11g. Dietary Exchanges: 1 Starch • 1 Medium-Fat Meat • ½ Fat OR 1 Carbohydrate • 1 Medium-Fat Meat • ½ Fat.

autumn pork roast dinner

PREP TIME: 15 MINUTES
READY TO SERVE: 8 HOURS 15 MINUTES
SERVINGS: 6

✳ slow cooked

1 rolled boneless pork loin roast (1¾- to 2-lb.)

¼ teaspoon salt

⅛ teaspoon pepper

3 large dark-orange sweet potatoes, peeled, thinly sliced

1 medium onion, sliced, separated into rings

¾ teaspoon dried thyme leaves

1 quart apple juice (4 cups)

1. Sprinkle pork roast with salt and pepper; place in 3½- to 4-quart slow cooker. Place sliced sweet potatoes around and on top of pork. Top with onion. Sprinkle with thyme. Pour apple juice over onion.

2. Cover; cook on Low setting for at least 8 hours.

3. Remove pork from slow cooker; place on serving platter. With slotted spoon, remove sweet potatoes and onion from slow cooker. If desired, serve pork and vegetables with juices from slow cooker.

Nutrition Information Per Serving: 380 Calories • Total Fat 11g • Saturated Fat 4g • Cholesterol 90mg • Sodium 170mg • Total Carbohydrate 37g • Dietary Fiber 2g • Sugars 21g • Protein 34g. Dietary Exchanges: 1½ Starch • 1 Fruit • 4 Lean Meat OR 2½ Carbohydrate • 4 Lean Meat.

honey-mustard chicken and carrots

PREP TIME: 30 MINUTES
SERVINGS: 4

2 teaspoons margarine or butter

4 boneless skinless chicken breast halves

½ cup apple juice

2 cups frozen baby cut carrots

2 tablespoons sweet honey mustard

3 tablespoons coarsely chopped honey-roasted peanuts

1. Melt margarine in large nonstick skillet over medium-high heat. Add chicken; cook 5 to 8 minutes or until chicken is browned on both sides.

2. Add apple juice. Reduce heat to medium; cover and cook 5 minutes. Add carrots; cover and cook 5 to 10 minutes or until chicken is fork-tender, its juices run clear and carrots are crisp-tender.

3. With slotted spoon, remove chicken and carrots from skillet; cover to keep warm. Stir mustard into liquid in skillet. Spoon mustard sauce over chicken and carrots; sprinkle with peanuts.

Nutrition Information Per Serving: Calories 250 • Total Fat 9g • Saturated 2g • Cholesterol 75mg • Sodium 210mg • Total Carbohydrate 13g • Dietary Fiber 3g • Sugars 9g • Protein 29g. Dietary Exchanges: ½ Fruit • 1 Vegetable • 4 Very Lean Meat • 1 Fat OR ½ Carbohydrate • 1 Vegetable • 4 Very Lean Meat • 1 Fat.

slow-cooked corned beef dinner

PREP TIME: 15 MINUTES
READY TO SERVE: 10 HOURS 15 MINUTES
SERVINGS: 6

* slow cooked

6 carrots, cut into 1-inch pieces

4 medium potatoes, unpeeled, cut into 1-inch cubes

1 large onion, cut into thin wedges

1 corned beef brisket (2- to 2½-lb.)

4 to 5 cups water

¼ teaspoon coarsely ground black pepper

6 whole cloves

1 bay leaf

1. In 3½ to 4-quart slow cooker, combine carrots, potatoes and onion; mix well.

2. If necessary, cut brisket to fit into slow cooker. Place brisket over vegetables. Add enough of the water to cover. If brisket is packaged with spice packet, add contents of spice packet and omit pepper, cloves and bay leaf. If not, add pepper, cloves and bay leaf.

3. Cover; cook on Low setting for 10 to 12 hours or until brisket and vegetables are tender. Remove and discard bay leaf. Cut brisket into thin slices.

Nutrition Information Per Serving: Calories 370 • Total Fat 18g • Saturated 6g • Cholesterol 90mg • Sodium 1070mg • Total Carbohydrate 31g • Dietary Fiber 5g • Sugars 7g • Protein 20g. Dietary Exchanges: 2 Starch • 2 High-Fat Meat OR 2 Carbohydrate • 2 High-Fat Meat.

fish and rice bundles

PREP TIME: 35 MINUTES
SERVINGS: 4

1 box (6.25-oz.) quick-cooking white and wild rice mix

4 sole or flounder fillets, each about 9x4 inches (¾ to 1 lb.)

Paprika

Lemon wedges, if desired

1. Heat oven to 450°F. Line 15x10-inch pan with sides with foil. Cook rice as directed on box.

2. Spoon ¾ cup cooked rice mixture down center of each sole fillet. Starting at narrow end, roll up each; secure with toothpick. With pancake turner, place roll-ups in pan. Sprinkle lightly with paprika. Cover loosely with foil.

3. Bake 15 to 20 minutes or until fish flakes easily with fork. If desired, garnish with lemon wedges.

Nutrition Information Per Serving: Calories 160 • Total Fat 1g • Saturated Fat 0g • Trans Fat 0g • Cholesterol 40mg • Sodium 340mg • Total Carbohydrate 20g • Dietary Fiber 0g • Sugars 0g • Protein 16g. Dietary Exchanges: 1½ Starch • 1½ Very Lean Meat.

layered santa fe salad

PREP TIME: 10 MINUTES
SERVINGS: 4

* super fast

¾ cup chunky-style salsa

1 teaspoon sugar

3 teaspoons chili powder

1 bag (10-oz.) mixed salad greens (8 cups loosely packed)

1 cup diced cooked chicken

1 container (8-oz.) fat-free sour cream

1 cup shredded reduced-fat Cheddar cheese (4-oz.)

2 tablespoons sliced ripe olives (from 3.8-oz. can), drained

1 cup broken baked tortilla chips

1. In small bowl, mix salsa, sugar and chili powder.

2. In 13x9-inch (3-quart) glass baking dish, arrange salad greens. Top with chicken. Spoon salsa mixture evenly over chicken. Top with spoonfuls of sour cream. Sprinkle with cheese, olives and chips. Serve immediately.

Nutrition Information Per Serving: Calories 250 • Total Fat 6g • Saturated Fat 2g • Trans Fat 0g • Cholesterol 40mg • Sodium 780mg • Total Carbohydrate 30g • Dietary Fiber 4g • Sugars 6g • Protein 22g. Dietary Exchanges: 2 Starch • 2 Lean Meat.

skillet turkey and dressing

READY TO SERVE: 20 MINUTES
SERVINGS: 4

* super fast

4 fresh turkey breast slices (about ³/₄ lb.)

¹/₂ cup chopped green bell pepper

2 tablespoons water

1 jar (12-oz.) fat-free turkey gravy

1 cup ready-to-serve fat-free chicken broth with ¹/₃ less sodium (from 14¹/₂-oz. can)

3 cups dry cubed sage and onion stuffing

1 package (6-oz.) dried fruit bits

1. Spray large nonstick skillet with nonstick cooking spray. Heat over medium-high heat until hot. Add turkey breast slices; if desired, sprinkle with salt and pepper. Cook 2 to 4 minutes or until turkey is golden brown and no longer pink in center, turning once. Remove turkey from skillet; cover to keep warm.

2. In same skillet, combine bell pepper and water; cover and cook 1 to 2 minutes. Reserve ¹/₄ cup gravy. Add remaining gravy and broth to skillet; mix well. Bring to a boil. Remove skillet from heat. Stir in stuffing and fruit bits until well moistened.

3. Return turkey to skillet; drizzle with reserved gravy. Cover; let stand 5 minutes before serving.

Nutrition Information Per Serving: Calories 390 • Total Fat 2g • Saturated Fat 0g • Cholesterol 55mg • Sodium 1220mg • Total Carbohydrate 65g • Dietary Fiber 7g • Sugars 18g • Protein 29g. **Dietary Exchanges:** 2¹/₂ Starch • 1¹/₂ Fruit • 3 Very Lean Meat OR 4 Carbohydrate • 3 Very Lean Meat.

hamburger hash skillet supper

hamburger hash skillet supper

READY TO SERVE: 25 MINUTES
SERVINGS: 5

* super fast

1 lb. lean (at least 80%) ground beef

1 bag (1-lb. 4-oz.) refrigerated diced potatoes with onions

½ cup chopped red onion

⅓ cup whipping cream

1 tablespoon Worcestershire sauce

1 teaspoon celery salt

¼ teaspoon pepper

2 medium tomatoes, chopped (1¼ cups)

1. In 12-inch nonstick skillet, cook ground beef, potatoes and red onion over medium heat for 10 to 15 minutes or until beef is thoroughly cooked and potatoes are tender, stirring frequently. Drain well.

2. Stir cream, Worcestershire sauce, celery salt and pepper into beef mixture; blend well. Cook an additional 2 to 5 minutes or until mixture is bubbly around edges, stirring frequently. Gently stir in tomatoes.

Nutrition Information Per Serving: Calories 350 • Total Fat 18g • Saturated Fat 8g • Cholesterol 70mg • Sodium 660mg • Total Carbohydrate 27g • Dietary Fiber 2g • Sugars 4g • Protein 20g. **Dietary Exchanges:** 2 Starch • 2 Medium-Fat Meat • 1½ Fat.

peppered cube steaks with potatoes and gravy

PREP TIME: 30 MINUTES
SERVINGS: 4

4 beef cube steaks (about 1 lb.)

1 teaspoon garlic-pepper blend

1⅓ cups water

2 tablespoons margarine or butter

½ cup milk

1⅓ cups mashed potato flakes

1 cup beef broth

¼ cup water

1 tablespoon cornstarch

1. Sprinkle both sides of each cube steak with garlic-pepper blend. Spray 12-inch nonstick skillet with nonstick cooking spray. Heat over medium-high heat until hot. Add steaks; cook 6 to 8 minutes, turning once.

2. Meanwhile, in medium saucepan, combine 1⅓ cups water and margarine. Bring to a boil. Remove from heat. Stir in milk and potato flakes with fork until potatoes are of desired consistency.

3. Remove steaks from skillet; cover to keep warm. In same skillet, combine broth, ¼ cup water and cornstarch; cook until bubbly and thickened, stirring constantly. Serve gravy over steaks and potatoes.

Nutrition Information Per Serving: Calories 300 • Total Fat 11g • Saturated Fat 3g • Cholesterol 65mg • Sodium 440mg • Total Carbohydrate 22g • Dietary Fiber 2g • Sugars 2g • Protein 28g. **Dietary Exchanges:** 1½ Starch • 3½ Very Lean Meat • 1½ Fat OR 1½ Carbohydrate • 3½ Very Lean Meat • 1½ Fat.

herbed chicken and stuffing supper

PREP TIME: 15 MINUTES
READY TO SERVE: 6 HOURS 35 MINUTES
SERVINGS: 6

* slow cooked

3 lb. bone-in chicken pieces, skin removed

1 can (10¾-oz.) condensed cream of chicken with herbs soup

4 medium dark-orange sweet potatoes, peeled, cut into ½-inch slices

1 package (6-oz.) chicken-flavor stuffing mix

1¼ cups water

¼ cup margarine or butter, melted

1 cup frozen cut green beans, thawed

1. Place chicken pieces in 5- to 6-quart slow cooker. Spoon soup over chicken. Top with sweet potatoes. In medium bowl, combine stuffing mix, water and margarine; mix well. Spoon over sweet potatoes.

2. Cover; cook on Low setting for 4 to 6 hours.

3. About 20 minutes before serving, sprinkle green beans over stuffing. Cover; cook on Low setting an additional 15 to 20 minutes or until beans are tender.

Nutrition Information Per Serving: Calories 620 • Total Fat 24g • Saturated Fat 6g • Cholesterol 150mg • Sodium 1070mg • Total Carbohydrate 52g • Dietary Fiber 5g • Sugars 16g • Protein 54g. **Dietary Exchanges:** 3 Starch • 1 Vegetable • 6 Lean Meat • 1 Fat OR 3½ Carbohydrate • 1 Vegetable • 6 Lean Meat • 1 Fat.

family-favorite beef stew

* slow cooked

1½ lb. beef stew meat cut into ¾-inch cubes

5 tablespoons all-purpose flour

1 teaspoon salt

½ teaspoon pepper

1 tablespoon oil

1 lb. small (2½- to 3-inch) red potatoes, quartered

1½ cups frozen pearl onions (from 16-oz. pkg.)

1 package (1-lb.) fresh baby carrots

1 jar (12-oz.) beef gravy

1 can (14.5-oz.) diced tomatoes, undrained

¼ cup cold water

1. On waxed paper, sprinkle beef with 2 tablespoons of the flour, salt and pepper; toss to coat. Heat oil in large skillet over medium-high heat until hot. Add coated beef; cook and stir 4 to 6 minutes or until browned, stirring occasionally.

2. In 4- to 6-quart slow cooker, layer potatoes, onions and carrots. Add browned beef; sprinkle with any remaining flour mixture. Top with gravy and tomatoes.

3. Cover; cook on Low setting for 8 to 10 hours.

4. About 10 minutes before serving, blend water and remaining 3 tablespoons flour until smooth. Stir into stew. Increase heat setting to High; cover and cook an additional 10 minutes or until thickened.

Nutrition Information Per Serving: Calories 380 • Total Fat 10g • Saturated Fat 3g • Cholesterol 80mg • Sodium 910mg • Total Carbohydrate 41g • Dietary Fiber 6g • Sugars 10g • Protein 31g. **Dietary Exchanges:** 1½ Starch • ½ Fruit • 2 Vegetable • 3 Lean Meat OR 2 Carbohydrate • 2 Vegetable • 3 Lean Meat.

easy seafood dinner

SERVINGS: 6

NANCY SIGNORELLI * MIAMI, FLORIDA

1 can (8-oz.) refrigerated crescent dinner rolls

1 can (4¼-oz.) tiny shrimp, drained, reserving liquid

1 lb. frozen cod or haddock, thawed, cut into ½-inch cubes

4 green onions, sliced

⅓ cup all-purpose flour

1 cup milk

1 tablespoon dried parsley flakes

½ to 1 teaspoon garlic powder

1 cup dairy sour cream

3 tablespoons dry sherry, if desired

1½ cups frozen sweet peas (from 1-lb. pkg.), thawed, drained

1 can (8-oz.) sliced water chestnuts, drained

1 jar (2.5-oz.) sliced mushrooms, drained

1. Heat oven to 350°F. Remove dough from can in rolled sections; do not unroll. Cut each section into 6 slices. Place on ungreased cookie sheet; slightly flatten each slice. Bake at 350°F for 13 to 16 minutes or until golden brown. Set aside.

2. In large skillet, combine reserved shrimp liquid, cod and green onions. Bring to a boil. Reduce heat; cover and simmer 3 to 5 minutes or until fish flakes easily with fork. Remove from heat; do not drain.

3. In medium saucepan using wire whisk, stir flour into milk. Cook over medium heat about 2 minutes or until mixture thickens and boils, stirring constantly. Stir in parsley flakes, garlic powder, sour cream and sherry. Add shrimp, peas, water chestnuts and mushrooms; mix well. Gently blend sour cream mixture into fish mixture in skillet. Heat over low heat about 5 minutes, stirring occasionally. To serve, place 2 baked crescent pinwheels on plate; spoon about 1 cup of fish mixture over pinwheels.

Nutrition Information Per Serving: Calories 420 • Total Fat 18g • Sodium 500mg • Total Carbohydrate 37g • Protein 26g.

MAKE-AHEAD SIMPLICITY

You can assemble the majority of Easy Seafood Dinner the day before, making dinnertime a snap. Simply prepare the fish mixture as directed, through the point where the sour cream is added.

Just before serving, bake the crescent pinwheels as directed in the recipe. Heat the seafood mixture, covered over low heat, stirring occasionally. Serve with the pinwheels as noted above.

family-favorite beef stew

creamy bow tie pasta with broccoli and ham

creamy bow tie pasta with broccoli and ham

READY TO SERVE: 20 MINUTES
SERVINGS: 5

* super fast

6 oz. uncooked bow tie pasta (farfalle) (2 cups)

2 cups frozen broccoli florets

1 container (10-oz.) refrigerated Alfredo sauce

2 cups diced cooked ham (about ¾ lb.)

1 can (4-oz.) mushroom pieces and stems, drained

1. Cook pasta to desired doneness as directed on package, adding broccoli during last 3 minutes of cooking time. Drain; return to saucepan.

2. Add Alfredo sauce, ham and mushrooms; cook over medium-low heat until thoroughly heated, stirring occasionally.

Nutrition Information Per Serving: Calories 410 • Total Fat 22g • Saturated Fat 11g • Cholesterol 65mg • Sodium 1130mg • Total Carbohydrate 32g • Dietary Fiber 2g • Sugars 3g • Protein 20g. Dietary Exchanges: 2 Starch • 1 Vegetable • 1½ Lean Meat • 3 Fat OR 2 Carbohydrate • 1 Vegetable • 1½ Lean Meat • 3 Fat.

gnocchi alfredo casserole

SERVINGS: 6

KELLY LYNNE BAXTER * OLYMPIA, WASHINGTON

1 package (16-oz.) potato gnocchi

¼ cup butter

1 garlic clove, minced

1 cup whipping cream

6 oz. shredded Romano cheese (1½ cups)

¼ lb. cooked ham, coarsely chopped (¾ cup)

1 package (10-oz.) frozen cut broccoli in a cheese-flavored sauce in a pouch, thawed

2 jars (4.5-oz. each) sliced mushrooms, drained

½ cup Parmesan dry bread crumbs

1. Heat oven to 400°F. Cook gnocchi as directed on package, omitting salt.

2. Meanwhile, melt butter in large nonstick skillet over medium heat. Add garlic; cook and stir 3 minutes. Add cream and mix well. Gradually add 1 cup of the cheese, stirring after each addition until melted.

3. Add ham, broccoli in sauce, mushrooms and cooked gnocchi; mix well. Spoon into ungreased 8- or 9-inch square (2-quart) glass baking dish. In small bowl, combine bread crumbs and remaining ½ cup cheese; mix well. Sprinkle over casserole.

4. Bake at 400°F for 30 minutes or until golden brown. Cool 5 minutes before serving.

Nutrition Information Per Serving: Calories 550 • Total Fat 33g • Sodium 1630mg • Total Carbohydrate 42g • Protein 20g.

slow-cooked turkey dinner

PREP TIME: 15 MINUTES
READY TO SERVE: 7 HOURS 45 MINUTES
SERVINGS: 4 SERVINGS

* slow cooked

6 small red potatoes (about 2½ inches in diameter), unpeeled, quartered

2 cups sliced fresh carrots

1½ lb. turkey thighs, skinned

¼ cup all-purpose flour

2 tablespoons dry onion soup mix

⅓ cup chicken broth or water

1 can (10¾-oz.) condensed 98% fat-free cream of mushroom soup with 30% less sodium

1. Place potatoes and carrots in a 3½- to 4-quart slow cooker.

2. In a medium bowl, combine all remaining ingredients; blend well. Pour over turkey.

3. Cover; cook on High setting for 30 minutes.

4. Reduce heat to Low setting; cook at least 7 hours.

Nutrition Information Per Serving: Calories 410 • Total Fat 8g • Saturated Fat 3g • Cholesterol 65mg • Sodium 1130mg • Total Carbohydrate 57g • Dietary Fiber 6g • Sugars 9g • Protein 28g. Dietary Exchanges: 3½ Starch • 1 Vegetable • 2 Lean Meat OR 3½ Carbohydrate • 1 Vegetable • 2 Lean Meat.

navajo taco salad

READY TO SERVE: 20 MINUTES
SERVINGS: 4

* super fast

1 medium green bell pepper, coarsely chopped (1 cup)

1 medium onion, coarsely chopped (1/2 cup)

1 can (15-oz.) kidney beans, drained

1 cup chunky-style salsa

1/2 cup frozen whole kernel corn (from 1-lb. bag)

4 oz. baked tortilla chips (about 5 1/2 cups)

6 cups torn romaine

1 cup shredded Cheddar cheese (4 oz.)

1/4 cup fat-free sour cream

Fresh cilantro leaves, if desired

1. Heat 10-inch nonstick skillet over medium-high heat. Add bell pepper and onion; cook 5 minutes, stirring frequently, until almost tender. Stir in kidney beans, salsa and corn. Cover; simmer 3 minutes, stirring occasionally, until vegetables are tender and mixture is hot.

2. Meanwhile, arrange chips on individual dinner plates. Top each with romaine. Spoon vegetable-bean mixture over lettuce. Sprinkle each with cheese. Top with sour cream and cilantro, if desired.

Nutrition Information Per Serving: Calories 420 • Total Fat 11g • Saturated Fat 6g • Trans Fat 0g • Cholesterol 30mg • Sodium 710mg • Total Carbohydrate 64g • Dietary Fiber 12g • Sugars 8g • Protein 22g. Dietary Exchanges: 4 Starch • 1 1/2 Medium-Fat Meat.

speedy layered chicken enchilada pie

SERVINGS: 6

KAREN HALL * MINNEAPOLIS, MINNESOTA

1 package (11.5-oz.) flour tortillas (8 tortillas)

2 cups cubed cooked chicken

1/2 cup uncooked instant white rice

8 oz. shredded reduced-fat Monterey Jack cheese (2 cups)

1 can (15-oz.) black beans, drained, rinsed

1 can (19-oz.) red enchilada sauce

1 cup frozen shoepeg white corn (from 1-lb. pkg.), thawed

1 cup chunky-style salsa

2 tablespoons thinly sliced green onions

Reduced-fat dairy sour cream, if desired

Additional chopped green onions, if desired

1. Heat oven to 350°F. Spray 9-inch round (2-quart) glass baking dish or casserole with nonstick cooking spray. Cut 5 of the tortillas in half. Cut remaining tortillas into 2 1/2-inch-wide strips. In large bowl, combine chicken, rice, 1 cup of the cheese, beans and 1 cup of the enchilada sauce; mix well.

2. Layer 4 tortilla halves in bottom of sprayed baking dish. Top with 1/4 cup enchilada sauce and half of the chicken mixture. Top with 2 tortilla halves; fill in empty spaces with 3 tortilla strips. Spoon corn over tortillas. Spread salsa over corn. Layer with 2 tortilla halves and 3 strips. Top with remaining half of chicken mixture. Continue layering with remaining 2 tortilla halves and strips, enchilada sauce, cheese and 2 tablespoons of the green onions.

3. Bake at 350°F for 35 to 45 minutes or until mixture is thoroughly heated and cheese is melted. Cool 5 minutes. Top with sour cream and green onions.

Nutrition Information Per Serving: Calories 540 • Total Fat 19g • Sodium 1410mg • Total Carbohydrate 57g • Protein 35g.

TIME-SAVING STRATIGIES

It's easy to shave minutes off the clock when preparing the enchilada pie:

* Use a pizza cutter and cutting board to quickly slice the flour tortillas. Or, cut them with a pair of kitchen shears.

* If you don't have any leftover chicken, pick up a box of cubed, cooked chicken from the supermarket.

* Thaw the corn by setting it in a colander and rinsing with warm water.

chicken and noodle supper

READY TO SERVE: 20 MINUTES
SERVINGS: 4

* super fast

2½ cups water

2 packages (3-oz. each) chicken-flavor ramen noodle soup mix

1½ cups cubed cooked chicken

1 cup frozen peas and carrots

2 tablespoons chopped onion or 2 teaspoons instant chopped onion

1 jar (2.5-oz.) sliced mushrooms, drained

1. Bring water to a boil in large saucepan. Add ramen noodles, contents of soup mix seasoning packets, chicken, peas and carrots and onion; mix well. Cook over medium-high heat for 4 to 6 minutes or until vegetables are tender.

2. Stir in mushrooms; cook until thoroughly heated.

Nutrition Information Per Serving: Calories 320 • Total Fat 12g • Saturated Fat 5g • Cholesterol 45mg • Sodium 800mg • Total Carbohydrate 32g • Dietary Fiber 2g • Sugars 3g • Protein 21g. **Dietary Exchanges:** 2 Starch • 2 Very Lean Meat • 2 Fat OR 2 Carbohydrate • 2 Very Lean Meat • 2 Fat.

chicken à la king

chicken à la king

1 can (12-oz.) refrigerated fluffy buttermilk biscuits

¼ cup margarine or butter

⅓ cup all-purpose flour

1 can (10¼-oz.) condensed chicken broth

1¼ cups milk

2 cups cubed cooked chicken

1 cup frozen sweet peas

1 can (4-oz.) mushroom pieces and stems, drained

1 jar (2-oz.) diced pimientos, drained

¼ teaspoon salt

¼ teaspoon pepper

1. Bake biscuits as directed on can.

2. Meanwhile, melt margarine in large saucepan over medium-low heat. Add flour; blend well. Add broth and milk. Cook, stirring constantly, until the mixture boils and thickens.

3. Add all remaining ingredients; simmer 5 to 10 minutes or until mixture is thoroughly heated through.

4. Split warm biscuits; place on serving plates. Spoon hot chicken mixture over biscuits.

Nutrition Information Per Serving: Calories 500 • Total Fat 23g • Saturated Fat 6g • Cholesterol 55mg • Sodium 1600mg • Total Carbohydrate 44g • Dietary Fiber 3g • Sugars 9g • Protein 28g. Dietary Exchanges: 3 Starch • 2½ Lean Meat • 2½ Fat OR 3 Carbohydrate • 2½ Lean Meat • 2½ Fat.

hot tuna salad

1 can (10¾-oz.) condensed 98% fat-free cream of celery soup

1 can (8-oz.) crushed pineapple in unsweetened juice, undrained

1 can (8-oz.) sliced water chestnuts, drained

1 jar (4-oz.) sliced pimientos, drained

1½ cups uncooked instant white or brown rice

1½ cups sliced celery

⅔ cup raisins

1 tablespoon salt-free lemon-pepper seasoning

1½ cups water

1 can (12-oz.) water-packed chunk light tuna, drained, flaked

1 cup fat-free mayonnaise or salad dressing

½ cup sliced almonds

1. Heat oven to 400°F. Spray 13x9-inch (3-quart) baking dish with nonstick cooking spray.

2. In large nonstick saucepan, combine soup, pineapple, water chestnuts, pimientos, rice, celery, raisins, lemon-pepper seasoning and water; mix well. Bring to a boil. Remove from heat. Stir in tuna and mayonnaise; mix well. Spoon into sprayed baking dish. Top with almonds.

3. Bake at 400°F for 15 to 20 minutes or until thoroughly heated.

Nutrition Information Per Serving: Calories 270 • Total Fat 5g • Saturated Fat 1g • Cholesterol 10mg • Sodium 670mg • Total Carbohydrate 44g • Dietary Fiber 4g • Sugars 15g • Protein 13g. Dietary Exchanges: 2 Starch • 1 Fruit • 1 Very Lean Meat • ½ Fat OR 3 Carbohydrate • 1 Very Lean Meat • ½ Fat.

EASY ALTERATIONS

Want to customize Hot Tuna Salad to your own taste? Consider replacing the raisins with some peeled and diced apple or try using dried cranberries if the sweet gems suit your family better.

Experiment with different seasonings, too. Swap out the lemon-pepper for dried thyme or rosemary or even a little curry or Chinese five spice powder. Heat things up by stirring some hot pepper sauce or red pepper flakes in with the tuna and mayonnaise.

---

skillet meatballs with linguine

READY TO SERVE: 25 MINUTES
SERVINGS: 4

8 oz. uncooked linguine

1 package (10.5-oz.) frozen cooked light Italian meatballs

1 can (15-oz.) Italian-style tomato sauce

1 can (10.75-oz.) condensed 98% fat-free cream of mushroom soup with 30% less sodium

1 jar (2.5-oz.) sliced mushrooms, drained

1/4 cup chopped fresh parsley, if desired

1. Cook linguine as directed on package. Drain; cover to keep warm.

2. Meanwhile, in 10-inch skillet, combine all remaining ingredients except parsley; mix well. Bring to a boil over medium-high heat. Reduce heat to medium-low; cover and cook 8 to 10 minutes or until meatballs are thoroughly heated, stirring occasionally.

3. Serve meatballs with sauce over cooked linguine. Sprinkle with parsley.

Nutrition Information Per Serving: Calories 430 • Total Fat 10g • Saturated Fat 4g • Cholesterol 30mg • Sodium 1250mg • Total Carbohydrate 61g • Dietary Fiber 5g • Sugars 12g • Protein 25g. Dietary Exchanges: 3 Starch • 1/2 Fruit • 1 Vegetable • 2 Medium-Fat Meat.

SIMPLE KITCHEN SECRET

Dried pasta is a staple in most homes, but you can beat the clock with the refrigerated variety. For instance, use one 9-ounce package of refrigerated linguine instead of the dried type called for in this recipe. Not only does it offer a fresher taste, but it cooks much quicker than dried pasta. Just follow the package directions and you'll be happily surprised to see that the linguine is table-ready in just a couple of minutes.

pineapple chicken and rice

READY TO SERVE: 50 MINUTES
SERVINGS: 4

2 tablespoons oil

4 bone-in chicken breast halves, skin removed, if desired

1 can (14.5-oz.) ready-to-serve chicken broth

1/2 cup purchased sweet-and-sour sauce

1 can (8-oz.) pineapple tidbits in unsweetened juice, drained, reserving juice

1 cup uncooked regular long-grain white rice

1/2 cup chopped red bell pepper

1/2 cup chopped green bell pepper

1/2 cup sliced green onions

1. Heat oil in large skillet over medium-high heat until hot. Add chicken; cook 2 to 3 minutes or each side, or until browned. Remove chicken from skillet.

2. Add chicken broth, sweet-and-sour sauce, pineapple liquid and rice to skillet; blend well. Bring to a boil. Add chicken breast halves, meaty side down. Reduce heat to low; cover and simmer 25 to 30 minutes, or until most of the liquid is absorbed, chicken is fork tender and juices run clear.

3. Remove chicken from skillet; cover to keep warm. Add bell peppers, green onions and pineapple tidbits to rice mixture. Cook an additional 5 minutes, or until peppers are crisp-tender. Spoon rice mixture onto platter; top with chicken.

Nutrition Information Per Serving: Calories 510 • Total Fat 15g • Saturated Fat 3g • Cholesterol 80mg • Sodium 500mg • Dietary Fiber 2g. Dietary Exchanges: 3 Starch • 1 Fruit • 4 Lean Meat OR 4 Carbohydrate • 4 Lean Meat.

easy moo goo gai pan

READY TO SERVE: 40 MINUTES
SERVINGS: 4

4 boneless skinless chicken breast halves, cut into thin strips

3 tablespoons cornstarch

1 tablespoon dry sherry

2 tablespoons soy sauce

1 cup chicken broth

4 teaspoons cornstarch

1 tablespoon oil

1 teaspoon grated gingerroot

2 garlic cloves, minced

8 oz. fresh snow pea pods, trimmed, cut diagonally in half

1 can (8-oz.) bamboo shoots, drained

1 jar (4.5-oz.) whole mushrooms, drained

3 green onions, cut into ½-in. pieces

4 cups cooked rice (cooked as directed on package)

1. In a medium bowl, combine chicken, 1 tablespoon cornstarch, sherry and soy sauce; mix well.

2. In a small bowl, combine broth and 4 teaspoons cornstarch; mix well.

3. Heat oil in large skillet or wok over medium-high heat until hot. Add chicken mixture, gingerroot and garlic; cook and stir 3 to 4 minutes, or until the chicken is no longer pink.

4. Add pea pods, bamboo shoots and mushrooms; cook and stir 3 to 4 minutes, or until vegetables are crisp-tender.

5. Add broth mixture and green onions; cook until thickened and bubbly, stirring constantly. Serve over rice.

Nutrition Information Per Serving: Calories 450 • Total Fat 8g • Saturated Fat 2g • Cholesterol 70mg • Sodium 920mg • Dietary Fiber 4g. Dietary Exchanges: 3 Starch • 3 Vegetable • 3 Lean Meat OR 3 Carbohydrate • 3 Vegetable • 3 Lean Meat.

twenty-minute cassoulet

READY TO SERVE: 20 MINUTES
SERVINGS: 8

∗ super fast

1 lb. smoked kielbasa sausage or turkey sausage, cut in half lengthwise, sliced

1 cup sliced celery

½ cup chopped onion

2 garlic cloves, minced

½ teaspoon dried thyme leaves

½ teaspoon dried rosemary leaves, crushed

2 cans (15.5-oz. each) great northern beans, drained, rinsed

1 can (15.5- or 15-oz.) light red kidney beans, drained, rinsed

1 can (14.5-oz.) diced tomatoes, undrained

1 teaspoon brown sugar

¼ cup sliced green onions

1. In nonstick Dutch oven or large saucepan, brown sausage over medium heat, stirring frequently. With slotted spoon, remove sausage; set aside.

2. Reserve 1/2 teaspoon drippings in Dutch oven. Add celery, onion, garlic, thyme and rosemary; cook and stir 5 minutes or until vegetables are crisp-tender.

3. Add cooked sausage and remaining ingredients except green onions. Bring to a boil. Reduce heat to low; cover and simmer 10 minutes or until thoroughly heated.

4. Top each serving with sliced green onions.

Nutrition Information Per Serving: Calories 320 • Total Fat 16g • Saturated Fat 6g • Cholesterol 40mg • Sodium 920mg • Total Carbohydrate 27g • Dietary Fiber 8g • Sugars 4g • Protein 16g. Dietary Exchanges: 2 Starch • 1½ High-Fat Meat • ½ Fat OR 2 Carbohydrate • 1½ High-Fat Meat • ½ Fat.

santa fe chicken bread bowls

READY TO SERVE: 30 MINUTES
SERVINGS: 6

MAUREEN GILL ✸ GARFIELD HEIGHTS, OHIO

2 cans (11-oz. each) refrigerated French loaf

1 tablespoon olive or vegetable oil

2 boneless skinless chicken breast halves, cut into ½-inch pieces

1 red bell pepper, chopped

¼ cup chopped red onion

1 can (16-oz.) chili beans, drained

1 can (11-oz.) vacuum-packed super sweet yellow and white corn, drained

1 can (10-oz.) red enchilada sauce

¾ cup dairy sour cream

½ cup ketchup

1 package (1.25-oz.) taco seasoning mix

1 tablespoon dried parsley flakes

1 teaspoon dried basil leaves

2 oz. shredded Cheddar cheese (½ cup), if desired

1. Heat oven to 350°F. Spray cookie sheet with nonstick cooking spray. Remove dough from cans. Cut each loaf into 3 pieces; shape each into ball, placing seam at bottom so dough is smooth on top. Place dough balls, seam side down, on sprayed cookie sheet. Bake at 350°F for 22 to 26 minutes or until golden brown.

2. Meanwhile, heat oil in large saucepan over medium-high heat until hot. Add chicken, bell pepper and onion; cook 5 to 7 minutes or until chicken is no longer pink in center, stirring occasionally. Add all remaining ingredients except cheese; mix well. Bring to a boil. Reduce heat to medium-low; simmer 7 minutes or until thoroughly heated, stirring occasionally.

3. With sharp knife, cut small portion off top of each loaf. Lightly press center of bread down to form bowls. Place each bread bowl on individual serving plate. Spoon about 1 cup chicken mixture into each. Sprinkle evenly with cheese. Place top of each bread bowl next to filled bread bowl.

Nutrition Information Per Serving: Calories 590 • Total Fat 18g • Sodium 1960mg • Total Carbohydrate 78g • Protein 26g.

SERVE A NO-FUSS SENSATION

Bread bowls are easy when you start with refrigerated, crusty French loaf dough. Just cut, shape and bake for an impressive dinner that takes only a few moments to create.

While the bread is baking, you can whip up whatever taste sensation you are filling the bowls with. Try the bowls with your favorite soup recipe (thick, creamy soups work best), or ladle in some heartwarming chili or an old-fashioned stew.

chunky skillet sausage stew

READY TO SERVE: 35 MINUTES
SERVINGS: 6

1 lb. smoked sausage, cut into 1½- to 2-inch chunks

6 small new red potatoes, unpeeled, quartered

1 small onion, cut into 8 wedges

1 can (14.5-oz.) stewed tomatoes, undrained

⅛ teaspoon pepper

½ medium head cabbage, cut into 6 wedges

1. In large skillet, combine all ingredients except cabbage; mix well. Arrange cabbage wedges over top.

2. Bring to a boil. Reduce heat to medium-low; cover and cook 15 to 20 minutes or until vegetables are tender. Spoon sauce from skillet over cabbage wedges before serving.

Nutrition Information Per Serving: Calories 390 • Total Fat 23g • Saturated Fat 8g • Cholesterol 55mg • Sodium 890mg • Total Carbohydrate 32g • Dietary Fiber 5g • Sugars 6g • Protein 14g. Dietary Exchanges: 1½ Starch • 2 Vegetable • 1 High-Fat Meat • 3 Fat OR 1½ Carbohydrate • 2 Vegetable • 1 High-Fat Meat • 3 Fat.

smothered buttermilk chicken over biscuits

PREP TIME: 25 MINUTES
READY TO SERVE: 8 HOURS 45 MINUTES
SERVINGS: 5

✳ slow cooked

- 1 lb. boneless skinless chicken thighs, cut into ¾-inch pieces
- 3 medium carrots, sliced
- ⅓ cup chopped onion
- ½ cup water
- 2 tablespoons margarine or butter, melted
- ¼ teaspoon salt
- ¼ teaspoon pepper
- 1 bay leaf
- 1 package (1.2-oz.) roasted chicken gravy mix
- ⅓ cup buttermilk
- 2 teaspoons all-purpose flour
- 1 cup frozen sweet peas, thawed, drained
- 1 can (10.2-oz.) large refrigerated buttermilk biscuits (5 biscuits)

1. In 4- to 6-quart slow cooker, combine chicken, carrots, onion, water, margarine, salt, pepper and bay leaf; mix well.

2. Cover; cook on Low setting for 6 to 8 hours.

3. About 20 minutes before serving, stir gravy mix into chicken mixture. Remove and discard bay leaf. In measuring cup, blend buttermilk and flour until smooth. Stir flour mixture and peas into chicken mixture; mix well. Increase heat setting to High; cover and cook an additional 10 to 15 minutes or until peas are cooked.

4. Meanwhile, bake biscuits as directed on can. Serve chicken mixture over split biscuits.

Nutrition Information Per Serving: Calories 440 • Total Fat 21g • Saturated Fat 5g • Cholesterol 60mg • Sodium 170mg • Total Carbohydrate 39g • Dietary Fiber 3g • Sugars 10g • Protein 23g. **Dietary Exchanges:** 2 Starch • ½ Fruit • 2½ Lean Meat • 2½ Fat OR 2½ Carbohydrate • 2½ Lean Meat • 2½ Fat.

skillet chicken and winter vegetables

READY TO SERVE: 45 MINUTES
SERVINGS: 4

3 tablespoons all-purpose flour

$3/4$ teaspoon peppered seasoned salt

4 chicken drumsticks, skin removed

4 chicken thighs, skin removed

2 cups refrigerated red or new potato wedges (from 20-oz. pkg.)

1 cup fresh baby carrots

1 medium onion, cut into thin wedges

1 can (14.5-oz.) Italian-style stewed tomatoes, undrained

1. Spray 12-inch nonstick skillet with nonstick cooking spray. Heat over medium-high heat until hot. In shallow bowl, combine flour and seasoned salt; mix well. Coat chicken pieces with flour mixture; add to skillet. Cook 6 to 10 minutes or until browned on all sides.

2. Add all remaining ingredients; stir gently to mix. Increase heat to high; cook 2 minutes. Reduce heat to medium-low; cover and simmer 20 to 25 minutes or until chicken is fork-tender, its juices run clear and vegetables are tender, stirring occasionally.

Nutrition Information Per Serving: Calories 315 • Total Fat 8g • Saturated Fat 2g • Cholesterol 90mg • Sodium 690mg • Total Carbohydrate 30g • Dietary Fiber 4g • Sugars 6g • Protein 31g. Dietary Exchanges: $1^{1}/2$ Starch • 1 Vegetable • $3^{1}/2$ Lean Meat • 2 Carbohydrate Choices.

pork chop dinner with bacon and cider gravy

READY TO SERVE: 30 MINUTES
SERVINGS: 4

4 oz. uncooked extra-wide egg noodles ($2^{1}/2$ cups)

2 cups frozen cut green beans

3 slices bacon, cut into small pieces

4 boneless pork loin chops (4-oz. each)

$1/4$ cup chopped onion

1 cup apple cider or juice

1 teaspoon honey mustard

$1/4$ teaspoon salt

$1/4$ teaspoon dried thyme leaves

$1/8$ teaspoon pepper

1 tablespoon water

1 tablespoon cornstarch

1. Cook noodles to desired doneness as directed on package, adding green beans during last 4 minutes of cooking time. Drain; cover to keep warm.

2. Meanwhile, in large skillet, cook bacon over medium heat until brown and crisp. With slotted spoon remove bacon from skillet; drain on paper towels. Drain and discard all drippings from skillet.

3. Place pork chops in skillet near center. Sprinkle onion around pork chops. Cook 3 to 5 minutes or until pork chops are golden brown, turning once. In small bowl, combine cider, mustard, salt, thyme and pepper; mix well. Pour over chops. Reduce heat to low; cover and cook 10 to 15 minutes or until pork is no longer pink in center.

4. Arrange noodles and green beans on serving platter. Place pork chops on top of noodle mixture; cover to keep warm.

5. In small bowl, combine water and cornstarch; blend until smooth. Add to juices in skillet; mix well. Cook and stir over medium-low heat until bubbly and thickened; boil 1 minute. (If desired, gravy can be strained.)

6. To serve, pour gravy over pork chops and noodles. Sprinkle with bacon.

Nutrition Information Per Serving: Calories 340 • Total Fat 10g • Saturated Fat 3g • Cholesterol 85mg • Sodium 300mg • Total Carbohydrate 34g • Dietary Fiber 2g • Sugars 9g • Protein 28g. Dietary Exchanges: $1^{1}/2$ Starch • $1/2$ Fruit • 1 Vegetable • 3 Lean Meat OR 2 Carbohydrate • 1 Vegetable • 3 Lean Meat.

skillet chicken and winter vegetables

drumsticks with sweet potatoes and pineapple

PREP TIME: 15 MINUTES
READY TO SERVE: 10 HOURS 15 MINUTES
SERVINGS: 4

* slow cooked

- 2 medium dark-orange sweet potatoes, peeled, sliced (about 3 cups)
- 1 can (8-oz.) pineapple tidbits in unsweetened juice, undrained
- ½ cup chicken broth
- ¼ cup finely chopped onion
- 1 teaspoon grated gingerroot (if desired)
- ¼ cup barbecue sauce
- ¼ teaspoon pepper
- 2 tablespoons honey
- ½ teaspoon dry mustard
- 8 chicken drumsticks (about 1½ lb.), skin removed

1. In 4- to 6-quart slow cooker, combine sweet potatoes, pineapple with liquid, broth onion and gingerroot; mix well.

2. In a small bowl, combine barbecue sauce, honey and dry mustard; mix well. Coat chicken drumsticks well with barbecue sauce mixture. Arrange chicken in single layer over potato mixture in slow cooker; overlapping slightly if necessary. Spoon any remaining barbecue sauce mixture over chicken.

3. Cover and cook on Low setting for 7 to 10 hours.

Nutrition Information Per Serving: Calories 300 • Total Fat 6g • Saturated Fat 2g • Cholesterol 80mg • Sodium 300mg • Total Carbohydrate 34g • Dietary Fiber 3g • Sugars 25g • Protein 28g. Dietary Exchanges: 1 Starch • 1½ Fruit • 3 Lean Meat OR 2½ Carbohydrate • 3 Lean Meat.

salmon à la king

READY TO SERVE: 25 MINUTES
SERVINGS: 4

* **super fast**

1 can (11-oz.) refrigerated soft breadsticks

¼ cup margarine or butter

½ cup coarsely chopped green bell pepper

½ cup sliced celery

3 tablespoons all-purpose flour

¼ teaspoon salt

1½ cups milk

1 can (14¾-oz.) salmon, drained, flaked

1 jar (2-oz.) chopped pimientos, drained

Fresh dill, if desired

1. Heat oven to 350°F. Separate breadsticks. Stack 3 breadsticks together; stretch to a 10-inch rope. Twist rope; shape into ring, pinching ends to seal. Place on ungreased cookie sheet. Repeat with remaining breadsticks. Bake at 350°F for 18 to 22 minutes or until golden brown.

2. Meanwhile, melt margarine in large skillet over medium-high heat. Add bell pepper and celery; cook and stir 1 minute. Stir in flour and salt; cook until mixture is smooth and bubbly. Gradually add milk. Cook until mixture boils and thickens, stirring constantly.

3. Gently fold in salmon and pimientos; cook until thoroughly heated. Serve over baked breadsticks rings. Garnish with fresh dill.

Nutrition Information Per Serving: Calories 530 • Total Fat 24g • Saturated Fat 6g • Cholesterol 45mg • Sodium 1350mg • Total Carbohydrate 48g • Dietary Fiber 2g • Sugars 10g • Protein 28g. Dietary Exchanges: 3 Starch • 3 Lean Meat • 3 Fat OR 3 Carbohydrate • 3 Lean Meat • 3 Fat.

tarragon grilled fish and vegetables

READY TO SERVE: 35 MINUTES
SERVINGS: 4

2 tablespoons olive or vegetable oil

2 carrots cut into julienne strips (1½x¼x¼-inch)

1 zucchini, cut into julienne strips (1½x¼x¼-inch)

1 small red bell pepper, cut into thin strips

½ cup sliced red onion

4 orange roughy fillets (6-oz. each)

Salt, if desired

Pepper, if desired

4 teaspoons chopped fresh tarragon or 1½ teaspoons dried tarragon leaves

2 tablespoons margarine or butter, chilled

1. Heat grill. Heat oil in medium skillet over medium-high heat until hot. Add carrots, zucchini, bell pepper and onion; cook and stir 2 to 3 minutes or until vegetables are crisp-tender.

2. Cut four 18x12-inch pieces of heavy-duty foil. Place 1 orange roughy fillet on each; sprinkle with salt and pepper, if desired. Top each fillet with ¼ of vegetable mixture, tarragon and margarine. Wrap each packet securely using double-fold seal, allowing room for heat expansion.

3. When ready to grill, place packets, seam side up, on gas grill over medium heat or on charcoal grill 4 to 6 inches from medium coals. Cook 12 to 18 minutes or until fish flakes easily with fork, rearranging packets several times during cooking. Open packets carefully to allow hot steam to escape.

Nutrition Information Per Serving: Calories 260 • Total Fat 14g • Saturated Fat 2g • Cholesterol 35mg • Sodium 190mg • Total Carbohydrate 8g • Dietary Fiber 2g • Sugars 5g • Protein 26g. Dietary Exchanges: 1½ Vegetable • 3½ Very Lean Meat • 2 Fat.

soups & sandwiches

spaghetti and meatball soup ✳ p. 74

fast fajita and vegetable pita ✳ p. 85

turkey-vegetable-cheddar soup ✳ p. 89

sandwiches on a stick ✳ p. 109

bistro burger

onion-topped burger

bistro burgers

READY TO SERVE: 25 MINUTES
SERVINGS: 4

* super fast

1½ lb. lean (at least 80%) ground beef

¼ teaspoon salt

¼ teaspoon pepper

4 kaiser rolls, split

¼ cup creamy mustard-mayonnaise sauce

4 thin slices sweet onion (Walla Walla, Maui or Texas Sweet)

4 tomato slices

4 oz. thinly sliced fresh Parmesan cheese

½ cup fresh basil leaves

1. Heat gas or charcoal grill. In medium bowl, combine ground beef, salt and pepper; mix well. Shape mixture into 4 (½-inch-thick) patties.

2. When grill is heated, place patties on gas grill over medium heat or on charcoal grill 4 to 6 inches from medium coals. Cook covered 11 to 13 minutes or until meat thermometer inserted in center of patties reads 160°F, turning once.

3. To toast rolls, during last 1 to 2 minutes of cooking time, place rolls, cut sides down, on grill.

4. Spread cut sides of rolls with mustard-mayonnaise sauce. Place patties on bottom halves of rolls. Top each with onion, tomato, cheese, basil and top half of roll.

Nutrition Information Per Serving: Calories 640 • Total Fat 35g • Saturated Fat 15g • Cholesterol 125mg • Sodium 1160mg • Total Carbohydrate 35g • Dietary Fiber 2g • Sugars 2g • Protein 46g. Dietary Exchanges: 2 Starch • 5½ Medium-Fat Meat • 1 Fat.

onion-topped burgers

READY TO SERVE: 25 MINUTES
SERVINGS: 4

* super fast

1 lb. lean (at least 80%) ground beef

¼ cup fresh bread crumbs

¼ cup beef broth or water

2 tablespoons dry French onion soup mix (from 1-oz. package)

1 large sweet onion (Walla Walla, Maui or Texas Sweet), cut into ⅛-inch-thick slices, separated into rings

2 tablespoons beef broth or water

¼ teaspoon salt

¼ teaspoon pepper

4 burger buns, split

1. Heat gas or charcoal grill. In medium bowl, combine ground beef, bread crumbs, ¼ cup beef broth and soup mix; mix well. Shape mixture into 4 (½-inch-thick) patties. Place sliced onion, 2 tablespoons beef broth, salt and pepper in foil grilling bag or foil packet.

2. When grill is heated, place patties and grilling bag with onion mixture on gas grill over medium heat or on charcoal grill 4 to 6 inches from medium coals. Cook 11 to 13 minutes or until meat thermometer inserted in center of patties reads 160°F, turning patties once and turning grilling bag frequently.

3. To toast buns, during last 1 to 2 minutes of cooking time, place buns, cut side down, on grill.

4. Place patties on bottom halves of buns. Top each with onions and top half of bun.

Nutrition Information Per Serving: Calories 370 • Total Fat 17g • Saturated Fat 6g • Cholesterol 70mg • Sodium 830mg • Total Carbohydrate 30g • Dietary Fiber 3g • Sugars 9g • Protein 25g. Dietary Exchanges: 2 Starch • 3 Medium-Fat Meat.

quick chicken subs

READY TO SERVE: 15 MINUTES
SANDWICHES: 4

* super fast

¼ cup fat-free mayonnaise or salad dressing

4 hoagie buns (2-oz. each), split

1½ cups shredded lettuce

¼ lb. thinly sliced 98%-fat-free cooked chicken breast

1 large tomato, cut into 8 slices

2 oz. reduced-fat hot pepper cheese, shredded (½ cup)

1. Spread mayonnaise on cut sides of hoagie buns.

2. Layer remaining ingredients evenly on bottom halves of buns. Top with top halves of buns. Wrap each sandwich securely with foil or plastic wrap; take with you for an on-the-go dinner.

Nutrition Information Per Serving: Calories 260 • Total Fat 6g • Saturated Fat 3g • Trans Fat 0g • Cholesterol 35mg • Sodium 590mg • Total Carbohydrate 35g • Dietary Fiber 3g • Sugars 8g • Protein 17g. Dietary Exchanges: 2 Starch • 1 Vegetable • 1 Very Lean Meat • 1 Fat.

spaghetti and meatball soup

READY TO SERVE: 20 MINUTES
SERVINGS: 5

* super fast

- 4 cups water
- 4 oz. uncooked ready-cut spaghetti (short curved pasta) (1 cup)
- 20 frozen cooked meatballs
- 1 jar (27- to 30-oz.) spaghetti sauce

1. Bring water to a boil in large saucepan. Add spaghetti and meatballs; cook about 10 minutes or until spaghetti is tender. Do not drain.

2. Stir in spaghetti sauce. Cook until thoroughly heated. If desired, sprinkle individual servings with grated Parmesan cheese.

Nutrition Information Per Serving: Calories 510 • Total Fat 29g • Saturated Fat 13g • Cholesterol 75mg • Sodium 1530mg • Total Carbohydrate 38g • Dietary Fiber 7g • Sugars 2g • Protein 24 g. Dietary Exchanges: 2½ Starch • 2½ High-Fat Meat • 1½ Fat OR 2½ Carbohydrate • 2½ High-Fat Meat • 1½ Fat.

garlicky turkey burgers

READY TO SERVE: 25 MINUTES
SERVINGS: 4

* super fast

- 1 lb. lean ground turkey
- ½ cup refrigerated shredded hash brown potatoes
- ¼ cup sliced green onions
- 2 tablespoons grated Parmesan cheese
- 2 teaspoons minced garlic
- ¼ teaspoon seasoned salt
- ⅛ teaspoon pepper
- ¼ cup mayonnaise or salad dressing, if desired
- 4 whole wheat hamburger buns, split
- 4 lettuce leaves
- 4 slices tomato, if desired

1. In medium bowl, combine all ingredients except mayonnaise, buns, lettuce and tomato; mix well. Shape into 4 (½-inch-thick) patties. Place patties on broiler pan.

2. Broil 4 to 6 inches from heat for 8 to 10 minutes or until thermometer inserted in center of patties reads 165°F.

3. Spread mayonnaise on cut sides of buns. Place lettuce, turkey burgers and tomato on bottom halves of buns. Cover with top halves of buns.

Nutrition Information Per Serving: Calories 300 • Total Fat 9g • Saturated Fat 3g • Cholesterol 80mg • Sodium 450mg • Total Carbohydrate 26g • Dietary Fiber 4g • Sugars 3g • Protein 31g. Dietary Exchanges: 1½ Starch • 3½ Very Lean Meat • 1 Fat.

barbecue chicken wraps

READY TO SERVE: 20 MINUTES
SERVINGS: 4

* super fast

- 2 cups refrigerated original barbecue sauce with shredded chicken (from 18-oz. container)
- 4 slices precooked bacon (from 2.1- or 2.8-oz. package), cut into pieces, if desired
- 4 flour tortillas (10- to 12-inch), heated
- 1 cup shredded Cheddar cheese (4 oz.)
- 1 cup creamy coleslaw

1. In 1-quart saucepan, cook barbecue sauce with shredded chicken and bacon over medium heat for 5 to 10 minutes or until thoroughly heated, stirring occasionally.

2. Spoon ½ cup chicken mixture down center of each warm tortilla. Top each with cheese. Spoon coleslaw down sides of each. Fold up bottom of each tortilla; fold in sides. If desired, enclose bottom of wraps in foil or waxed paper.

Nutrition Information Per Serving: Calories 620 • Total Fat 27g • Saturated Fat 9g • Cholesterol 75mg • Sodium 1540mg • Total Carbohydrate 65g • Dietary Fiber 3g • Sugars 15g • Protein 29g. Dietary Exchanges: 3½ Starch • 2½ Lean Meat • 3½ Fat • 1 Other Carbohydrate.

spaghetti and meatball soup

philadelphia meatball heroes

READY TO SERVE: 30 MINUTES
SERVINGS: 6

1 package (18-oz.) frozen cooked meatballs, thawed
1 jar (14-oz.) spaghetti sauce (2 cups)
1 cup sliced green bell peppers
1 cup sliced red bell peppers
1 onion, sliced
6 unsliced hot dog or hoagie buns
4 oz. shredded Cheddar cheese (1 cup)

1. In large saucepan, combine meatballs and spaghetti sauce; cook over medium heat for 10 to 12 minutes or until meatballs are hot, stirring occasionally.

2. Meanwhile, spray medium skillet with nonstick cooking spray. Add bell peppers and onion; cook over medium-high heat for 5 to 6 minutes or until peppers are crisp-tender, stirring frequently.

3. Split each bun lengthwise, cutting to but not through bottom; place on ungreased cookie sheet. Place meatballs in buns. Top each with pepper mixture and cheese. Broil 4 to 6 inches from heat for 2 to 3 minutes or until cheese is melted.

Nutrition Information Per Serving: Calories 580 • Total Fat 35g • Saturated Fat 15g • Cholesterol 70mg • Sodium 1490mg • Total Carbohydrate 43g • Dietary Fiber 6g • Sugars 11g • Protein 24g. Dietary Exchanges: 2 Starch • 1 Fruit • 2½ High-Fat Meat • 2½ Fat OR 3 Carbohydrate • 2½ High-Fat Meat • 2½ Fat.

cheesy pizza soup

READY TO SERVE: 15 MINUTES
SERVINGS: 4

* super fast

2 cans (19-oz. each) ready-to-serve tomato basil soup
½ cup chopped pepperoni
1½ cups shredded pizza cheese blend (6 oz.)
2 teaspoons chopped fresh basil or parsley, if desired

1. In 2-quart saucepan, combine soup, pepperoni and 1 cup of the cheese; mix well.

2. Cook over medium heat for 4 to 6 minutes or until thoroughly heated and cheese softens, stirring occasionally. (Cheese will not melt completely.) Top individual servings with remaining cheese and basil.

Nutrition Information Per Serving: Calories 400 • Total Fat 21g • Saturated Fat 10g • Cholesterol 40mg • Sodium 1840mg • Total Carbohydrate 33g • Dietary Fiber 2g • Sugars 18g • Protein 17g. Dietary Exchanges: 1½ Starch • 1½ Other Carbohydrate • 1½ High-Fat Meat.

turkey-wild rice tomato soup

READY TO SERVE: 35 MINUTES
SERVINGS: 6

½ lb. bulk turkey breakfast sausage
¾ cup uncooked instant white rice
¾ cup uncooked instant wild rice
1 package (2.4-oz.) tomato with basil soup mix
1 can (14.5-oz.) no-salt-added stewed tomatoes, undrained
4 cups water
1 cup beef broth
1 tablespoon all-purpose flour
1 can (12-oz.) evaporated skimmed milk

1. Heat nonstick Dutch oven or large saucepan over medium-high heat until hot. Add sausage; cook 4 to 5 minutes or until no longer pink. With slotted spoon, remove sausage from Dutch oven; drain on paper towels.

2. Wipe Dutch oven clean with paper towels. Return sausage to Dutch oven. Stir in all remaining ingredients except flour and milk. Bring to a boil. Reduce heat to medium-low; cover and cook 8 to 10 minutes or until rice is tender.

3. Meanwhile, in small bowl, combine flour and milk; blend well. Gradually stir into soup. Increase heat to medium-high; cook, stirring constantly, until bubbly.

Nutrition Information Per Serving: Calories 270 • Total Fat 6g • Saturated Fat 2g • Cholesterol 30mg • Sodium 930mg • Total Carbohydrate 39g • Dietary Fiber 1g • Sugars 11g • Protein 16g. Dietary Exchanges: 2½ Starch • 1½ Lean Meat OR 2½ Carbohydrate • 1½ Lean Meat.

tuna pita sandwiches

READY TO SERVE: 10 MINUTES
SERVINGS: 6

* super fast

1 can (6-oz.) tuna in water, drained, flaked

1 can (8-oz.) crushed pineapple, well drained

¼ cup shredded carrot

3 tablespoons light mayonnaise

3 whole wheat or white pita breads (6-inch)

Leaf lettuce, if desired

1. In small bowl, combine tuna, pineapple, carrot and mayonnaise; mix well.

2. Cut pita breads in half crosswise; open each half to form pocket. Place lettuce and ¼ cup tuna mixture in each pocket.

Nutrition Information Per Serving: Calories 160 • Total Fat 4g • Saturated Fat 1g • Cholesterol 10mg • Sodium 310mg • Total Carbohydrate 22g • Dietary Fiber 3g • Sugars 4g • Protein 9g. Dietary Exchanges: 1½ Starch • ½ Very Lean Meat • ½ Fat.

southwestern chicken rice soup

READY TO SERVE: 25 MINUTES
SERVINGS: 3

* super fast

2 flour tortillas (8-inch)

1 cup cubed cooked chicken

6 medium green onions, chopped (⅓ cup)

1 can (19-oz.) ready-to-serve tomato basil soup

1 can (14-oz.) chicken broth

¾ cup uncooked instant rice

1 teaspoon chopped fresh cilantro

2 teaspoons lime juice

1. Heat oven to 400°F. Cut tortillas into ¼-inch strips; cut strips into 2- to 3-inch lengths. Place strips on ungreased cookie sheet. Bake for 6 to 8 minutes or until brown.

2. Meanwhile, in 1½-quart saucepan, combine chicken, onions, soup and broth; mix well. Bring to a boil. Stir in rice. Remove from heat. Cover; let stand 5 minutes.

3. Stir cilantro and lime juice into soup. If necessary, simmer 5 minutes to heat thoroughly, stirring occasionally. Top individual servings with tortilla strips.

Nutrition Information Per Serving: Calories 340 • Total Fat 7g • Saturated Fat 2g • Cholesterol 40mg • Sodium 1160mg • Total Carbohydrate 48g • Dietary Fiber 2g • Sugars 8g • Protein 22g. Dietary Exchanges: 2½ Starch • 2 Lean Meat • ½ Other Carbohydrate.

mexican-style chicken-filled tortillas

PREP TIME: 20 MINUTES
SERVINGS: 4

* super fast

4 boneless skinless chicken breast halves, cut into thin bite-sized strips

1 cup frozen whole kernel corn

1 cup chunky-style salsa

1 can (2¼-oz.) sliced ripe olives, well drained

4 fat-free flour tortillas (8- to 10-inch)

1. Spray large nonstick skillet with nonstick cooking spray. Heat over medium-high heat until hot. Add chicken; cook and stir 5 to 6 minutes or until no longer pink.

2. Stir in corn, salsa and olives. Reduce heat to medium; cook 4 to 6 minutes or until thoroughly heated.

3. Meanwhile, warm tortillas as directed on package. Spoon ¼ of chicken mixture onto half of each tortilla. Fold tortillas over. If desired, serve with light sour cream and additional salsa.

Nutrition Information Per Serving: Calories 420 • Total Fat 5g • Saturated Fat 1g • Cholesterol 75mg • Sodium 1170mg • Total Carbohydrate 59g • Dietary Fiber 3g • Sugars 5g • Protein 34g. Dietary Exchanges: 4 Starch • 3 Very Lean Meat OR 4 Carbohydrate • 3 Very Lean Meat.

tuna pita sandwiches

shrimp-vegetable noodle soup

monte cristo folds

SERVINGS: 4

KELLY B. EVERHART ✳ SEFFNER, FLORIDA

¼ lb. chopped cooked ham

¼ lb. chopped cooked turkey

4 oz. sliced Swiss cheese, chopped (1 cup)

1 can (16.3-oz.) large refrigerated buttermilk biscuits

1 egg

1 tablespoon milk

¼ teaspoon cinnamon

¼ teaspoon nutmeg

Powdered sugar

Raspberry jam

1. Heat oven to 375°F. In medium bowl, combine ham, turkey and cheese; mix well.

2. Separate the dough into 8 biscuits. Press or roll each to form 6- to 7-inch round. Place scant ⅓ cup ham mixture on one side of each biscuit. Fold dough over filling; press edges to seal. Place on ungreased cookie sheet.

3. In small bowl, combine egg, milk, cinnamon and nutmeg; beat well. Brush over tops of filled biscuits.

4. Bake at 375°F for 12 to 19 minutes or until golden brown. Sprinkle with powdered sugar. Serve with jam.

Nutrition Information Per Serving: Calories 550 • Total Fat 23g • Sodium 1650mg • Total Carbohydrate 64g • Protein 21g.

shrimp-vegetable noodle soup

READY TO SERVE: 25 MINUTES
SERVINGS: 4

✳ **super fast**

2 cans (14-oz. each) chicken broth

1 cup water

2 medium carrots, diagonally sliced (1 cup)

1 medium stalk celery, diagonally sliced (½ cup)

1 package (3-oz.) shrimp- or chicken-flavor ramen noodle soup mix, noodles partially broken

1½ teaspoons grated gingerroot or ½ teaspoon ground ginger

1 teaspoon finely shredded lemon peel

⅛ teaspoon pepper

4 oz. fresh snow pea pods, cut in half diagonally (1 cup)

12 oz. uncooked peeled deveined medium shrimp, tails removed

1. In 3-quart saucepan, combine broth, water, carrots, celery, contents of seasoning packet from soup mix, gingerroot, lemon peel and pepper. Bring to a boil over medium-high heat. Cook 1 minute.

2. Add broken ramen noodles and pea pods; mix well. Reduce heat; simmer 2 minutes.

3. Stir in shrimp. Cook 3 to 4 minutes or until shrimp are pink and firm and soup is thoroughly heated, stirring occasionally.

Nutrition Information Per Serving: Calories 220 • Total Fat 6g • Saturated Fat 3g • Cholesterol 120mg • Sodium 1150mg • Total Carbohydrate 21g • Dietary Fiber 2g • Sugars 4g • Protein 20g. **Dietary Exchanges:** 1½ Starch • 2 Very Lean Meat • ½ Fat.

SMART SHOPPING

You can streamline the preparation of Shrimp-Vegetable Noodle Soup by using cooked shrimp. Add 12 ounces of the cooked shrimp right at the end of the cooking time. They only need to cook 1 to 2 minutes, just long enough to heat them through.

If you plan on purchasing fresh shrimp, be sure to look for those with a firm texture and mild aroma. Unless you are purchasing Tiger Shrimp, you should avoid shrimp that have a yellow color to the meat or black spots. Similarly, don't purchase those with

dark rings on the shells or meat.

Fresh shrimp are best when used the day they are purchased, but you can store them in the refrigerator for a day by setting them on ice and covering them with a damp paper towel to prevent them from drying out. Never re-freeze shrimp that were previously frozen.

Shrimp are done cooking when they turn pink and opaque. Watch closely to avoid overcooking because shrimp that have been overcooked are often dense and chewy.

caesar chicken wraps

READY TO SERVE: 20 MINUTES
SERVINGS: 4

1 package (7.5-oz.) complete Caesar salad mix

1 cup chopped cooked chicken

4 garden vegetable or plain flour tortillas (8- to 9-inch)

2 tablespoons shredded fresh Parmesan cheese

1. Crush croutons from salad mix; set aside. In large bowl, combine remaining Caesar salad mix ingredients and chicken; mix well.

2. Spoon salad mixture evenly onto tortillas; spread to within 1 inch of edges. Sprinkle each with shredded cheese and crushed croutons. Roll up each tortilla.

Nutrition Information Per Serving: Calories 330 • Total Fat 14g • Saturated Fat 3g • Cholesterol 35mg • Sodium 760mg • Total Carbohydrate 32g • Dietary Fiber 2g • Sugars 1g • Protein 18g. Dietary Exchanges: 1½ Starch • 1½ Vegetable • 1½ Lean Meat • 2 Fat OR 1½ Carbohydrate • 1½ Vegetable • 1½ Lean Meat • 2 Fat.

pasta cheeseburger soup

READY TO SERVE: 25 MINUTES
SERVINGS: 4

1½ cups uncooked rotini pasta (4 oz.)

½ lb. lean (at least 80%) ground beef

2 small zucchini, chopped (2 cups)

½ teaspoon dried oregano leaves

1 tablespoon all-purpose flour

¼ teaspoon salt

1 cup milk

1 cup chicken broth

1 jar (8-oz.) pasteurized process cheese sauce

1. Cook rotini as directed on package. Drain well.

2. Meanwhile, in 2½-quart saucepan, cook ground beef, zucchini and oregano over medium-high heat for 5 to 7 minutes or until thoroughly cooked, stirring frequently. Drain.

3. Stir in flour and salt. Add milk, chicken broth, cheese sauce and cooked rotini to ground beef mixture; mix gently. Simmer about 5 minutes or until cheese is melted, stirring occasionally.

Nutrition Information Per Serving: Calories 430 • Total Fat 22g • Saturated Fat 11g • Cholesterol 80mg • Sodium 1500mg • Total Carbohydrate 34g • Dietary Fiber 2g • Sugars 8g • Protein 25g. Dietary Exchanges: 2 Starch • 2-1/2 Medium-Fat Meat • 1½ Fat.

italian patty melts

PREP TIME: 30 MINUTES
SERVINGS: 4

1 lb. lean ground beef

2 tablespoons grated Parmesan cheese

1 teaspoon dried Italian seasoning

2 teaspoons oil

1 medium green bell pepper, cut into 8 rings

4 slices (¾-oz. each) mozzarella cheese

4 sandwich buns, split

1. In medium bowl, combine ground beef, Parmesan cheese and Italian seasoning; mix well. Shape mixture into four 4-inch patties.

2. Heat oil in large skillet over medium-high heat until hot. Add bell pepper rings; cook 2 to 3 minutes or until crisp-tender. Remove from skillet.

3. Place patties in same skillet. Reduce heat to medium; cook 10 to 12 minutes or until thoroughly cooked, turning once. Top each patty with 2 bell pepper rings and 1 slice of the cheese. Cover; cook 1 to 2 minutes or until cheese is melted. Serve in buns.

Nutrition Information Per Serving: Calories 440 • Total Fat 24g • Saturated Fat 9g • Cholesterol 85mg • Sodium 460mg • Total Carbohydrate 24g • Dietary Fiber 2g • Sugars 6g • Protein 31g. Dietary Exchanges: 1½ Starch • 4 Medium-Fat Meat • ½ Fat OR 1½ Carbohydrate • 4 Medium-Fat Meat • ½ Fat.

caesar chicken wraps

mixed vegetable clam chowder

READY TO SERVE: 20 MINUTES
SERVINGS: 2

* super fast

1. In medium saucepan, combine all ingredients except cheese; stir to blend.

2. Cook over medium heat until thoroughly heated, stirring frequently. Sprinkle individual servings with cheese.

Nutrition Information Per Serving: Calories 270 • Total Fat 13g • Saturated Fat 4g • Cholesterol 25mg • Sodium 1070mg • Total Carbohydrate 29g • Dietary Fiber 3g • Sugars 4g • Protein 10g. **Dietary Exchanges:** 1½ Starch • 1 Vegetable • 1/2 High-Fat Meat • 1½ Fat OR 1½ Carbohydrate • 1 Vegetable • ½ High-Fat Meat • 1½ Fat.

- 1 can (18.5-oz.) ready-to-serve New England clam chowder
- 1 cup frozen mixed vegetables, thawed
- ⅛ teaspoon dried thyme leaves
- 2 tablespoons shredded Cheddar cheese

MADE-IN-MINUTES MEAL PLAN

To set a hearty soup dinner on the table quickly, make Mixed Vegetable Clam Chowder your main course.

Thaw the recipe's frozen vegetables by soaking the bag briefly in a bowl of hot water. You can also open the bag, spread the veggies on a microwavable dish and cook on High for 2 minutes or until the ice has melted. When the vegetables have thawed, combine the soup ingredients, simmering it all on the stovetop. As the soup warms, slice a few pears, an apple or even some oranges for a refreshing side dish.

oriental pork tortillas

PREP TIME: 15 MINUTES
SERVINGS: 4

* super fast

- ⅓ cup plum jam
- 1 tablespoon cornstarch
- ½ teaspoon ginger
- ½ teaspoon dry mustard
- ¼ teaspoon garlic powder
- 2 tablespoons soy sauce
- 2 teaspoons red wine vinegar
- 4 flour tortillas (10-inch)
- 1 teaspoon oil
- ¾ lb. boneless butterflied pork loin chops, cut into thin strips
- 6 cups purchased coleslaw blend (from 16-oz. pkg.)

1. In small bowl, combine jam, cornstarch, ginger, dry mustard, garlic powder, soy sauce and vinegar; mix well. Set aside. Heat tortillas as directed on package.

2. Meanwhile, heat oil in 12-inch nonstick skillet over medium-high heat until hot. Add pork; cook and stir 4 to 5 minutes or until no longer pink.

3. Add jam mixture and coleslaw blend; cook and stir until sauce is bubbly and thickened. Spoon mixture evenly down center of each warm tortilla; roll up.

Nutrition Information Per Serving: Calories 420 • Total Fat 11g • Saturated Fat 3g • Cholesterol 45mg • Sodium 850mg • Total Carbohydrate 57g • Dietary Fiber 2g • Sugars 19g • Protein 24g. **Dietary Exchanges:** 3½ Starch • 1 Vegetable • 2 Lean Meat OR 3½ Carbohydrate • 1 Vegetable • 2 Lean Meat.

A RAPID REPLACEMENT

Can't find the plum jam needed for this recipe? Substitute it with apricot or cherry preserves. Or, head over to the Asian-food section of your grocery store and pick up a small jar of plum sauce. This tangy sauce is a sweet-and-sour delight that is made from plums, apricots, sugar and seasonings. Use it anytime you want to jazz up a meal without much work. The popular sauce is wonderful when it's mixed into stir-fries or brushed over grilled chicken.

fast fajita and vegetable pita

READY TO SERVE: 10 MINUTES
SERVINGS: 6

* super fast

¼ cup Italian dressing

2 to 3 teaspoons lime juice

½ lb. thinly sliced, cooked roast beef, cut into strips (2 cups)

½ cup chopped fresh broccoli

1 small tomato, chopped (½ cup)

3 pita breads (6-inch), cut in half to form pockets

6 leaves lettuce

1. In medium bowl, mix dressing and lime juice. Add roast beef, broccoli and tomato; toss to coat.

2. To serve, line pita bread halves with lettuce. Fill each with about ½ cup beef mixture. If desired, drizzle with additional Italian dressing.

Nutrition Information Per Serving: Calories 240 • Total Fat 11g • Saturated Fat 3g • Trans Fat 0g • Cholesterol 35mg • Sodium 280mg • Total Carbohydrate 19g • Dietary Fiber 1g • Sugars 2g • Protein 15g. Dietary Exchanges: 1 Starch • 1½ Lean Meat • 1½ Fat.

savory crescent chicken squares

SERVINGS: 4

DORIS CASTLE ✳ RIVER FOREST, ILLINOIS

1 package (3-oz.) cream cheese, softened

1 tablespoon margarine or butter, softened

2 cups cubed cooked chicken

1 tablespoon chopped chives or onion

¼ teaspoon salt

⅛ teaspoon pepper

2 tablespoons milk

1 tablespoon chopped pimiento, if desired

1 can (8-oz.) refrigerated crescent dinner rolls

1 tablespoon margarine or butter, melted

¾ cup seasoned croutons, crushed

1. Heat oven to 350°F. In medium bowl, beat cream cheese and 1 tablespoon softened margarine until smooth. Add chicken, chives, salt, pepper, milk and pimiento; mix well.

2. Separate crescent dough into 4 rectangles. Firmly press perforations to seal. Spoon ½ cup of chicken mixture onto center of each rectangle. Pull 4 corners of dough to center of chicken mixture; twist firmly. Pinch edges to seal. Place on ungreased cookie sheet. Brush tops of sandwiches with 1 tablespoon melted margarine; sprinkle with crushed croutons.

3. Bake at 350°F for 25 to 30 minutes or until golden brown.

Nutrition Information Per Serving: Calories 500 • Total Fat 31g • Sodium 890mg • Total Carbohydrate 28g • Protein 27g.

italian pasta sausage soup

SERVINGS: 6

JULIE WINTER ✳ GROSSE POINTE WOODS, MICHIGAN

1 lb. hot or sweet Italian sausage links

1 can (28-oz.) whole tomatoes, undrained, cut up

1 can (14½-oz.) ready-to-serve chicken broth

1 can (8-oz.) tomato sauce

1 teaspoon dried basil leaves

1 teaspoon dried oregano leaves

1 package (16-oz.) frozen pasta, broccoli, corn and carrots in a garlic-seasoned sauce

Grated fresh Parmesan cheese

1. Place sausage links in large saucepan or 5-quart Dutch oven. Add water to a depth of about ½ inch. Bring to a boil. Reduce heat; cover and simmer 10 minutes or until sausage is partially cooked. Drain.

2. Slice sausage into ½-inch slices; return to saucepan. Add tomatoes, broth, tomato sauce, basil and oregano; blend well. Bring to a boil. Reduce heat; cover and simmer 20 minutes, stirring occasionally. Stir in frozen vegetables with pasta. Cover; bring to a boil. Reduce heat; simmer 3 to 5 minutes or until vegetables are crisp-tender. Sprinkle with Parmesan cheese.

Nutrition Information Per Serving: Calories 310 • Total Fat 17g • Sodium 1600mg • Total Carbohydrate 23g • Protein 17g.

turkey, ham and cheese bagel-wiches

READY TO SERVE: 15 MINUTES
SERVINGS: 4

✳ super fast

2 tablespoons fat-free mayonnaise or salad dressing

1 teaspoon honey mustard

4 multigrain bagels, split, toasted

4 slices (1.5-oz. each) cooked turkey breast

4 slices (1-oz. each) cooked ham

1 slice (1.5-oz.) provolone cheese, cut into quarters

4 thin slices tomato

1. Set oven control to broil. In small bowl, mix mayonnaise and mustard. Place toasted bottom halves of bagels on ungreased cookie sheet. Spread each with mayonnaise mixture. Top each evenly with turkey, ham and cheese.

2. Broil 4 to 6 inches from heat 2 to 3 minutes or until cheese is melted. Top each with tomato slice and toasted top half of bagel.

Nutrition Information Per Serving: Calories 300 • Total Fat 6g • Saturated Fat 2.5g • Trans Fat 0g • Cholesterol 60mg • Sodium 720mg • Total Carbohydrate 39g • Dietary Fiber 3g • Sugars 6g • Protein 27g. Dietary Exchanges: 2 Starch • ½ Other Carbohydrate • 3 Very Lean Meat • ½ Fat.

nacho bean soup

PREP TIME: 20 MINUTES
SERVINGS: 3

✳ super fast

1 can (14½-oz.) ready-to-serve vegetable broth

1 cup milk

2 tablespoons all-purpose flour

1 can (15.5- or 15-oz.) pinto beans, drained, rinsed

1 can (4.5-oz.) chopped green chiles

8 oz. shredded taco-flavored cheese blend (2 cups)

2 tablespoons chopped fresh cilantro

1 cup broken tortilla or corn chips

1. In large saucepan, combine broth, milk and flour; blend well. Cook and stir over medium heat until mixture comes to a boil.

2. Stir in beans, chiles, cheese and cilantro. Cook 5 minutes or until thoroughly heated and cheese is melted, stirring constantly. Sprinkle individual servings with tortilla chips.

Nutrition Information Per Serving: Calories 590 • Total Fat 33g • Saturated Fat 19g • Cholesterol 80mg • Sodium 1690mg • Total Carbohydrate 46g • Dietary Fiber 8g • Sugars 8g • Protein 28g. Dietary Exchanges: 3 Starch • 3 High-Fat Meat • 1 Fat OR 3 Carbohydrate • 3 High-Fat Meat • 1 Fat.

italian beef dippers

READY TO SERVE: 30 MINUTES
SERVINGS: 6

1 can (18.5-oz.) ready-to-serve French onion soup

½ teaspoon dried Italian seasoning

¾ pound thinly sliced Italian- or garlic-seasoned cooked roast beef

6 crusty French rolls (each 3 to 4 inches long)

6 slices (¾-oz. each) provolone cheese

1. Combine the soup and Italian seasoning in a medium (2 quart) saucepan.

2. Heat the soup over medium heat until warmed through; stirring occasionally. Add the slices of beef. Continue to heat the soup and the beef for 4 to 6 minutes, stirring occasionally, until heated through.

3. Cut the rolls in half. Use the slotted spoon to remove the slices of beef from the soup. Put the beef on the bottom halves of the rolls. Put a few onions from the soup on the beef.

4. Cut each slice of cheese into 2 pieces. Put 2 pieces of cheese on top of the beef on each sandwich. Cover the beef and cheese with the top halves of the rolls.

5. Divide the soup between six custard cups. Serve the sandwiches with the warm soup for dipping.

Nutrition Information Per Serving: Calories 280 • Total Fat 10g • Sodium 1410mg • Total Carbohydrate 28g • Sugars 3g • Protein 20g. **Dietary Exchanges:** 2 Starch • 2 Very Lean Meat • 1 Fat.

turkey-vegetable-cheddar soup

turkey-vegetable-cheddar soup

READY TO SERVE: 20 MINUTES
SERVINGS: 4

* super fast

1 package (1-lb.) frozen pasta, broccoli and carrots in creamy Cheddar sauce

1 cup cubed smoked deli turkey breast (5 oz.)

⅛ teaspoon pepper

1¾ cups water

1 can (14½-oz.) ready-to-serve chicken broth

1. In large saucepan, combine all ingredients; stir to blend. Bring to a boil.

2. Reduce heat; simmer 5 minutes or until vegetables are tender, stirring occasionally.

Nutrition Information Per Serving: Calories 200 • Total Fat 6g • Saturated Fat 2g • Cholesterol 20mg • Sodium 1070mg • Total Carbohydrate 22g • Dietary Fiber 3g • Sugars 3g • Protein 14g. Dietary Exchanges: 1½ Starch • 1 Very Lean Meat • 1 Fat OR 1½ Carbohydrate • 1 Very Lean Meat • 1 Fat.

tuna melt biscuits

PREP TIME: 30 MINUTES
SERVINGS: 5

1 can (10.2-oz.) large refrigerated buttermilk biscuits (5 biscuits)

2 cans (6-oz. each) water-packed chunk light tuna, well drained

⅓ cup chopped celery

⅓ cup well-drained crushed pineapple

2 tablespoons finely chopped onion

¼ cup purchased honey mustard salad dressing

5 slices (¾-oz. each93) American cheese

1. Heat oven to 375°F. Bake biscuits as directed on can. Cool slightly.

2. Meanwhile, in medium bowl, combine tuna, celery, pineapple, onion and salad dressing; mix well.

3. Split biscuits; arrange, cut side up, on cookie sheet. Spoon mixture evenly onto biscuit halves. Cut cheese slices in half diagonally; place 1 piece on each topped biscuit half.

4. Bake at 375°F for 5 to 7 minutes or until filling is hot and cheese is melted.

Nutrition Information Per Serving: Calories 370 • Total Fat 18g • Saturated Fat 7g • Cholesterol 40mg • Sodium 1190mg • Total Carbohydrate 30g • Dietary Fiber 1g • Sugars 10g • Protein 23g. Dietary Exchanges: 1½ Starch • ½ Fruit • 2½ Very Lean Meat • 3 Fat OR 2 Carbohydrate • 2½ Very Lean Meat • 3 Fat.

chili mac

PREP TIME: 25 MINUTES
SERVINGS: 6

* super fast

4 oz. uncooked elbow macaroni (1 cup)

½ lb. extra-lean ground beef

1 cup chopped green bell pepper or celery

1 medium onion, chopped

4 cans (8-oz. each) no-salt-added tomato sauce

1 can (15-oz.) spicy chili beans, undrained

½ teaspoon salt

1. Cook macaroni to desired doneness as directed on package.

2. Meanwhile, spray large nonstick saucepan or skillet with nonstick cooking spray. Add ground beef, bell pepper and onion; cook over medium-high heat until beef is browned.

3. Drain macaroni. Add to ground beef mixture with all remaining ingredients. Cook until thoroughly heated.

Nutrition Information Per Serving: Calories 250 • Total Fat 6g • Saturated 2g • Cholesterol 25mg • Sodium 500mg • Total Carbohydrate 34g • Dietary Fiber 4g • Sugars 7g • Protein 15g. Dietary Exchanges: 2 Starch • 1 Vegetable • 1 Medium-Fat Meat OR 2 Carbohydrate • 1 Vegetable • 1 Medium-Fat Meat.

roast beef panini

READY TO SERVE: 15 MINUTES
SERVINGS: 4

1 package (10-oz.) ready-to-serve Italian pizza crusts (two 6-inch crusts)

4 tablespoons light garlic-and-herb spreadable cheese (from 4- to 6.5-oz. container)

1 cup spinach leaves

¼ lb. thinly sliced 97%-fat-free cooked Italian roast beef (from deli)

1 large tomato, sliced

¼ cup sliced ripe olives

2 tablespoons shredded Parmesan cheese

1. Spread top side of 1 pizza crust and bottom side of other pizza crust with spreadable cheese.

2. On crust with top spread with cheese, layer remaining ingredients. Top with second crust, cheese side down. Cut into 8 wedges.

Nutrition Information Per Serving: Calories 320 • Total Fat 13g • Saturated Fat 6g • Trans Fat 0g • Cholesterol 45mg • Sodium 590mg • Total Carbohydrate 35g • Dietary Fiber 3g • Sugars 2g • Protein 19g. **Dietary Exchanges:** 2½ Starch • 1½ Very Lean Meat • 2 Fat.

great northern bean stew

READY TO SERVE: 30 MINUTES
SERVINGS: 6

ELLEN ANDERS * BIG BEND, WISCONSIN

1 lb. bulk pork sausage

1 cup coarsely chopped onions

1 cup thinly sliced carrots

2 cups chopped cabbage

1 tablespoon brown sugar

1 can (28-oz.) whole tomatoes, undrained, cut up

1 can (15.5-oz.) great northern beans, drained

½ teaspoon paprika

½ teaspoon dried thyme leaves

¼ to ½ teaspoon salt

½ teaspoon pepper

1 tablespoon vinegar

¼ teaspoon hot pepper sauce

⅓ cup chopped fresh parsley or 1 tablespoon dried parsley flakes

1. In large saucepan or 4-quart Dutch oven, brown sausage and onions; drain.

2. Stir in all remaining ingredients; bring to a boil. Reduce heat; cover and simmer 15 minutes.

Nutrition Information Per Serving: Calories 200 • Total Fat 10g • Sodium 840mg • Total Carbohydrate 20g • Protein 11g.

SIMPLE INGREDIENT SWITCHES

Great Northern Bean Stew is the perfect way to chase winter's chill and satisfy the heartiest of appetites…even when you're tight on time.

Best of all, you can adjust the dish to fit your family's tastes and substitute some of the ingredients with household staples you likely have on hand. Consider the following alternatives to the comforting recipe. They'll have you out of the kitchen and enjoying dinner with your gang in no time.

* While the stew features great northern beans, feel free to use kidney beans or whatever 15.5-oz. can of beans you have in your cupboard.

* Out of hot sauce? Just stir in a little salsa instead or add a dash of red pepper flakes.

* If you don't have pork sausage, use ground beef. Season it with fennel seed if you have it on your spice rack.

90 * Pillsbury Everyday Family Suppers 2007

roast beef panini

chicken, vegetable and cream cheese sandwiches

READY TO SERVE: 10 MINUTES
SERVINGS: 4

* super fast

8 slices pumpernickel rye bread

1 container (6.5-oz.) gourmet spreadable cheese with garlic and herbs (1 cup)

16 thin slices cucumber

1 lb. sliced cooked chicken (from deli)

1 medium tomato, sliced

1 slice (¼-inch thick) sweet onion (Walla Walla, Maui or Texas Sweet), separated into rings

1 cup coleslaw mix (from 16-oz. bag)

1. Spread one side of all slices of bread with spreadable cheese.

2. Top 4 bread slices, cheese side up, evenly with cucumber, chicken, tomato, onion and coleslaw mix. Cover with remaining bread slices, cheese side down.

Nutrition Information Per Serving: Calories 480 • Total Fat 28g • Saturated Fat 13g • Cholesterol 95mg • Sodium 2040mg • Total Carbohydrate 34g • Dietary Fiber 4g • Sugars 7g • Protein 23g. **Dietary Exchanges:** 2 Starch • 2½ Lean Meat • 4 Fat.

NO-STRESS SIDES FOR SANDWICHES

Serving sandwiches for supper? Soup and salad are classic additions, but you can also round out the meal with sliced fresh fruit or even canned mandarin oranges, peaches or pineapple. Fresh vegetables make great choices, too.

Consider serving carrot and celery sticks, tomato wedges or cucumber slices. Creamy pasta salads from the deli are an effortless way to complete a sandwich platter, as are pickle spears and potato chips.

monterey shrimp pitas

READY TO SERVE: 20 MINUTES
SERVINGS: 6

* super fast

⅔ cup nonfat plain yogurt

1 tablespoon chopped fresh dill or 1 teaspoon dried dill weed

1 teaspoon sugar

¼ teaspoon salt

1 tablespoon lemon juice

1 lb. shelled deveined cooked shrimp

1 can (14-oz.) artichoke hearts, drained, chopped

1 medium tomato, seeded, chopped

3 (6- to 8-inch) whole wheat pita (pocket) breads, halved

1. In medium bowl, combine yogurt, dill, sugar, salt and lemon juice; blend well. Add shrimp, artichoke hearts and tomato; stir just until combined.

2. Spoon shrimp mixture into pita bread halves.

Nutrition Information Per Serving: Calories 210 • Total Fat 2g • Saturated Fat 0g • Cholesterol 150mg • Sodium 490mg • Total Carbohydrate 26g • Dietary Fiber 5g • Sugars 4g • Protein 22g. **Dietary Exchanges:** 1½ Starch • 1 Vegetable • 2 Very Lean Meat OR 1½ Carbohydrate • 1 Vegetable • 2 Very Lean Meat.

garden-fresh tuna salad sandwiches

READY TO SERVE: 15 MINUTES
SERVINGS: 4

* super fast

1 can (6-oz.) water-packed tuna, drained, flaked

⅔ cup chopped seeded cucumber

½ cup shredded carrot

¼ cup chopped green onions

¼ cup fat-free mayonnaise or salad dressing

2 tablespoons nonfat sour cream

1 tablespoon lemon juice

4 leaves leaf lettuce

8 slices whole wheat bread, toasted if desired

1. In medium bowl, combine all ingredients except lettuce and bread; mix well.

2. Place 1 lettuce leaf on each of 4 slices of bread; spoon and spread ½ cup tuna mixture onto each. Top with remaining slices of bread.

Nutrition Information Per Serving: Calories 220 • Total Fat 3g • Saturated Fat 1g • Cholesterol 15mg • Sodium 550mg • Total Carbohydrate 32g • Dietary Fiber 5g • Sugars 5g • Protein 16g. **Dietary Exchanges:** 2 Starch • 2 Very Lean Meat OR 2 Carbohydrate • 2 Very Lean Meat.

HELPFUL TUNA TIPS

Most on-the-go moms agree…canned tuna is a mealtime lifesaver. The kitchen staple comes in three grades: solid or fancy offers the largest pieces, while flaked and grated contains the smallest. Chunk tuna falls between the two. You can use any variety in the recipe above.

While Garden-Fresh Tuna Salad Sandwiches are a great way to serve tuna when time's tight, you may also want to consider whipping up your standard tuna salad recipe with a little curry powder stirred in for fun. You can also try tossing in a handful of chopped walnuts or water chestnuts. If you usually use mayonnaise in your family's tuna salad, consider replacing it with Italian salad dressing for a tasty change of pace when the clock is ticking.

chicken-tortellini soup

READY TO SERVE: 20 MINUTES
SERVINGS: 4

* super fast

- 2 cans (14-oz. each) fat-free chicken broth with 1/3 less sodium
- 3 cups water
- 5 to 6 medium green onions, sliced (1/3 cup)
- 1/2 teaspoon dried basil leaves
- 2 cloves garlic, minced
- 1/2 lb. precut chicken breast chunks or 2 boneless, skinless chicken breasts (1/2 lb.), cut into 1/2-inch pieces
- 1 package (9-oz.) refrigerated cheese-filled tortellini
- 1 cup chopped fresh spinach
- 1 cup frozen sweet peas (from 1-lb. bag)

1. In 3-quart saucepan or Dutch oven, mix broth, water, onions, basil and garlic. Heat to boiling. Stir in chicken and tortellini. Reduce heat to medium; simmer uncovered for 4 minutes.

2. Add spinach and peas; cook for 5 minutes, stirring occasionally, until spinach is wilted, tortellini is tender and chicken is no longer pink in center. If desired, season to taste with pepper.

Nutrition Information Per Serving: Calories 190 • Total Fat 6g • Saturated Fat 2.5g • Trans Fat 0g • Cholesterol 90mg • Sodium 500mg • Total Carbohydrate 17g • Dietary Fiber 2g • Sugars 3g • Protein 19g. Dietary Exchanges: 1 Starch • 2 1/2 Very Lean Meat • 1 Fat.

buffalo chicken sandwiches

READY TO SERVE: 30 MINUTES
SERVINGS: 4

1 tablespoon margarine or butter, melted

1 tablespoon hot pepper sauce

4 frozen breaded chicken patties

4 leaves leaf lettuce

4 sandwich buns, split

4 tablespoons purchased blue cheese salad dressing

1. Heat oven to 400°F. In small cup, combine margarine and hot pepper sauce; mix well. Brush margarine mixture over chicken patties; place on ungreased cookie sheet.

2. Bake at 400°F for 12 to 15 minutes or until thoroughly heated.

3. Place lettuce on bottom halves of buns. Top each with chicken patty and blue cheese dressing. Cover with top halves of buns. If desired, serve with celery sticks.

Nutrition Information Per Serving: Calories 520 • Total Fat 32g • Saturated Fat 6g • Cholesterol 45mg • Sodium 460mg • Total Carbohydrate 38g • Dietary Fiber 4g • Sugars 8g • Protein 19g. Dietary Exchanges: 2½ Starch • 1½ High-Fat Meat • 4 Fat OR 2½ Carbohydrate • 1½ High-Fat Meat • 4 Fat.

cheesy hot dog chowder

mediterranean wraps

✳ super fast

2 soft cracker breads, halved

1 container (8-oz.) hummus

½ cup chopped fresh parsley

¼ cup sliced ripe olives

1 medium cucumber,
thinly sliced

1 tomato, seeded, chopped

2 oz. crumbled feta cheese
(½ cup)

CRACKER BREADS

Cracker breads may be labeled as "Lavosh" in the ethnic-cooking aisle of your grocery store. It is an Armenian bread that's available in a crisp variety good for dipping and a soft version that is ideal for sandwich wraps and roll-ups. If you can't find soft cracker breads, try using flour tortillas or thick slices of deli-bought turkey or ham when assembling the Mediterranean Wraps.

1. Spread each bread half evenly with hummus to within ½ inch of edges.

2. Arrange parsley, olives, cucumber, tomato and cheese over hummus. Roll up each bread half.

Nutrition Information Per Serving: Calories 400 • Total Fat 12g • Saturated Fat 2g • Cholesterol 15mg • Sodium 970mg • Total Carbohydrate 58g • Dietary Fiber 5g • Sugars 8g • Protein 16g. Dietary Exchanges: 4 Starch • ½ High-Fat Meat • 1 Fat OR 4 Carbohydrate • ½ High-Fat Meat • 1 Fat.

cheesy hot dog chowder

✳ super fast

2 cans (18.5-oz. each) ready-
to-serve 99% fat-free white
Cheddar and potato soup

1 cup milk

1 cup frozen whole kernel
corn (from 1-lb. bag)

4 hot dogs, thinly sliced

1 cup shredded American
and Cheddar cheese blend
(4 oz.)

Shredded American and
Cheddar cheese blend,
if desired

1. In 3-quart saucepan, combine soup, milk, corn and hot dogs; mix well. Bring to a boil. Reduce heat to medium-low; simmer 6 to 8 minutes or until the corn is tender, stirring occasionally.

2. Add 1 cup cheese; stir until it is melted. Top individual servings with additional shredded cheese.

Nutrition Information Per Serving: Calories 315 • Total Fat 23g • Saturated Fat 11g • Cholesterol 60mg • Sodium 850mg • Total Carbohydrate 13g • Dietary Fiber 1g • Sugars 6g • Protein 15g. Dietary Exchanges: 1 Starch • 2 High-Fat Meat • 1 Fat.

creamy chicken-vegetable chowder

PREP TIME: 25 MINUTES
SERVINGS: 6

* super fast

chowder

1½ cups milk or half-and-half

1 cup chicken broth

1 can (10¾-oz.) condensed cream of potato soup

1 can (10¾-oz.) condensed cream of chicken soup

2 cups cubed cooked chicken or turkey

⅓ cup chopped green onions

1 can (11-oz.) whole kernel corn with red and green peppers, drained

1 jar (11-oz.) sliced mushrooms, drained

1 can (4.5-oz.) chopped green chiles

6 oz. shredded Cheddar cheese (1½ cups)

crescent rolls

1 can (8-oz.) refrigerated crescent dinner rolls

¼ cup crushed nacho-flavored tortilla chips

1. In 4-quart saucepan or Dutch oven, combine milk, broth, potato soup and chicken soup; blend well. Add all remaining chowder ingredients except cheese; mix well. Cook over medium heat for 5 to 8 minutes or until onions are tender, stirring occasionally. Remove from heat. Add cheese; stir until melted.

2. While chowder is heating, bake crescent rolls. Heat oven to 375°F. Shape dough as directed on can. Gently press top of each roll in crushed chips. Place on ungreased cookie sheet.

3. Bake at 375°F for 11 to 13 minutes or until golden brown. Serve chowder with crescent rolls.

Nutrition Information Per Serving: Calories 535 • Total Fat 25g • Saturated Fat 11g • Cholesterol 80mg • Sodium 1920mg • Total Carbohydrate 47g • Dietary Fiber 3g • Sugars 12g • Protein 30g. Dietary Exchanges: 3 Starch • 3 Lean Meat • 3 Fat.

SPECIAL TOUCHES MADE EASY

To gussy up Creamy Chicken-Vegetable Chowder without much work, drain a small jar of diced pimientos and stir it into the heartwarming dish. For even more flair, replace 1 of the cups of cooked chicken with a cup of cooked and cubed ham.

Garnish individual servings with additional chopped green onions or a little fresh parsley. To keep the kids excited about dinner, let them crush a few of the nacho-flavored tortilla chips leftover from the crescent rolls, and sprinkle them into their bowls.

---

italian toast toppers

READY TO SERVE: 15 MINUTES
SERVINGS: 8 SANDWICHES

* super fast

¾ lb. lean ground turkey

1 jar (28-oz.) tomato pasta sauce

8 slices Italian bread

8 teaspoons grated Parmesan cheese

½ cup shredded mozzarella cheese (2 oz.)

1. Set oven control to broil. In 8-inch skillet, cook ground turkey over medium heat, stirring frequently, until no longer pink; drain. Stir in pasta sauce. Cook, stirring occasionally, until thoroughly heated.

2. Meanwhile, place slices of bread on ungreased cookie sheet. Broil 4 to 6 inches from heat 30 to 60 seconds or until lightly toasted.

3. Turn bread slices over; top each with 1 teaspoon Parmesan cheese. Broil 1 to 1½ minutes or until top is golden brown.

4. Remove from broiler. Spoon turkey mixture evenly onto bread. Top each with mozzarella cheese. Return to broiler; broil 30 to 60 seconds longer or until cheese is melted.

Nutrition Information Per Serving: Calories 250 • Total Fat 9g • Saturated Fat 2.5g • Trans Fat 0g • Cholesterol 35mg • Sodium 710mg • Total Carbohydrate 29g • Dietary Fiber 2g • Sugars 7g • Protein 15g. Dietary Exchanges: 1½ Starch • ½ Other Carbohydrate • 1½ Medium-Fat Meat.

chicken and apple "clams"

READY TO SERVE: 15 MINUTES
SERVINGS: 6

* super fast

3 tablespoons mayonnaise
  or salad dressing

3 tablespoons plain fat-free
  yogurt

⅛ teaspoon seasoned salt

1 cup chopped cooked
  chicken breast

1 medium tart-sweet red
  apple, cored, cut into bite-
  size pieces (about ¾ cup)

3 tablespoons thinly
  sliced celery

6 whole wheat or white
  mini pita breads

1. In medium bowl, mix mayonnaise, yogurt and seasoned salt. Gently stir in chicken, apple and celery to coat.

2. Cut slit in side of each pita bread to open and form pocket. Fill each with ⅓ cup chicken mixture.

Nutrition Information Per Serving: Calories 170 • Total Fat 2.5g • Saturated Fat 0.5g • Trans Fat 0g • Cholesterol 20mg • Sodium 350mg • Total Carbohydrate 29g • Dietary Fiber 4g • Sugars 6g • Protein 12g. Dietary Exchanges: 2 Starch • 1 Very Lean Meat.

grilled chicken club sandwiches

grilled chicken club sandwiches

READY TO SERVE: 20 MINUTES
SERVINGS: 2

2 boneless skinless chicken
  breast halves

4 thin slices Canadian bacon

2 kaiser rolls, cut horizontally
  into thirds

3 tablespoons mayonnaise
  or salad dressing

4 lettuce leaves

2 slices tomato

1. Heat grill. Place 1 chicken breast half, boned side up, between 2 pieces of plastic wrap or waxed paper. Working from center, gently pound chicken with flat side of meat mallet or rolling pin until about 1/2-inch thick; remove wrap. Repeat with remaining chicken breast half.

2. Place chicken on gas grill over medium heat or on charcoal grill 4 to 6 inches from medium coals. Cook 6 to 8 minutes or until fork-tender and juices run clear, turning once. Add bacon during last 5 minutes of cooking time; turn once. If desired, toast kaiser rolls, cut side down, during last 3 minutes of cooking time.

3. Spread all cut sides of rolls with mayonnaise. Cut each chicken breast half into 2 pieces. On bottom section of each roll, place 2 chicken pieces, overlapping if necessary. Top with lettuce, tomato and middle section of roll. Place 2 Canadian bacon slices on top of middle section. Top with lettuce and top of roll. Press each sandwich slightly; spear each with 2 long toothpicks. Cut sandwiches in half between toothpicks.

Nutrition Information Per Serving: Calories 540 • Total Fat 26g • Saturated Fat 5g • Cholesterol 115mg • Sodium 1290mg • Total Carbohydrate 32g • Dietary Fiber 2g • Sugars 3g • Protein 44g. Dietary Exchanges: 2 Starch • 5 1/2 Very Lean Meat • 4 Fat OR 2 Carbohydrate • 5 1/2 Very Lean Meat • 4 Fat.

hamburger-noodle soup

PREP TIME: 10 MINUTES
READY TO SERVE: 8 HOURS 30 MINUTES
SERVINGS: 5

1. Brown ground beef in large skillet until thoroughly cooked, stirring frequently. Drain well.

2. In 3 1/2- to 4-quart slow cooker, combine ground beef and all remaining ingredients except mixed vegetables and noodles; mix well.

3. Cover; cook on Low setting for 6 to 8 hours.

4. About 20 minutes before serving, stir thawed vegetables and noodles into soup. Increase heat setting to High; cover and cook an additional 15 to 20 minutes or until vegetables are crisp-tender and noodles are tender.

Nutrition Information Per Serving: Calories 310 • Total Fat 13g • Saturated Fat 5g • Cholesterol 65mg • Sodium 700mg • Total Carbohydrate 26g • Dietary Fiber 4g • Sugars 6g • Protein 21g. Dietary Exchanges: 1 Starch • 2 Vegetable • 2 Lean Meat • 1 1/2 Fat OR 1 Carbohydrate • 2 Vegetable • 2 Lean Meat • 1 1/2 Fat.

1 lb. lean or extra-lean
  ground beef

1/2 cup coarsely chopped onion

1 medium stalk celery, cut into
  1/4-inch slices

1 package (1.15-oz.) dry beefy
  mushroom recipe soup mix

1 can (14.5-oz.) diced
  tomatoes, undrained

3 cups water

2 cups frozen mixed
  vegetables, thawed, drained

2 oz. uncooked fine egg
  noodles (1 cup)

"SOUP-ER" IDEAS FOR SUPPER

Serve up steaming bowlfuls of the Hamburger-Noodle Soup with freshly baked refrigerated French bread or Parmesan breadsticks. A simple side dish of sliced pears or a small side salad is also a great touch. Slice refrigerated cookie dough as soon as you get home from work, and bake the cookies as directed on the package. They'll bake to yummy perfection while you enjoy the satisfying soup.

Don't have the fine egg noodles noted in the recipe? Consider frozen, home-style egg noodles instead. They cook quickly and add down-home flavor to this family favorite. And if the only can of diced tomatoes you have on hand includes garlic, peppers, chiles or specific herb and seasonings, feel free to use it in place of the plain tomatoes the recipe calls for. After all, you'll just increase this dish's delightful taste.

SOUPS & SANDWICHES * **101**

sassy southwestern burgers

READY TO SERVE: 20 MINUTES
SERVINGS: 4

* super fast

1 lb. lean ground beef

6 tablespoons salsa

2 tablespoons taco seasoning mix (from 1.25-oz. pkg.)

4 burger buns, split

4 slices (1-oz. each) hot pepper Monterey Jack cheese

1. Heat grill. In medium bowl, combine ground beef, 2 tablespoons of the salsa and the taco seasoning mix; mix well. Shape mixture into 4 patties, ½-inch thick.

2. When ready to grill, place patties on gas grill over medium heat or on charcoal grill 4 to 6 inches from medium coals. Cook 11 to 13 minutes or until patties are thoroughly cooked, turning once.

3. Meanwhile, place buns, cut side down, on grill. Cook 1 to 2 minutes or until buns are lightly toasted. Place 1 slice of cheese on each patty; cook an additional 1 minute or until cheese is melted.

4. Place patties on bottom halves of buns. Top each with 1 tablespoon salsa and top half of bun.

Nutrition Information Per Serving: Calories 460 • Total Fat 26g • Saturated Fat 12g • Cholesterol 100mg • Sodium 910mg • Total Carbohydrate 26g • Dietary Fiber 1g • Sugars 6g • Protein 30g. Dietary Exchanges: 1½ Starch • 3½ Medium-Fat Meat • 1½ Fat OR 1½ Carbohydrate • 3½ Medium-Fat Meat • 1½ Fat.

ham and vegetable tortilla rolls

READY TO SERVE: 25 MINUTES
SERVINGS: 4

* super fast

4 flour tortillas (8- to 10-inch)

4 tablespoons reduced-fat garden vegetable cream cheese spread (from 8-oz. container)

1 package (6-oz.) thinly sliced 97%-fat-free cooked ham

1 cup shredded lettuce

8 thin slices tomato

1 small cucumber, cut into thin strips

½ green bell pepper, cut into thin strips

½ cup shredded mozzarella or smoked provolone cheese (2 oz.)

1. Spread each tortilla evenly with 1 tablespoon cream cheese spread. Top evenly with remaining ingredients.

2. Roll up tortillas. Cut each diagonally in half; secure with toothpicks.

Nutrition Information Per Serving: Calories 280 • Total Fat 10g • Saturated Fat 4.5g • Trans Fat 0.5g • Cholesterol 40mg • Sodium 780mg • Total Carbohydrate 30g • Dietary Fiber 2g • Sugars 4g • Protein 18g. Dietary Exchanges: 1½ Starch • 1 Vegetable • 1½ Very Lean Meat • 1½ Fat.

GRAB-AND-GO GREATS

Looking for a fast, handheld dinner to enjoy on the way to soccer practice? Give these rolls a try!

They are ideal for picnics, fishing trips and even as take-alongs on hiking excursions. After cutting the rolls in half and securing with toothpicks, just wrap each roll with foil or plastic wrap. Double or triple the recipe, and you'll have a simple (and popular) contribution to potluck gatherings, church suppers and other bring-a-dish events.

sassy southwestern burgers

pepperoni 'n cheese crescents

pepperoni 'n cheese crescents

READY TO SERVE: 40 MINUTES
SERVINGS: 4

1 can (8-oz.) refrigerated crescent dinner rolls

24 slices pepperoni (about 5 oz.)

½ cup shredded mozzarella cheese (2 oz.)

1 cup tomato pasta sauce or pizza sauce

1. Heat the oven to 375°F.

2. Separate the dough into 8 triangles, stretching each triangle slightly.

3. Put 3 pepperoni slices lengthwise down the center of each triangle, overlapping slightly. Put about 1 tablespoon of cheese on the top of each triangle.

4. Roll up each of the triangles, starting with the shortest side and rolling to the opposite point. Put the rolls, point side down, on an ungreased cookie sheet.

5. Bake the rolls at 375°F for 10 to 14 minutes or until golden brown.

6. Meanwhile, pour the tomato pasta sauce into a small saucepan (1 quart). Heat over medium-low heat until warmed through, stirring occasionally.

7. Serve the crescents with the pasta sauce for dipping.

Nutrition Information Per Serving: Calories 480 • Total Fat 29g • Sodium 1790mg • Total Carbohydrate 40g • Sugars 14g • Protein 16g. Dietary Exchanges: 1 High-Fat Meat • 4 Fat.

turkey poorboy sandwiches

READY TO SERVE: 10 MINUTES
SERVINGS: 4

✳ super fast

1 medium carrot, shredded (¾ cup)

¼ cup raisins

½ cup vanilla fat-free yogurt

3 tablespoons fat-free mayonnaise or salad dressing

4 French rolls (2-oz. each), halved lengthwise

½ lb. thinly sliced cooked lean turkey breast

4 leaves leaf lettuce

1. In small bowl, mix carrots, raisins, yogurt and mayonnaise.

2. Spread cut sides of both halves of each roll with carrot mixture. Fill each roll with turkey and lettuce leaf.

Nutrition Information Per Serving: Calories 300 • Total Fat 3g • Saturated Fat 1g • Trans Fat 0g • Cholesterol 50mg • Sodium 480mg • Total Carbohydrate 45g • Dietary Fiber 3g • Sugars 13g • Protein 24g. Dietary Exchanges: 2 Starch • 1 Other Carbohydrate • 2½ Very Lean Meat.

SANDWICH STACKERS...THEN AND NOW

In the southern region of the USA, hearty handheld delights that come together quickly...without much fuss or expense...are sometimes referred to as "poorboy" or "po'boy" sandwiches.

Traditionally, the classic, submarine-like stackers were loaded with meats and cheeses and featured plenty of mustard; but today, anything goes! Poorboys now offer a limitless combination of tasty fillings, so let your kitchen creativity run wild.

easy steak sandwiches

⅓ cup beef broth

½ teaspoon garlic powder

1 teaspoon Worcestershire sauce

Dash pepper

¾ lb. beef round sandwich tip steaks (⅛-inch thick)

1 small onion, thinly sliced

4 French rolls (4- to 6-inch), split

4 leaves romaine lettuce, if desired

1. In large nonstick skillet, combine broth, garlic powder, Worcestershire sauce and pepper. Bring to a boil. Add steaks and onion; cook over medium-high heat for 2 to 4 minutes or until beef is of desired doneness, turning once.

2. To serve, drizzle cooking liquid over cut surfaces of rolls. Layer lettuce, steak and onion in rolls.

Nutrition Information Per Serving: Calories 300 • Total Fat 6g • Saturated Fat 2g • Cholesterol 45mg • Sodium 540mg • Total Carbohydrate 38g • Dietary Fiber 2g • Sugars 4g • Protein 23g. Dietary Exchanges: 2½ Starch • 2 Lean Meat OR 2½ Carbohydrate • 2 Lean Meat.

FAST AND FILLING DINNER

Drizzled with savory pan juices, these mouthwatering sandwiches are best when served on crusty rolls. Don't despair if all you have is soft bread, though. Just toast the bread first, then serve the sandwiches with a knife and fork.

Regardless of the bread you use, consider adding deli-bought three-bean salad to the menu as well as instant pudding for dessert. Tossing some sliced bananas into the pudding right before serving adds a fun touch to the effortless treat. Or prepare some tapioca as an after-dinner surprise. Just be sure to prepare it before you begin making the sandwiches, so it's ready by dessert time.

tuna cheese flips

SERVINGS: 5 (2 SANDWICHES EACH)

MARILYN BELSCHNER * AMHERST, NEBRASKA

2 cans (6-oz. each) tuna, drained, flaked

⅛ teaspoon lemon-pepper seasoning

⅓ cup sliced ripe or green olives, drained

⅓ cup mayonnaise or salad dressing

2 oz. shredded Monterey Jack or Cheddar cheese (½ cup)

1 can (12-oz.) refrigerated flaky biscuits

1 egg, beaten or 2 tablespoons milk

1 cup crushed potato chips

1. Heat oven to 375°F. In small bowl, combine tuna, lemon-pepper seasoning, olives, mayonnaise and cheese.

2. Separate dough into 10 biscuits. Press or roll out each to 5-inch circle. Spoon about ¼ cup tuna mixture onto center of each circle. Fold dough in half over filling; press edges with fork to seal.

3. Brush both sides of each sandwich with egg; press both sides in chips.

4. Place on ungreased cookie sheet. With sharp knife, make two or three ½-inch slits in top of each sandwich. Bake at 375°F for 18 to 24 minutes or until deep golden brown.

Nutrition Information Per Serving: Calories 260 • Total Fat 15g • Sodium 620mg • Total Carbohydrate 18g • Protein 12g.

hearty steak and tater soup

PREP TIME: 20 MINUTES
READY TO SERVE: 9 HOURS 55 MINUTES
SERVINGS: 8

✳ slow cooked

1 lb. boneless beef round steak, trimmed of fat, cut into 1¼x1-inch pieces

1 lb. small red potatoes, cut into ¼-inch slices (4 cups)

2 medium stalks celery, chopped (1 cup)

2 medium carrots, chopped (1 cup)

½ cup chopped onion

2 garlic cloves, minced

1 tablespoon beef-flavor instant bouillon

½ teaspoon salt

½ teaspoon pepper

4 cans (14-oz. each) beef broth

1 jar (6-oz.) sliced mushrooms, undrained

½ cup water

½ cup all-purpose flour

1. In 4- to 5-quart slow cooker, combine all ingredients except water and flour; mix well.

2. Cover; cook on Low setting for 8 to 9 hours.

3. About 35 minutes before serving, blend water and flour until smooth. Gradually stir into soup. Increase heat setting to High; cover and cook an additional 30 minutes or until slightly thickened.

Nutrition Information Per Serving: Calories 190 • Total Fat 3g • Saturated Fat 1g • Cholesterol 30mg • Sodium 1690mg • Total Carbohydrate 27g • Dietary Fiber 3g • Sugars 3g • Protein 17g. Dietary Exchanges: 1 Starch • 2 Vegetable • 1½ Very Lean Meat OR 1½ Carbohydrate • 2 Vegetable • 1½ Very Lean Meat.

GIVE LUMPY CHEESE BREAD A TRY

Lumpy Cheese Bread is a great accompaniment to any soup. To start, separate a 16.3-oz. can of large refrigerated biscuits into 8 biscuits. Cut each biscuit into 8 pieces and place them in a bowl. Mix with an 8-oz. can of pizza sauce as well as 1 cup of finely shredded mozzarella cheese. Spread the mixture into an ungreased 9-in. square glass baking dish. Sprinkle with another cup of the finely shredded mozzarella cheese. Bake at 375°F for 22 to 28 minutes or until the bread is golden brown and bubbly.

sandwiches on a stick

italian turkey soup

PREP TIME: 25 MINUTES
SERVINGS: 6

* super fast

½ lb. lean ground turkey

½ teaspoon fennel seed, crushed

½ teaspoon anise seed, crushed

2 garlic cloves, minced

2 cans (14.5-oz. each) no-salt-added stewed tomatoes, undrained

1 can (8-oz.) no-salt-added tomato sauce

2 cups water

1 teaspoon dried basil leaves

1 teaspoon dried oregano leaves

½ teaspoon salt

½ cup uncooked orzo or rosamarina

1. Spray nonstick Dutch oven or large saucepan with nonstick cooking spray. Add turkey, fennel seed, anise seed and garlic; cook over medium-high heat until turkey is no longer pink.

2. Add all remaining ingredients except orzo; mix well. Bring to a boil. Add orzo; return to a boil. Reduce heat to medium-low; cover and cook 12 minutes or until orzo is tender.

Nutrition Information Per Serving: Calories 150 • Total Fat 4g • Saturated Fat 1g • Cholesterol 30mg • Sodium 240mg • Total Carbohydrate 19g • Dietary Fiber 2g • Sugars 5g • Protein 10g. **Dietary Exchanges:** 1 Starch • 1 Vegetable • 1 Lean Meat OR 1 Carbohydrate • 1 Vegetable • 1 Lean Meat.

BE SURE TO USE YOUR NOODLE

Orzo is a rice-shaped pasta that cooks quickly, making it a natural addition to boiling pots of soup and a key ingredient in weeknight suppers. If you don't have this change-of-pace pasta at home, use small shell pasta instead. No matter which variety you add to soups, be careful to use only the amount in the recipe. Pasta continues to absorb a soup's liquid as it sits, turning the pasta soggy. This affects the soup's texture, particularly the leftovers.

sandwiches on a stick

READY TO SERVE: 40 MINUTES
SERVINGS: 4

¼ cup mayonnaise

2 tablespoons Thousand Island salad dressing

6 slices bacon

1 medium tomato

9 slices white or whole wheat sandwich bread

6 lettuce leaves

6 slices deli chicken or turkey (about 6 ounces)

4 cherry tomatoes

4 pickle chunks

1. Combine the mayonnaise and Thousand Island salad dressing in a small bowl.

2. On a microwave-safe plate, microwave the bacon on High 5 to 6 minutes, until crisp. Cool.

3. Cut the tomato into 6 slices.

4. Toast the slices of bread. Spread the mayonnaise mixture onto 1 side of each slice of toast.

5. Put 1 lettuce leaf and 2 slices of chicken on top of each of 3 slices of bread. Top with remaining bread, spread side down. Top each of these slices of bread with 1 lettuce leaf, 2 tomato slices and 2 crisp bacon slices. Cover the bacon with the last 3 slices of bread, spread side down.

6. Cut each sandwich diagonally into 4 pieces.

7. Take a wooden skewers and stick the food on the skewer in this order: 1 sandwich piece, 1 cherry tomato, 1 sandwich piece, 1 pickle chunk, 1 sandwich piece.

Nutrition Information Per Serving: Calories 420 • Total Fat 24g • Sodium 740mg • Total Carbohydrate 32g • Sugars 5g • Protein 21g. **Dietary Exchanges:** 2 Starch • 2 Lean Meat.

beef & ground beef

pizza skillet hot dish * p. 121

caramelized onion pot roast * p. 129

cheesy italian tortellini * p. 134

beef and bean tamale pie * p. 138

bistro beef ✽ p. 131

spicy beef and vegetables

spicy beef and vegetables

READY TO SERVE: 30 MINUTES
SERVINGS: 4

pasta
4 oz. uncooked vermicelli

sauce
2 tablespoons soy sauce

2 tablespoons hoisin sauce

1 tablespoon honey

1 teaspoon cornstarch

½ teaspoon crushed red pepper flakes

stir-fry
¾ lb. boneless beef sirloin steak, cut into thin bite-sized strips

1 medium onion, cut into thin wedges

2 medium zucchini, cut into 2x¼x¼-inch strips

1 small red bell pepper, cut into thin strips

1 garlic clove, minced

1 can (14-oz.) baby corn nuggets, drained, rinsed, if desired

1. Cook vermicelli to desired doneness as directed on package. Drain; cover to keep warm.

2. Meanwhile, in small bowl, combine all sauce ingredients; blend well. Set aside.

3. Spray large nonstick skillet with nonstick cooking spray. Heat over medium-high heat until hot. Add beef and onion; cook and stir 3 to 5 minutes or until beef is no longer pink and onion is crisp-tender.

4. Add zucchini, bell pepper and garlic; cook and stir 2 to 4 minutes or until vegetables are crisp-tender. Stir sauce well. Add sauce and corn to skillet; cook 2 to 4 minutes or until sauce is bubbly and thickened, stirring frequently. Serve beef mixture over vermicelli.

Nutrition Information Per Serving: Calories 290 • Total Fat 5g • Saturated Fat 2g • Cholesterol 45mg • Sodium 720mg • Total Carbohydrate 39g • Dietary Fiber 4g • Sugars 13g • Protein 22g. Dietary Exchanges: 1 Starch • 1 Fruit • 1 Vegetable • 2½ Lean Meat OR 2 Carbohydrate • 1 Vegetable • 2½ Lean Meat.

REFRESHING ACCOMPANIMENT

Often served at Chinese New Year celebrations, fresh oranges are said to bring good luck. In addition, the juicy fruits make a fast, change-of-pace addition to dinners, so go ahead and set a few orange wedges alongside individual servings of Spicy Beef and Vegetables. Or, consider garnishing vanilla pudding with thin orange slices for dessert. While you are waiting for the pasta water to boil, cut up the stir-fry ingredients and slice the oranges.

teriyaki beef and mushrooms

READY TO SERVE: 30 MINUTES
SERVINGS: 4

1⅓ cups uncooked regular long-grain white rice

2⅔ cups water

⅓ cup teriyaki sauce

2 tablespoons dry sherry

2 teaspoons cornstarch

1 teaspoon grated gingerroot

1 tablespoon oil

¾ lb. boneless beef top sirloin steak, cut into thin bite-sized strips

6 to 7 oz. fresh shiitake mushrooms, sliced

2 cups frozen sugar snap peas

4 oz. fresh bean sprouts (1 cup)

1. Cook rice in water as directed on package.

2. Meanwhile, in small bowl, combine teriyaki sauce, sherry, cornstarch and gingerroot; blend well. Set aside.

3. Heat oil in large skillet or wok over medium-high heat until hot. Add beef; cook and stir 3 to 4 minutes or until beef is browned and of desired doneness. Remove beef from skillet; cover to keep warm.

4. In same skillet, combine mushrooms and sugar snap peas. Cover; cook over medium-high heat for 4 to 5 minutes or until peas are crisp-tender, stirring once or twice.

5. Stir cornstarch mixture until smooth. Add cornstarch mixture, beef and sprouts to skillet; cook and stir until sauce is bubbly and thickened. Serve over rice.

Nutrition Information Per Serving: Calories 420 • Total Fat 8g • Saturated Fat 2g • Cholesterol 45mg • Sodium 1000mg • Total Carbohydrate 64g • Dietary Fiber 4g • Sugars 7g • Protein 24g. Dietary Exchanges: 3½ Starch • ½ Fruit • 1 Vegetable • 1½ Lean Meat OR 4 Carbohydrate • 1 Vegetable • 1½ Lean Meat.

steak and potato salad

READY TO SERVE: 30 MINUTES
SERVINGS: 4

½ lb. small new red potatoes, halved

⅔ cup fat-free honey Dijon dressing

¾ lb. boneless beef sirloin steak (¾-inch thick)

¼ teaspoon salt

¼ teaspoon coarse ground black pepper

4 cups torn romaine

2 medium tomatoes, cut into thin wedges

½ cup thinly sliced red onion

1. Heat gas or charcoal grill. In 2-quart saucepan, place potatoes and enough water to cover. Heat to boiling. Reduce heat to medium; cook 5 to 8 minutes or just until potatoes are fork-tender.

2. Drain potatoes; place in medium bowl. Gently stir in 2 tablespoons of the dressing to coat. Brush steak with 1 tablespoon of the remaining dressing; sprinkle with salt and pepper.

3. When grill is heated, place steak and potatoes on gas grill over medium heat or on charcoal grill over medium coals; cover grill. Cook 8 to 15 minutes, turning once, until steak is desired doneness and potatoes are golden brown.

4. Arrange lettuce, tomatoes and onion on large serving platter. Cut steak into thin slices; arrange on platter. Top with potatoes. Drizzle salad with remaining dressing. If desired, sprinkle with additional black pepper.

Nutrition Information Per Serving: Calories 210 • Total Fat 3g • Saturated Fat 1g • Trans Fat 0g • Cholesterol 45mg • Sodium 610mg • Total Carbohydrate 29g • Dietary Fiber 4g • Sugars 10g • Protein 20g. Dietary Exchanges: 1 Starch • 1 Other Carbohydrate • 2½ Very Lean Meat.

chuck wagon cheeseburger skillet

SERVINGS: 5
ROSEMARY WARMUTH ✳ WHEELING, WEST VIRGINIA

4 slices bacon

1 lb. lean ground beef

3 tablespoons chopped onion

3 tablespoons oil

2½ cups frozen hash-brown potatoes, thawed

1 can (11-oz.) vacuum-packed whole kernel corn with red and green peppers, drained

1 can (4.5-oz.) chopped green chiles, drained

½ cup barbecue sauce

8 oz. shredded Cheddar cheese (2 cups)

¼ teaspoon salt, if desired

¼ teaspoon pepper, if desired

1 can (16.3-oz.) large refrigerated buttermilk biscuits or reduced-fat buttermilk biscuits

1. Heat oven to 400°F. Cook bacon until crisp. Drain on paper towel; crumble. Set aside. In 12-inch cast-iron or ovenproof skillet, cook ground beef and onion over medium heat until beef is thoroughly cooked, stirring frequently. Drain. Place beef mixture in medium bowl; cover to keep warm.

2. Add oil to same skillet. Heat over medium-high heat until hot. Add potatoes; cook 3 to 5 minutes or until browned, stirring constantly. Add cooked ground beef, corn, chiles, barbecue sauce, cheese, salt and pepper; mix well. Cook until thoroughly heated, stirring occasionally. Sprinkle with bacon.

3. Separate dough into 8 biscuits. Arrange biscuits over hot mixture. Bake at 400°F for 16 to 24 minutes or until biscuits are deep golden brown and bottoms are no longer doughy.

Nutrition Information Per Serving: Calories 880 • Total Fat 53g • Sodium 1950mg • Total Carbohydrate 62g • Protein 38g.

MEAL-IN-ONE IS VERSATILE, TOO

This meat-and-potato dish is a surefire family pleaser. It's a one-pan meal with meat, vegetables, cheese and biscuits all baked in a large ovenproof skillet. To save time, you can use 1 tablespoon bacon flavored bits instead of cooking the bacon. You can also adjust the ingredients for your gang. Stir some sliced olives into the hot mixture just before adding the bacon, or, sprinkle sesame seeds over the biscuits before popping the dish in the oven.

beef 'n bean tostadas

READY TO SERVE: 20 MINUTES
SERVINGS: 6

* super fast

 1 can (16-oz.) refried beans

 1 can (4.5-oz.) chopped green
   chiles, drained

12 tostada shells

 1 lb. lean ground beef

 1 jar (16-oz.) salsa

1½ cups shredded lettuce

 3 oz. shredded
   Cheddar cheese (¾ cup)

¾ cup diced tomato

1. Heat oven to 375°F. In medium bowl, combine beans and chiles; mix well. Spread 2 to 3 tablespoons bean mixture on each tostada shell; place on ungreased large cookie sheet. Bake at 375°F for 5 to 7 minutes or until hot.

2. Meanwhile, brown ground beef in large skillet over medium heat until thoroughly cooked, stirring frequently. Drain. Stir in 1½ cups of the salsa. Cook for 2 to 3 minutes or until thoroughly heated.

3. Serve tostada shells topped with hot beef mixture, shredded lettuce, cheese, tomato and remaining salsa.

Nutrition Information Per Serving: Calories 410 • Total Fat 20g • Saturated Fat 8g • Cholesterol 60mg • Sodium 1240mg • Total Carbohydrate 33g • Dietary Fiber 7g • Sugars 5g • Protein 24g. **Dietary Exchanges:** 2 Starch • 2 Medium-Fat Meat • 2 Fat OR 2 Carbohydrate • 2 Medium-Fat Meat • 2 Fat.

beef and ramen noodle bowls

sunburst ground beef casserole

PREP TIME: 25 MINUTES
READY TO SERVE: 55 MINUTES
SERVINGS: 6

1 lb. ground beef
¼ cup chopped onion
1 can (14½-oz.) cut green beans, drained
2 cans (8-oz. each) tomato sauce
¼ teaspoon dried basil leaves
⅛ teaspoon pepper
1 can (7.5-oz.) refrigerated buttermilk biscuits
4 oz. Cheddar cheese cut into ½-inch cubes (1 cup)
2 tablespoons margarine or butter, melted
1 tablespoon sesame seeds

1. Heat oven to 375°F. In 10-inch ovenproof skillet, brown ground beef and onion until beef is thoroughly cooked. Drain. Add green beans, tomato sauce, basil and pepper; mix well. Simmer while preparing biscuits.

2. Separate dough into 10 biscuits. Cut hole in center of each biscuit. Fold cheese cubes into hot meat mixture. Pull edges of biscuit rings to form oval; place around outer edge of skillet. Place biscuit holes in center of skillet. Brush biscuit pieces with margarine; sprinkle with sesame seeds.

3. Bake at 375°F for 23 to 28 minutes or until golden brown.

Nutrition Information Per Serving: Calories 400 • Total Fat 24g • Saturated Fat 10g • Cholesterol 65mg • Sodium 1080mg • Total Carbohydrate 24g • Dietary Fiber 3g • Sugars 6g • Protein 21g. Dietary Exchanges: 1½ Starch • 1 Vegetable • 2 Medium-Fat Meat • 2½ Fat OR 1½ Carbohydrate • 1 Vegetable • 2 Medium-Fat Meat • 2½ Fat.

beef and ramen noodle bowls

READY TO SERVE: 20 MINUTES
SERVINGS: 4

* super fast

1 tablespoon vegetable oil
1 medium onion, cut into thin wedges
1 bag (1-lb. 5-oz.) frozen stir-fry vegetables with traditional teriyaki sauce meal starter
¾ cup water
1 tablespoon peanut butter
1 package (3-oz.) oriental-flavor ramen noodle soup mix
¾ lb. cooked roast beef (from deli), cut into thin bite-size strips
¼ cup chopped peanuts

1. In 10-inch skillet, heat oil over medium-high heat until hot. Add onion; cook and stir 1 minute. Add frozen sauce from meal starter, water, peanut butter and 1 teaspoon of the seasoning from soup mix; discard remaining seasoning. Cook 2 to 3 minutes or until sauce is thawed, stirring occasionally.

2. Break up ramen noodles (from soup mix) into skillet. Add frozen vegetables; cover and cook an additional 8 to 10 minutes or until vegetables are crisp-tender, stirring occasionally.

3. Add beef; cook and stir until thoroughly heated. Spoon mixture into individual serving bowls. Sprinkle with peanuts.

Nutrition Information Per Serving: Calories 340 • Total Fat 16g • Saturated Fat 3g • Cholesterol 40mg • Sodium 1850mg • Total Carbohydrate 30g • Dietary Fiber 5g • Sugars 11g • Protein 24g. Dietary Exchanges: 1 Starch • 1 Vegetable • 3 Lean Meat • 1½ Fat.

MAKE MEALTIME A SNAP

When planning to serve this comforting entree, keep the following in mind for no-fuss assembly and preparation:

* To break up the ramen noodles before adding them to the skillet, gently pound the unopened package with a rolling pin or a wooden spoon.

* Breadsticks, egg rolls and green tea pair well with this main course.

* For a time-saving dessert, stir a drop or two of almond extract into vanilla pudding or pick up almond or fortune cookies at the grocery store. Lemon sherbet also caps off the meal easily

beef brisket with cranberry gravy

PREP TIME: 10 MINUTES
READY TO SERVE: 10 HOURS 10 MINUTES
SERVINGS: 8

* slow cooker

1 (2½-lb.) fresh beef brisket (not corned beef)

½ teaspoon salt

¼ teaspoon pepper

1 can (16-oz.) whole berry cranberry sauce

1 can (8-oz.) tomato sauce

½ cup chopped onion

1 tablespoon prepared mustard

1. Rub surface of beef brisket with salt and pepper. Place beef in 4- to 6-quart slow cooker. In small bowl, combine all remaining ingredients; mix well. Pour over beef.

2. Cover; cook on Low setting for 8 to 10 hours.

3. Remove beef from slow cooker. Cut beef across grain into thin slices. If desired, skim fat from cranberry sauce in slow cooker. Serve beef with sauce.

Nutrition Information Per Serving: Calories 305 • Total Fat 10g • Saturated Fat 4g • Cholesterol 80mg • Sodium 440mg • Total Carbohydrate 26g • Dietary Fiber 2g • Sugars 22g • Protein 30g. Dietary Exchanges: 1½ Fruit • 1 Vegetable • 4 Very Lean Meat • 1 Fat OR 1½ Carbohydrate • 1 Vegetable • 4 Very Lean Meat • 1 Fat.

chili cornbread bake

PREP TIME: 25 MINUTES
READY TO SERVE: 1 HOUR 5 MINUTES
SERVINGS: 8

chili

1 lb. ground beef

1 cup chopped onion

½ cup chopped green bell pepper

1 garlic clove, minced

1 can (15½- or 15-oz.) light red kidney beans, drained, rinsed

1 can (8-oz.) tomato sauce

1 package (1¼-oz.) taco seasoning mix

cornbread

1 cup all-purpose flour

1 cup yellow cornmeal

2 tablespoons sugar

3 teaspoons baking powder

½ teaspoon salt

1 can (8½-oz.) cream-style corn, undrained

½ cup milk

1 egg

4 oz. shredded Cheddar cheese (1 cup)

1. Heat oven to 350°F. Grease 2-quart casserole. In large skillet, cook ground beef, onions, bell pepper and garlic over medium-high heat until beef is thoroughly cooked. Drain. Stir in kidney beans, tomato sauce and taco seasoning mix. Reduce heat; simmer 10 minutes.

2. Meanwhile, in medium bowl, combine flour, cornmeal, sugar, baking powder and salt; mix well. In small bowl, combine corn, milk and egg; beat well. Add to dry ingredients; stir just until moistened.

3. Spoon ½ the cornbread mixture into greased casserole; sprinkle with ½ the cheese. Spoon chili over cheese; sprinkle with remaining cheese. Spoon remaining cornbread mixture evenly over cheese, spreading gently to cover.

4. Bake at 350°F for 30 to 40 minutes or until top is golden brown. Let stand 5 minutes before serving.

Nutrition Information Per Serving: Calories 420 • Total Fat 16g • Saturated Fat 7g • Cholesterol 75mg • Sodium 1110mg • Total Carbohydrate 47g • Dietary Fiber 6g • Sugars 11g • Protein 21g. Dietary Exchanges: 3 Starch • 1½ Medium-Fat Meat • 1½ Fat OR 3 Carbohydrate • 1½ Medium-Fat Meat • 1½ Fat.

MAKING TIME FOR A FAST FIESTA

With the recipe for Chili Cornbread Bake and a little bit of planning, you can surprise your family with a mouthwatering menu made up of Southwestern delights…even on a busy weeknight!

Start the evening before by quickly cooking up the beef and bean mixture on the stovetop. Next, stir together the batter for the cornbread. Store both items in separate containers in the refrigerator. When you're ready to simmer up dinner the following night, assemble the entree per the directions.

While the casserole is baking, prepare some Spanish rice from a box mix and toss together a green salad featuring your favorite tangy, bottled dressing. You'll have an outstanding dinner on the table in no time!

beefy tortilla casserole

PREP TIME: 20 MINUTES
READY TO SERVE: 8 HOURS 20 MINUTES
SERVINGS: 6

* slow cooker

1½ lb. lean ground beef

1 can (14.5-oz.) diced tomatoes with green chiles, undrained

1 can (10¾-oz.) condensed cream of onion soup

1 package (1.25-oz.) taco seasoning mix

¼ cup water

6 corn tortillas, (5- or 6-inch) cut into ½-inch strips

½ cup sour cream

4 oz. shredded Cheddar cheese (1 cup)

3 tablespoons sliced green onions

1. Cook ground beef in large skillet over medium heat until thoroughly cooked, stirring frequently. Drain.

2. In 3½- to 5-quart slow cooker, combine ground beef, tomatoes, soup, taco seasoning mix and water; mix well. Add tortilla strips; stir in gently.

3. Cover; cook on Low setting for 7 to 8 hours.

4. About 5 minutes before serving, spread sour cream over casserole. Sprinkle with cheese. Cover; let stand about 5 minutes or until cheese is melted. Sprinkle with onions.

Nutrition Information Per Serving: Calories 470 • Total Fat 29g • Saturated Fat 14g • Cholesterol 100mg • Sodium 950mg • Total Carbohydrate 26g • Dietary Fiber 3g • Sugars 9g • Protein 30g. Dietary Exchanges: 2 Starch • 3 High-Fat Meat OR 2 Carbohydrate • 3 High-Fat Meat.

pizza skillet hot dish

pizza skillet hot dish

READY TO SERVE: 30 MINUTES
SERVINGS: 4

½ lb. lean ground beef

2 oz. sliced pepperoni, chopped (½ cup)

1 jar (14-oz.) spaghetti sauce (2 cups)

¾ cup water

7 oz. uncooked ready-cut spaghetti (short curved pasta) (2 cups)

¼ cup sliced ripe olives

½ green bell pepper, cut into bite-sized strips

4 oz. shredded mozzarella cheese (1 cup)

1. Brown ground beef in large skillet over medium-high heat until thoroughly cooked, stirring frequently. Add pepperoni; cook 1 minute.

2. Stir in spaghetti sauce, water a
heat to medium-low. Cover; co
doneness, stirring occasion

3. Add olives; stir
Remove from h

Nutrition Information Pe
Sodium 990mg • Total Carb
3 Starch • 4½ Medium-Fat Me

biscuit-topped italian casserole

SERVINGS: 10

ROBERT WICK ✳ ALTAMONTE SPRINGS, FLORIDA

1 lb. ground beef

½ cup chopped onion

1 tablespoon oil, if desired

¾ cup water

½ teaspoon salt, if desired

¼ teaspoon pepper

1 can (8-oz.) tomato sauce

1 can (6-oz.) tomato paste

8 oz. shredded mozzarella cheese (2 cups)

1½ cups frozen mixed vegetables (from 1-lb. pkg.), thawed

2 cans (12-oz. each) refrigerated flaky biscuits

1 tablespoon margarine or butter, melted

½ teaspoon dried oregano leaves, crushed

1. Heat oven to 375°F. Grease 13x9-inch (3-quart) baking dish. In large skillet, brown ground beef and onion in oil until beef is thoroughly cooked; drain. Stir in water, salt, pepper, tomato sauce and tomato paste; simmer 15 minutes, stirring occasionally. Place half of hot meat mixture in greased baking dish; sprinkle with ⅔ cup of the cheese.

2. Spoon mixed vegetables evenly over cheese; sprinkle an additional ⅔ cup cheese over vegetables. Spoon remaining hot meat mixture evenly over cheese and vegetables; sprinkle with remaining ⅔ cup cheese.

3. Separate dough into 20 biscuits. Separate each biscuit into 3 layers. Arrange layers over hot meat mixture, overlapping, in 3 rows of 20 layers each. Gently brush biscuits with margarine; sprinkle with oregano. Bake at 375°F for 22 to 27 minutes or until biscuit topping is golden brown.

Nutrition Information Per Serving: Calories 420 • Total Fat 22g • Sodium 1240mg • Total Carbohydrate 36g • Protein 19g.

ADDING EYE APPEAL

Even on your busiest nights, you'd be surprised at how easy it is to dress up foods, making them more appealing to the picky eaters in your family.

By arranging the meat mixture, cheese and the vegetables in layers and completing the Biscuit-Topped Italian Casserole with an overlapping layer of split biscuits, you'll create an eye-catching dish without a lot of extra effort. Brushing the biscuits with melted butter and sprinkling them with oregano, adds even more interest to the attractive main course.

steak neapolitan

READY TO SERVE: 20 MINUTES
SERVINGS: 4

* super fast

1 teaspoon vegetable oil

2 tablespoons lemon juice

4 beef tenderloin steaks (4-oz. each and about 1-inch thick)

1 cup finely chopped onions (2 medium)

1 cup dry Marsala wine

2 tablespoons chopped fresh Italian parsley

1. Heat oil in large skillet over medium-high heat until hot. Add lemon juice and steaks; cook 8 to 10 minutes or until of desired doneness, turning once. Remove steaks from skillet; cover to keep warm.

2. Add onions and wine to juice mixture in skillet; cook and stir 4 minutes or until liquid is reduced to about ½ cup.

3. To serve, spoon onion mixture over steaks. Sprinkle with parsley.

Nutrition Information Per Serving: Calories 290 • Total Fat 10g • Saturated Fat 3g • Cholesterol 65mg • Sodium 65mg • Total Carbohydrate 11g • Dietary Fiber 1g • Sugars 4g • Protein 25g. Dietary Exchanges: 3 Medium-Fat Meat • 1 Other Carbohydrate.

rib-eye steaks with avocado salsa

READY TO SERVE: 30 MINUTES
SERVINGS: 4

salsa

½ cup salsa

1 medium avocado, peeled, pitted and coarsely chopped

2 tablespoons finely chopped red onion

2 tablespoons chopped fresh cilantro

steaks

4 boneless beef rib-eye steaks (¾-inch thick)

1 teaspoon garlic salt

1. Heat grill. In medium bowl, combine all salsa ingredients; mix well.

2. When ready to grill, sprinkle both sides of each steak with garlic salt. Place steaks on gas grill over medium heat or on charcoal grill 4 to 6 inches from medium coals. Cook 8 to 12 minutes or until of desired doneness, turning once or twice. Serve steaks with salsa.

Nutrition Information Per Serving: Calories 400 • Total Fat 22g • Saturated Fat 7g • Cholesterol 115mg • Sodium 800mg • Total Carbohydrate 6g • Dietary Fiber 3g • Sugars 2g • Protein 44g. Dietary Exchanges: ½ Starch • 6 Lean Meat • 1 Fat OR ½ Carbohydrate • 6 Lean Meat • 1 Fat.

best west tex-mex burgers

READY TO SERVE: 25 MINUTES
SERVINGS: 6

* super fast

¼ cup corn flake crumbs

⅔ cup chunky-style salsa

1 lb. extra-lean (at least 90%) ground beef

¾ cup fat-free sour cream

2 tablespoons chopped green chiles (from 4.5-oz. can)

¼ teaspoon ground cumin

6 fat-free flour tortillas (8 to 10 inch)

1½ cups chopped leaf lettuce

1. Heat gas or charcoal grill. In large bowl, mix corn flake crumbs and 3 tablespoons of the salsa. Stir in ground beef. Shape mixture into 6 round or long, narrow (hot dog-shaped) patties, ½-inch thick.

2. In small bowl, mix sour cream, green chiles and cumin; set aside.

3. When grill is heated, place patties on gas grill over medium heat or on charcoal grill over medium coals; cover grill. Cook 11 to 13 minutes, turning once, until patties are no longer pink in center and juice is clear and thermometer inserted in center of patties reads 160°F. Just before burgers are done, wrap tortillas in foil; place on grill for 1 minute to heat.

4. To serve, sprinkle ¼ cup lettuce down center of each tortilla. Top each with patty. Spoon sour cream mixture evenly over patties. Roll up tortillas. Serve with remaining salsa.

Nutrition Information Per Serving: Calories 320 • Total Fat 7g • Saturated Fat 2.5g • Trans Fat 0g • Cholesterol 50mg • Sodium 730mg • Total Carbohydrate 42g • Dietary Fiber 4g • Sugars 3g • Protein 22g. Dietary Exchanges: 1½ Starch • 1½ Other Carbohydrate • 2½ Very Lean Meat • 1 Fat.

steak neapolitan

fettuccine with beef and peppers

* super fast

1 package (9-oz.) refrigerated fettuccine

1 lb. lean (at least 80%) ground beef

1 medium green bell pepper, cut into thin bite-size strips

1 medium red bell pepper, cut into thin bite-size strips

½ cup half-and-half

⅓ cup basil pesto

½ teaspoon salt

⅛ teaspoon pepper

1. Cook fettuccine as directed on package. Drain; cover to keep warm.

2. Meanwhile, in 10-inch skillet, cook ground beef over medium-high heat for 5 to 7 minutes or until thoroughly cooked, stirring frequently. Drain. Add bell peppers; cook 4 to 6 minutes or until crisp-tender, stirring occasionally.

3. Add half-and-half, pesto, salt, pepper and cooked fettuccine. Reduce heat to medium; cook an additional 3 to 5 minutes or until thoroughly heated, stirring occasionally.

Nutrition Information Per Serving: Calories 560 • Total Fat 31g • Saturated Fat 10g • Cholesterol 150mg • Sodium 510mg • Total Carbohydrate 40g • Dietary Fiber 2g • Sugars 5g • Protein 31g. Dietary Exchanges: 2½ Starch • 3½ Medium-Fat Meat • 2½ Fat.

BEATING THE KITCHEN CLOCK

On days when you are pressed for time, reach for a package of frozen mixed bell pepper and onion stir-fry medley. As a substitute for the bell peppers in the fettuccine recipe, the frozen blend is a real time-saver that offers an extra flavor boost from its onions.

You can also prepare the dinner with leftover cooked ground beef or even steak or sirloin tips to really speed up your meal preparation. Or try replacing the half-and-half, basil pesto, salt and pepper with your favorite creamy Italian salad dressing.

sirloin and mushrooms in rich beef-dijon sauce

8 oz. uncooked angel hair pasta

1 lb. boneless beef top sirloin steak, cut into 1-inch pieces

2 garlic cloves, minced

1 package (8-oz.) sliced fresh mushrooms (3 cups)

1 cup beef broth

¼ cup diagonally sliced green onions

2 tablespoons all-purpose flour

3 tablespoons milk

2 tablespoons Dijon mustard

Coarse ground black pepper

1. Cook pasta to desired doneness as directed on package.

2. Meanwhile, spray 12-inch nonstick skillet with nonstick cooking spray. Heat over medium-high heat until hot. Add beef and garlic; cook about 4 minutes, stirring frequently. Add mushrooms, broth and onions. Reduce heat; cover and cook 3 minutes. Uncover; cook an additional 2 to 3 minutes.

3. In small bowl, combine flour and milk; blend until smooth. Add to skillet; cook and stir 2 minutes or until slightly thickened. Stir in mustard until smooth.

4. Drain pasta; arrange on serving platter. Spoon beef-mushroom mixture and sauce over pasta. Sprinkle with pepper.

Nutrition Information Per Serving: Calories 400 • Total Fat 9g • Saturated Fat 3g • Cholesterol 50mg • Sodium 340mg • Total Carbohydrate 50g • Dietary Fiber 2g • Sugars 3g • Protein 29g. Dietary Exchanges: 3 Starch • 1 Vegetable • 2½ Lean Meat OR 3 Carbohydrate • 1 Vegetable • 2½ Lean Meat.

beef and vegetable packets

READY TO SERVE: 30 MINUTES
SERVINGS: 4

4 medium potatoes, thinly sliced (4 cups)

8 large mushrooms, sliced (2 cups)

4 large carrots, thinly sliced (2 cups)

2 medium onions, sliced

½ lb. extra-lean (at least 90%) ground beef

1 cup barbecue sauce

1. Heat gas or charcoal grill. Cut 4 (20 x 18-inch) sheets of heavy-duty foil. Fold each in half to form 18x10-inch rectangles.

2. In large bowl, mix potatoes, mushrooms, carrots and onions. Crumble ground beef over vegetables. Add barbecue sauce; toss until well coated. Spoon ¼ of mixture onto each sheet of foil. Wrap each packet securely using double-fold seals, allowing room for heat expansion.

3. When grill is heated, place packets on gas grill over medium heat or on charcoal grill over medium coals; cover grill. Cook 20 minutes, turning packets over once, until vegetables are tender and beef is brown. Carefully open packets to allow steam to escape.

Nutrition Information Per Serving: Calories 340 • Total Fat 5g • Saturated Fat 2g • Trans Fat 0g • Cholesterol 35mg • Sodium 680mg • Total Carbohydrate 61g • Dietary Fiber 7g • Sugars 24g • Protein 16g. Dietary Exchanges: 1½ Starch • 2½ Other Carbohydrate • 1½ Lean Meat.

skillet beef and green beans

PREP TIME: 45 MINUTES
SERVINGS: 4

1 teaspoon oil

1 lb. boneless beef top round steak, cut into thin strips

¼ cup chopped onion

3 cups sliced new red potatoes

2 cups frozen cut green beans

¾ cup beef broth

½ teaspoon dried thyme leaves

¼ teaspoon pepper

1 teaspoon Worcestershire sauce

¼ cup water

2 teaspoons cornstarch

¼ cup chopped fresh parsley

1. Heat oil in large nonstick skillet or wok over medium-high heat until hot. Add beef and onion; cook and stir 2 to 3 minutes or until beef is browned. Remove beef from skillet; cover to keep warm.

2. In same skillet, combine potatoes, green beans, broth, thyme, pepper and Worcestershire sauce. Bring to a boil. Reduce heat; cover and simmer 15 to 20 minutes or until vegetables are tender.

3. In small bowl, blend water and cornstarch. Add beef, cornstarch mixture and parsley to vegetables; cook and stir until bubbly.

Nutrition Information Per Serving: Calories 310 • Total Fat 5g • Saturated Fat 2g • Cholesterol 65mg • Sodium 170mg • Total Carbohydrate 36g • Dietary Fiber 5g • Sugars 3g • Protein 29g. Dietary Exchanges: 2 Starch • 1 Vegetable • 3 Lean Meat OR 2 Carbohydrate • 1 Vegetable • 3 Lean Meat.

12 QUICK SKILLET STIR-INS

It's simple (and fun) to add items to stir-fry and stovetop dishes. When you're preparing Skillet Beef and Green Beans for instance, feel free to mix in any of the following ingredients after you add the beef broth:

* Fresh cauliflower florets

* Canned baby corn

* Chopped celery

* Sliced mushrooms

* Frozen broccoli florets

* Julienned carrots

* Sesame seeds

* Slivered almonds

* Frozen corn

* Dried marjoram

* Crushed rosemary

* Minced garlic

texas chili

beef with mushrooms and noodles

READY TO SERVE: 20 MINUTES
SERVINGS: 4

* super fast

3½ cups uncooked medium egg noodles (6 oz.)

½ lb. boneless beef sirloin steak, cut into thin bite-size strips

¼ teaspoon peppered seasoned salt

1 can (15-oz.) Italian-style tomato sauce

1 package (8-oz.) sliced fresh mushrooms (3 cups)

6 small green onions, cut into ½-inch pieces

1. Cook and drain noodles as directed on package, omitting salt. Place on serving platter or in serving bowl; cover to keep warm.

2. Meanwhile, sprinkle beef with seasoned salt. Heat 10-inch nonstick skillet over medium-high heat. Add beef; cook and stir 2 minutes or until brown.

3. Stir in tomato sauce, mushrooms and onions (if necessary, break up larger pieces of tomatoes with spoon). Heat to boiling. Reduce heat to low; simmer uncovered 3 to 5 minutes, stirring occasionally, until vegetables are tender. Pour beef mixture over noodles; toss gently to mix.

Nutrition Information Per Serving: Calories 340 • Total Fat 7g • Saturated Fat 1.5g • Trans Fat 0g • Cholesterol 65mg • Sodium 640mg • Total Carbohydrate 50g • Dietary Fiber 4g • Sugars 9g • Protein 20g. Dietary Exchanges: 3 Starch • 1 Vegetable • 1 Lean Meat • ½ Fat.

sweet-and-sour meatball kabobs

PREP TIME: 25 MINUTES
SERVINGS: 4

* super fast

1 large green bell pepper, cut into 12 pieces

8 thin wedges red onion

12 small fresh mushrooms

½ teaspoon seasoned salt

16 frozen cooked meatballs, thawed

¾ cup sweet-and-sour sauce

1. Heat gas or charcoal grill. In large bowl, combine bell pepper, onion and mushrooms. Sprinkle with seasoned salt; toss to coat.

2. Onto four 12- to 14-inch metal skewers, alternately thread meatballs, bell pepper, onion and mushrooms.

3. When grill is heated, place kabobs on gas grill over medium heat or on charcoal grill 4 to 6 inches from medium coals. Cook covered 10 to 15 minutes or until meatballs are thoroughly heated and vegetables are crisp-tender, brushing generously with half of the sweet-and-sour sauce and turning frequently. Heat remaining sweet-and-sour sauce to a boil; boil 1 minute. Serve sauce with kabobs for dipping.

Nutrition Information Per Serving: Calories 405 • Total Fat 21g • Saturated Fat 8g • Cholesterol 125mg • Sodium 1000mg • Total Carbohydrate 30g • Dietary Fiber 2g • Sugars 14g • Protein 24g. Dietary Exchanges: 1 Starch • 3 Medium-Fat Meat • 1 Fat • 1 Other Carbohydrate.

texas chili

PREP TIME: 15 MINUTES
READY TO SERVE: 10 HOURS 15 MINUTES
SERVINGS: 6

* slow cooked

1½ lb. beef top round steak, trimmed of fat, cut into ¾-inch cubes

1 small onion, finely chopped

2 garlic cloves, minced

1 can (28-oz.) diced tomatoes, undrained

1 can (8-oz.) tomato sauce

1 can (15- or 15.5-oz.) pinto beans, undrained

1 can (4.5-oz.) chopped green chiles

3 teaspoons chili powder

1 teaspoon cumin

1. In 4- to 6-quart slow cooker, combine all ingredients; mix well.

2. Cover; cook on Low setting for 8 to 10 hours.

Nutrition Information Per Serving: Calories 250 • Total Fat 4g • Saturated Fat 1g • Cholesterol 60mg • Sodium 710mg • Total Carbohydrate 31g • Dietary Fiber 9g • Sugars 7g • Protein 31g. Dietary Exchanges: 2 Starch • 3 Very Lean Meat OR 2 Carbohydrate • 3 Very Lean Meat.

petite lasagna

PREP TIME: 20 MINUTES
READY TO SERVE: 55 MINUTES
SERVINGS: 3

½ lb. lean ground beef or bulk mild Italian sausage

¼ cup chopped onion

¼ cup chopped green bell pepper

¼ cup chopped fresh mushrooms

1 jar (14-oz.) spaghetti sauce

¾ cup low-fat ricotta cheese

2 tablespoons grated Parmesan cheese

2 tablespoons chopped fresh parsley

1 egg, beaten

3 frozen precooked lasagna noodles (1 sheet), thawed

4 oz. shredded mozzarella cheese (1 cup)

1. Heat oven to 350°F. Spray medium nonstick skillet with nonstick cooking spray. Add ground beef, onion and bell pepper. Cook and stir until browned; drain. Reduce heat to low; stir in mushrooms and spaghetti sauce. Simmer 5 minutes, stirring occasionally.

2. In small bowl, combine ricotta cheese, Parmesan cheese, parsley and egg; mix well. If lasagna noodles are in perforated sheet, separate at perforations. Cut 1 of the lasagna noodles in half lengthwise.

3. Spread ¼ cup meat mixture in bottom of ungreased 9x5-inch (2-quart) loaf baking dish. Top with 1½ lasagna noodles, ½ the ricotta mixture, ½ the remaining meat mixture and ½ the mozzarella cheese. Repeat layers, starting with noodles and ending with mozzarella cheese.

4. Bake at 350°F for 30 to 35 minutes or until thoroughly heated and bubbly.

Nutrition Information Per Serving: Calories 460 • Total Fat 17g • Saturated Fat 6g • Cholesterol 85mg • Sodium 980mg • Total Carbohydrate 34g • Dietary Fiber 3g • Sugars 2g • Protein 42g. Dietary Exchanges: 2 Starch • 1 Vegetable • 5 Lean Meat OR 2 Carbohydrate • 1 Vegetable • 5 Lean Meat.

mexican beef skillet dinner

READY TO SERVE: 20 MINUTES
SERVINGS: 5

* super fast

1 lb. lean (at least 80%) ground beef

1 small onion, chopped (⅓ cup)

1 garlic clove, minced or ⅛ teaspoon garlic powder

1 can (10.75-oz.) condensed cream of mushroom soup

1 can (4.5-oz.) chopped green chiles

1 can (10-oz.) enchilada sauce

2 cups tortilla chips, broken slightly

1 cup shredded Cheddar cheese (4 oz.)

2 tablespoons chopped fresh cilantro, if desired

1. In 10-inch skillet, cook ground beef, onion and garlic over medium-high heat for 5 to 7 minutes or until beef is thoroughly cooked, stirring frequently. Drain.

2. Stir in soup, chiles, enchilada sauce and chips. Reduce heat to medium; cook and stir 3 to 4 minutes or until thoroughly heated and bubbly.

3. Sprinkle with cheese. Cover; cook an additional 2 to 3 minutes or until cheese is melted. Sprinkle with cilantro.

Nutrition Information Per Serving: Calories 480 • Total Fat 31g • Saturated Fat 12g • Cholesterol 80mg • Sodium 1030mg • Total Carbohydrate 24g • Dietary Fiber 3g • Sugars 4g • Protein 25g. Dietary Exchanges: 1½ Starch • 3 Medium-Fat Meat • 3 Fat.

SPEEDY KITCHEN STAPLES

Many of today's busy family cooks keep a few items on hand to speed up the dinnertime rush. Jars of minced and chopped garlic really help beat the clock and make cleanup a snap. You'll find the prepared garlic in the produce area of the grocery store. Just follow the jar's label for the amount to use in your favorite recipes. Similarly, cans of chopped chiles add plenty of zip to dishes, without the chopping required of fresh chiles.

caramelized onion pot roast

PREP TIME: 25 MINUTES
READY TO SERVE: 10 HOURS 25 MINUTES
SERVINGS: 12

* slow cooked

1 tablespoon olive or vegetable oil

1 boneless beef chuck roast (4 lb.)

1 teaspoon salt

½ teaspoon pepper

6 medium onions, sliced

1½ cups beef broth

¾ cup beer or nonalcoholic beer

2 tablespoons brown sugar

3 tablespoons Dijon mustard

2 tablespoons cider vinegar

1. Heat oil in large skillet over medium-high heat until hot. Add beef roast; cook about 10 minutes or until browned on all sides, turning occasionally. Sprinkle with salt and pepper.

2. Place onions in 3½- to 6-quart slow cooker. Place beef on onions. In small bowl, combine all remaining ingredients; mix well. Pour over beef and onions.

3. Cover; cook on Low setting for 8 to 10 hours.

4. With slotted spoon, remove beef and onions from slow cooker. Cut beef into slices. If desired, skim fat from beef juices in slow cooker. Serve beef with juices.

Nutrition Information Per Serving: Calories 330 • Total Fat 19g • Saturated Fat 7g • Cholesterol 95mg • Sodium 500mg • Total Carbohydrate 9g • Dietary Fiber 1g • Sugars 7g • Protein 32g. **Dietary Exchanges:** ½ Starch • 2 Vegetable • 4½ Lean Meat • 1 Fat OR ½ Carbohydrate • 2 Vegetable • 4½ Lean Meat • 1 Fat.

bistro beef

sloppy joe loaf

SERVINGS: 6

HELENA CRUTCHER ✱ HAZEL GREEN, ALABAMA

1 lb. extra-lean ground beef

1 small onion, chopped

1 can (8-oz.) tomato sauce

1 tablespoon all-purpose flour

¼ teaspoon dried basil leaves

¼ teaspoon dried oregano leaves

¼ teaspoon fennel seed

1 can (11-oz.) refrigerated French loaf

4 oz. shredded mozzarella cheese (1 cup)

1. Heat oven to 350°F. Spray cookie sheet and large skillet with nonstick cooking spray. In sprayed skillet, cook ground beef and onion over medium-high heat until beef is thoroughly cooked, stirring frequently. Drain. Add tomato sauce, flour, basil, oregano and fennel seed; mix well. Reduce heat to medium-low; simmer 5 minutes. Remove from heat.

2. Meanwhile, remove dough from can; place on lightly floured surface. Cut loaf in half lengthwise. Roll each half to form 16x4-inch rectangles. Place 1 dough rectangle on sprayed cookie sheet, being careful not to change shape.

3. Stir ½ cup of the cheese into ground beef mixture. Spoon and spread mixture over dough rectangle on cookie sheet. Sprinkle with remaining ½ cup cheese. Top with remaining dough rectangle.

4. Bake at 350°F for 25 to 30 minutes or until golden brown. Cut into slices.

Nutrition Information Per Serving: Calories 340 • Total Fat 14g • Sodium 680mg • Total Carbohydrate 28g • Protein 25g.

bistro beef

READY TO SERVE: 30 MINUTES
SERVINGS: 4

8 slices French bread, diagonally sliced ½-inch thick

Nonstick cooking spray

2 tablespoons grated Parmesan cheese

1 tablespoon olive or vegetable oil

¾ lb. beef sirloin or flank steak, cut into thin bite-sized strips

1 small onion, sliced

1 teaspoon minced garlic (1 to 2 cloves)

1½ cups frozen bell pepper and onion stir-fry

2 tablespoons water

2 teaspoons cornstarch

1 teaspoon Worcestershire sauce

1. Place bread slices on ungreased cookie sheet. Spray bread with nonstick cooking spray; sprinkle with Parmesan cheese.

2. Broil 4 to 6 inches from heat for 1 to 2 minutes or until lightly browned. Set aside.

3. Heat oil in large skillet over medium-high heat until hot. Add beef, onion and garlic; cook 3 to 4 minutes or until beef is browned, stirring occasionally. Add bell pepper and onion stir-fry; cook 2 to 3 minutes or until crisp-tender.

4. In small bowl, combine water, cornstarch and Worcestershire sauce; blend well. Add to beef mixture; cook and stir until slightly thickened.

5. Place 2 toasted bread slices on each of 4 individual serving plates. Top each with beef mixture.

Nutrition Information Per Serving: Calories 300 • Total Fat 10g • Saturated Fat 3g • Cholesterol 45mg • Sodium 400mg • Total Carbohydrate 31g • Dietary Fiber 3g • Sugars 4g • Protein 21g. Dietary Exchanges: 2 Starch • 2 Lean Meat • ½ Fat OR 2 Carbohydrate • 2 Lean Meat • ½ Fat.

SWIFT BUT SPECIAL TOUCH

For a weeknight dinner that is as memorable as it is easy, serve the open-faced beef sandwiches with a broccoli side dish. Simply steam or microwave the broccoli spears just before you begin to cook the beef. Season the spears with a pinch of garlic or onion salt. Right before serving, top the hot broccoli with grated or shredded Parmesan cheese.

steaks with lemon-chive butter

READY TO SERVE: 25 MINUTES
SERVINGS: 4

* super fast

1. Heat gas or charcoal grill. In small bowl, combine all butter ingredients; blend well. Set aside.

2. In another small bowl, combine pepper and garlic salt; mix well. Rub pepper mixture onto all surfaces of steaks.

3. When grill is heated, place steaks on gas grill over medium-high heat or on charcoal grill 4 to 6 inches from medium-high coals. Cook covered 8 to 12 minutes or until of desired doneness, turning once. Serve steaks with butter.

Nutrition Information Per Serving: Calories 430 • Total Fat 17g • Saturated Fat 11g • Cholesterol 150mg • Sodium 290mg • Total Carbohydrate 1g • Dietary Fiber 0g • Sugars 0g • Protein 47g. Dietary Exchanges: 6½ Lean Meat • 1 Fat.

butter

- 3 tablespoons butter or margarine, softened
- 2 teaspoons chopped fresh or ¾ teaspoon dried chives
- ½ teaspoon grated lemon peel
- 1 teaspoon lemon juice

steaks

- 2 teaspoons coarse ground pepper
- ½ teaspoon garlic salt
- 4 beef top loin steaks, 1-inch thick, (New York, Kansas City or strip steaks)

MAKE IT EVEN QUICKER

Don't have time to heat up the grill? See how easy it is to broil the steaks in your oven instead.

Season the beef top loin steaks as directed above, and set them on a broiler pan. Broil them 4 to 6 inches from the heat, using the times noted in the recipe, turning once.

And if you are pressed for time, there is no need to wait for the butter to soften either. Just microwave it in a small microwavable dish on Low or Defrost for 20 to 30 seconds or until it is soft. Mix in the chives, lemon peel and lemon juice and you will be good to go!

mexi-lasagna

PREP TIME: 25 MINUTES
READY TO SERVE: 45 MINUTES
SERVINGS: 6

- 4 oz. uncooked mini-lasagna noodles (2 cups)
- ½ lb. ground beef
- 1 can (15½- or 15-oz.) kidney beans, drained
- 1 can (14½-oz.) chili-style tomatoes, undrained
- 1 can (8-oz.) tomato sauce
- 8 oz. shredded Monterey Jack cheese (2 cups)
- 1 can (4½-oz.) chopped green chiles

1. Heat oven to 350°F. Spray 12x8-inch (2-quart) baking dish with nonstick cooking spray. Cook noodles to desired doneness as directed on package. Drain.

2. Meanwhile, in large skillet, cook ground beef over medium-high heat until thoroughly cooked. Drain. Add kidney beans, tomatoes and tomato sauce; cook until thoroughly heated, stirring occasionally.

3. Spoon cooked noodles evenly into sprayed baking dish. Sprinkle with 1 cup of the cheese, all of the beef mixture, green chiles and remaining 1 cup cheese.

4. Bake at 350°F for 20 minutes or until the edges are bubbly and the mixture is thoroughly heated.

Nutrition Information Per Serving: Calories 370 • Total Fat 17g • Saturated Fat 9g • Cholesterol 55mg • Sodium 770mg • Total Carbohydrate 32g • Dietary Fiber 5g • Sugars 4g • Protein 22g. Dietary Exchanges: 2 Starch • 1 Vegetable • 2 High-Fat Meat OR 2 Carbohydrate • 1 Vegetable • 2 High-Fat Meat.

tortilla dip supper

READY TO SERVE: 20 MINUTES
SERVINGS: 5

＊ super fast

1 lb. lean ground beef
1 can (16-oz.) refried beans
1 can (8-oz.) tomato sauce
1 cup salsa
½ cup sour cream
4 oz. shredded Cheddar cheese (1 cup)
2 cups shredded lettuce
2 medium tomatoes, chopped
8 oz. tortilla chips (5 cups)

1. Brown ground beef in large skillet over medium-high heat until thoroughly cooked, stirring frequently. Drain.

2. Add refried beans, tomato sauce and salsa; mix well. Cook and stir 4 to 5 minutes or until thoroughly heated and bubbly.

3. In small bowl, combine sour cream and cheese; mix well. Spoon over beef mixture. Cover; cook over low heat for 3 to 4 minutes or until thoroughly heated. Remove from heat. To serve, top with lettuce and tomatoes. Serve with tortilla chips for dipping.

Nutrition Information Per Serving: Calories 670 • Total Fat 37g • Saturated Fat 15g • Cholesterol 90mg • Sodium 1520mg • Total Carbohydrate 52g • Dietary Fiber 9g • Sugars 8g • Protein 31g. Dietary Exchanges: 3 Starch • 1 Vegetable • 3 Medium-Fat Meat • 4 Fat OR 3 Carbohydrate • 1 Vegetable • 3 Medium-Fat Meat • 4 Fat.

speedy meat loaf

PREP TIME: 10 MINUTES
READY TO SERVE: 40 MINUTES
SERVINGS: 4

¾ lb. extra-lean ground beef
½ cup Italian-style bread crumbs
⅓ cup chopped green bell pepper
¼ cup ketchup
1 tablespoon Worcestershire sauce
2 teaspoons onion powder
1 egg white
2 tablespoons ketchup

1. Heat oven to 475°F. Spray broiler pan rack with nonstick cooking spray; if desired, also line pan with foil.

2. In medium bowl, combine all ingredients except 2 tablespoons ketchup; mix well. Place mixture on sprayed broiler pan rack; shape mixture firmly into 8x4-inch rectangle. Spread with 2 tablespoons ketchup.

3. Bake at 475°F for 20 to 25 minutes or until center is no longer pink. Let stand for 5 minutes before serving.

Nutrition Information Per Serving: Calories 250 • Total Fat 11g • Saturated Fat 4g • Cholesterol 55mg • Sodium 580mg • Total Carbohydrate 18g • Dietary Fiber 1g • Sugars 3g • Protein 19g. Dietary Exchanges: 1 Starch • 2 Lean Meat • 1 Fat OR 1 Carbohydrate • 2 Lean Meat • 1 Fat.

beef and spinach roll-ups

READY TO SERVE: 25 MINUTES
SERVINGS: 4

＊ super fast

1 package (9-oz.) frozen spinach in a pouch, thawed, squeezed to drain
½ teaspoon garlic powder
½ teaspoon salt-free lemon-pepper seasoning
1 lb. boneless beef sirloin steak (½-inch thick)
⅛ teaspoon pepper
4 pieces heavy thread or dental floss

1. In small bowl, combine spinach, garlic powder and lemon-pepper seasoning; mix well.

2. Place beef sirloin on cutting board. (Beef should be rectangular in shape.) Sprinkle with pepper. Spread spinach mixture evenly over beef. Beginning with long edge, roll up jelly-roll fashion. To secure roll-up, tie beef in 4 places with thread. With sharp knife, cut roll into 4 equal pieces.

3. Place rolls, cut side up, on broiler pan. Broil 4 to 6 inches from heat for 12 to 16 minutes or until beef is of desired doneness, turning once.

Nutrition Information Per Serving: Calories 150 • Total Fat 5g • Saturated Fat 2g • Cholesterol 60mg • Sodium 190mg • Total Carbohydrate 3g • Dietary Fiber 1g • Sugars 0g • Protein 22g. Dietary Exchanges: 1 Vegetable • 2½ Lean Meat.

cheesy italian tortellini

PREP TIME: 15 MINUTES
READY TO SERVE: 8 HOURS 30 MINUTES
SERVINGS: 4

✳ slow cooked

½ lb. lean ground beef

½ lb. bulk Italian pork sausage

1 cup sliced fresh mushrooms

1 container (15-oz.) refrigerated marinara sauce

1 can (14.5-oz.) diced tomatoes with Italian seasonings, undrained

1 package (9-oz.) refrigerated cheese-filled tortellini

4 oz. shredded mozzarella cheese or pizza cheese blend (1 cup)

1. In large skillet, break ground beef and sausage into large pieces. Cook over medium heat about 10 minutes or until browned, stirring occasionally.

2. Spray 4- to 5-quart slow cooker with nonstick cooking spray. Combine meat mixture, mushrooms, marinara sauce and tomatoes in sprayed slow cooker; mix well.

3. Cover; cook on Low setting for 7 to 8 hours.

4. About 15 minutes before serving, add tortellini to slow cooker; stir gently to mix. Sprinkle with cheese. Cover; cook on Low setting for an additional 15 minutes or until tortellini are tender.

Nutrition Information Per Serving: Calories 575 • Total Fat 33g • Saturated Fat 13g • Cholesterol 135mg • Sodium 1330mg • Total Carbohydrate 39g • Dietary Fiber 3g • Sugars 12g • Protein 34g. Dietary Exchanges: 2½ Starch • 4 Medium-Fat Meat • 1½ Fat OR 2½ Carbohydrate • 4 Medium-Fat Meat • 1½ Fat.

beef, bacon and barley soup

PREP TIME: 25 MINUTES
READY TO SERVE: 8 HOURS 25 MINUTES
SERVINGS: 8

✳ slow cooked

4 slices bacon, cut into ½-inch pieces

1½ lb. boneless beef round steak, cut into ½-inch pieces

1 medium onion, chopped (½ cup)

4 small red potatoes, unpeeled, cut into ½-inch cubes (about 2 cups)

1½ cups fresh baby carrots, cut in half lengthwise

1 cup frozen whole kernel corn

½ cup uncooked regular pearl barley

2 cans (14-oz. each) beef broth

1 can (14.5-oz.) diced tomatoes with basil, garlic and oregano, undrained

1 jar (12-oz.) beef gravy

1. Cook bacon in large nonstick skillet over medium-high heat for 3 minutes, stirring frequently. Add beef and onion; cook 3 to 5 minutes or until beef is browned, stirring occasionally.

2. In 3½- to 4-quart slow cooker, layer potatoes, carrots, corn and barley. Top with beef mixture. Pour broth, tomatoes and gravy over top. Do not stir.

3. Cover; cook on Low setting for 7 to 8 hours. Stir before serving.

Nutrition Information Per Serving: Calories 260 • Total Fat 6g • Saturated Fat 2g • Cholesterol 50mg • Sodium 860mg • Total Carbohydrate 32g • Dietary Fiber 5g • Sugars 4g • Protein 24g. Dietary Exchanges: 2 Starch • 2½ Very Lean Meat • 1 Fat.

SAVING TIME WITH A SLOW COOKER

As today's pace speeds up, family cooks are slowing down the dinnertime rush with their slow cookers. Even though the handy kitchen devices don't require much clock watching, there are a few tips you may want to keep in mind to get the most out of your slow cooker:

✳ Recipes often use the Low setting because a longer cooking time usually fits better with daily work schedules. The cooking time can be decreased, however, by using the High setting. In general, 1 hour at High is equal to 2 hours at Low.

✳ Smaller foods don't always cook faster. Baby carrots, for instance, take longer to cook than some other veggies. Always check items for doneness.

✳ Most cooked food can be held in a slow cooker for up to 1 hour without overcooking. Items such as dips and spreads can usually be kept on Low for several hours.

✳ Resist the temptation to lift the lid. Removing the lid allows heat to escape and can add as much as 20 minutes of cooking time.

cheesy italian tortellini

baked steak burritos

SERVINGS: 6

BECKY FULLER ✻ WESTMONT, ILLINOIS

Bake-Off

- ½ cup butter
- 1 package (1.25-oz.) taco seasoning mix
- 1½ lb. boneless beef sirloin tip steak, cut into thin bite-sized strips
- 1 can (16-oz.) refried beans
- 1 package (10.5-oz.) flour tortillas for soft tacos and fajitas (12 tortillas)
- 8 oz. shredded Cheddar cheese (2 cups)
- 3 green onions, thinly sliced
- 1 can (10-oz.) red enchilada sauce
- 4 oz. shredded Mexican cheese blend (1 cup)

1. Heat oven to 400°F. Melt butter in large skillet over medium heat. Stir in taco seasoning mix. Add beef strips; cook 5 to 6 minutes or until desired doneness, stirring frequently. Drain.

2. Meanwhile, place refried beans in microwavable dish. Microwave on High for 2 minutes, stirring once or twice.

3. Spread each tortilla with refried beans to within ¼ inch of edge. Top each with beef, Cheddar cheese and onions. Fold opposite sides over filling; roll up. Place seam side down in ungreased 13x9-inch (3-quart) glass baking dish. Pour enchilada sauce over burritos. Sprinkle with Mexican cheese blend.

4. Bake at 400°F for 7 to 12 minutes or until burritos are thoroughly heated and cheese is melted.

Nutrition Information Per Serving: Calories 750 • Total Fat 45g • Sodium 1990mg • Total Carbohydrate 45g • Protein 42g.

saucy pepper steak

PREP TIME: 20 MINUTES
READY TO SERVE: 9 HOURS 35 MINUTES
SERVINGS: 6

* slow cooked

1½ lb. boneless beef round steak, trimmed of fat, cut into 6 serving pieces

2 medium onions, cut into ¼-inch slices

1 garlic clove, minced

½ teaspoon grated gingerroot or ¼ teaspoon ginger

1 cup beef broth

3 tablespoons soy sauce

¼ cup cold water

2 tablespoons cornstarch

2 medium green bell peppers, cut into ¾-inch strips

2 medium tomatoes, each cut into 8 wedges

1. Spray 12-inch skillet with nonstick cooking spray. Heat over medium-high heat until hot. Add beef; cook about 8 minutes or until browned, turning once.

2. Layer beef, onions, garlic and gingerroot in 3½- to 6-quart slow cooker. In small bowl, combine broth and soy sauce; mix well. Pour over beef.

3. Cover; cook on Low setting for 7 to 9 hours.

4. About 15 minutes before serving, in small bowl, blend water and cornstarch until smooth. Gradually stir into beef mixture. Stir in bell peppers. Increase heat setting to high; cover and cook an additional 10 to 12 minutes or until slightly thickened. Add tomatoes; cover and cook an additional 3 minutes or just until tomatoes are thoroughly heated.

Nutrition Information Per Serving: Calories 170 • Total Fat 4g • Saturated Fat 1g • Cholesterol 60mg • Sodium 680mg • Total Carbohydrate 11g • Dietary Fiber 2g • Sugars 4g • Protein 25g. Dietary Exchanges: 2 Vegetable • 3 Very Lean Meat.

beef tenderloin with mushroom-shallot sauce

READY TO SERVE: 20 MINUTES
SERVINGS: 2

* super fast

2 beef tenderloin (filet mignon) steaks (½ lb. each)

1 large clove garlic, peeled, halved

¼ teaspoon coarse ground black pepper

1 teaspoon butter or margarine

1 cup fresh whole mushrooms, halved

2 shallots, thinly sliced

¼ cup Cabernet Sauvignon or other dry red wine

¼ cup beef broth

1 teaspoon cornstarch

1. Set oven control to broil. Line 15x10-inch pan with sides with foil. Rub both sides of each steak with cut side of garlic. Sprinkle each side with pepper; place steaks in pan.

2. Broil 4 to 6 inches from heat 12 to 16 minutes, turning once, until desired doneness.

3. Meanwhile, in 7-inch nonstick skillet, melt butter over medium heat. Add mushrooms and shallots; cook 4 to 6 minutes, stirring frequently, until shallots are tender and mushrooms begin to brown. Add wine; cook 1 minute, stirring occasionally.

4. In small bowl, mix broth and cornstarch until smooth. Gradually stir into mushroom mixture, cooking and stirring until bubbly and thickened. Serve sauce over steaks.

Nutrition Information Per Serving: Calories 210 • Total Fat 10g • Saturated Fat 4g • Trans Fat 0g • Cholesterol 70mg • Sodium 200mg • Total Carbohydrate 5g • Dietary Fiber 0g • Sugars 0g • Protein 26g. Dietary Exchanges: ½ Starch • 3½ Lean Meat.

FORK & KNIFE DELIGHT

Instead of serving bread alongside Beef Tenderloin with Mushroom-Shallot Sauce, why not turn the recipe into an easy meal-in-one? Simply cut off a few slices from a loaf of crusty French bread. Set the pieces under your broiler for a few minutes. Once the slices are toasted, remove to a dinner plate, position a steak on each slice, and pour the sauce over the steak.

For extra flair, top each with a flavorful cheese such as Swiss. Served with a simple green salad or steamed vegetables, the open-faced sandwiches will make a hearty addition to your weeknight lineup.

keep-it-simple lasagna

PREP TIME: 15 MINUTES
READY TO SERVE: 50 MINUTES
SERVINGS: 6

6 oz. mini lasagna noodles (3 cups)

1 medium zucchini, sliced

1 cup low-fat cottage cheese

1 egg white

2 oz. shredded mozzarella cheese (½ cup)

1 can (2¼ oz.) sliced ripe olives, drained

¼ lb. extra-lean ground beef

1 jar (25.5-oz.) reduced-fat, reduced sodium chunky vegetable spaghetti sauce

1 teaspoon fennel seed, crushed

¼ cup grated fresh Parmesan cheese

1. Cook noodles to desired doneness as directed on package, adding zucchini during last 2 minutes of cooking time.

2. Meanwhile, heat oven to 400°F. Spray 9-inch square pan with nonstick cooking spray. In small bowl, combine cottage cheese, egg white and ¼ cup of the mozzarella cheese; mix well. Set aside.

3. In large nonstick skillet over medium-high heat, brown ground beef; drain. Stir in spaghetti sauce and fennel; simmer 5 minutes.

4. Drain noodles and zucchini. Spread small amount of sauce in bottom of sprayed pan. Layer half each of noodles, zucchini, cottage cheese mixture and sauce; repeat layers. Top with remaining ¼ cup mozzarella cheese and Parmesan cheese.

5. Bake at 400°F for 25 to 35 minutes or until lasagna is bubbly and top is golden brown.

Nutrition Information Per Serving: Calories 280 • Total Fat 7g • Saturated Fat 3g • Cholesterol 20mg • Sodium 680mg • Total Carbohydrate 35g • Dietary Fiber 3g • Sugars 12g • Protein 19g. Dietary Exchanges: 2 Starch • 1 Vegetable • 2 Lean Meat OR 2 Carbohydrate • 1 Vegetable • 2 Lean Meat.

beef and bean tamale pie

PREP TIME: 15 MINUTES
READY TO SERVE: 6 HOURS 15 MINUTES
SERVINGS: 4

✳ slow cooked

½ lb. lean ground beef

½ cup chopped onion

1 can (15- or 15.5-oz.) kidney beans, drained, rinsed

1 can (10-oz.) enchilada sauce

1 pouch (6.5-oz.) golden corn muffin and bread mix

⅓ cup milk

2 tablespoons margarine or butter, melted

1 egg

2 oz. shredded Colby-Monterey Jack cheese (½ cup)

1 can (6.5-oz.) chopped green chiles

¼ cup sour cream

¼ cup chopped green onions

1. In large skillet, cook ground beef and onion over medium heat for 5 to 7 minutes or until beef is thoroughly cooked, stirring frequently. Drain. Stir in beans and enchilada sauce. Place beef mixture in 3½- to 4½-quart slow cooker.

2. In small bowl, combine corn muffin mix, milk, margarine and egg; stir just until moistened. (Batter will be lumpy.) Add cheese and chiles; stir gently to mix. Spoon over beef mixture in slow cooker.

3. Cover; cook on Low setting for 5 to 6 hours or until toothpick inserted in center of cornbread comes out clean. Top individual servings with sour cream and onions.

Nutrition Information Per Serving: Calories 615 • Total Fat 29g • Saturated Fat 11g • Cholesterol 115mg • Sodium 1340mg • Total Carbohydrate 69g • Dietary Fiber 10g • Sugars 22g • Protein 30g. Dietary Exchanges: 4½ Starch • 2 High-Fat Meat • 1 Fat OR 4½ Carbohydrate • 2 High-Fat Meat • 1 Fat.

MORNING MEAL PLAN

With just an ounce of planning, it's a snap to assemble zesty Beef and Bean Tamale Pie in your slow cooker before you head out the door in the morning.

The night before, prepare the beef mixture by browning the beef and stirring in the beans and enchilada sauce. Store the combination in the refrigerator. Next, stir together the cornbread batter, including the cheese and chiles.

Set the batter in the refrigerator as well. In the morning, you'll merely have to assemble the ingredients in your slow cooker, for a meal you'll turn to time and again.

beef and bean tamale pie

mom's skillet goulash

READY TO SERVE: 30 MINUTES
SERVINGS: 6

8 oz. uncooked rotini
(spiral pasta) (2⅔ cups)

1 lb. lean ground beef

1½ cups sliced celery

1 cup chopped onions

2 cans (14.5-oz. each) diced
tomatoes, undrained

1 can (10¾-oz.) condensed
tomato soup

1 teaspoon dried basil leaves

½ teaspoon salt

¼ teaspoon pepper

1. Cook rotini to desired doneness as directed on package. Drain.

2. Meanwhile, in 12-inch skillet or Dutch oven, combine ground beef, celery and onions. Cook over medium heat until beef is thoroughly cooked, stirring frequently. Drain.

3. Add cooked rotini and all remaining ingredients; mix well. Bring to a boil. Reduce heat; simmer 10 minutes, stirring occasionally.

Nutrition Information Per Serving: Calories 370 • Total Fat 12g • Saturated Fat 4g • Cholesterol 45mg • Sodium 730mg • Total Carbohydrate 44g • Dietary Fiber 3g • Sugars 9g • Protein 21g. Dietary Exchanges: 2½ Starch • 1 Vegetable • 1½ Medium-Fat Meat • ½ Fat OR 2½ Carbohydrate • 1 Vegetable • 1½ Medium-Fat Meat • ½ Fat.

sloppy joe confetti tacos

READY TO SERVE: 20 MINUTES
SERVINGS: 6

* super fast

1 lb. lean (at least 80%)
ground beef

1 package (4.6-oz.) taco shells
(12 shells)

1 can (15.5-oz.) sloppy joe sauce

1 small red bell pepper,
chopped

1 can (11-oz.) vacuum-packed
whole kernel corn, drained

1 can (2¼-oz.) sliced ripe
olives, drained

1 cup thinly sliced
romaine lettuce

½ cup shredded Colby-
Monterey Jack cheese (2 oz.)

1. Heat oven to 350°F. In 10-inch skillet, cook ground beef over medium-high heat for 5 to 7 minutes or until thoroughly cooked, stirring frequently. Drain.

2. Meanwhile, heat taco shells as directed on package.

3. Stir sloppy joe sauce, bell pepper and corn into ground beef. Cook an additional 2 to 3 minutes or until mixture is hot and bubbly.

4. Spoon about ¼ cup beef mixture into each warm taco shell. Top each with olives, lettuce and cheese.

Nutrition Information Per Serving: Calories 495 • Total Fat 29g • Saturated Fat 11g • Cholesterol 90mg • Sodium 860mg • Total Carbohydrate 30g • Dietary Fiber 3g • Sugars 6g • Protein 29g. Dietary Exchanges: 2 Starch • 3½ Medium-Fat Meat • 2 Fat.

HERE'S A QUICK FIX

Turn popular Sloppy Joe Confetti Tacos into a "no-chop" recipe. Look for packages of frozen, chopped bell pepper with the frozen vegetables at your supermarket. Does your grocery store have a salad bar in the produce department? If so, you could even consider purchasing chopped pepper from there. You'll also find bags of torn or shredded romaine lettuce in the produce section, which will help you beat the clock at home.

pepper steak salad

* super fast

dressing

- ¼ cup vegetable oil
- 3 tablespoons red wine vinegar
- 2 tablespoons Dijon mustard
- 1 tablespoon soy sauce
- ¼ teaspoon pepper
- 1 garlic clove, minced, or ⅛ teaspoon garlic powder

salad

- 2½ cups shredded Chinese (napa) cabbage
- ½ lb. cooked roast beef, cut into strips or chunks (about 1⅓ cups)
- 1 cup cherry tomatoes, halved
- 1 cup sliced fresh mushrooms
- 2 medium stalks celery, sliced (½ cup)
- ½ large green bell pepper, cut into bite-size strips

1. In large bowl, combine dressing ingredients; blend well.

2. Add all salad ingredients; toss gently to coat. Serve immediately.

Nutrition Information Per Serving: Calories 230 • Total Fat 16g • Saturated Fat 2g • Cholesterol 25mg • Sodium 1070mg • Total Carbohydrate 7g • Dietary Fiber 2g • Sugars 2g • Protein 14g. Dietary Exchanges: 1 Vegetable • 1½ Medium-Fat Meat • 2 Fat.

MUSHROOMS DRESS UP DINNER...EASILY

The sliced and packaged fresh mushrooms that are found in the produce department are perfect for preparing a meal in minutes. Today, family cooks have an assortment of fresh mushrooms to choose from, helping to mix up workweek dinners and shake the supper-time doldrums. If you're preparing Pepper Steak Salad, consider using one of these varieties and bring a new flavor to the table.

* Portobello. This is a large-capped mushroom that offers a robust flavor.

* Shiitake. Often used in Asian recipes, this variety has an umbrella-shaped cap and a soft texture.

* Oyster. This mushroom is rather delicate and has a velvety texture.

* Crimini. While this may look like a button mushroom, its flavor is stronger.

---

sweet 'n spicy meat and potato loaves

sauce

- 1 can (8-oz.) jellied cranberry sauce (¾ cup)
- ¼ cup chili or barbecue sauce
- 1 teaspoon dried mustard

meat loaves

- 1 lb. extra-lean ground beef
- 2 cups refrigerated shredded hash-brown potatoes (from 20-oz. package)
- ½ cup finely chopped onion
- 2 egg whites
- 1 teaspoon Worcestershire sauce
- ½ teaspoon ground sage

1. Heat oven to 400°F. Place roasting rack in shallow pan; spray rack with nonstick cooking spray.

2. In small bowl, combine all sauce ingredients; beat with wire whisk until smooth.

3. In large bowl, combine all meat loaf ingredients and ¼ cup of the sauce; mix well. Shape mixture into 6 oval loaves, about ¾-inch thick; place on sprayed rack in pan. Spoon about 1 teaspoon sauce over each loaf.

4. Bake at 400°F for 15 minutes. Spoon an additional 1 teaspoon sauce over each loaf. Bake an additional 15 minutes or until no longer pink in center. Serve with the remaining sauce.

Nutrition Information Per Serving: Calories 260 • Total Fat 10g • Saturated Fat 4g • Cholesterol 45mg • Sodium 200mg • Total Carbohydrate 26g • Dietary Fiber 1g • Sugars 15g • Protein 17g. Dietary Exchanges: 1 Starch • ½ Fruit • 2 Medium-Fat Meat OR 1½ Carbohydrate • 2 Medium-Fat Meat.

chicken & turkey

barbecued turkey and vegetables ✻ p. 153

salsa chicken ✻ p. 157

ranch club salad ✻ p. 179

savory turkey breast ✻ p. 149

cajun chicken salad * p. 154

grilled teriyaki-apricot chicken

grilled teriyaki-apricot chicken

READY TO SERVE: 30 MINUTES
SERVINGS: 4

4 boneless skinless chicken breast halves

¼ teaspoon salt

¼ teaspoon coarsely ground black pepper

⅓ cup apricot preserves, large pieces finely chopped

3 tablespoons purchased teriyaki baste and glaze

½ teaspoon grated gingerroot

1. Heat grill. Sprinkle chicken with salt and pepper. In small bowl, combine all remaining ingredients; mix well. Set aside.

2. When ready to grill, place chicken on gas grill over medium heat or on charcoal grill 4 to 6 inches from medium coals. Cook 15 to 20 minutes or until chicken is fork-tender and juices run clear, turning once and brushing with teriyaki-apricot mixture during last 5 minutes of cooking time.

Nutrition Information Per Serving: Calories 220 • Total Fat 3g • Saturated Fat 1g • Cholesterol 75mg • Sodium 510mg • Total Carbohydrate 21g • Dietary Fiber 0g • Sugars 16g • Protein 27g. Dietary Exchanges: 1½ Fruit • 4 Very Lean Meat OR 1½ Carbohydrate • 4 Very Lean Meat.

chicken con queso

READY TO SERVE: 20 MINUTES
SERVINGS: 4

* super fast

4 frozen breaded cooked chicken patties

2 cups uncooked instant white rice

2 cups water

1½ cups chunky-style salsa

2 cups shredded American cheese (8 oz.)

1. Cook chicken patties as directed on package.

2. Meanwhile, cook rice in water as directed on package. Stir ½ cup of the salsa into rice. Cover to keep warm.

3. In 1½-quart saucepan, combine remaining 1 cup salsa and the cheese; cook over low heat until cheese is melted, stirring occasionally.

4. Place cooked rice on individual serving plates. Top each serving with warm chicken patty. Spoon cheese sauce over top.

Nutrition Information Per Serving: Calories 620 • Total Fat 31g • Saturated Fat 14g • Cholesterol 85mg • Sodium 1510mg • Total Carbohydrate 58g • Dietary Fiber 4g • Sugars 6g • Protein 27g. Dietary Exchanges: 4 Starch • 2 High-Fat Meat • 2½ Fat.

citrus chicken salad

READY TO SERVE: 10 MINUTES
SERVINGS: 4

* super fast

6 cups torn romaine

1 can (15-oz.) mandarin orange segments, drained

1 can (10-oz.) 98%-fat-free chicken breast chunks in water, drained

⅓ cup fat-free poppy seed dressing

Fresh mint leaves, if desired

1. In large bowl, gently toss lettuce, orange segments and chicken.

2. Drizzle dressing over salad. If desired, garnish with fresh mint leaves.

Nutrition Information Per Serving: Calories 150 • Total Fat 1.5g • Saturated Fat 0g • Trans Fat 0g • Cholesterol 25mg • Sodium 380mg • Total Carbohydrate 19g • Dietary Fiber 3g • Sugars 13g • Protein 17g. Dietary Exchanges: 1 Other Carbohydrate • 2½ Very Lean Meat.

bayou sausage jambalaya

READY TO SERVE: 30 MINUTES
SERVINGS: 4

¼ lb. smoked turkey kielbasa, cut into ½-inch-thick slices

2 boneless skinless chicken breast halves, cut into bite-sized pieces

2 cups salsa

1½ cups uncooked instant white rice

1 cup water

Hot pepper sauce, if desired

1. Spray large nonstick skillet or Dutch oven with nonstick cooking spray. Heat over medium-high heat until hot. Add kielbasa and chicken; cook and stir 5 to 8 minutes or until chicken is no longer pink.

2. Add salsa, rice and water; mix well. Bring to a boil. Reduce heat; cover and simmer 5 to 10 minutes or until rice is tender. If desired, add salt and pepper to taste. Serve with hot pepper sauce.

Nutrition Information Per Serving: Calories 280 • Total Fat 3g • Saturated Fat 1g • Cholesterol 55mg • Sodium 1280mg • Total Carbohydrate 41g • Dietary Fiber 2g • Sugars 5g • Protein 23g. Dietary Exchanges: 2 Starch • ½ Fruit • 2½ Very Lean Meat OR 2½ Carbohydrate • 2½ Very Lean Meat.

chicken packets milano

READY TO SERVE: 35 MINUTES
SERVINGS: 4

4 boneless skinless chicken breasts (1 lb.)

¼ cup reduced-calorie zesty Italian or Italian Parmesan dressing

4 slices tomato

12 fresh sage leaves or ½ teaspoon ground sage

1. Heat oven to 450°F. Cut 4 (12x12-inch) sheets of heavy-duty foil. Place 1 chicken breast in center of each. Top each with 1 tablespoon dressing, 1 slice of tomato and 3 sage leaves.

2. Wrap each packet securely using double-fold seals, allowing room for heat expansion. Place packets on ungreased cookie sheet.

3. Bake 20 to 25 minutes or until juice of chicken is no longer pink when centers of thickest pieces are cut and thermometer inserted in center reads 165°F. Carefully open packets to allow steam to escape.

Nutrition Information Per Serving: Calories 160 • Total Fat 6g • Saturated Fat 1.5g • Trans Fat 0g • Cholesterol 70mg • Sodium 260mg • Total Carbohydrate 2g • Dietary Fiber 0g • Sugars 1g • Protein 25g. Dietary Exchanges: 3½ Very Lean Meat • 1 Fat.

chili turkey tenderloins

READY TO SERVE: 25 MINUTES
SERVINGS: 4

* super fast

1 lb. fresh turkey breast tenderloins, cut crosswise into ½-inch slices

½ teaspoon salt

½ teaspoon cumin

1 cup frozen whole kernel corn (from 1-lb. bag)

1 cup chunky-style salsa

¼ cup raisins

¼ cup chili sauce

¼ cup water

1. Sprinkle turkey slices with salt and cumin.

2. Heat 10-inch nonstick skillet over medium-high heat until hot. Add turkey; cook 2 to 4 minutes or until brown on both sides.

3. Add corn, salsa, raisins, chili sauce and water; mix well. Reduce heat to low; cover and simmer 8 to 10 minutes or until turkey is no longer pink in center and corn is hot, stirring occasionally.

Nutrition Information Per Serving: Calories 220 • Total Fat 1g • Saturated Fat 0g • Cholesterol 75mg • Sodium 1010mg • Total Carbohydrate 23g • Dietary Fiber 2g • Sugars 13g • Protein 30g. Dietary Exchanges: ½ Starch • ½ Fruit • 4 Very Lean Meat • ½ Other Carbohydrate.

bayou sausage
jambalaya

savory turkey breast

savory turkey breast

PREP TIME: 15 MINUTES
READY TO SERVE: 9 HOURS 15 MINUTES
SERVINGS: 12

✳ slow cooked

1 (6- to 6½-lb.) bone-in
  turkey breast
½ cup chopped onion
½ cup chopped celery
1 bay leaf
1 teaspoon salt
½ teaspoon coarsely ground
  black pepper
1 teaspoon chicken-flavor
  instant bouillon
½ cup water

1. Remove gravy packet or extra parts from turkey breast. Place onion, celery and bay leaf in cavity of turkey. Place turkey in 5- to 6-quart slow cooker. Sprinkle salt and pepper over turkey.

2. In small bowl, combine bouillon and water; stir until dissolved. Pour over turkey.

3. Cover; cook on Low setting for 8 to 9 hours. Remove and discard bay leaf before serving.

Nutrition Information Per Serving: Calories 305 • Total Fat 13g • Saturated Fat 4g • Cholesterol 125mg • Sodium 410mg • Total Carbohydrate 0g • Dietary Fiber 0g • Sugars 0g • Protein 47g. Dietary Exchanges: 7 Very Lean Meat • 1 Fat.

garden chicken sauté

READY TO SERVE: 20 MINUTES
SERVINGS: 4

✳ super fast

2 teaspoons olive or
  vegetable oil
2 boneless skinless chicken
  breast halves, cut into
  1-inch pieces
2 garlic cloves, minced
2 cups water
1 cup fresh baby carrots,
  halved crosswise
1 teaspoon dried Italian
  seasoning
2 packages (3-oz. each)
  chicken-flavor ramen
  noodle soup mix

1. Heat oil in large nonstick skillet over medium-high heat until hot. Add chicken and garlic; cook and stir 4 to 5 minutes or until chicken is browned.

2. Stir in water, carrots, Italian seasoning and contents of 1 of the soup mix seasoning packets. (Discard remaining seasoning packet or reserve for a later use.) Bring to a boil. Reduce heat; cover and cook 6 to 7 minutes or until carrots are crisp-tender.

3. Gently break each block of ramen noodles in half; add noodles and zucchini to skillet. Bring to a boil. Boil, uncovered, 5 to 6 minutes or until zucchini is tender and noodles are cooked, separating noodles gently as they soften.

Nutrition Information Per Serving: Calories 320 • Total Fat 12g • Saturated Fat 5g • Cholesterol 35mg • Sodium 710mg • Total Carbohydrate 33g • Dietary Fiber 2g • Sugars 4g • Protein 19g. Dietary Exchanges: 2 Starch • 1 Vegetable • 1½ Very Lean Meat • 2 Fat OR 2 Carbohydrate • 1 Vegetable • 1½ Very Lean Meat • 2 Fat.

hunter's stew with chicken

PREP TIME: 15 MINUTES
READY TO SERVE: 6 HOURS 15 MINUTES
SERVINGS: 4

✳ slow cooked

1 medium onion, thinly sliced
1 medium green bell pepper,
  cut into 1-inch pieces
3 boneless skinless chicken
  breast halves, cut into
  2x1-inch pieces
1 can (15-oz.) garbanzo beans,
  drained
1 jar (14-oz.) spaghetti sauce
1 can (8-oz.) mushroom pieces
  and stems, drained

1. In a 3½- to 4-quart slow cooker, combine all ingredients; mix well.

2. Cover; cook on Low setting for at least 6 hours.

Nutrition Information Per Serving: Calories 290 • Total Fat 6g • Saturated Fat 1g • Cholesterol 55mg • Sodium 790mg • Total Carbohydrate 30g • Dietary Fiber 9g • Sugars 3g • Protein 29g. Dietary Exchanges: 2 Starch • 3 Very Lean Meat • ½ Fat OR 2 Carbohydrate • 3 Very Lean Meat • ½ Fat.

overnight chicken enchilada bake

PREP TIME: 30 MINUTES
READY TO SERVE: 9 HOURS 40 MINUTES
SERVINGS: 8

* plan ahead

1 lb. boneless skinless chicken breast halves, cut into thin bite-sized pieces

1 can (10¾-oz.) condensed cream of chicken soup

1 container (8-oz.) sour cream

1 can (4.5-oz.) chopped green chiles

2 cans (10-oz. each) enchilada sauce

12 corn tortillas (6-inch), quartered

8 oz. shredded Cheddar cheese (2 cups)

¼ cup sliced green onions

1. Spray 13x9-inch (3-quart) glass baking dish and 16x12-inch sheet of foil with nonstick cooking spray. Heat large nonstick skillet over medium-high heat until hot. Add chicken; cook 3 to 4 minutes or until chicken is no longer pink in center, stirring frequently. Remove from heat. Stir in soup, sour cream and chiles.

2. Spread ¼ cup of the enchilada sauce in sprayed baking dish. Arrange half of the tortilla pieces over sauce, overlapping as necessary. Spoon and spread 1 cup enchilada sauce evenly over tortillas. Spread half of chicken mixture over sauce. Top with 1 cup of the cheese. Repeat layers, starting with tortilla pieces. Cover tightly with sprayed foil. Refrigerate at least 8 hours or overnight.

3. To serve, heat oven to 375°F. Bake covered for 30 minutes. Uncover baking dish; bake an additional 20 to 25 minutes or until sauce is bubbly and cheese begins to brown. Let stand 15 minutes before serving. Sprinkle with onions.

Nutrition Information Per Serving: Calories 390 • Total Fat 20g • Saturated Fat 11g • Cholesterol 85mg • Sodium 930mg • Total Carbohydrate 28g • Dietary Fiber 3g • Sugars 5g • Protein 25g. Dietary Exchanges: 2 Starch • 2½ Very Lean Meat • 3½ Fat.

mandarin–smoked turkey salad

READY TO SERVE: 15 MINUTES
SERVINGS: 6

* super fast

dressing

½ cup orange marmalade

2 tablespoons soy sauce

4 teaspoons cider vinegar

⅛ teaspoon ginger

salad

4 cups shredded Chinese napa cabbage

2 cups shredded iceberg lettuce

2½ cups cubed smoked turkey (about ¾ lb.)

1 cup fresh pea pods, trimmed, cut diagonally into 1-inch pieces

1 can (15-oz.) mandarin orange segments, drained

1. In 1-quart saucepan, mix dressing ingredients until well blended. Heat over medium heat, stirring frequently, until marmalade is melted. Cool 5 minutes.

2. Meanwhile, in large bowl, toss cabbage, lettuce, turkey and pea pods.

3. Gently stir orange segments into salad. Pour dressing over salad; toss gently to coat. Serve immediately.

Nutrition Information Per Serving: Calories 210 • Total Fat 3g • Saturated Fat 1g • Trans Fat 0g • Cholesterol 50mg • Sodium 390mg • Total Carbohydrate 27g • Dietary Fiber 2g • Sugars 20g • Protein 20g. Dietary Exchanges: ½ Starch • 1 Other Carbohydrate • 1 Vegetable • 2½ Very Lean Meat.

SPUR-OF-THE-MOMENT SALAD FIXINGS

It doesn't take much time or effort to jazz up the entree Mandarin-Smoked Turkey Salad.

For a crunchy treat, leave the croutons on the shelf and top the refreshing dish with a sprinkling of chow mien noodles, sunflower kernels, slivered almonds or even some finely chopped peanuts.

Trying to get your little ones to eat more veggies? Chop a red or green bell pepper and toss it into the salad. Slices of carrot, celery, zucchini or cucumber make healthy additions as well.

While the recipe calls for smoked turkey, feel free to use last night's cooked chicken. You'll clean out the fridge and set dinner on the table all at once. And if you're looking to streamline the salad's assembly a bit, pick up a bag of fresh spinach leaves or coleslaw mix from your grocer's produce department on your way home from work.

chicken breasts supreme

PREP TIME: 25 MINUTES
READY TO SERVE: 4 HOURS 40 MINUTES
SERVINGS: 6

✳ slow cooked

2 slices bacon

6 boneless skinless chicken breast halves (about 1½ lb.)

1 jar (4.5-oz.) sliced mushrooms, drained

1 can (4.5-oz.) condensed cream of chicken soup

2 tablespoons dry sherry, if desired

3 oz. sliced Swiss cheese

1 tablespoon chopped fresh chives

3 cups frozen broccoli florets

1. Cook bacon in large skillet over medium heat until crisp. Remove bacon from skillet; drain on paper towels. Refrigerate until needed. Reserve bacon drippings in skillet.

2. Add chicken breast halves to bacon drippings in skillet; cook over medium-high heat for 3 to 5 minutes or until lightly browned, turning once. Transfer chicken to 4- to 6-quart slow cooker. Top with mushrooms. In same skillet, stir together soup and sherry. Spoon over mushrooms.

3. Cover; cook on Low setting for 3 to 4 hours.

4. Top mixture in slow cooker with cheese slices. Sprinkle with chives. Crumble bacon over cheese. Increase heat setting to High; cover and cook an additional 10 to 15 minutes or until cheese is melted.

5. Meanwhile, microwave broccoli in covered microwave-safe dish on High for 6 to 8 minutes or until crisp-tender.

6. With slotted spoon, remove chicken, broccoli and mushrooms from slow cooker; arrange on serving platter. Serve with cooking juices from slow cooker.

Nutrition Information Per Serving: Calories 285 • Total Fat 12g • Saturated Fat 5g • Cholesterol 90mg • Sodium 610mg • Total Carbohydrate 11g • Dietary Fiber 3g • Sugars 2g • Protein 36g. Dietary Exchanges: 2 Vegetable • 4½ Very Lean Meat.

barbecued turkey
and vegetables

barbecued turkey and vegetables

PREP TIME: 20 MINUTES
READY TO SERVE: 10 HOURS 20 MINUTES
SERVINGS: 4

* **slow cooked**

1 cup barbecue sauce

½ cup hot water

2 bone-in turkey thighs
(1½ lb.), skin removed

3 medium potatoes,
unpeeled, each cut into
8 pieces

6 medium carrots,
cut into 2½x½-inch sticks

1. In medium bowl, combine barbecue sauce and water; mix well. In 3½- to 4-quart slow cooker, layer turkey, potatoes and carrots. Pour sauce mixture over top.

2. Cover; cook on Low setting for 8 to 10 hours.

3. With slotted spoon, remove turkey and vegetables from slow cooker; place on serving platter. Remove turkey meat from bones and cut into pieces; discard bones. Spoon cooking juices from slow cooker over turkey and vegetables.

Nutrition Information Per Serving: Calories 350 • Total Fat 4g • Saturated Fat 1g • Cholesterol 105mg • Sodium 740mg • Total Carbohydrate 53g • Dietary Fiber 5g • Sugars 23g • Protein 30g. Dietary Exchanges: 3 Starch • 2 Vegetable • 2 Very Lean Meat OR 3 Carbohydrate • 2 Vegetable • 2 Very Lean Meat.

chicken parmesan italiano

PREP TIME: 30 MINUTES
SERVINGS: 2

2 tablespoons Italian-style
bread crumbs

2 tablespoons shredded fresh
Parmesan cheese

½ teaspoon dried oregano
leaves

1 tablespoon lemon juice

1 small garlic clove, minced

2 boneless skinless chicken
breast halves

Nonstick cooking spray

1. Heat oven to 425°F. Line cookie sheet with foil; spray foil with nonstick cooking spray.

2. In shallow dish, combine bread crumbs, cheese and oregano; mix well. In small cup or bowl, combine lemon juice and garlic.

3. Brush both sides of chicken with lemon juice mixture; coat with bread crumb mixture. Place on sprayed foil-lined cookie sheet. Lightly spray chicken with cooking spray.

4. Bake at 425°F for 15 to 20 minutes or until chicken is fork-tender and juices run clear.

Nutrition Information Per Serving: Calories 210 • Total Fat 7g • Saturated Fat 2g • Cholesterol 80mg • Sodium 280mg • Total Carbohydrate 6g • Dietary Fiber 0g • Sugars 0g • Protein 30g. Dietary Exchanges: ½ Starch • 4 Very Lean Meat • ½ Fat OR ½ Carbohydrate • 4 Very Lean Meat • ½ Fat.

honey-mustard turkey tenderloins

PREP TIME: 30 MINUTES
SERVINGS: 6

2 fresh turkey breast
tenderloins (¾-lb. each)

1 tablespoon olive oil

½ teaspoon salt

¼ teaspoon pepper

1 cup purchased honey-
mustard salad dressing

¼ cup chopped fresh basil

1. Heat grill. Brush turkey tenderloins with oil; sprinkle with salt and pepper. In small saucepan, combine salad dressing and basil; mix well.

2. When ready to grill, place turkey on gas grill over medium heat or on charcoal grill 4 to 6 inches from medium coals. Cook 15 to 20 minutes or until turkey is fork-tender and juices run clear, turning and brushing with salad dressing mixture 2 or 3 times.

3. To serve, bring any remaining salad dressing mixture to a boil. Serve with turkey.

Nutrition Information Per Serving: Calories 360 • Total Fat 23g • Saturated Fat 3g • Cholesterol 110mg • Sodium 360mg • Total Carbohydrate 6g • Dietary Fiber 0g • Sugars 5g • Protein 33g. Dietary Exchanges: ½ Fruit • 4½ Very Lean Meat • 4 Fat OR ½ Carbohydrate • 4½ Very Lean Meat • 4 Fat.

cajun chicken salad

dressing

- 2 tablespoons cider vinegar
- 2 to 3 teaspoons dried Cajun seasoning
- ⅓ cup vegetable oil

salad

- 1 package (9-oz.) frozen diced cooked chicken breast, thawed
- 2 cups cold cooked rice
- 3 stalks celery, diced (1 cup)
- 6 medium green onions, chopped (⅓ cup)
- 1 large tomato, diced (1 cup)
- 1 medium green bell pepper, diced (1 cup)

1. In large bowl, combine vinegar and Cajun seasoning; mix well with wire whisk. Gradually beat in oil until well blended.

2. Add salad ingredients; toss to coat. Serve immediately, or cover and refrigerate until serving time.

Nutrition Information Per Serving: Calories 485 • Total Fat 22g • Saturated Fat 4g • Cholesterol 55mg • Sodium 300mg • Total Carbohydrate 47g • Dietary Fiber 2g • Sugars 3g • Protein 25g. Dietary Exchanges: 3 Starch • 2½ Very Lean Meat • 4 Fat.

PLANNING AHEAD LEADS TO A QUICK FIX

Like many soups, casseroles and one-dish recipes, this salad calls for cooked rice. Some cooks swing by an Asian restaurant and pick up white rice to ease dinner prep, but you could save time by serving the salad when other rice dishes appear on your weekly menu plan. When cooking rice for another recipe, add an extra cup of uncooked rice to the pot. Store the extra rice in the refrigerator, and make this salad in the next day or two.

chicken cheese enchiladas

SERVINGS: 6

BARBIE LEE * TAVERNIER, FLORIDA

- 1 package (1.25-oz.) taco seasoning mix
- 1 tablespoon olive oil
- ½ cup water
- 1 lb. boneless skinless chicken breasts, cut into bite-sized pieces or strips
- 12 oz. shredded Monterey Jack cheese (3 cups)
- ⅓ cup chopped fresh cilantro
- ½ teaspoon salt
- 1 container (15-oz.) ricotta cheese
- 1 can (4.5-oz.) chopped green chiles
- 1 egg
- 1 jar (16-oz.) chunky-style salsa
- 1 package (10.5-oz.) flour tortillas for soft tacos and fajitas (12 tortillas)

1. Heat oven to 350°F. In resealable food storage plastic bag, combine taco seasoning mix, oil and ¼ cup of the water; seal bag and mix well. Add chicken pieces; reseal and turn bag to mix. Refrigerate 5 minutes or up to 12 hours to marinate.

2. In medium bowl, combine 2½ cups of the Monterey Jack cheese, cilantro, salt, ricotta cheese, chiles and egg; mix well. Heat large nonstick skillet over medium-high heat until hot. Add chicken with marinade; cook 5 to 10 minutes or until chicken is no longer pink in center, stirring frequently.

3. In ungreased 13x9-inch (3-quart) glass baking dish, combine ½ cup of the salsa and remaining ¼ cup water; mix well. Spread evenly in bottom of baking dish. Spoon ⅓ cup cheese mixture down center of a tortilla. Top with chicken; roll up. Place filled tortilla, seam side down, over salsa mixture in baking dish. Repeat with remaining tortillas. Drizzle enchiladas with remaining salsa. Sprinkle with remaining ½ cup Monterey Jack cheese.

4. Bake at 350°F for 20 to 25 minutes or until cheese is melted.

Nutrition Information Per Serving: Calories 630 • Total Fat 33g • Sodium 2160mg • Total Carbohydrate 40g • Protein 44g.

cajun chicken salad

salsa chicken

salsa chicken

PREP TIME: 10 MINUTES
READY TO SERVE: 9 HOURS 10 MINUTES
SERVINGS: 6

* slow cooked

1 tablespoon oil

12 boneless skinless chicken thighs (about 2½ lb.)

1 teaspoon salt

½ cup chunky-style salsa

1 can (15-oz.) black beans, drained, rinsed

1 can (11-oz.) vacuum-packed whole kernel corn, drained

2 tablespoons chopped fresh cilantro

1. Heat oil in 12-inch skillet over medium-high heat until hot. Sprinkle chicken thighs with salt; add to skillet. Cook about 4 minutes or until browned, turning once.

2. In 3½- to 5-quart slow cooker, combine salsa, beans and corn; mix well. Top with chicken.

3. Cover; cook on Low setting for 7 to 9 hours. Sprinkle chicken and vegetables with cilantro before serving.

Nutrition Information Per Serving: Calories 440 • Total Fat 17g • Saturated Fat 5g • Cholesterol 115mg • Sodium 980mg • Total Carbohydrate 30g • Dietary Fiber 6g • Sugars 4g • Protein 48g. Dietary Exchanges: 2 Starch • 6 Very Lean Meat • 1½ Fat OR 2 Carbohydrate • 6 Very Lean Meat • 1½ Fat.

quick turkey stroganoff

PREP TIME: 20 MINUTES
SERVINGS: 4

* super fast

8 oz. uncooked egg noodles (4 cups)

2 cups cubed cooked turkey

1 jar (4.5-oz.) sliced mushrooms, drained

1 can (10¾-oz.) condensed cream of mushroom soup

1 cup sour cream

1 jar (2-oz.) diced pimientos, drained

1. Cook noodles to desired doneness as directed on package. Drain.

2. Meanwhile, in large skillet, combine turkey, mushrooms and soup; mix well. Cook over medium heat until bubbly, stirring frequently. Stir in sour cream and pimientos. Cook until thoroughly heated. Do not boil.

3. Serve turkey mixture over noodles.

Nutrition Information Per Serving: Calories 550 • Total Fat 24g • Saturated Fat 11g • Cholesterol 135mg • Sodium 810mg • Total Carbohydrate 51g • Dietary Fiber 3g • Sugars 6g • Protein 33g. Dietary Exchanges: 3½ Starch • 3 Very Lean Meat • 4 Fat OR 3½ Carbohydrate • 3 Very Lean Meat • 4 Fat.

curried chicken and rice

PREP TIME: 20 MINUTES
READY TO SERVE: 40 MINUTES
SERVINGS: 4

¾ lb. boneless skinless chicken breast halves, cut into bite-sized pieces

1⅓ cups water

1 can (14.5-oz.) stewed tomatoes, undrained

⅓ cup raisins

1 tablespoon brown sugar

1 tablespoon fresh lemon juice

1 teaspoon chicken-flavor instant bouillon

1 teaspoon curry powder

½ teaspoon cinnamon

¼ teaspoon salt

¼ teaspoon ginger

1 cup uncooked basmati rice, rinsed, or regular long-grain rice

1. In large saucepan, combine all ingredients except rice. Bring to a boil.

2. Stir in rice. Reduce heat; cover and simmer 20 minutes or until chicken is no longer pink, rice is tender and liquid is absorbed.

Nutrition Information Per Serving: Calories 340 • Total Fat 3g • Saturated Fat 1g • Cholesterol 55mg • Sodium 490mg • Total Carbohydrate 55g • Dietary Fiber 2g • Sugars 14g • Protein 24g. Dietary Exchanges: 3 Starch • ½ Fruit • 2 Very Lean Meat OR 3½ Carbohydrate • 2 Very Lean Meat.

SEASONING WITH CURRY POWDER

Curry powder is a delightful blend of herbs and seasonings that usually includes coriander, turmeric and cumin. It is often thought of as spicy, but many of the varieties found in the spice aisle at the supermarket are quite mild. Regardless of which brand or type you use, curry powder is bright yellow and very fragrant. Due to its warm, bold flavor, a little goes a long way.

creamy chicken-topped potatoes

PREP TIME: 20 MINUTES
SERVINGS: 2

* super fast

2 medium baking potatoes

1 package (9-oz.) frozen broccoli, peas, carrots and low-fat creamy Alfredo sauce

1 cup chopped cooked chicken

1 tablespoon diced pimientos

½ cup sour cream

¼ cup grated Parmesan cheese

Salt, if desired

Pepper, if desired

1. Pierce potatoes several times with fork. Place on microwave-safe paper towel in microwave oven. Microwave on High for 6 to 8 minutes or until tender, turning potatoes over and rearranging halfway through cooking. Let stand 3 minutes.

2. Meanwhile, open pouch of vegetables; pour into medium saucepan. Add chicken and pimientos; cook over medium-low heat until vegetables are tender and mixture is thoroughly heated, stirring frequently. Stir in sour cream and 2 tablespoons of the cheese. Cook until thoroughly heated.

3. To serve, cut potatoes in half lengthwise; place on individual plates. Mash potatoes slightly with fork. Spoon vegetable mixture over potatoes. Top with remaining cheese. If desired, add salt and pepper to taste.

Nutrition Information Per Serving: Calories 530 • Total Fat 24g • Saturated Fat 13g • Cholesterol 105mg • Sodium 820mg • Total Carbohydrate 44g • Dietary Fiber 6g • Sugars 8g • Protein 34g. Dietary Exchanges: 2½ Starch • 1 Vegetable • 3½ Lean Meat • 2½ Fat OR 2½ Carbohydrate • 1 Vegetable • 3½ Lean Meat • 2½ Fat.

easy chinese chicken

READY TO SERVE: 30 MINUTES
SERVINGS: 4

1 package (6-oz.) uncooked rice noodles

2 teaspoons light sesame or vegetable oil

4 boneless skinless chicken breast halves, cut into thin bite-sized strips

2 cups fresh bean sprouts

1 package (9-oz.) frozen cut broccoli in a pouch, thawed, drained

1 can (8-oz.) bamboo shoots, drained

½ cup water

2 tablespoons soy sauce

4 teaspoons cornstarch

1 teaspoon sugar

½ teaspoon chicken-flavor instant bouillon

1. Cook noodles to desired doneness as directed on package. Drain; cover to keep warm.

2. Meanwhile, heat oil in large skillet over medium-high heat until hot. Add chicken; cook and stir 3 to 6 minutes or until chicken is no longer pink in center. Add bean sprouts, broccoli and bamboo shoots; cook and stir about 5 minutes or until vegetables are tender.

3. In small bowl, combine all remaining ingredients; blend well. Stir into chicken mixture; cook and stir until bubbly and thickened. Serve chicken mixture over noodles.

Nutrition Information Per Serving: Calories 370 • Total Fat 6g • Saturated Fat 1g • Cholesterol 75mg • Sodium 820mg • Total Carbohydrate 48g • Dietary Fiber 3g • Sugars 3g • Protein 31g. Dietary Exchanges: 3 Starch • 1 Vegetable • 3 Very Lean Meat OR 3 Carbohydrate • 1 Vegetable • 3 Very Lean Meat.

STIR-FRY SECRETS REVEALED

When preparing the Easy Chinese Chicken, be sure all of the vegetables drain thoroughly before you begin cooking. Patting them dry on a paper towel helps eliminate extra moisture so the veggies stir-fry rather than steam.

Because stir-frying is such a fast cooking method, it's a good idea to chop and assemble all of the ingredients before you begin.

Once the rice noodles are cooked and drained, you may want to toss them with sesame or peanut oil before returning them to the pot. This will prevent them from sticking together while you stir-fry the chicken and vegetables. Cover the noodles to keep them warm until you are ready to serve your gang this tangy, all-time family favorite.

easy chinese chicken

simple sweet-and-sour chicken

PREP TIME: 15 MINUTES
SERVINGS: 4

✳ super fast

1 package (10½-oz.) frozen chicken nuggets

1 tablespoon oil

1 green bell pepper, cut into squares

1 small onion, cut into thin wedges

½ cup purchased sweet-and-sour sauce

1 can (8-oz.) pineapple chunks in unsweetened juice, undrained

1. Prepare chicken nuggets as directed on package.

2. Meanwhile, heat oil in medium skillet over medium-high heat until hot. Add bell pepper and onion; cook and stir until crisp-tender. Stir in sweet-and-sour sauce and pineapple; cook until thoroughly heated. Serve over chicken nuggets.

Nutrition Information Per Serving: Calories 320 • Total Fat 16g • Saturated Fat 13g • Cholesterol 45mg • Sodium 6550mg • Total Carbohydrate 31g • Dietary Fiber 1g • Sugars 16g • Protein 13g. Dietary Exchanges: 1 Starch • 1 Fruit • 1½ Medium-Fat Meat • 1½ Fat OR 2 Carbohydrate • 1½ Medium-Fat Meat • ½ Fat.

honey-dijon turkey medallions

PREP TIME: 30 MINUTES
SERVINGS: 4

1¼ lb. fresh turkey breast tenderloins

2 tablespoons Dijon mustard

2 tablespoons honey

⅛ teaspoon hot pepper sauce

1. Line broiler pan and rack with foil; cut slits in foil on rack. Cut turkey tenderloins crosswise into 1½-inch-thick slices; place cut side up on foil-lined rack in pan.

2. In small bowl, combine all remaining ingredients; mix well. Generously brush tops of turkey slices with about half of mustard mixture.

3. Broil 3 to 4 inches from heat for 6 to 8 minutes. Turn turkey slices; generously brush with remaining mustard mixture. Broil an additional 6 to 8 minutes or until turkey is no longer pink in center.

Nutrition Information Per Serving: Calories 180 • Total Fat 1g • Saturated Fat 0g • Cholesterol 95mg • Sodium 250mg • Total Carbohydrate 9g • Dietary Fiber 0g • Sugars 9g • Protein 34g. Dietary Exchanges: ½ Fruit • 5 Very Lean Meat OR ½ Carbohydrate • 5 Very Lean Meat.

chicken broccoli stroganoff

SERVINGS: 6

PATRICIA KIEWIET ✳ LAGRANGE, ILLINOIS

2 cups frozen cut broccoli (from 1-lb. pkg.)

1 tablespoon margarine or butter

¼ cup chopped onion

3 tablespoons all-purpose flour

1 can (10½-oz.) condensed chicken broth

2 cups cubed cooked chicken

1 jar (2.5-oz.) sliced mushrooms, drained

1 container (8-oz.) dairy sour cream (1 cup)

Hot cooked noodles

Chopped fresh parsley

1. Cook broccoli in microwave according to package directions until crisp-tender. Drain; set aside.

2. In 2-quart microwave-safe casserole, microwave margarine on High for 20 seconds or until melted. Add onion; toss to coat. Cover with microwave-safe plastic wrap. Microwave on High for 2 minutes or until crisp-tender. Add flour; blend well.

3. Using wire whisk, stir broth into onion mixture; blend well. Microwave on High for 4 to 6 minutes or until mixture thickens and bubbles, stirring the mixture once halfway through cooking.

4. Add chicken, cooked broccoli, mushrooms and sour cream; blend well. Microwave on High for 3 to 5 minutes or until mixture is thoroughly heated and bubbles around edges, stirring once halfway through cooking.

5. Serve over noodles; garnish with parsley.

Nutrition Information Per Serving: Calories 490 • Total Fat 17g • Sodium 445mg • Total Carbohydrate 58g • Protein 26g.

soft-shell turkey tacos

PREP TIME: 25 MINUTES
SERVINGS: 4

* super fast

- ¾ lb. ground turkey breast
- 1 teaspoon chili powder
- 1 can (14.5-oz.) Mexican-style stewed tomatoes, undrained, cut up
- 8 flour tortillas (7-in.), heated
- ½ cup shredded reduced-fat Monterey Jack cheese (2 oz.)
- 1 cup shredded lettuce

1. Heat 8-inch nonstick skillet over medium-high heat. Add ground turkey and chili powder; cook 5 to 6 minutes, stirring frequently, until turkey is no longer pink. Stir in tomatoes. Reduce heat to medium; cook 10 minutes, stirring occasionally, until liquid has evaporated.

2. Spoon turkey mixture evenly down center of each tortilla. Top each with cheese and lettuce. Roll tortillas into cone shape.

Nutrition Information Per Serving: Calories 400 • Total Fat 13g • Saturated Fat 4.5g • Trans Fat 1g • Cholesterol 65mg • Sodium 780mg • Total Carbohydrate 45g • Dietary Fiber 3g • Sugars 6g • Protein 29g. Dietary Exchanges: 3 Starch • 3 Lean Meat.

speedy turkey cutlets and zucchini

PREP TIME: 30 MINUTES
SERVINGS: 4

- 2 tablespoons tarragon vinegar
- 1 teaspoon dried basil leaves
- 2 garlic cloves, minced
- 1 lb. fresh turkey cutlets or turkey breast slices
- 3 tablespoons oil
- 4 cups sliced zucchini (3 to 4 medium)
- 1½ cups sliced fresh mushrooms
  Salt, if desired
  Pepper, if desired

1. In small bowl, combine vinegar, basil and garlic; mix well. Brush over both sides of turkey.

2. Heat 2 tablespoons of the oil in large nonstick skillet over medium-high heat until hot. Add turkey cutlets; cook about 4 minutes or until turkey is no longer pink in center, turning once. Remove from skillet; place on serving platter. Cover to keep warm.

3. In same skillet, heat remaining 1 tablespoon oil until hot. Add zucchini and mushrooms; cook and stir until zucchini is crisp-tender. If desired, add salt and pepper to taste. Arrange vegetables on platter with turkey.

Nutrition Information Per Serving: Calories 240 • Total Fat 11g • Saturated Fat 2g • Cholesterol 75mg • Sodium 50mg • Total Carbohydrate 6g • Dietary Fiber 2g • Sugars 3g • Protein 29g. Dietary Exchanges: 1 Vegetable • 4 Very Lean Meat • 1½ Fat.

southwest chicken and fettuccine

PREP TIME: 20 MINUTES
SERVINGS: 4

* super fast

- 1 package (9-oz.) refrigerated fettuccine
- 1 can (14.5-oz.) diced tomatoes with green chiles or jalapeño chiles, undrained
- 1 package (9-oz.) frozen southwestern-flavored cooked chicken breast strips, thawed
- 1 cup shredded Monterey Jack cheese (4 oz.)
- 1 medium avocado, pitted, peeled and chopped, if desired

1. Cook fettuccine in 3-quart saucepan as directed on package. Drain in colander; cover to keep warm.

2. In same saucepan, combine tomatoes and chicken; mix well. Cook over medium heat until thoroughly heated, stirring occasionally. Stir in cooked fettuccine. Sprinkle individual servings with cheese and avocado.

Nutrition Information Per Serving: Calories 405 • Total Fat 19g • Saturated Fat 8g • Cholesterol 100mg • Sodium 830mg • Total Carbohydrate 27g • Dietary Fiber 3g • Sugars 6g • Protein 31g. Dietary Exchanges: 1½ Starch • 1 Vegetable • 3½ Lean Meat • 1½ Fat.

smoked turkey and salsa pizzas

READY TO SERVE: 30 MINUTES
SERVINGS: 8

1 can (1-lb., 0.3-oz.) large refrigerated buttermilk biscuits

1 cup salsa

½ lb. smoked turkey breast (from deli), cut into 2x1-inch strips (2 cups)

6 oz. shredded 4-cheese Mexican cheese blend (1½ cups)

1. Heat oven to 350°F. Lightly grease cookie sheets. Separate dough into 8 biscuits. Press or roll each biscuit to form 5½-inch round. Place on greased cookie sheets. Bake at 350°F for 10 minutes. Cool.

2. Spread each biscuit with 2 tablespoons salsa. Top each with ¼ cup turkey strips and 3 tablespoons cheese.

3. Return to oven; bake an additional 5 to 7 minutes or until thoroughly heated and cheese is melted.

Nutrition Information Per Serving: Calories 310 • Total Fat 16g • Saturated Fat 7g • Cholesterol 30mg • Sodium 1240mg • Total Carbohydrate 27g • Dietary Fiber 1g • Sugars 5g • Protein 14g. Dietary Exchanges: 2 Starch • 1 Very Lean Meat • 2½ Fat OR 2 Carbohydrate • 1 Very Lean Meat • 2½ Fat.

simple chicken parmigiana

READY TO SERVE: 30 MINUTES
SERVINGS: 4

- ¼ cup unseasoned dry bread crumbs
- 2 tablespoons grated Parmesan cheese
- 2 tablespoons chopped fresh Italian parsley
- 4 boneless skinless chicken breast halves
- 1 egg, beaten
- 2 tablespoons olive or vegetable oil
- ⅔ cup spaghetti sauce
- 2 oz. shredded mozzarella cheese (½ cup)

1. In medium bowl, combine bread crumbs, Parmesan cheese and parsley; mix well. Dip chicken in beaten egg; coat with bread crumb mixture.

2. Heat oil in large nonstick skillet over medium-high heat until hot. Add chicken; reduce heat to medium. Cook 20 to 23 minutes or until chicken is fork-tender and juices run clear, turning once.

3. Meanwhile, heat spaghetti sauce. Sprinkle chicken with mozzarella cheese; cover skillet to melt cheese. Serve sauce with chicken.

Nutrition Information Per Serving: Calories 320 • Total Fat 16g • Saturated Fat 4g • Cholesterol 135mg • Sodium 420mg • Total Carbohydrate 9g • Dietary Fiber 1g • Sugars 1g • Protein 35g. **Dietary Exchanges:** ½ Starch • 4½ Very Lean Meat • 2½ Fat OR ½ Carbohydrate • 4½ Very Lean Meat • 2½ Fat.

quick-topped vegetable chicken casserole

SERVINGS: 6

BERNICE MALINOWSKI ✳ CUSTER, WISCONSIN

casserole
- 1 can (10¾-oz.) condensed cream of chicken soup
- 1 package (3-oz.) cream cheese, softened
- ½ cup milk
- ½ cup chopped celery
- ½ cup chopped onion
- ¼ cup grated Parmesan cheese
- ¼ cup chopped green bell pepper
- ¼ cup shredded carrot
- 2 to 3 cups cubed cooked chicken
- 1 package (9-oz.) frozen cut broccoli in a pouch, cooked, drained

topping
- 1 cup complete or buttermilk pancake mix
- ¼ cup slivered almonds
- 4 oz. shredded Cheddar cheese (1 cup)
- ¼ cup milk
- 1 tablespoon oil
- 1 egg, slightly beaten

1. Heat oven to 375°F. In large saucepan, combine soup, cream cheese, ½ cup milk, celery, onion, Parmesan cheese, bell pepper and carrot. Cook over medium heat until mixture is hot and cream cheese is melted, stirring frequently. Stir in chicken and broccoli. Pour into ungreased 2-quart casserole or 12x8-inch (2-quart) baking dish.

2. In medium bowl, combine all topping ingredients; blend well. Spoon tablespoonfuls of topping over hot chicken mixture.

3. Bake at 375°F for 20 to 30 minutes or until topping is golden brown and chicken mixture bubbles around edges.

Nutrition Information Per Serving: Calories 510 • Total Fat 28g • Sodium 1140mg • Total Carbohydrate 29g • Protein 35g.

MAKE IT AN ALL-TIME FAVORITE

Made with a pancake mix, the fast and easy spoon-on crust is what puts a tasty twist on this old-fashioned chicken and vegetable pie.

When mixing up the topping, feel free to use a cup of whatever shredded cheese you have in the refrigerator. You can also give the top crust your own touch by stirring dried rosemary, oregano, basil or your favorite herb into the batter. If you like things a bit spicer, mix in a dash of hot pepper sauce or a few tablespoons of chopped chiles.

Even though the bubbling casserole makes a filling meal on its own, you can serve the dish with cups of soup, a spinach salad, canned cranberry sauce or spears of steamed asparagus. For dessert, pop open a can of fruit medley or surprise your family with scoops of ice cream.

chicken-chile stromboli

SERVINGS: 6

DEBRA KELLY ✳ WHEELING, ILLINOIS

1 can (10-oz.) chunk white and dark chicken in water, drained

1 can (4.5-oz.) chopped green chiles

4 oz. ⅓-less-fat cream cheese (Neufchâtel), softened

¼ cup chopped roasted red bell peppers (from a jar)

1 tablespoon honey

Dash salt

Dash pepper

1 can (11-oz.) refrigerated French loaf

1 egg

1 teaspoon water

Dash dried parsley flakes

6 thin strips roasted red bell peppers (from a jar)

1 tablespoon butter, melted

Dash garlic powder

1. Heat oven to 350°F. Grease cookie sheet. In medium bowl, combine chicken, chiles, cream cheese, ¼ cup roasted peppers, honey, salt and pepper; mix well.

2. Remove dough from can; place on lightly floured surface. Carefully unroll dough. Spread chicken mixture evenly over dough to within 1 inch of edges. With lightly floured hands, carefully but firmly reroll dough. Gently press edges to seal; fold ends under. Place loaf on greased cookie sheet.

3. In small bowl, combine egg and water; beat well. Brush over top of loaf; sprinkle with parsley. Arrange roasted pepper strips about 2 inches apart on top of loaf. With sharp knife, cut 5 or 6 diagonal slices, ½-inch deep, on top of loaf.

4. Bake at 350°F for 25 to 30 minutes or until edges are deep golden brown.

5. In small bowl, combine butter and garlic powder. Brush over warm loaf. Cut loaf into slices.

Nutrition Information Per Serving: Calories 290 • Total Fat 11g • Sodium 710mg • Total Carbohydrate 28g • Protein 17g.

chicken and sausage stew

PREP TIME: 30 MINUTES
SERVINGS: 4

1 tablespoon vegetable oil

3 boneless skinless chicken thighs, cut into bite-sized pieces

1 medium carrot, chopped

1 medium onion, chopped

1 medium stalk celery, chopped

1 cup frozen whole kernel corn

1 teaspoon cumin

1 can (15-oz.) tomato sauce

1 can (14.5-oz.) diced tomatoes, undrained

4 oz. fully cooked smoked sausage, cut into thin slices

¼ cup grated Parmesan

1. Heat oil in large saucepan or Dutch oven over medium-high heat until hot. Add chicken, carrot, onion and celery; cook 5 minutes, stirring frequently.

2. Stir in all remaining ingredients except cheese. Bring to a boil. Reduce heat; cover and simmer 5 to 10 minutes or until chicken is no longer pink in center and vegetables are tender. Sprinkle with cheese.

Nutrition Information Per Serving: Calories 315 • Total Fat 16g • Saturated Fat 5g • Cholesterol 50mg • Sodium 1130mg • Total Carbohydrate 25g • Dietary Fiber 4g • Sugars 10g • Protein 18g. Dietary Exchanges: 1 Starch • 2 Vegetable • 1½ Lean Meat • 2 Fat.

QUICK-AND-EASY REPLACEMENTS

If chicken thighs aren't a staple in your kitchen, you can prepare Chicken and Sausage Stew with 2 boneless chicken breasts instead.

When it comes to the smoked sausage in the recipe, feel free to use your favorite Polish, turkey, reduced-fat beef or even venison sausage in its place. They all make delicious options in this chill-chasing stew.

chicken-chile stromboli

quick italian chicken and rice

READY TO SERVE: 20 MINUTES
SERVINGS: 3

* super fast

3 packages (4-oz. each) refrigerated tomato and herb with basil-seasoned boneless skinless chicken breast fillet

2 teaspoons oil

1 can (14.5-oz.) Italian-style stewed tomatoes, undrained

¾ cup water

1½ cups uncooked instant white rice

1. Cut chicken fillets into small bite-sized strips.

2. Heat oil in large nonstick skillet over medium-high heat until hot. Add chicken; cook and stir 4 to 5 minutes or until browned and no longer pink in center.

3. Add tomatoes and water; mix well. Bring to a boil. Stir in rice. Cover; remove from heat. Let stand 5 minutes or until liquid is absorbed.

Nutrition Information Per Serving: Calories 350 • Total Fat 4g • Saturated Fat 0g • Cholesterol 55mg • Sodium 1120mg • Total Carbohydrate 51g • Dietary Fiber 2g • Sugars 3g • Protein 27g. **Dietary Exchanges:** 3 Starch • 1 Vegetable • 2½ Very Lean Meat OR 3 Carbohydrate • 1 Vegetable • 2½ Very Lean Meat.

roasted chicken and vegetables

PREP TIME: 15 MINUTES
READY TO SERVE: 1 HOUR 20 MINUTES
SERVINGS: 4

✳ plan ahead

chicken and vegetables

- 3 to 3½ lb. cut-up frying chicken, skin removed
- 6 to 8 small new red potatoes, unpeeled, quartered
- 1 large red onion, cut into 8 wedges
- 4 oz. fresh whole mushrooms (1⅓ cups)

sauce

- ¼ cup creamy mustard-mayonnaise sauce
- 1 tablespoon oil
- ¼ teaspoon peppered seasoned salt

1. Heat oven to 375°F. Arrange chicken, meaty side up, in ungreased 15x10x1-inch baking pan. Arrange vegetables around chicken.

2. In small bowl, combine all sauce ingredients; mix well. Brush sauce over chicken and vegetables. Bake at 375°F for 45 minutes.

3. Baste chicken and vegetables with pan juices. Bake an additional 15 to 20 minutes or until chicken is fork-tender, its juices run clear and vegetables are tender. Serve pan juices with chicken and vegetables. If desired, sprinkle with 2 tablespoons chopped fresh parsley.

Nutrition Information Per Serving: Calories 480 • Total Fat 16g • Saturated Fat 4g • Cholesterol 115mg • Sodium 320mg • Total Carbohydrate 43g • Dietary Fiber 5g • Sugars 4g • Protein 41g. Dietary Exchanges: 2½ Starch • 1 Vegetable • 4½ Lean Meat OR 2½ Carbohydrate • 1 Vegetable • 4½ Lean Meat.

chicken vegetable alfredo

PREP TIME: 30 MINUTES
SERVINGS: 6

- 6 oz. uncooked linguine
- 2 cups fresh broccoli florets
- 2 cups thinly sliced carrots
- 2 tablespoons margarine or butter
- ½ cup chopped onion
- 1 garlic clove, minced
- 3 tablespoons all-purpose flour
- 2 teaspoons very low-sodium chicken-flavor instant bouillon
- ½ teaspoon salt
- ¼ teaspoon pepper
- 2 cups skim milk
- 1½ cups cubed cooked chicken
- 1 container (8-oz.) light sour cream
- ⅓ cup grated Parmesan cheese
- ¼ cup sliced ripe olives, if desired

1. Cook linguine to desired doneness as directed on package.

2. Meanwhile, in medium saucepan, bring 4 cups water to a boil. Add broccoli and carrots; return to a boil. Reduce heat; cook about 5 minutes or until crisp-tender. Drain well.

3. Melt margarine in large nonstick saucepan or Dutch oven over medium heat. Add onion and garlic; cook until onion is tender. Stir in flour, bouillon, salt and pepper. Gradually stir in milk. Cook until mixture boils and thickens, stirring constantly.

4. Stir in cooked broccoli and carrots, chicken, sour cream and ¼ cup of the Parmesan cheese. Cook until thoroughly heated. Do not boil.

5. Drain linguine. Add to vegetable mixture; toss to mix. Place on serving platter; sprinkle with remaining Parmesan cheese and olives, if desired.

Nutrition Information Per Serving: Calories 360 • Total Fat 12g • Saturated Fat 5g • Cholesterol 50mg • Sodium 510mg • Total Carbohydrate 41g • Dietary Fiber 3g • Sugars 11g • Protein 22g. Dietary Exchanges: 2½ Starch • 1 Vegetable • 2 Lean Meat • 1 Fat OR 2½ Carbohydrate • 1 Vegetable • 2 Lean Meat • 1 Fat.

COOKING CHICKEN BREASTS

Boneless skinless chicken breasts make a great supper-time option when you're racing against the clock. Not only do they cook quickly, but they are a healthy choice for family cooks who are looking for low-fat main courses.

When preparing chicken breasts, remember to trim any visible fat from the chicken before cooking. Cook the meat until it is no longer pink, but be careful not to overcook it as chicken can dry out easily.

pineapple-glazed chicken breasts

READY TO SERVE: 30 MINUTES
SERVINGS: 4

¼ cup Dijon mustard

¼ cup frozen pineapple juice concentrate, thawed

2 cloves garlic, minced

2 tablespoons chopped fresh rosemary or 1 teaspoon dried rosemary leaves

½ teaspoon salt

¼ teaspoon pepper

4 boneless skinless chicken breast halves (5-oz. each)

2 teaspoons olive oil

4 slices (½-in. thick) fresh pineapple, rind removed

1. Heat gas or charcoal grill. In small bowl, mix mustard and juice concentrate; reserve 2 tablespoons. Into remaining mixture, stir garlic, rosemary, salt and pepper; set aside.

2. When grill is heated, rub chicken breast halves with oil. Place chicken on gas grill over medium heat or on charcoal grill over medium coals; cover grill. Cook 5 minutes.

3. Add pineapple to grill; brush with rosemary mixture. Turn chicken; brush with rosemary mixture. Cover grill; cook 6 to 8 minutes longer, brushing chicken occasionally with rosemary mixture and turning chicken and pineapple once, until chicken is fork-tender and juice is no longer pink when centers of thickest pieces are cut. Discard any remaining rosemary mixture.

4. Place chicken on serving plates. Spoon reserved 2 tablespoons mustard mixture over chicken. Halve or quarter pineapple slices; serve with chicken.

Nutrition Information Per Serving: Calories 270 • Total Fat 8g • Saturated Fat 1.5g • Trans Fat 0g • Cholesterol 85mg • Sodium 750mg • Total Carbohydrate 17g • Dietary Fiber 1g • Sugars 12g • Protein 32g. Dietary Exchanges: 1 Fruit • 4½ Very Lean Meat • 1 Fat.

chicken fajita pizza

SERVINGS: 8

ELIZABETH DANIELS ✳ KULA, MAUI, HAWAII

1 can (10-oz.) refrigerated pizza crust

1 tablespoon olive oil or vegetable oil

4 boneless skinless chicken breast halves, cut into thin, bite-sized strips

1 to 2 teaspoons chili powder

½ to 1 teaspoon salt

½ teaspoon garlic powder

1 cup thinly sliced onions

1 cup green or red bell pepper strips (2x¼-inch)

½ cup mild picante salsa

8 oz. shredded Monterey Jack cheese (2 cups)

1. Heat oven to 425°F. Spray 12-inch pizza pan or 13x9-inch pan with nonstick cooking spray. Unroll dough; place in sprayed pan. Starting at center, press out with hands. Bake at 425°F for 7 to 9 minutes or until very light golden brown.

2. Meanwhile, heat oil in large skillet over medium-high heat until hot. Add chicken; sprinkle with chili powder, salt and garlic powder. Cook and stir 3 to 5 minutes or until lightly browned. Add onions and bell pepper strips; cook and stir an additional 2 to 3 minutes or until chicken is no longer pink and vegetables are crisp-tender.

3. Remove crust from oven. Spoon chicken mixture evenly over partially baked crust. Spoon salsa over chicken. Sprinkle with cheese.

4. Return to oven; bake an additional 14 to 18 minutes or until crust is golden brown.

Nutrition Information Per Serving: Calories 290 • Total Fat 13g • Sodium 830mg • Total Carbohydrate 20g • Protein 24g.

ADDING PIZZAZZ TO PIZZA

The key to great pizza is in the crust, and using a can of refrigerated dough gets dinner prep off to a good start. Make sure the oven is preheated to the right temperature. Good pizza crusts depend on hot ovens.

Not only can you customize pizza toppings to fit your family's taste, but you can experiment with the crust, too. Season the dough with basil before baking it, or sprinkle the greased pan with cornmeal before pressing out the dough.

chicken fajita pizza

apple-honey-mustard chicken

PREP TIME: 25 MINUTES
SERVINGS: 4

1 jar (12-oz.) apple jelly

1 teaspoon ground ginger

½ teaspoon garlic powder

2 tablespoons soy sauce

2 tablespoons honey mustard

4 boneless skinless chicken breast halves

1. Heat gas or charcoal grill. In 1-quart saucepan, combine all ingredients except chicken; mix well. Bring to a boil over medium heat. Boil 1 minute, stirring constantly.

2. When grill is heated, lightly brush glaze on one side of each chicken breast half. Place chicken, glaze side down, on gas grill over medium heat or on charcoal grill 4 to 6 inches from medium coals. Lightly brush glaze over chicken; cook covered 10 to 16 minutes or until juice is clear when center of thickest part is cut (170°F).

3. Heat remaining glaze to a boil; boil 1 minute. Serve chicken with glaze.

Nutrition Information Per Serving: Calories 355 • Total Fat 4g • Saturated Fat 1g • Cholesterol 75mg • Sodium 660mg • Total Carbohydrate 52g • Dietary Fiber 1g • Sugars 37g • Protein 28g. Dietary Exchanges: 4 Very Lean Meat • 3½ Other Carbohydrates.

chicken puff pie

READY TO SERVE: 30 MINUTES
SERVINGS: 4

2 cups frozen mixed vegetables

2 cans (10¾-oz. each) condensed 98% fat-free cream of chicken soup with 30% less sodium

½ cup chicken broth

2 cups cubed cooked chicken or turkey

2 tablespoons chopped fresh parsley or 1 teaspoon dried parsley flakes

½ teaspoon poultry seasoning

⅛ teaspoon white pepper

1 can (4-oz.) mushroom pieces and stems, drained

1 can (8-oz.) refrigerated crescent dinner rolls

Additional chopped fresh parsley or dried parsley flakes

1. Heat oven to 375°F. Cook frozen vegetables as directed on package. Drain.

2. In large saucepan, combine cooked vegetables and all remaining ingredients except crescent rolls and additional parsley. Cook over medium heat until mixture is bubbly and thoroughly heated, stirring occasionally.

3. Meanwhile, separate dough into 8 triangles. Place 2 triangles together, stacking one on top of the other; press together slightly. (If necessary, gently press triangles until 6 inches long.) Repeat with remaining dough. Place triangles on ungreased cookie sheet. Bake triangles at 375°F for 9 to 12 minutes.

4. To serve, spoon hot chicken mixture into ungreased 12x8-inch (2-quart) baking dish. Arrange warm triangles, side by side, on top of chicken mixture, alternating short sides of triangles. Sprinkle with additional parsley.

Nutrition Information Per Serving: Calories 490 • Total Fat 20g • Saturated Fat 5g • Cholesterol 70mg • Sodium 1310mg • Total Carbohydrate 47g • Dietary Fiber 3g • Sugars 6g • Protein 30g. Dietary Exchanges: 3 Starch • 1 Vegetable • 2½ Lean Meat • 2 Fat OR 3 Carbohydrate • 1 Vegetable • 2½ Lean Meat • 2 Fat.

crunchy asian chicken salad

READY TO SERVE: 20 MINUTES
SERVINGS: 4

salad

- 1 tablespoon butter or margarine
- 1 package (3-oz.) oriental-flavor ramen noodle soup mix, noodles crushed
- 2 cups coleslaw blend (from 16-oz. bag)
- 2 cups shredded lettuce
- 1 package (9-oz.) frozen diced cooked chicken, thawed, larger pieces cut up if necessary
- ¼ cup chopped peanuts
- 2 medium green onions, sliced (2 tablespoons)

dressing

- ⅓ cup rice vinegar or white vinegar
- ¼ cup creamy peanut butter
- 3 tablespoons sugar
- 2 tablespoons vegetable oil
- Contents of seasoning packet from soup mix

1. In 8-inch skillet, melt butter over medium heat. Add crushed ramen noodles; cook 4 to 5 minutes or until toasted, stirring constantly.

2. Meanwhile, in large bowl, combine dressing ingredients; blend well.

3. Add toasted noodles, coleslaw blend, lettuce and chicken; toss to coat. If desired, serve on lettuce-lined plates. Sprinkle with peanuts and onions.

Nutrition Information Per Serving: Calories 420 • Total Fat 26g • Saturated Fat 6g • Cholesterol 60mg • Sodium 460mg • Total Carbohydrate 20g • Dietary Fiber 3g • Sugars 13g • Protein 27g. Dietary Exchanges: 1 Starch • 1 Vegetable • 3 Very Lean Meat • 4½ Fat.

TIME-EASING SUBSTITUTIONS

The homemade dressing for Crunchy Asian Chicken Salad is simply delicious and comes together quite easily. If you are particularly pressed for time, however, you should go ahead and substitute about ¾ cup purchased Asian salad dressing. You'll find a variety to choose from in the salad dressing aisle of your grocery store.

If you have leftover chicken sitting in the refrigerator, feel free to use that in place of the frozen chicken the dish calls for. You'll find that the salad is wonderful when grilled chicken is used that was seasoned with soy sauce, garlic, gingerroot, Chinese five-spice powder or bottled teriyaki or sweet-and-sour sauce.

turkey scaloppine

READY TO SERVE: 20 MINUTES
SERVINGS: 4

- 1 lb. fresh turkey breast slices
- ½ teaspoon salt
- ½ cup Italian-style dry bread crumbs
- 4 teaspoons margarine or butter
- ½ cup dry white wine
- 2 tablespoons lemon juice
- Lemon slices
- Chopped fresh Italian parsley

1. Sprinkle turkey slices with salt; coat slices on both sides with bread crumbs.

2. Generously spray large nonstick skillet with nonstick cooking spray. Heat over medium-high heat until hot. Add turkey; cook 2 to 4 minutes or until no longer pink in center, turning once. Remove turkey from skillet; place on serving platter. Cover to keep warm.

3. Add margarine, wine and lemon juice to same skillet; bring to a boil. Pour sauce over turkey. Top with lemon slices and parsley.

Nutrition Information Per Serving: Calories 220 • Total Fat 5g • Saturated Fat 1g • Cholesterol 75mg • Sodium 580mg • Total Carbohydrate 11g • Dietary Fiber 1g • Sugars 1g • Protein 29g. Dietary Exchanges: ½ Starch • 4 Very Lean Meat • 1 Fat OR ½ Carbohydrate • 4 Very Lean Meat • 1 Fat.

honey-glazed chicken thighs

READY TO SERVE: 20 MINUTES
SERVINGS: 4

* super fast

¼ cup honey

2 tablespoons soy sauce

2 garlic cloves, minced, or ¼ teaspoon garlic powder

4 boneless skinless chicken thighs (about 1 lb.)

2 tablespoons olive or vegetable oil

¼ teaspoon salt

¼ teaspoon coarsely ground black pepper

1. Heat gas or charcoal grill. In small bowl, combine honey, soy sauce and garlic; blend well with wire whisk. Set aside. Brush chicken thighs with oil; sprinkle with salt and pepper.

2. When grill is heated, place chicken on gas grill over medium heat or on charcoal grill 4 to 6 inches from medium coals. Cook covered 8 to 12 minutes or until juice is clear when center of thickest part is cut (180°F), turning once and brushing with honey mixture during last 2 minutes of cooking time.

Nutrition Information Per Serving: Calories 190 • Total Fat 10g • Saturated Fat 3g • Cholesterol 70mg • Sodium 220mg • Total Carbohydrate 5g • Dietary Fiber 0g • Sugars 4g • Protein 20g. **Dietary Exchanges:** 3 Lean Meat • ½ Other Carbohydrate.

turkey and twists in tomato-cream sauce

READY TO SERVE: 30 MINUTES
SERVINGS: 4

3 cups uncooked rotini pasta (8 oz.)

⅓ lb. fully cooked, honey-roasted turkey breast

1 container (15-oz.) refrigerated marinara sauce

½ cup reduced-fat sour cream

2 tablespoons finely shredded Parmesan cheese

2 tablespoons chopped fresh parsley

1. In 3-quart saucepan, cook pasta as directed on package, omitting salt. Drain; cover to keep warm.

2. Meanwhile, cut turkey into 1x¼x¼-inch strips. In 8-inch skillet, heat marinara sauce over medium heat. Stir in sour cream until well blended. Stir in turkey; cook until thoroughly heated.

3. Serve cooked sauce over pasta. Sprinkle with cheese and parsley.

Nutrition Information Per Serving: Calories 430 • Total Fat 8g • Saturated Fat 2.5g • Trans Fat 0g • Cholesterol 45mg • Sodium 860mg • Total Carbohydrate 68g • Dietary Fiber 5g • Sugars 13g • Protein 24g. **Dietary Exchanges:** 3½ Starch • 1 Other Carbohydrate • 2 Lean Meat.

chicken cordon bleu stromboli

SERVINGS: 5

DEE DEE GLICK * CLINTON, MONTANA

1 can (11-oz.) refrigerated French loaf

½ cup grated Parmesan cheese

4 oz. thinly sliced cooked ham

6 oz. thinly sliced cooked chicken

1 jar (6-oz.) sliced mushrooms, drained

1 large green bell pepper, thinly sliced

4 oz. shredded mozzarella cheese (1 cup)

6 oz. shredded Swiss cheese (1½ cups)

¼ cup purchased honey-Dijon salad dressing

1. Heat oven to 375°F. Spray cookie sheet with butter-flavored nonstick cooking spray. Unroll dough onto sprayed cookie sheet. Press to form 14x12-inch rectangle.

2. Reserve 2 tablespoons of the Parmesan cheese. Sprinkle remaining Parmesan cheese lengthwise in 4-inch-wide strip down center of dough to within ¼ inch of each end. Top with ham, chicken, mushrooms, bell pepper, cheeses and salad dressing.

3. Bring one long side of dough up and over filling, completely covering filling. Repeat with remaining long side, overlapping dough. Press edge to seal. Fold ends under. With sharp knife, cut 5 slits in top of dough to allow steam to escape. Sprinkle with reserved 2 tablespoons Parmesan cheese.

4. Bake at 375°F for 18 to 24 minutes or until golden brown. Cool 5 minutes. Cut into slices.

Nutrition Information Per Serving: Calories 520 • Total Fat 25g • Sodium 1470mg • Total Carbohydrate 34g • Protein 38g.

orange chicken stir-fry

READY TO SERVE: 15 MINUTES
SERVINGS: 4

* super fast

- 2 cups uncooked instant rice
- 2 cups water
- 3 tablespoons frozen orange juice concentrate, thawed
- 2 tablespoons low-sodium soy sauce
- ½ teaspoon cornstarch
- ¼ teaspoon garlic powder
- 1 lb. chicken breast strips for stir-fry
- 1 bag (1-lb.) frozen broccoli, carrots and water chestnuts, thawed, drained

  Chopped green onions, if desired

1. Cook rice in water as directed on package, omitting salt.

2. Meanwhile, in small bowl, mix orange juice concentrate, soy sauce, cornstarch and garlic powder until smooth.

3. Heat 10-inch nonstick skillet over medium-high heat. Add chicken; cook 5 to 8 minutes, stirring frequently, until chicken is no longer pink in center.

4. Stir in juice concentrate mixture and vegetables. Reduce heat to medium; cover and cook 6 to 8 minutes, stirring occasionally, until vegetables are crisp-tender. Serve over rice. If desired, garnish with chopped green onions.

Nutrition Information Per Serving: Calories 410 • Total Fat 4g • Saturated Fat 1g • Trans Fat 0g • Cholesterol 70mg • Sodium 370mg • Total Carbohydrate 61g • Dietary Fiber 4g • Sugars 9g • Protein 31g. **Dietary Exchanges:** 3 Starch • ½ Other Carbohydrate • 1 Vegetable • 3 Very Lean Meat.

easy tostada pizzas

sesame chicken nuggets

READY TO SERVE: 20 MINUTES
SERVINGS: 4

✳ super fast

2 tablespoons sesame seeds

1 lb. precut chicken breast chunks, or 4 boneless skinless chicken breast halves, cut into 1-inch chunks

1 tablespoon oil

¾ cup purchased sweet-and-sour or barbecue sauce or ½ cup honey

1. In large nonstick skillet over medium heat, toast sesame seeds until golden brown, stirring frequently. Sprinkle toasted sesame seeds over chicken chunks.

2. Heat oil in same skillet over medium-high heat until hot. Add chicken; cook and stir 5 to 6 minutes or until chicken is no longer pink. Serve chicken nuggets with sauce.

Nutrition Information Per Serving: Calories 230 • Total Fat 8g • Saturated Fat 1g • Cholesterol 65mg • Sodium 210mg • Total Carbohydrate 14g • Dietary Fiber 0g • Sugars 11g • Protein 35g. Dietary Exchanges: 1 Fruit • 3 Very Lean Meat • 1 Fat OR 1 Carbohydrate • 3 Very Lean Meat • 1 Fat.

easy tostada pizzas

READY TO SERVE: 45 MINUTES
SERVINGS: 4

1 package (9-oz.) frozen southwestern-seasoned cooked chicken breast strips

1 can (15-oz.) refrigerated cornbread twists

1 cup shredded Mexican cheese blend (4 oz.)

½ cup thick 'n chunky salsa

1. Heat the oven to 375°F.

2. Set the frozen chicken strips on a microwavable plate. Microwave on Low for 2 to 3 minutes, until thawed.

3. Unroll the cornbread dough and separate it into 4 rectangles, each made of 4 strips. Lay the rectangles on an ungreased cookie sheet. Press out each rectangle to measure 5½x4½-inches.

4. Divide the chicken strips into 4 piles. Put 1 pile of chicken on each rectangle. Sprinkle each pile with cheese.

5. Bake the pizzas for 15 to 20 minutes or until the edges are deep golden brown. Serve the pizzas with salsa.

Nutrition Information Per Serving: Calories 480 • Total Fat 23g • Sodium 1260mg • Total Carbohydrate 36g • Sugars 9g • Protein 33g. Dietary Exchange: 2 Fat.

cheesy tomato-chicken skillet

READY TO SERVE: 30 MINUTES
SERVINGS: 4

7 oz. uncooked pasta nuggets (radiatore) (2 cups)

¾ lb. chicken breast strips for stir-frying

1 can (10¾-oz.) condensed cream of chicken soup

1½ cups (5 to 6 medium) chopped Italian plum tomatoes

½ cup milk

2 tablespoons chopped fresh basil

4 oz. shredded mozzarella cheese (1 cup)

1. Cook pasta to desired doneness as directed on package. Drain; cover to keep warm.

2. Meanwhile, spray large nonstick skillet with nonstick cooking spray. Heat over medium-high heat until hot. Add chicken strips; cook and stir 4 to 6 minutes or until chicken is no longer pink in center. Reduce heat to medium. Add soup, tomatoes, milk and basil; mix well.

3. Add cooked pasta; cook and stir until bubbly and thoroughly heated. Sprinkle with cheese. Remove from heat. Cover; let stand 2 to 3 minutes or until cheese is melted.

Nutrition Information Per Serving: Calories 450 • Total Fat 13g • Saturated Fat 5g • Cholesterol 75mg • Sodium 820mg • Total Carbohydrate 48g • Dietary Fiber 2g • Sugars 5g • Protein 36g. Dietary Exchanges: 3 Starch • 4 Lean Meat OR 3 Carbohydrate • 4 Lean Meat.

turkey meat loaves

READY TO SERVE: 40 MINUTES
SERVINGS: 6

1½ lb. ground turkey breast

¾ cup old-fashioned or quick-cooking oats

1 small red bell pepper, finely chopped

½ cup apple juice

3 teaspoons onion powder

1 teaspoon salt

1 teaspoon dried sage leaves, crushed

½ teaspoon pepper

¼ teaspoon garlic powder

2 tablespoons apple juice

1. Heat oven to 375°F. Spray 12 regular-size muffin cups with cooking spray. In medium bowl, mix all ingredients except 2 tablespoons apple juice.

2. Spoon mixture evenly into muffin cups, mounding tops. Brush tops with 2 tablespoons apple juice.

3. Bake 20 to 30 minutes or until thermometer inserted in center of loaf reads 165°F.

Nutrition Information Per Serving: Calories 210 • Total Fat 7g • Saturated Fat 2g • Trans Fat 0g • Cholesterol 75mg • Sodium 470mg • Total Carbohydrate 12g • Dietary Fiber 1g • Sugars 4g • Protein 27g. Dietary Exchanges: ½ Starch • 3½ Very Lean Meat • 1 Fat.

caramelized garlic chicken

READY TO SERVE: 25 MINUTES
SERVINGS: 4

* super fast

2 teaspoons olive oil

4 garlic cloves

4 teaspoons brown sugar

4 boneless skinless chicken breast halves

1. Heat oven to 500°F. Line shallow roasting pan with foil; spray foil with nonstick cooking spray.

2. Heat oil in small nonstick skillet over medium-low heat until hot. Add garlic; cook 1 to 2 minutes or until garlic begins to soften. Remove from heat; stir in brown sugar until well mixed.

3. Place chicken breast halves in sprayed foil-lined pan; spread garlic mixture evenly over chicken.

4. Bake at 500°F for 10 to 15 minutes or until chicken is fork-tender and juices run clear.

Nutrition Information Per Serving: Calories 170 • Total Fat 5g • Saturated Fat 1g • Cholesterol 75mg • Sodium 65mg • Total Carbohydrate 5g • Dietary Fiber 0g • Sugars 5g • Protein 27g. Dietary Exchanges: ½ Fruit • 4 Very Lean Meat OR ½ Carbohydrate • 4 Very Lean Meat.

barbecued chicken pizza

PREP TIME: 30 MINUTES
SERVINGS: 6

2 cups shredded cooked chicken breast

⅓ cup barbecue sauce

1 prebaked thin-crust Italian bread shell (12-inch)

3 Italian plum tomatoes, sliced

4 oz. shredded reduced-fat Monterey Jack cheese (1 cup)

Fresh cilantro leaves

1. Heat oven to 450°F. In small bowl, combine chicken and barbecue sauce; mix well. Place bread shell on ungreased cookie sheet; spread chicken mixture over shell. Arrange tomatoes over chicken; sprinkle with cheese.

2. Bake at 450°F for 10 minutes or until cheese is melted and bread shell is browned. Sprinkle with cilantro.

Nutrition Information Per Serving: Calories 270 • Total Fat 8g • Saturated Fat 3g • Cholesterol 55mg • Sodium 510mg • Total Carbohydrate 24g • Dietary Fiber 1g • Sugars 2g • Protein 26g. Dietary Exchanges: 1½ Starch • 3 Very Lean Meat • 1 Fat OR 1½ Carbohydrate • 3 Very Lean Meat • 1 Fat.

turkey meat loaves

ranch club salad

ranch club salad

READY TO SERVE: 15 MINUTES
SERVINGS: 4

✳ super fast

8 cups shredded lettuce

1 chunk (¾-lb.) cooked turkey breast (from deli), cut into two 3¼-inch strips

4 slices purchased cooked bacon, cut into ½-inch pieces

1 small tomato, chopped

1 cup seasoned croutons

½ cup ranch salad dressing

1. In large bowl, combine all ingredients except dressing.

2. Add dressing; toss to coat.

Nutrition Information Per Serving: Calories 340 • Total Fat 22g • Saturated Fat 5g • Cholesterol 70mg • Sodium 540mg • Total Carbohydrate 12g • Dietary Fiber 2g • Sugars 3g • Protein 24g. Dietary Exchanges: 3½ Lean Meat • 2 Fat • 1 Other Carbohydrate.

presto chicken primavera potatoes

PREP TIME: 25 MINUTES
SERVINGS: 4

✳ super fast

4 medium baking potatoes (about 2 lb.)

1 teaspoon oil

¾ cup chopped zucchini

½ cup chopped red bell pepper

1 tablespoon all-purpose flour

¼ teaspoon garlic powder

⅛ teaspoon pepper

1½ cups skim milk

⅓ cup grated Parmesan cheese

2 cups cubed cooked chicken breast

1. Pierce potatoes with fork; place on microwave-safe paper towel or roasting rack in microwave. Microwave on High for 10 to 15 minutes or until tender, turning once halfway through cooking. Cover; let stand 5 minutes.

2. Meanwhile, heat oil in medium nonstick saucepan over medium-high heat until hot. Add zucchini and bell pepper; cook and stir until zucchini is crisp-tender. Stir in flour, garlic powder and pepper. Add milk; stir until well blended. Cook and stir until thickened and bubbly. Stir in cheese and chicken; cook until thoroughly heated.

3. To serve, cut potatoes in half lengthwise, cutting to but not through bottom of potatoes. Mash slightly with fork. Spoon chicken mixture over potatoes.

Nutrition Information Per Serving: Calories 350 • Total Fat 7g • Saturated Fat 3g • Cholesterol 70mg • Sodium 260mg • Total Carbohydrate 39g • Dietary Fiber 4g • Sugars 7g • Protein 32g. Dietary Exchanges: 2½ Starch • 3 Lean Meat OR 2½ Carbohydrate • 3 Lean Meat.

cacciatore with a twist

READY TO SERVE: 30 MINUTES
SERVINGS: 4

2 teaspoons olive or vegetable oil

1 medium onion, sliced

1 small green pepper

2 garlic cloves, minced

4 fresh turkey breast slices (about ½ lb.), cut into strips

3 oz. uncooked rotini (spiral pasta) (1 cup)

1 can (15-oz.) tomato sauce

1 can (15-oz.) garbanzo beans, drained, rinsed

¾ teaspoon dried oregano leaves

1. Heat oil in large nonstick skillet over medium heat until hot. Add onion, bell pepper, garlic and turkey; cook and stir 5 to 10 minutes or until turkey is no longer pink.

2. Meanwhile, cook rotini to desired doneness as directed on package.

3. Add tomato sauce, beans and oregano to turkey mixture; mix well. Bring to a boil. Reduce heat; cover and simmer 10 minutes or until thoroughly heated.

4. Drain rotini. Serve turkey mixture over rotini.

Nutrition Information Per Serving: Calories 290 • Total Fat 4g • Saturated Fat 1g • Cholesterol 35mg • Sodium 870mg • Total Carbohydrate 42g • Dietary Fiber 6g • Sugars 7g • Protein 21g. Dietary Exchanges: 2½ Starch • 1 Vegetable • 2 Very Lean Meat OR 2½ Carbohydrate • 1 Vegetable • 2 Very Lean Meat.

dilled chicken-potato hash

READY TO SERVE: 30 MINUTES
SERVINGS: 4

- 2 teaspoons margarine
  or butter
- 1 lb. fresh chicken breast
  tenders, cut into 1-inch pieces
- 2 cups frozen bell pepper
  and onion stir-fry
- 1 package (16-oz.) frozen
  southern-style hash-brown
  potatoes
- 1 teaspoon dried dill weed
- ½ teaspoon salt
- ¼ teaspoon cracked black
  pepper
- ½ cup chicken broth

1. Melt margarine in large nonstick skillet over medium-high heat. Add chicken; cook and stir 5 to 7 minutes or until chicken is no longer pink in center.

2. Add bell pepper and onion stir-fry; cook and stir 2 minutes. Add potatoes, dill, salt and pepper; cook and stir 5 minutes or until potatoes are lightly browned and mixture is hot.

3. Stir in broth; cook 1 minute.

Nutrition Information Per Serving: Calories 260 • Total Fat 6g • Saturated Fat 1g • Cholesterol 65mg • Sodium 480mg • Total Carbohydrate 23g • Dietary Fiber 3g • Sugars 2g • Protein 28g. Dietary Exchanges: 1 Starch • 1 Vegetable • 3 Very Lean Meat • 1 Fat OR 1 Carbohydrate • 1 Vegetable • 3 Very Lean Meat • 1 Fat.

grilled chicken breasts with georgia peach salsa

READY TO SERVE: 30 MINUTES
SERVINGS: 4

salsa

- 1 cup chopped peeled ripe peaches
- 1 tablespoon fresh lime juice
- 2 teaspoons brown sugar
- ½ cup diced red bell pepper
- 2 tablespoons thinly sliced green onions
- 1 tablespoon minced jalapeno chile pepper
- Dash salt

chicken

- 4 boneless skinless chicken breast halves
- ⅛ teaspoon salt
- ⅛ teaspoon pepper

1. Heat grill. In medium bowl, combine peaches, lime juice and brown sugar; mix well. Stir in bell pepper, onions, chile and dash of salt.

2. Place 1 chicken breast half between 2 pieces of plastic wrap or waxed paper. Working from center, gently pound with flat side of mallet or rolling pin until about ¼-inch thick; remove wrap. Repeat with remaining chicken breast halves.

3. When ready to grill, oil grill rack. Lightly sprinkle chicken with ⅛ teaspoon salt and pepper. Place chicken on gas grill over medium heat or on charcoal grill 4 to 6 inches from medium coals. Cook 6 to 10 minutes or until chicken is fork-tender and juices run clear, turning once. Serve chicken with salsa.

Nutrition Information Per Serving: Calories 160 • Total Fat 3g • Saturated Fat 1g • Cholesterol 75mg • Sodium 180mg • Total Carbohydrate 6g • Dietary Fiber 1g • Sugars 5g • Protein 27g. Dietary Exchanges: ½ Fruit • 4 Very Lean Meat OR ½ Carbohydrate • 4 Very Lean Meat.

two-cheese chicken with couscous

READY TO SERVE: 25 MINUTES
SERVINGS: 6

* super fast

chicken mixture

- 1 tablespoon vegetable or olive oil
- 1¼ lb. boneless skinless chicken breast halves, cut into ½- to ¾-inch pieces
- ½ teaspoon garlic-pepper blend
- 1 jar (26- to 28-oz.) chunky pasta sauce
- 1 jar (4.5-oz.) sliced mushrooms, drained
- ¾ cup shredded mozzarella cheese (3 oz.)

couscous

- 2 cups water
- 1 cup uncooked couscous
- ½ teaspoon garlic-pepper blend
- ¼ teaspoon salt
- ¼ cup grated Parmesan cheese

1. In 10-inch skillet, heat oil over medium-high heat until hot. Add chicken; sprinkle with ½ teaspoon garlic-pepper blend. Cook 2 to 4 minutes or until brown, stirring frequently.

2. Add pasta sauce and mushrooms. Bring to a boil. Reduce heat to medium; cook 5 to 7 minutes or until sauce is of desired consistency and chicken is no longer pink in center, stirring occasionally.

3. Meanwhile, bring water to a boil. Remove from heat. Stir in couscous, ½ teaspoon garlic-pepper blend and salt; mix well. Cover; let stand 5 minutes.

4. Stir mozzarella cheese into chicken mixture. Fluff couscous with fork; stir in Parmesan cheese. Serve chicken mixture over couscous. If desired, sprinkle with additional Parmesan cheese.

Nutrition Information Per Serving: Calories 410 • Total Fat 12g • Saturated Fat 3g • Cholesterol 65mg • Sodium 970mg • Total Carbohydrate 44g • Dietary Fiber 5g • Sugars 13g • Protein 32g. Dietary Exchanges: 2½ Starch • 3½ Lean Meat.

CHICKEN TENDERS TO THE RESCUE!

Chicken tenders will shorten the preparation time for this recipe. Just cut the tenders into ½- to ¾-inch pieces. Look for chicken tenders near other cut and packaged chicken in your grocer's meat department.

For a change-of-pace dinner, swap out the chicken with an equal amount of sliced sausage. Polish sausage, Kielbasa and turkey sausage all make zesty substitutes in this popular, meal-in-one skillet dish.

california chicken salad

READY TO SERVE: 15 MINUTES
SERVINGS: 10

✳ super fast

salad

- 3½ cups torn leaf lettuce
- 3½ cups torn romaine
- 3 boneless skinless chicken breasts (¾-lb. each), cooked, cut into bite-sized pieces
- 2 oz. Canadian bacon, sliced, cut into thin strips (1 cup)
- 6 medium green onions, sliced (6 tablespoons)
- 1 medium tomato, chopped (¾ cup)

vinaigrette

- ¼ cup balsamic vinegar
- 2 tablespoons canola or soybean oil
- 1 teaspoon Dijon mustard
- 1 clove garlic, minced

1. In large bowl, mix salad ingredients.

2. In small bowl, mix vinaigrette ingredients until well blended. Just before serving, pour vinaigrette over salad; toss gently.

Nutrition Information Per Serving: Calories 190 • Total Fat 11g • Saturated Fat 1.5g • Trans Fat 0g • Cholesterol 50mg • Sodium 250mg • Total Carbohydrate 5g • Dietary Fiber 2g • Sugars 3g • Protein 19g. Dietary Exchanges: 1 Vegetable • 2½ Very Lean Meat • 2 Fat.

IMPROVISE WITH LEFTOVER CHICKEN

This salad recipe is a tasty way to use up any extra, cooked chicken you may have on hand. Another good idea is to heat leftover chicken in a skillet with a few chopped onions, curry powder, raisins and a bit of broth. Serve the mixture over rice for an effortless meal-in-one. You can also add some cooked chicken to a can of chicken broth and heat it through on the stove. Stir in a handful of frozen peas, chives and chopped parsley for instant soup!

light and lemony chicken

READY TO SERVE: 25 MINUTES
SERVINGS: 4

✳ super fast

rice

- 3 cups hot cooked instant rice (cooked as directed on package, omitting margarine and salt)

sauce

- ⅔ cup ready-to-serve fat-free chicken broth with ⅓ less sodium
- 1 teaspoon light soy sauce
- 1 teaspoon grated lemon peel
- ¼ cup lemon juice
- 1 tablespoon sugar
- 1 tablespoon cornstarch
- Dash pepper

stir-fry

- 4 boneless skinless chicken breast halves, cut into bite-sized strips
- 8 green onions, cut into 1-inch pieces
- 1 lb. fresh asparagus spears, trimmed, cut into 1-inch pieces (3 cups)
- 2 cups frozen baby cut carrots

1. While rice is cooking, combine all sauce ingredients; mix well. Set aside.

2. Spray large nonstick skillet or wok with nonstick cooking spray. Heat over high heat until hot. Add chicken and onions; cook and stir until chicken is lightly browned and no longer pink. Remove skillet from heat; place chicken and onions on plate.

3. Spray skillet again with cooking spray. Heat over high heat about 1 minute. Add asparagus and carrots; cook and stir 3 to 4 minutes or until vegetables are crisp-tender.

4. Return chicken and onions to skillet. Stir sauce well; pour over chicken and vegetables. Cook and stir just until sauce thickens. Serve over rice.

Nutrition Information Per Serving: Calories 350 • Total Fat 4g • Saturated Fat 1g • Cholesterol 75mg • Sodium 260mg • Total Carbohydrate 45g • Dietary Fiber 6g • Sugars 10g • Protein 33g. Dietary Exchanges: 2½ Starch • 2 Vegetable • 3 Very Lean Meat OR 2½ Carbohydrate • 2 Vegetable • 3 Very Lean Meat.

CHICKEN WITHOUT STICKIN'

Two innovations help saute chicken without much oil: nonstick cooking spray and nonstick skillets. Nonstick spray relies on an aerosol can to disperse the oil in a thinner layer than is possible with butter. A nonstick pan is also a key kitchen tool. To help your pan last for years, don't use metal utensils as they mar finishes. Also, do not wash the pan with steel wool or abrasive powders. Use hot, soapy water and a sponge instead.

chicken manicotti olé

SERVINGS: 5

RENÉE McWILLIAMS ✳ LINCOLN, NEBRASKA

10 uncooked manicotti

1 lb. ground chicken or
    ground turkey breast

1 jar (16-oz.) chunky-style
    salsa

1 can (15-oz.) black beans,
    drained, rinsed

¼ teaspoon garlic powder

¼ teaspoon pepper

4 oz. shredded Colby-Monterey
    Jack cheese blend (1 cup)

1. Heat oven to 350°F. Spray 13x9-inch (3-quart) glass baking dish with nonstick cooking spray. Cook manicotti to desired doneness as directed on package. Drain; rinse with cold water.

2. In large bowl, combine ground chicken, ¾ cup of the salsa, ¾ cup of the beans, garlic powder and pepper; mix well. In small bowl, combine remaining salsa and beans; mix well. Cover; reserve for topping.

3. Stuff manicotti with chicken mixture. Arrange in sprayed baking dish. Cover with foil.

4. Bake at 350°F for 30 minutes. Uncover baking dish; top with reserved salsa mixture and cheese. Bake, uncovered, an additional 15 to 20 minutes or until chicken is thoroughly cooked and cheese is melted.

Nutrition Information Per Serving: Calories 440 • Total Fat 16g • Sodium 1010mg • Total Carbohydrate 43g • Protein 30g.

spicy picnic chicken

SERVINGS: 4

YVONNE DEL BIAGGIO ✷ SACRAMENTO, CALIFORNIA

1 cup buttermilk

1 package (1.25-oz.) taco seasoning mix

1 cup Parmesan dry bread crumbs

¼ cup all-purpose flour

1 to 2 teaspoons salt

½ teaspoon pepper

8 pieces bone-in chicken, skin removed, if desired

3 tablespoons butter, melted

1. Heat oven to 400°F. Spray broiler pan with nonstick cooking spray. In shallow bowl, combine buttermilk and 1 tablespoon of the taco seasoning mix; mix well. In another shallow bowl, combine remaining taco seasoning mix, bread crumbs, flour, salt and pepper; mix well.

2. Dip chicken pieces in buttermilk mixture; coat with bread crumb mixture. Place on sprayed broiler pan. Let stand 10 minutes. Discard any remaining buttermilk and coating mixture.

3. Drizzle chicken with butter. Bake at 400°F for 45 to 55 minutes or until chicken is fork-tender and juices run clear.

Nutrition Information Per Serving: Calories 430 • Total Fat 18g • Sodium 2990mg • Total Carbohydrate 31g • Protein 37g.

turkey slice saute with vegetables

READY TO SERVE: 35 MINUTES
SERVINGS: 5

½ lb. fresh whole green beans
  or 2 cups frozen cut green
  beans

½ to 2 cups sliced carrots

1 cup celery

1 to 1¼ lb. fresh turkey breast
  slices

1 cup sliced fresh mushrooms

¼ cup sliced green onions or 2
  tablespoons finely chopped
  shallots

¼ cup dry white wine

2 tablespoons lemon juice

½ teaspoon salt

¼ teaspoon pepper

1. Place green beans, carrots and celery in steamer basket over boiling water. Reduce heat; cover and steam 10 minutes or until vegetables are crisp-tender. Cover to keep vegetables warm.

2. Meanwhile, melt margarine in large skillet over medium heat. Add turkey breast slices; cook 2 to 3 minutes, turning once.

3. Add mushrooms, onions, wine and lemon juice to skillet. Reduce heat; cover and simmer 2 to 3 minutes or until turkey is no longer pink. Sprinkle with salt and pepper.

4. Arrange steamed vegetables and turkey slices on warm serving platter. Spoon mixture over turkey.

Nutrition Information Per Serving: Calories 210 • Total Fat 5g • Saturated Fat 1g • Cholesterol 75mg • Sodium 360mg • Total Carbohydrate 10g • Dietary Fiber 4g • Sugars 5g • Protein 29g. **Dietary Exchanges:** 2 Vegetable • 3½ Very Lean Meat • ½ Fat.

chicken and spinach calzones

PREP TIME: 35 MINUTES
READY TO SERVE: 50 MINUTES
SERVINGS: 4

1 tablespoon cornmeal,
  if desired

2 boneless skinless chicken
  breast halves, cut into
  ½-inch cubes

1 small onion

2 garlic cloves, minced

½ cup pizza sauce

2 tablespoons grated Romano
  cheese

2 cups frozen cut leaf spinach,
  thawed, squeezed to drain
  and coarsely chopped

3 oz. mozzarella cheese, cut
  into ¼-inch cubes (⅔ cup)

1 can (10-oz.) refrigerated
  pizza crust

1. Heat oven to 425°F. Line cookie sheet with foil; spray foil with nonstick cooking spray. Sprinkle with cornmeal.

2. Spray medium nonstick skillet with cooking spray. Heat over medium-high heat until hot. Add chicken; cook and stir 5 to 6 minutes or until no longer pink. Add onion and garlic; cook 1 to 2 minutes or until onion is tender.

3. Stir in pizza sauce and Romano cheese. Remove from heat; stir in spinach and mozzarella cheese.

4. Remove pizza dough from can; do not unroll. Cut roll of dough into 4 equal portions. Press or roll each portion into 6- to 7-inch round.

5. Spoon ¼ of spinach mixture onto half of each round. Fold untopped half of dough over filling; press edges together with fork to seal. Place calzones on cookie sheet; reshape into semicircles, if necessary. If desired, spray tops lightly with cooking spray.

6. Bake at 425°F for 10 to 15 minutes or until crusts are golden brown.

Nutrition Information Per Serving: Calories 370 • Total Fat 9g • Saturated Fat 4g • Cholesterol 50mg • Sodium 810mg • Total Carbohydrate 41g • Dietary Fiber 3g • Sugars 5g • Protein 29g. **Dietary Exchanges:** 2 Starch • 2 Vegetable • 3 Lean Meat OR 2 Carbohydrate • 2 Vegetable • 3 Lean Meat.

pork & sausage

basil-pork and asian noodles ✳ p. 197

italian sausage lasagna ✳ p. 194

individual pepperoni pizzas ✳ p. 205

saucy medallions with coucous ✳ p. 202

honey-orange glazed pork chops ✳ p. 206

key west ribs

key west ribs

PREP TIME: 10 MINUTES
READY TO SERVE: 9 HOURS 10 MINUTES
SERVINGS: 4

* slow cooked

- 2½ lb. country-style pork loin ribs
- ¼ cup finely chopped onion
- ¼ cup barbecue sauce
- 1 teaspoon grated orange peel
- 1 teaspoon grated lime peel
- ½ teaspoon salt
- ¼ cup orange juice
- 2 tablespoons lime juice

1. Place pork ribs in 3½- to 4-quart slow cooker. In small bowl, combine all remaining ingredients; mix well. Pour over ribs.

2. Cover; cook on Low setting for 7 to 9 hours. Spoon sauce over ribs.

Nutrition Information Per Serving: Calories 520 • Total Fat 39g • Saturated Fat 14g • Cholesterol 140mg • Sodium 470mg • Total Carbohydrate 5g • Dietary Fiber 1g • Sugars 2g • Protein 36g. Dietary Exchanges: ½ Fruit • 5 High-Fat Meat OR ½ Carbohydrate • 5 High-Fat Meat.

baked macaroni, ham and cheese

PREP TIME: 30 MINUTES
READY TO SERVE: 1 HOUR
SERVINGS: 4

- 8 oz. uncooked bow tie pasta (farfalle) (3½ cups)
- ¼ cup butter
- 1 small garlic clove, minced
- ¼ cup all-purpose flour
- 2 cups milk
- 6 oz. shredded extra-sharp Cheddar cheese (1½ cups)
- 4 drops hot pepper sauce
- 1 cup julienne-cut (1½x¼x¼-inch) cooked ham

1. Heat oven to 375°F. Spray 1½-quart casserole with nonstick cooking spray.

2. Cook pasta to desired doneness as directed on package. Drain; return to saucepan.

3. Meanwhile, melt butter in medium saucepan over medium heat. Add garlic; cook 1 minute. With wire whisk, blend in flour; cook and stir 1 minute. Add milk; cook until mixture boils and thickens, stirring occasionally. Reduce heat to low. Add cheese; stir until melted.

4. Stir in hot pepper sauce. If desired, add salt and pepper to taste. Add ham; mix well. Add cheese sauce to cooked pasta; stir until well mixed. Spoon into sprayed casserole.

5. Bake at 375°F for 25 to 30 minutes or until lightly browned and bubbly.

Nutrition Information Per Serving: Calories 620 • Total Fat 31g • Saturated Fat 18g • Cholesterol 100mg • Sodium 950mg • Total Carbohydrate 55g • Dietary Fiber 2g • Sugars 9g • Protein 30g. Dietary Exchanges: 3½ Starch • 3 High-Fat Meat • 1 Fat OR 3½ Carbohydrate • 3 High-Fat Meat • 1 Fat.

barbecued pork fajitas

READY TO SERVE: 20 MINUTES
SERVINGS: 4

* super fast

- 1 teaspoon ground cumin
- ½ teaspoon garlic-pepper blend
- 1 lb. boneless pork loin chops, cut into thin, bite-size strips
- ½ medium red bell pepper, cut into thin, bite-size strips
- ½ medium green bell pepper, cut into thin, bite-size strips
- ½ cup red onion slices or 1 medium onion, sliced
- ⅓ cup barbecue sauce
- 4 fat-free flour tortillas (8- to 10-inch)

1. In resealable plastic food-storage bag, place cumin and garlic-pepper blend. Seal bag; shake to blend. Add pork; seal bag and shake to coat.

2. Heat 10-inch nonstick skillet over medium-high heat. Add pork; cook and stir 2 minutes.

3. Add bell peppers and onion; cook 2 to 3 minutes, stirring frequently, until pork is no longer pink in center and vegetables are crisp-tender. Stir in barbecue sauce; cook and stir until thoroughly heated. Serve pork mixture in tortillas.

Nutrition Information Per Serving: Calories 380 • Total Fat 9g • Saturated Fat 3g • Trans Fat 0g • Cholesterol 70mg • Sodium 710mg • Total Carbohydrate 44g • Dietary Fiber 4g • Sugars 7g • Protein 31g. Dietary Exchanges: 2½ Starch • 1 Vegetable • 3 Lean Meat.

lime-marinated pork tenderloins

READY TO SERVE: 30 MINUTES
SERVINGS: 6

2 pork tenderloins (¾-lb. each)

¼ cup frozen limeade concentrate, thawed

1 tablespoon oil

2 garlic cloves, minced

½ teaspoon salt

¼ teaspoon seasoned pepper blend

1. Cut each pork tenderloin in half lengthwise, cutting to but not through bottom; open and flatten. Place tenderloins in food storage plastic bag or shallow nonmetal dish.

2. In small bowl, combine all remaining ingredients; mix well. Pour over tenderloins; turn to coat. Seal bag or cover dish; let stand at room temperature for 10 minutes to marinate.

3. Line 13x9-inch pan with foil. Place tenderloins, cut side up, in foil-lined pan. Broil 4 to 6 inches from heat for 12 to 15 minutes or until pork is no longer pink in center, turning once. Cut into slices.

Nutrition Information Per Serving: Calories 170 • Total Fat 6g • Saturated Fat 2g • Cholesterol 65mg • Sodium 240mg • Total Carbohydrate 6g • Dietary Fiber 0g • Sugars 5g • Protein 24g. Dietary Exchanges: ½ Fruit • 3½ Very Lean Meat • ½ Fat OR ½ Carbohydrate • 3½ Very Lean Meat • ½ Fat.

breaded honey mustard pork

READY TO SERVE: 20 MINUTES
SERVINGS: 4

* super fast

2 tablespoons honey mustard

1 egg

½ cup unseasoned dry bread crumbs

½ teaspoon garlic-pepper blend

¼ teaspoon salt

1 lb. pork tenderloin, cut crosswise into 8 pieces

1 to 2 tablespoons vegetable oil

1. In shallow bowl, combine mustard and egg; beat well. In another shallow bowl, combine bread crumbs, garlic-pepper blend and salt; mix well.

2. To flatten each pork piece, place pork between 2 pieces of plastic wrap or waxed paper. Working from center, gently pound pork with flat side of meat mallet or rolling pin until about ¼-inch thick; remove wrap.

3. Heat oil in 10-inch nonstick skillet over medium-high heat until hot. Coat each pork piece with mustard mixture, then crumbs; place in skillet. Cook 6 to 8 minutes or until brown on both sides and slightly pink in center, turning once.

Nutrition Information Per Serving: Calories 280 • Total Fat 13g • Saturated Fat 3g • Cholesterol 120mg • Sodium 440mg • Total Carbohydrate 13g • Dietary Fiber 1g • Sugars 2g • Protein 27g. Dietary Exchanges: 1 Starch • 3½ Lean Meat • ½ Fat.

easy italian spiced pork

READY TO SERVE: 30 MINUTES
SERVINGS: 4

1 package (0.6-oz.) Italian dressing mix

¼ cup balsamic vinegar

½ teaspoon Italian seasoning

¼ teaspoon crushed red pepper

1 tablespoon extra-virgin olive oil or canola oil

4 boneless pork loin chops, ¾-inch thick (1 lb. each)

Paprika

1. In small bowl, beat dressing mix, vinegar, Italian seasoning and red pepper with wire whisk until mix is dissolved. Beat in oil until well blended.

2. In shallow glass baking dish, arrange pork chops in single layer. Spread oil mixture over both sides of pork. Let stand at room temperature 15 minutes to marinate.

3. Meanwhile, heat gas or charcoal grill.

4. When grill is heated, remove pork from marinade; discard marinade. Place pork on gas grill over medium-high heat or on charcoal grill over medium-high coals. Sprinkle pork with paprika. Cook uncovered 4 minutes. Turn pork; sprinkle with paprika. Cook uncovered 3 to 6 minutes longer or until pork is slightly pink in center and thermometer inserted in center of pork reads 160°F.

Nutrition Information Per Serving: Calories 220 • Total Fat 12g • Saturated Fat 3.5g • Trans Fat 0g • Cholesterol 70mg • Sodium 680mg • Total Carbohydrate 4g • Dietary Fiber 0g • Sugars 3g • Protein 24g. Dietary Exchanges: ½ Other Carbohydrate • 3½ Lean Meat.

lime-marinated pork tenderloins

home-style pork stew

easy ham and noodles

READY TO SERVE: 20 MINUTES
SERVINGS: 4

＊ super fast

1 can (14-oz.) chicken broth

1 cup water

3 cups uncooked dumpling egg noodles (6 oz.)

2 packages (10-oz. each) frozen broccoli, cauliflower and carrots in cheese-flavored sauce

2 cups cubed cooked ham

1. In medium saucepan, bring broth and water to a boil. Add noodles; return to a boil. Cook 8 to 10 minutes or until noodles are tender and most of liquid is absorbed. Do not drain.

2. Meanwhile, cook vegetables as directed on package.

3. Add vegetables in cheese sauce and ham to noodle mixture; toss gently to mix.

Nutrition Information Per Serving: Calories 350 • Total Fat 11g • Saturated Fat 4g • Cholesterol 80mg • Sodium 2090mg • Total Carbohydrate 38g • Dietary Fiber 3g • Sugars 4g • Protein 25g. Dietary Exchanges: 2 Starch • 2 Vegetable • 2 Lean Meat • 1 Fat.

corn, pork and bean bundles

READY TO SERVE: 30 MINUTES
SERVINGS: 4

¾ lb. boneless pork loin chops, cut into 2x¼-inch strips

1 can (15-oz.) red beans, rinsed

½ cup barbecue sauce

1 cup frozen whole kernel corn (from 1-lb. bag), thawed

4 thin slices onion

1. Heat gas or charcoal grill. Cut 4 (15x12-inch) sheets of foil. In medium bowl, mix pork, beans and barbecue sauce. Divide pork mixture evenly onto center of each sheet of foil. Sprinkle corn evenly over top. Place onion slice on top of each.

2. To form bundles, bring short sides of foil together; make several 1-inch folds. Fold open edges of foil to seal.

3. When grill is heated, place bundles on gas grill over medium heat or on charcoal grill over medium coals; cover grill. Cook 18 to 20 minutes or until pork is no longer pink in center. Carefully open bundles to allow steam to escape.

Nutrition Information Per Serving: Calories 340 • Total Fat 7g • Saturated Fat 2.5g • Trans Fat 0g • Cholesterol 50mg • Sodium 350mg • Total Carbohydrate 44g • Dietary Fiber 8g • Sugars 10g • Protein 29g. Dietary Exchanges: 2 Starch • 1 Other Carbohydrate • 3 Very Lean Meat • ½ Fat.

home-style pork stew

PREP TIME: 15 MINUTES
READY TO SERVE: 8 HOURS 35 MINUTES
SERVINGS: 6

＊ slow cooked

1 tablespoon oil

1½ lb. boneless pork shoulder roast, cut into 1½-inch pieces

⅛ teaspoon salt

⅛ teaspoon pepper

8 small red potatoes, unpeeled, quartered

2 cups fresh baby carrots, cut in half lengthwise

1 jar (12-oz.) pork gravy

¼ cup ketchup

½ teaspoon dried rosemary leaves

¼ teaspoon pepper

⅛ teaspoon ground sage

1½ cups frozen cut green beans, thawed

1. Heat oil in large skillet over high heat until hot. Add pork; sprinkle with salt and ⅛ teaspoon pepper. Cook 3 to 5 minutes or until browned, stirring frequently.

2. In 4- to 6-quart slow cooker, combine pork and all remaining ingredients except green beans.

3. Cover; cook on Low setting for 6 to 8 hours.

4. About 20 minutes before serving, stir green beans into stew. Increase heat setting to High; cover and cook an additional 15 to 20 minutes or until beans are tender.

Nutrition Information Per Serving: Calories 380 • Total Fat 12g • Saturated Fat 3g • Cholesterol 50mg • Sodium 530mg • Total Carbohydrate 47g • Dietary Fiber 5g • Sugars 6g • Protein 20g. Dietary Exchanges: 3 Starch • 1 Vegetable • 1½ Lean Meat • 1 Fat OR 3 Carbohydrate • 1 Vegetable • 1½ Lean Meat • 1 Fat.

italian sausage lasagna

PREP TIME: 25 MINUTES
READY TO SERVE: 8 HOURS 25 MINUTES
SERVINGS: 6

✳ slow cooked

¾ lb. bulk Italian pork sausage

½ cup chopped onion

2 cans (15-oz. each) Italian-style tomato sauce

2 teaspoons dried basil leaves

½ teaspoon salt

1 container (15-oz.) part-skim ricotta cheese

1 cup grated Parmesan cheese

12 oz. shredded mozzarella cheese (3 cups)

12 oz. uncooked lasagna noodles (12 noodles)

1. In large skillet, cook sausage and onion over medium heat for 6 to 8 minutes or until sausage is no longer pink, stirring occasionally. Drain. Add tomato sauce, basil and salt; mix well.

2. In medium bowl, combine ricotta cheese, Parmesan cheese and 2 cups of the mozzarella cheese.

3. Spoon ¼ of the sausage mixture into 3½- to 5-quart slow cooker. Top with 4 noodles, broken into pieces to fit. Top with half of the cheese mixture and ¼ of the sausage mixture. Top with 4 noodles, remaining cheese mixture and ¼ of the sausage mixture. Top with remaining 4 noodles and remaining sausage mixture.

4. Cover; cook on Low setting for 6 to 8 hours.

5. About 10 minutes before serving, sprinkle top of lasagna with remaining 1 cup mozzarella cheese. Cover; let stand about 10 minutes or until cheese is melted. Cut lasagna into pieces.

Nutrition Information Per Serving: Calories 770 • Total Fat 37g • Saturated Fat 18g • Cholesterol 100mg • Sodium 1980mg • Total Carbohydrate 66g • Dietary Fiber 4g • Sugars 15g • Protein 47g. Dietary Exchanges: 3 Starch • 1 Low-Fat Milk • 2 Vegetable • 4 High-Fat Meat OR 4½ Carbohydrate • 2 Vegetable • 4 High-Fat Meat.

chips 'n salsa taco salad

READY TO SERVE: 20 MINUTES
SERVINGS: 4

✳ super fast

salad

¾ lb. coarse ground pork for chow mein or coarse ground beef for chili

1 medium onion, sliced, separated into rings

2 tablespoons taco seasoning mix (from 1.25-oz. package)

¾ cup chunky-style salsa

4 cups shredded lettuce

2 cups broken tortilla chips

2 medium tomatoes, chopped

1 cup shredded Mexican cheese blend or Cheddar cheese (4 oz.)

dressing

½ cup chunky-style salsa

¼ cup French salad dressing

garnishes

Sliced or cubed avocado

Sliced ripe olives

Sour cream

Chunky-style salsa

Whole tortilla chips

1. Spray 10-inch nonstick skillet with cooking spray. Add pork and onion; cook over medium heat 7 to 10 minutes or until no longer pink, stirring frequently.

2. Stir in taco seasoning mix and ¾ cup salsa. Cook 2 to 3 minutes or until thoroughly heated and sauce is of desired consistency, stirring occasionally.

3. In large bowl, combine dressing ingredients; blend well. Add meat mixture, lettuce, broken chips and tomatoes; toss to mix. Spoon onto individual serving plates. Sprinkle salads with cheese. Garnish as desired.

Nutrition Information Per Serving: Calories 800 • Total Fat 51g • Saturated Fat 18g • Cholesterol 85mg • Sodium 2220mg • Total Carbohydrate 56g • Dietary Fiber 10g • Sugars 14g • Protein 29g. Dietary Exchanges: 3½ Starch • 1 Vegetable • 2½ High-Fat Meat • 6 Fat • 1 Other Carbohydrate.

NEW USES FOR AN OLD FAVORITE

When it comes to avoiding a sticky situation, nonstick cooking spray can't be beat. Even so, the following uses for the spray may surprise you:

✳ Adding an avocado half to your taco salad? Keep the other half looking fresh by lightly spraying the exposed flesh with cooking spray. Wrap the leftover avocado in foil and refrigerate.

✳ For fast and easy flipping, spray both sides of a spatula with cooking spray when making pancakes or egg dishes.

✳ Give kitchen scissors a spritz when you cut dried fruit or marshmallows.

✳ Lightly spray your colander or strainer with nonstick cooking spray before draining pasta or potatoes.

italian sausage lasagna

basil-pork and asian noodles

basil-pork and asian noodles

READY TO SERVE: 25 MINUTES
SERVINGS: 4

✻ super fast

8 oz. uncooked capellini (angel hair) pasta

2 teaspoons sesame oil

1 tablespoon sesame seeds

1 lb. pork tenderloin, halved lengthwise, thinly sliced

1 medium onion, cut into thin wedges

1/2 cup stir-fry sauce

2 tablespoons honey

2 cups frozen sugar snap peas (from 1-lb. bag)

1/4 cup sliced fresh basil

Toasted sesame seeds

1. Cook pasta as directed on package. Drain; return to saucepan. Add sesame oil; toss to coat. Cover to keep warm.

2. Meanwhile, heat 10-inch nonstick skillet over medium-high heat until hot. Add sesame seeds; cook and stir 2 to 3 minutes or until golden brown. (Watch carefully to prevent burning.) Remove from skillet.

3. In same skillet, cook pork and onion over medium-high heat for 3 to 4 minutes or until no longer pink, stirring frequently.

4. Add stir-fry sauce, honey and sugar snap peas; mix well. Reduce heat to medium; cook 3 to 4 minutes or until peas are crisp-tender, stirring occasionally. Add basil; cook and stir 1 minute. Serve pork mixture over cooked pasta. Sprinkle with toasted sesame seeds.

Nutrition Information Per Serving: Calories 500 • Total Fat 9g • Saturated Fat 2g • Cholesterol 70mg • Sodium 1660mg • Total Carbohydrate 67g • Dietary Fiber 5g • Sugars 18g • Protein 38g. Dietary Exchanges: 4 Starch • 1 Vegetable • 3½ Lean Meat.

saucy manicotti

PREP TIME: 40 MINUTES
READY TO SERVE: 1 HOUR 20 MINUTES
SERVINGS: 8

✻ plan ahead

manicotti
8 uncooked manicotti
filling
1/2 lb. bulk mild Italian sausage

1/2 cup chopped onion

1 can (4-oz.) mushroom pieces and stems, drained

1½ cups finely chopped cooked turkey or chicken

2 egg yolks

1 pkg. (9-oz.) frozen spinach in a pouch, thawed, squeezed to drain

4 oz. shredded mozzarella cheese (1 cup)

1/2 cup grated Parmesan cheese

1 jar (14-oz.) spaghetti sauce
white sauce
2 tablespoons margarine or butter

2 tablespoons all-purpose flour

1½ cups whipping cream

1/3 cup grated Parmesan cheese

Dash garlic powder

Dash nutmeg

1. Cook manicotti to desired doneness as directed on package. Drain; place in cold water.

2. Meanwhile, heat oven to 350°F. In large skillet, brown sausage, onion and mushrooms. Remove from skillet; drain on paper towels. In large bowl, combine sausage mixture, turkey, egg yolks, spinach, mozzarella and ½ cup Parmesan cheese; mix well.

3. Drain manicotti; fill each with sausage mixture. Pour ½ the spaghetti sauce into ungreased 13x9-inch (3-quart) baking dish. Place filled manicotti side by side over sauce in dish.

4. Melt margarine in medium saucepan over medium heat. Stir in flour; cook until smooth and bubbly, stirring constantly. Gradually stir in cream; cook until slightly thickened, stirring constantly. Stir in 1/3 cup Parmesan cheese, garlic powder and nutmeg; blend well. Pour white sauce over manicotti in baking dish. Pour remaining spaghetti sauce over top.

5. Bake at 350°F for 35 to 40 minutes or until bubbly.

Nutrition Information Per Serving: Calories 490 • Total Fat 33g • Saturated Fat 17g • Cholesterol 170mg • Sodium 880mg • Total Carbohydrate 23g • Dietary Fiber 2g • Sugars 3g • Protein 26g. Dietary Exchanges: 1½ Starch • 3 Lean Meat • 4½ Fat OR 1½ Carbohydrate • 3 Lean Meat • 4½ Fat.

MAKE-AHEAD CONVENIENCE

For a stress-free, weeknight dinner that can't be beat, prepare Saucy Manicotti ahead of time and clear your schedule of kitchen duty later in the week. Simply prepare the recipe as directed, but do not bake the casserole. Instead, cover it with foil and freeze. When ready to use the main course, you don't even have to thaw it. Just bake it, covered, at 350°F for 1 hour 25 minutes. Uncover and bake 15 minutes longer or until it's heated through.

garlic and basil pork and pasta

READY TO SERVE: 30 MINUTES
SERVINGS: 4

4 oz. uncooked linguine, broken in half

2 medium zucchini (6- to 8-inches long)

$\frac{1}{2}$ lb. ground pork

2 garlic cloves, minced

1 tablespoon oil

2 medium tomatoes, seeded, coarsely chopped

3 tablespoons chopped fresh basil

$\frac{1}{2}$ teaspoon salt

$\frac{1}{8}$ teaspoon pepper

$\frac{1}{4}$ cup grated Parmesan cheese

1. Cook linguine to desired doneness as directed on package.

2. Meanwhile, cut zucchini lengthwise into $\frac{1}{4}$-inch-thick slices. Cut each slice lengthwise into long $\frac{1}{4}$-inch-thick strips. Set aside.

3. Heat large skillet or wok over medium-high heat until hot. Add pork and 1 of the minced garlic cloves; cook and stir until pork is no longer pink, gently breaking pork into large bite-sized pieces. Remove from skillet; drain.

4. In same skillet, heat oil until hot. Add zucchini and remaining minced garlic clove; cook and stir 5 to 7 minutes or until zucchini is tender.

5. Drain linguine; cover to keep warm.

6. To zucchini in skillet, add tomatoes, basil, salt and pepper; cook and stir until tomatoes are thoroughly heated. Add cooked linguine and pork; cook and stir until thoroughly heated. Sprinkle with cheese.

Nutrition Information Per Serving: Calories 310 • Total Fat 14g • Saturated Fat 5g • Cholesterol 40mg • Sodium 420mg • Total Carbohydrate 28g • Dietary Fiber 3g • Sugars 4g • Protein 18g. Dietary Exchanges: 1$\frac{1}{2}$ Starch • 1 Vegetable • 2 Lean Meat • 1$\frac{1}{2}$ Fat OR 1$\frac{1}{2}$ Carbohydrate • 1 Vegetable • 2 Lean Meat • 1$\frac{1}{2}$ Fat.

caesar tortellini with ham

READY TO SERVE: 20 MINUTES
SERVINGS: 4

* super fast

1 package (9-oz.) refrigerated cheese-filled tortellini

1$\frac{1}{2}$ cups frozen broccoli florets (from 14-oz. bag)

1$\frac{1}{2}$ cups cubed cooked ham

$\frac{2}{3}$ cup creamy Caesar salad dressing

3 cups shredded romaine lettuce (from 10-oz. bag)

2 tablespoons shredded Parmesan cheese

1. In 3-quart saucepan, bring 2 quarts (8 cups) water to a boil. Add tortellini and broccoli; cook as directed on tortellini package until tortellini are tender. Drain; return to saucepan.

2. Add ham and salad dressing; stir gently to mix. Cook over medium-low heat just until thoroughly heated, stirring occasionally.

3. Arrange lettuce on individual plates. Spoon tortellini mixture over lettuce. Sprinkle with cheese.

Nutrition Information Per Serving: Calories 375 • Total Fat 25g • Saturated Fat 7g • Cholesterol 100mg • Sodium 1250mg • Total Carbohydrate 17g • Dietary Fiber 3g • Sugars 3g • Protein 21g. Dietary Exchanges: 1 Starch • 1 Vegetable • 2$\frac{1}{2}$ Lean Meat • 3$\frac{1}{2}$ Fat.

spiced apple pork chops

READY TO SERVE: 20 MINUTES
SERVINGS: 4

* super fast

4 boneless pork loin chops ($\frac{3}{4}$-inch thick and 1-lb. each)

$\frac{1}{2}$ teaspoon pumpkin pie spice

$\frac{1}{4}$ teaspoon salt

$\frac{1}{8}$ teaspoon pepper

1 tablespoon apple or crabapple jelly, melted

1. Set oven control to broil. Line broiler pan without rack with foil; spray foil with cooking spray. Sprinkle both sides of pork chops with pumpkin pie spice, salt and pepper; place in pan.

2. Broil 4 to 6 inches from heat 7 to 10 minutes, turning once, until pork is no longer pink and thermometer inserted in center of pork reads 160°F. Brush pork with melted jelly; broil 30 to 60 seconds longer to glaze.

Nutrition Information Per Serving: Calories 190 • Total Fat 9g • Saturated Fat 3g • Trans Fat 0g • Cholesterol 70mg • Sodium 190mg • Total Carbohydrate 3g • Dietary Fiber 0g • Sugars 2g • Protein 24g. Dietary Exchange: 3$\frac{1}{2}$ Lean Meat.

barbecued pork tenderloin

READY TO SERVE: 30 MINUTES
SERVINGS: 4

¼ cup ketchup

¼ cup chili sauce

1 tablespoon brown sugar

2 tablespoons finely chopped
onion

⅛ teaspoon celery seed

Dash garlic powder

1½ teaspoons cider vinegar

1½ teaspoons Worcestershire
sauce

1 teaspoon prepared mustard

⅛ teaspoon Liquid Smoke

2 pork tenderloins
(½-lb. each)

1. In small saucepan, combine all ingredients except pork; mix well. Bring to a boil. Reduce heat; simmer 5 minutes. Cool slightly.

2. Heat grill. Cut each pork tenderloin in half lengthwise, cutting to but not through bottom; open and flatten.

3. When ready to grill, place flattened pork on gas grill over medium-high heat or on charcoal grill 4 to 6 inches from medium-high coals. Spoon half of sauce over pork; cook 5 to 7 minutes. Turn pork; spoon remaining sauce over pork. Cook an additional 5 to 7 minutes or until pork is no longer pink in center.

Nutrition Information Per Serving: Calories 180 • Total Fat 4g • Saturated Fat 1g • Cholesterol 65mg • Sodium 520mg • Total Carbohydrate 13g • Dietary Fiber 0g • Sugars 9g • Protein 24g. Dietary Exchanges: ½ Fruit • 3 Lean Meat OR ½ Carbohydrate • 3 Lean Meat.

chicken fried pork chops

READY TO SERVE: 25 MINUTES
SERVINGS: 4

* super fast

- 4 boneless pork loin chops (4-oz. each)
- ¼ cup all-purpose flour
- ½ teaspoon seasoned salt
- ¼ teaspoon garlic powder
- 2 to 3 tablespoons milk
- ½ cup Italian-style dry bread crumbs
- 2 tablespoons vegetable oil

1. To flatten each pork chop, place pork between 2 pieces of plastic wrap or waxed paper. Working from center, gently pound pork with flat side of meat mallet or rolling pin until about ¼ inch thick; remove wrap.

2. In shallow bowl, combine flour, seasoned salt and garlic powder; mix well. Place milk and bread crumbs in separate shallow bowls. Dip each pork chop in flour mixture; dip in milk. Coat well with bread crumbs.

3. Heat oil in 10-inch skillet over medium heat until hot. Add pork chops; cook 6 to 8 minutes or until slightly pink in center.

Nutrition Information Per Serving: Calories 300 • Total Fat 15g • Saturated Fat 4g • Cholesterol 60mg • Sodium 450mg • Total Carbohydrate 17g • Dietary Fiber 1g • Sugars 1g • Protein 24g. Dietary Exchanges: 1 Starch • 3 Very Lean Meat • 2½ Fat.

QUICK CLEANUP

It's easy to cut back on cleanup when it comes to the Chicken Fried Pork Chops, just use resealable storage bags. Leave the milk in a bowl, but combine the flour, seasoned salt and garlic powder in one bag and the bread crumbs in another. Shake the pork chops in each bag to coat as directed in the recipe. When done, you can toss the bags in the garbage, and you'll only have to wash out the milk bowl and the skillet you used to cook the pork.

easy italian sausage-vegetable soup

PREP TIME: 15 MINUTES
READY TO SERVE: 9 HOURS 45 MINUTES
SERVINGS: 7

* slow cooked

- ½ lb. bulk Italian pork sausage
- 1 cup sliced fresh carrots
- 1 large baking potato, peeled, cut into ½-inch cubes
- 1 garlic clove
- 2 cans (14½-oz. each) ready-to-serve beef broth
- 1 can (15-oz.) garbanzo beans drained
- 1½ cups waters
- ½ teaspoon dried Italian seasoning
- 1 bay leaf
- 1 cup julienne-cut (2x⅛x⅛-inch) zucchini
- Grated fresh Parmesan cheese

1. Brown sausage in a large skillet. Drain. In a 3½- to 4-quart slow cooker, combine cooked sausage and all remaining ingredients except zucchini and cheese; stir gently to mix.

2. Cover; cook on Low setting for 7 to 9 hours.

3. Remove and discard bay leaf. Gently stir in zucchini. Cover; cook on Low setting for an additional 30 minutes or until zucchini is tender.

4. To serve, ladle soup into bowls; sprinkle with cheese.

Nutrition Information Per Serving: Calories 220 • Total Fat 9g • Saturated Fat 3g • Cholesterol 20mg • Sodium 910mg • Total Carbohydrate 22g • Dietary Fiber 5g • Sugars 3g • Protein 12g. Dietary Exchanges: 1½ Starch • 1 High-Fat Meat OR 1½ Carbohydrate • 1 High Fat Meat.

honey-dijon pork roast

PREP TIME: 20 MINUTES
READY TO SERVE: 8 HOURS 20 MINUTES
SERVINGS: 8

* slow cooked

½ cup chopped onion

2 apples, peeled, sliced

1 tablespoon honey

1 tablespoon Dijon mustard

½ teaspoon coriander seed, crushed

¼ teaspoon salt

2- to 2½-lb. rolled boneless pork loin roast

2 tablespoons water

1 tablespoon cornstarch

1. In 4- to 6-quart slow cooker, combine onion and apples. In small bowl, combine honey, mustard, coriander and salt; mix well. Spread on all sides of pork roast. Place pork over onion and apples.

2. Cover; cook on Low setting for 7 to 8 hours.

3. Remove pork from slow cooker; place on serving platter. Cover with foil.

4. In small saucepan, blend water and cornstarch until smooth. Add apple mixture and juices from slow cooker; mix well. Cook over medium heat until mixture boils, stirring occasionally. Cut pork into slices. Serve pork with sauce.

Nutrition Information Per Serving: Calories 250 • Total Fat 10g • Saturated Fat 4g • Cholesterol 85mg • Sodium 180mg • Total Carbohydrate 9g • Dietary Fiber 1g • Sugars 6g • Protein 31g. **Dietary** Exchanges: ½ Starch • 4 Lean Meat OR ½ Carbohydrate • 4 Lean Meat.

ham and cheese potato bake

PREP TIME: 20 MINUTES
READY TO SERVE: 40 MINUTES
SERVINGS: 8

1½ cups skim milk

¼ cup all-purpose flour

½ teaspoon salt

¼ teaspoon pepper

8 cups frozen potatoes O'Brien with onions and peppers (from two 24-oz. pkgs.), thawed, patted dry with paper towels

1½ cups chopped 97% fat-free cooked ham (about 8 oz.)

1 cup nonfat sour cream

6 oz. shredded reduced-fat Colby cheese (1½ cups)

1. Heat oven to 400°F. Spray 13x9-inch (3-quart) baking dish with nonstick cooking spray.

2. In medium saucepan, combine milk, flour, salt and pepper; blend well. Cook and stir over medium-high heat until bubbly and thickened.

3. In large bowl, combine potatoes, ham, sour cream, cooked sauce and 1 cup of the cheese; mix well. Spoon potato mixture into sprayed baking dish. Sprinkle top with remaining ½ cup cheese.

4. Bake at 400°F for 15 to 20 minutes or until casserole is bubbly and cheese is melted. Let stand 5 minutes before serving.

Nutrition Information Per Serving: Calories 230 • Total Fat 6g • Saturated Fat 3g • Cholesterol 30mg • Sodium 670mg • Total Carbohydrate 28g • Dietary Fiber 2g • Sugars 6g • Protein 16g. **Dietary Exchanges:** 2 Starch • 1½ Lean Meat OR 2 Carbohydrate • 1½ Lean Meat.

honey-maple pork chops

READY TO SERVE: 20 MINUTES
SERVINGS: 4

* super fast

2 tablespoons honey

2 tablespoons microwave-ready maple-flavored syrup

⅛ teaspoon allspice

4 pork loin chops (6-oz. each) (¾-inch thick)

¼ teaspoon salt

⅛ teaspoon pepper

1. Heat grill. In small bowl, combine honey, syrup and allspice; mix well. Sprinkle pork chops with salt and pepper.

2. When ready to grill, brush pork chops with honey mixture. Place chops on gas grill over medium heat or on charcoal grill 4 to 6 inches from medium coals. Cook 8 to 10 minutes or until pork is no longer pink in center, turning once and brushing occasionally with sauce.

Nutrition Information Per Serving: Calories 200 • Total Fat 9g • Saturated Fat 3g • Cholesterol 75mg • Sodium 190mg • Total Carbohydrate 4g • Dietary Fiber 0g • Sugars 3g • Protein 26g. **Dietary** Exchange: 3½ Lean Meat.

saucy medallions with spiced couscous

SERVINGS: 4

SUSAN RUNKLE ✳ WALTON, KENTUCKY

1 lb. pork tenderloins, cut into ½-inch-thick slices

1 teaspoon salt

½ teaspoon pepper

2 tablespoons butter

1 teaspoon minced gingerroot

1 teaspoon minced garlic

1 tablespoon cornstarch

1 cup apple juice

¼ cup water

2 tablespoons balsamic vinegar

2 jars (4.5-oz. each) sliced mushrooms, undrained

COUSCOUS

2 cups water

½ teaspoon salt

1¼ cups uncooked couscous

1 cup frozen gold and white super sweet corn (from 1-lb. pkg.)

½ medium red bell pepper, chopped

3 green onions, chopped

½ teaspoon Chinese five-spice powder

1. To flatten each pork slice, place pork between two pieces of plastic wrap or waxed paper. Working from center, gently pound pork with flat side of meat mallet or rolling pin until about ¼-inch thick; remove wrap. Sprinkle pork with 1 teaspoon salt and pepper.

2. Melt butter in 12-inch skillet over medium-high heat. Add pork; cook 8 minutes or until browned on both sides, turning once. Remove pork from skillet. Add gingerroot and garlic to skillet; cook and stir 1 minute or until tender. Remove from heat.

3. In medium bowl, combine cornstarch apple juice, ¼ cup water and vinegar; blend well. Add to mixture in skillet. Bring to a boil. Reduce heat to medium-low. Add mushrooms with liquid and pork; cook 10 minutes or until sauce is of desired consistency, stirring occasionally.

4. Meanwhile, in medium saucepan, combine 2 cups water and ½ teaspoon salt. Bring to a boil. Stir in couscous, corn, bell pepper, onions and five-spice powder; mix well. Remove from heat. Cover; let stand 5 minutes. Serve couscous with pork mixture.

Nutrition Information Per Serving: Calories 480 • Total Fat 11g • Sodium 1260mg • Total Carbohydrate 65g • Protein 35g.

EFFORTLESS MENU ADDITIONS

Saucy Medallions with Spiced Couscous is a hearty meal-in-one that comes together easily on the stovetop. If you'd like to jazz up your menu a bit, consider steaming some broccoli or carrots to serve alongside the main course. You could also stir-fry a few stalks of asparagus in butter and garlic or microwave some frozen brussels sprouts for a truly memorable dinner. Pick up a can of refrigerated French bread to help you round out the supper.

---

oven-roasted pork 'n vegetables

PREP TIME: 20 MINUTES
READY TO SERVE: 1 HOUR
SERVINGS: 8

2 to 3 pork tenderloins (about 1½ lb. each)

16 to 20 new potatoes (about 2 lb.), cut in half

6 to 8 carrots (about 1 lb.) peeled, cut into 2-inch pieces

1 medium onion, cut into wedges

1 tablespoon olive oil

2 tablespoons dried rosemary leaves, crushed

1 teaspoon dried sage leaves, crushed

¼ teaspoon pepper

1. Heat oven to 450°F. Generously spray roasting pan with nonstick cooking spray. Place pork tenderloins in sprayed pan. Insert meat thermometer into thickest part of 1 tenderloin.

2. Place potatoes, carrots and onion around tenderloins. Drizzle oil evenly over tenderloins and vegetables. Sprinkle with rosemary, sage and pepper.

3. Bake at 450°F for 30 to 40 minutes or until meat thermometer reaches 165°F and vegetables are tender, stirring vegetables occasionally.

Nutrition Information Per Serving: Calories 270 • Total Fat 5g • Saturated Fat 1g • Cholesterol 50mg • Sodium 65mg • Total Carbohydrate 36g • Dietary Fiber 5g • Sugars 5g • Protein 21g. Dietary Exchanges: 2 Starch • 1 Vegetable • 2 Lean Meat OR 2 Carbohydrate • 1 Vegetable • 2 Lean Meat.

saucy medallions with spiced couscous

individual pepperoni pizzas

individual pepperoni pizzas

READY TO SERVE: 20 MINUTES
SERVINGS: 4

* super fast

- 4 flour tortillas (8-inch)
- 2 teaspoons olive oil
- 1½ cups finely shredded Cheddar and Monterey Jack cheese blend (6 oz.)
- ½ cup sliced pimiento-stuffed green olives
- ½ cup diced tomato, well drained
- 24 slices pepperoni
- 1 teaspoon dried oregano leaves

1. Heat gas or charcoal grill. Place tortillas on ungreased cookie sheets. Brush with oil. Sprinkle with 1 cup of the cheese. Top evenly with olives, tomato and pepperoni. Sprinkle with remaining cheese and oregano.

2. When grill is heated, with broad spatula, carefully slide pizzas onto gas grill over medium heat or onto charcoal grill 4 to 6 inches from medium coals. Cook covered 3 to 6 minutes or until cheese is melted and crust is crisp. To remove from grill, slide pizzas back onto cookie sheets.

Nutrition Information Per Serving: Calories 515 • Total Fat 36g • Saturated Fat 15g • Cholesterol 70mg • Sodium 1590mg • Total Carbohydrate 27g • Dietary Fiber 1g • Sugars 3g • Protein 21g. Dietary Exchanges: 2 Starch • 2 High-Fat Meat • 4 Fat.

zesty skillet pork chops

READY TO SERVE: 20 MINUTES
SERVINGS: 4

* super fast

- 4 boneless pork loin chops (1¼ lb. each and ¾-inch thick)
- ½ teaspoon garlic-pepper blend
- ¼ teaspoon salt
- ¾ cup barbecue sauce
- ½ cup chunky-style salsa

1. Heat 10-inch nonstick skillet over medium-high heat until hot. Sprinkle both sides of pork chops with garlic-pepper blend and salt; add to hot skillet. Cook 2 to 3 minutes or until brown on both sides.

2. Add barbecue sauce and salsa; turn to coat chops. Reduce heat to low; cover and simmer 10 to 15 minutes or until chops are slightly pink in center, turning chops and stirring sauce once or twice. Serve pork chops with sauce.

Nutrition Information Per Serving: Calories 295 • Total Fat 11g • Saturated Fat 4g • Cholesterol 85mg • Sodium 810mg • Total Carbohydrate 19g • Dietary Fiber 1g • Sugars 14g • Protein 31g. Dietary Exchanges: 1 Starch • 4 Lean Meat.

saucy bean 'n bacon bake

SERVINGS: 8

JOY ANN KIDDER ***** GAINESVILLE, FLORIDA

- ½ lb. bacon, cut into ¾-inch pieces
- 3 cans (15.5-oz. each) butter beans, drained
- 1 jar (2-oz.) sliced pimiento, drained
- 1 cup chopped green onions
- ¾ cup dairy sour cream
- ⅓ cup firmly packed brown sugar
- 1 to 2 teaspoons dry mustard
- 1 teaspoon garlic powder
- ⅛ teaspoon ground red pepper (cayenne)
- 2 tablespoons chopped green onion tops

1. Heat oven to 350°F. Cook bacon in large skillet until crisp; drain. Set aside. In large bowl, combine all remaining ingredients except green onion tops; mix well. Pour into ungreased 8-inch square (1½-quart) baking dish or 2-quart casserole.

2. Bake uncovered at 350°F for 25 minutes. Sprinkle with cooked bacon and 2 tablespoons green onion tops; bake an additional 10 to 15 minutes or until thoroughly heated.

Nutrition Information Per Serving: Calories 220 • Total Fat 9g • Sodium 43mg • Total Carbohydrate 29g • Protein 10g.

HOT DISH IS LOADED WITH VERSATILITY

The bean-bacon bake is a fast and simple dinner when you don't have a second to spare. Keep it in mind when you need a quick side dish, too. It's terrific when paired with grilled foods, and makes even sandwich dinners seem extra special. It's a welcomed addition to potluck buffets as well.

honey-orange glazed pork chops

READY TO SERVE: 25 MINUTES
SERVINGS: 4

* super fast

- 4 boneless pork loin chops, ³⁄₄-inch thick each (1 lb.)
- 3 tablespoons Worcestershire sauce
- ¹⁄₃ cup honey
- 1 tablespoon grated orange peel
- ¹⁄₄ teaspoon salt

1. In shallow glass baking dish, place pork chops. Brush 1 tablespoon Worcestershire sauce over both sides of each. Let stand at room temperature 15 minutes to marinate.

2. Meanwhile, heat gas or charcoal grill. In 2-quart saucepan, mix remaining 2 tablespoons Worcestershire sauce, the honey, orange peel and salt until well blended. Heat to boiling over high heat. Reduce heat to medium; boil 1 minute.

3. When grill is heated, place pork on gas grill over medium-high heat or on charcoal grill over medium-high coals. Spoon half of honey mixture evenly over pork. Cook uncovered 5 minutes. Turn pork; spoon remaining honey mixture over pork. Cook uncovered 3 to 5 minutes longer or until pork is slightly pink in center and thermometer inserted in center of pork reads 160°F.

Nutrition Information Per Serving: Calories 280 • Total Fat 9g • Saturated Fat 3g • Trans Fat 0g • Cholesterol 70mg • Sodium 320mg • Total Carbohydrate 26g • Dietary Fiber 0g • Sugars 25g • Protein 24g. Dietary Exchanges: 1¹⁄₂ Other Carbohydrate • 3¹⁄₂ Lean Meat.

luau pork stir-fry

SERVINGS: 4

SALLY SIBTHORPE ✳ ROCHESTER HILLS, MICHIGAN

- 1 tablespoon olive oil
- ¹⁄₂ lb. pork tenderloin, cut into thin, bite-sized strips
- ¹⁄₂ cup coconut milk (from 14-oz. can)
- ¹⁄₄ cup crushed pineapple
- 2 teaspoons lime juice
- 1 package (1-lb.) frozen stir-fry vegetables and traditional teriyaki sauce meal starter
- ¹⁄₄ cup chopped macadamia nuts
- ¹⁄₄ cup coconut
- 4 cups hot cooked rice

1. Heat oil in large skillet or wok over medium-high heat until hot. Add pork strips; cook and stir 5 to 6 minutes or until browned.

2. Add coconut milk, pineapple and lime juice; mix well. Reduce heat to low; simmer 3 minutes, stirring occasionally.

3. Add frozen sauce and vegetables from meal starter; mix well. Cook 7 to 10 minutes or until vegetables are crisp-tender, stirring frequently. Stir in nuts and coconut. Serve over rice.

Nutrition Information Per Serving: Calories 540 • Total Fat 21g • Sodium 680mg • Total Carbohydrate 65g • Protein 22g.

BAKED GOODS MAKE USE OF EXTRAS

Not sure what to do with the leftover coconut milk from the pork stir-fry? Add the refrigerated leftovers to smoothies the following morning. The tangy taste of coconut is sure be a eye-opener for your gang. Or, use the milk to replace some of the liquid called for in your favorite cake or other baked goods. If you plan on baking cookies in the next day or two, add the milk to the recipe and toss in some of the extra macadamia nuts and coconut, too.

honey-orange glazed pork chops

braised pork chops in sour cream sauce

READY TO SERVE: 30 MINUTES
SERVINGS: 6

6 boneless pork loin chops
  (4-oz. each)
¼ teaspoon salt
⅛ teaspoon pepper
¾ cup beef broth
1 tablespoon barbecue sauce
⅓ cup evaporated skim milk
⅓ cup nonfat sour cream
3 tablespoons all-purpose flour

1. Sprinkle pork chops with salt and pepper. Spray large nonstick skillet with nonstick cooking spray. Heat over medium-high heat until hot. Add pork chops; cover and cook 4 to 6 minutes or until golden brown, turning once.

2. In small bowl, mix ½ cup of the broth and the barbecue sauce. Pour over pork chops; cover tightly. Reduce heat to medium-low; simmer 5 to 10 minutes or until pork is no longer pink in center. Remove pork chops from skillet; cover.

3. In same small bowl, combine remaining ¼ cup broth, milk, sour cream and flour; beat until smooth. Pour into same skillet; cook and stir over medium heat for 2 to 3 minutes or until bubbly and thickened. Serve sauce over pork chops.

Nutrition Information Per Serving: Calories 200 • Total Fat 8g • Saturated Fat 3g • Cholesterol 70mg • Sodium 300mg • Total Carbohydrate 6g • Dietary Fiber 0g • Sugars 3g • Protein 27g. **Dietary Exchanges:** ½ Starch • 3½ Lean Meat OR ½ Carbohydrate • 3½ Lean Meat.

tomato-bean stew

PREP TIME: 15 MINUTES
READY TO SERVE: 12 HOURS 45 MINUTES
SERVINGS: 6

* slow cooked

4 slices bacon

8 oz. dried bean blend (1¼ cups)

½ cup sliced celery

½ cup chopped onion

3 cups water

1 can (15¼-oz.) whole kernel corn, undrained

1 package (1¼-oz.) taco seasoning mix

1 can (28-oz.) whole tomatoes, undrained, cut up

2 teaspoons sugar

1. Cook bacon until crisp. Drain on paper towels; crumble. Sort bean blend. Rinse well; drain.

2. In a 3½- to 4-quart slow cooker, combine cooked bacon, bean blend and all remaining ingredients except tomatoes and sugar; mix well.

3. Cover; cook on Low setting for 10 to 12 hours or until beans are tender.

4. Add tomatoes and sugar; mix well. Cover; cook on Low setting for an additional 30 minutes or until thoroughly heated.

Nutrition Information Per Serving: Calories 250 • Total Fat 2g • Saturated Fat 1g • Cholesterol 4mg • Sodium 1140mg • Total Carbohydrate 47g • Dietary Fiber 15g • Sugars 10g • Protein 12g. **Dietary Exchanges:** 3 Starch • ½ Very Lean Meat OR 3 Carbohydrate • ½ Very Lean Meat.

pizza pork chops

PREP TIME: 15 MINUTES
READY TO SERVE: 6 HOURS 15 MINUTES
SERVINGS: 6

* slow cooked

6 pork loin chops (6-oz. each and about 1-inch thick)

½ teaspoon salt

¼ teaspoon pepper

1 tablespoon oil

½ cup chopped onion

2 cups tomato pasta sauce

4 oz. shredded mozzarella cheese (1 cup)

1. Sprinkle pork chops with salt and pepper. Heat oil in 12-inch skillet over medium-high heat until hot. Add pork; cook about 5 minutes or until browned, turning once.

2. Place pork in 3½- to 6-quart slow cooker. Sprinkle onion over pork. Pour pasta sauce over top.

3. Cover; cook on Low setting for 4 to 6 hours.

4. Remove pork from slow cooker; place on serving platter. Top with sauce. Sprinkle with cheese.

Nutrition Information Per Serving: Calories 335 • Total Fat 15g • Saturated Fat 5g • Cholesterol 85mg • Sodium 750mg • Total Carbohydrate 18g • Dietary Fiber 1g • Sugars 7g • Protein 33g. **Dietary Exchanges:** 1 Starch • 4½ Lean Meat OR 4½ Carbohydrate • 4½ Lean Meat.

sweet-and-sour pork

READY TO SERVE: 30 MINUTES
SERVINGS: 4

⅔ cup uncooked regular long-grain white rice

1⅓ cups water

1 lb. pork tenderloin, cut crosswise into thin slices

1 green bell pepper, cut into 1-inch squares

1 can (20-oz.) pineapple chunks in unsweetened juice, drained

½ cup purchased sweet-and-sour sauce

¼ teaspoon ginger

1. Cook rice in water as directed on package.

2. Meanwhile, spray large skillet with nonstick cooking spray. Heat over medium-high heat until hot. Add pork; cook and stir 3 to 5 minutes or until no longer pink in center.

3. Add bell pepper; cook and stir 4 to 6 minutes or until crisp-tender.

4. Stir in pineapple, sweet-and-sour sauce and ginger; cook and stir until thoroughly heated. Serve over rice.

Nutrition Information Per Serving: Calories 320 • Total Fat 4g • Saturated Fat 1g • Cholesterol 65mg • Sodium 150mg • Total Carbohydrate 44g • Dietary Fiber 2g • Sugars 19g • Protein 26g. **Dietary Exchanges:** 2 Starch • 1 Fruit • 2 Lean Meat OR 3 Carbohydrate • 2 Lean Meat.

kielbasa-vegetable kabobs

READY TO SERVE: 25 MINUTES
SERVINGS: 4

* super fast

12 oz. cooked kielbasa, cut into
   1-inch pieces

2 cans (15-oz. each) whole
   potatoes, drained, rinsed
   with cold water

16 cherry tomatoes

16 pieces zucchini, cut into
   1-inch pieces

½ cup honey-mustard
   barbecue sauce

1. Heat gas or charcoal grill. Onto eight 10- to 12-inch metal skewers, alternately thread all ingredients except barbecue sauce. Brush kabobs with barbecue sauce.

2. When grill is heated, place kabobs on gas grill over medium heat or on charcoal grill 4 to 6 inches from medium coals. Cook covered 5 to 8 minutes or until kielbasa is deep golden brown, turning frequently and brushing twice with barbecue sauce. If desired, serve with additional warm barbecue sauce.

Nutrition Information Per Serving: Calories 450 • Total Fat 24g • Saturated Fat 9g • Cholesterol 50mg • Sodium 2090mg • Total Carbohydrate 44g • Dietary Fiber 7g • Sugars 12g • Protein 14g. Dietary Exchanges: 2 Starch • 1 Vegetable • 1 High-Fat Meat • 3½ Fat.

BROIL THE KABOBS INSTEAD

You can broil the kabobs in your oven rather than heating up the gas or charcoal grill if you'd like. Just assemble the skewers as directed, and brush them with the honey-mustard barbecue sauce.

Place the kabobs on a broiler pan. Broil 4 to 6 inches from the heat, using the time noted in the recipe as a general guide. Turn the kabobs frequently, and brush them twice with the sauce.

southwest pork and black bean stir-fry

READY TO SERVE: 30 MINUTES
SERVINGS: 4

1 tablespoon olive or
   vegetable oil

¾ lb. pork tenderloin, cut into
   2x½x¼-inch strips

1 medium onion, cut into thin
   wedges

1 small red pepper, cut into
   strips

2 garlic cloves, minced

2 cups frozen whole kernel
   corn, thawed

1 can (15-oz.) black beans,
   drained, rinsed

1 small zucchini, chopped

½ cup chunky-style salsa

   Salt, if desired

   Pepper, if desired

1. Heat oil in large nonstick skillet over medium-high heat until hot. Add pork, onion, bell pepper and garlic; cook and stir 6 to 8 minutes or until pork is no longer pink and vegetables are crisp-tender.

2. Stir in corn, beans, zucchini and salsa; cover and simmer 5 minutes or until zucchini is crisp-tender and flavors are blended. If desired, season with salt and pepper to taste.

Nutrition Information Per Serving: Calories 310 • Total Fat 7g • Saturated Fat 2g • Cholesterol 50mg • Sodium 480mg • Total Carbohydrate 34g • Dietary Fiber 8g • Sugars 7g • Protein 27g. Dietary Exchanges: 2 Starch • 1 Vegetable • 2½ Lean Meat OR 2 Carbohydrate • 1 Vegetable • 2½ Lean Meat.

WRAP IT UP!

The stir-fry is terrific on its own or served over a bed of rice or noodles for a fast supper-in-one. You can also turn the pork-and-bean dish into something special by wrapping the mixture into warm, flour tortillas and serving sour cream, shredded cheese, extra salsa or prepared guacamole on the side. The wraps also make a hearty lunch the next day, or a handheld meal when you've got to load the kids in the car and eat and run.

ham and vegetable pasta salad

READY TO SERVE: 25 MINUTES
SERVINGS: 4

✳ super fast

dressing

- ¾ cup mayonnaise or salad dressing
- ¼ cup milk
- 2 tablespoons chopped fresh or 1½ teaspoons dried dill
- 2 tablespoons Dijon mustard

salad

- 2 cups uncooked small pasta shells (7 oz.)
- 1 cup diced cooked ham
- 1 small unpeeled cucumber, diced (1 cup)
- 1 small carrot, finely chopped (½ cup)
- ¼ cup chopped red bell pepper
- 4 medium green onions, finely chopped (¼ cup)

MUST-TRY ITEM

If you don't have any cooked ham for the salad, pick up a package of cooked and cubed ham. You'll find the ham cubes alongside packaged ham and sandwich meats at your grocery store. Best of all, you can freeze whatever ham you don't use for future in-a-hurry meals.

1. Cook pasta as directed on package. Drain; rinse with cold water to cool. Drain well.

2. Meanwhile, in large bowl, combine dressing ingredients; blend well.

3. Add cooked pasta and all remaining salad ingredients to dressing; toss to coat. Serve immediately, or cover and refrigerate until serving time.

Nutrition Information Per Serving: Calories 570 • Total Fat 37g • Saturated Fat 6g • Cholesterol 40mg • Sodium 950mg • Total Carbohydrate 43g • Dietary Fiber 2g • Sugars 6g • Protein 15g. Dietary Exchanges: 2½ Starch • 1 Vegetable • 1 Lean Meat • 6½ Fat.

supper ham frittata

READY TO SERVE: 20 MINUTES
SERVINGS: 4

✳ super fast

- 1½ cups frozen southern-style cubed hash-brown potatoes (from 32-oz. bag)
- 1 small zucchini, quartered lengthwise, sliced (1 cup)
- 1½ cups diced cooked ham
- 4 eggs
- ¼ cup milk
- ¼ teaspoon salt
- 1 cup shredded Cheddar cheese (4 oz.)

1. Heat 10-inch nonstick skillet over medium-high heat until hot. Add potatoes, zucchini and ham; cook 5 to 8 minutes or until zucchini is crisp-tender and potatoes are thoroughly cooked, stirring frequently.

2. Meanwhile, in medium bowl, beat eggs. Add milk and salt; beat well.

3. Pour egg mixture over mixture in skillet. Reduce heat to medium-low; cover and cook 5 to 7 minutes or until center is set, lifting edges occasionally to allow uncooked egg mixture to flow to bottom of skillet.

4. Sprinkle frittata with cheese. Cover; cook an additional 2 to 3 minutes or until cheese is melted. To serve, cut into wedges.

Nutrition Information Per Serving: Calories 360 • Total Fat 20g • Saturated Fat 9g • Cholesterol 275mg • Sodium 1170mg • Total Carbohydrate 18g • Dietary Fiber 1g • Sugars 3g • Protein 27g. Dietary Exchanges: 1 Starch • 3½ Medium-Fat Meat • ½ Fat.

pulled-pork burritos

pulled-pork burritos

PREP TIME: 10 MINUTES
READY TO SERVE: 10 HOURS 10 MINUTES
SERVINGS: 9

* slow cooked

1 boneless pork loin roast
  (2- to 2½-lb.)
1 medium onion, thinly sliced
2 cups barbecue sauce
¾ cup chunky-style salsa
3 tablespoons chili powder
3 teaspoons dried Mexican
  seasoning
9 flour tortillas (8- to 10-inch)

1. Place pork roast in 3½- to 6-quart slow cooker. Arrange onion on top. In small bowl, combine all remaining ingredients except tortillas; mix well. Pour over pork.

2. Cover; cook on Low setting for 8 to 10 hours.

3. Remove pork from slow cooker; place on large plate. With 2 forks, pull pork into shreds. Pour sauce from slow cooker into bowl; stir in pork. Spoon pork mixture onto each tortilla; roll up.

Nutrition Information Per Serving: Calories 435 • Total Fat 14g • Saturated Fat 4g • Cholesterol 80mg • Sodium 930mg • Total Carbohydrate 47g • Dietary Fiber 3g • Sugars 17g • Protein 33g. Dietary Exchanges: 2 Starch • 1 Fruit • 4 Lean Meat OR 3 Carbohydrate • 4 Lean Meat.

honey-mustard pork tenderloin

PREP TIME: 15 MINUTES
READY TO SERVE: 50 MINUTES
SERVINGS: 4

1 tablespoon honey
1 tablespoon Dijon mustard
2 teaspoons olive or vegetable
  oil
2 garlic cloves, minced
½ teaspoon dried oregano
  leaves
1 pork tenderloin (¾-lb.)

1. Heat over to 425°F. Line 15x10x1-inch baking pan with foil.

2. In small bowl, combine honey, mustard, oil, garlic and oregano; mix well. Brush pork tenderloin with mixture; place on foil-lined pan.

3. Bake at 425°F for 25 to 30 minutes or until pork is no longer pink in center. Let stand for 5 minutes. Cut diagonally into slices.

Nutrition Information Per Serving: Calories 150 • Total Fat 6g • Saturated Fat 1g • Cholesterol 50mg • Sodium 130mg • Total Carbohydrate 5g • Dietary Fiber 0g • Sugars 4g • Protein 18g. Dietary Exchanges: ½ Fruit • 2 Lean Meat OR ½ Carbohydrate • 2 Lean Meat.

maple-glazed pork chops

READY TO SERVE: 35 MINUTES
SERVINGS: 4

pork chops
4 pork chops (¾-inch thick
  each)
¼ teaspoon salt
¼ teaspoon coarsely ground
  black pepper
maple glaze
¾ cup pure maple syrup or
  maple-flavored syrup
2 tablespoons brown sugar
2 tablespoons ketchup
2 tablespoons prepared
  mustard
1 tablespoon Worcestershire
  sauce

1. Heat grill. Rub both sides of pork chops with salt and pepper. In small saucepan, combine all glaze ingredients; mix well. Bring to a boil, stirring constantly. Set aside.

2. When ready to grill, place pork chops on gas grill over medium heat or on charcoal grill 4 to 6 inches from medium coals. Cook 15 minutes, turning once.

3. Brush pork chops with glaze. Cook an additional 10 minutes or until no longer pink, turning once and brushing frequently with glaze. Bring any remaining glaze to a boil; serve with pork chops.

Nutrition Information Per Serving: Calories 370 • Total Fat 18g • Saturated Fat 4g • Cholesterol 50mg • Sodium 430mg • Total Carbohydrate 45g • Dietary Fiber 0g • Sugars 36g • Protein 20g. Dietary Exchanges: 3½ Fruit • 3 Lean Meat.

taco pork chops

READY TO SERVE: 20 MINUTES
SERVINGS: 4

* super fast

1 package (1.25-oz.) taco
   seasoning mix
2 tablespoons lime juice
1 tablespoon honey
4 boneless pork loin chops (4-
   oz. each and ½-inch thick)
1 ripe medium avocado,
   pitted, peeled and cut up
1 tablespoon chopped fresh
   cilantro, if desired

1. Heat gas or charcoal grill. Reserve 2 teaspoons taco seasoning mix for topping. In small bowl, combine remaining taco seasoning mix, 1 tablespoon of the lime juice and the honey; mix well. Brush mixture on both sides of each pork chop. Discard any remaining mixture.

2. When grill is heated, place pork chops on gas grill over medium heat or on charcoal grill 4 to 6 inches from medium coals. Cook covered 8 to 10 minutes or until pork is slightly pink in center, turning once or twice.

3. Meanwhile, in small bowl, combine avocado, reserved 2 teaspoons taco seasoning mix and remaining 1 tablespoon lime juice; mash with fork until almost smooth.

4. Serve pork chops topped with avocado mixture. Sprinkle with cilantro, if desired.

Nutrition Information Per Serving: Calories 300 • Total Fat 16g • Saturated Fat 4g • Cholesterol 70mg • Sodium 870mg • Total Carbohydrate 14g • Dietary Fiber 3g • Sugars 5g • Protein 26g. Dietary Exchanges: 1 Starch • 3½ Lean Meat • 1 Fat.

mu shu pork

PREP TIME: 30 MINUTES
READY TO SERVE: 1 HOUR
SERVINGS: 4

* plan ahead

½ lb. boneless pork loin chops,
   cut into 1x⅛x⅛-in. strips
1 tablespoon dry sherry
1 teaspoon sugar
1 teaspoon soy sauce
⅓ cup water
1 tablespoon cornstarch
½ teaspoon chicken-flavor
   instant bouillon
1 tablespoon margarine or
   butter
3 eggs, beaten
1 cup thinly sliced Chinese
   (napa) cabbage
½ cup fresh bean sprouts
½ cup chopped fresh
   mushrooms
2 green onions, halved
   lengthwise, cut into
   1-in. pieces
8 teaspoons hoisin sauce
8 flour tortillas (7-in.)

1. In medium bowl, combine pork strips, sherry, sugar and soy sauce; mix well. Refrigerate at least 30 minutes or up to 6 hours.

2. In small bowl, combine water, cornstarch and bouillon; blend well. Set aside.

3. Melt margarine in large skillet or wok over medium-high heat. Add eggs; cook 2 to 3 minutes or until firm, turning once. Remove eggs from skillet; cut into thin strips.

4. Add pork mixture to skillet; cook and stir 2 to 3 minutes or until no longer pink. Add cabbage, bean sprouts and mushrooms; cook and stir 1 minute or until crisp-tender. Add cornstarch mixture to skillet; cook and stir until thickened and bubbly. Add eggs and onions to skillet; stir gently to combine. Remove from heat.

5. Spread 1 teaspoon hoisin sauce on each tortilla. Top each with about ½ cup pork mixture; roll up. Serve immediately.

Nutrition Information Per Serving: Calories 440 • Total Fat 16g • Saturated Fat 4g • Cholesterol 195mg • Sodium 890mg • Total Carbohydrate 51g • Dietary Fiber 3g • Sugars 9g • Protein 24g. Dietary Exchanges: 3 Starch • 1 Vegetable • 2 Lean Meat • 1½ Fat OR 3 Carbohydrate • 1 Vegetable • 2 Lean Meat • 1½ Fat.

STIR-FRY STRATEGIES

When stir-frying the pork for the Mu Shu Pork, you'll find that it will cook more evenly if the visible fat has been trimmed away and the meat is cut into pieces that are uniform in size and shape. It's also best to keep the skillet hot after you cook the eggs and before you add the strips of pork. If the skillet is too small, you'll risk the chance of steaming the meat and veggies. In this event, stir-fry the meat and vegetables in batches.

bean and sausage bake

SERVINGS: 6

MARJORIE FORTIER ✳ WEST REDDING, CONNECTICUT

¾ lb. bulk hot Italian sausage

½ cup coarsely chopped onion

½ cup coarsely chopped green
bell pepper

½ cup coarsely chopped red
bell pepper

1 tablespoon finely minced
garlic cloves

¾ cup ketchup

3 teaspoons chili powder

2 teaspoons dried cilantro
leaves, crushed, or
1 tablespoon chopped
fresh cilantro

¾ teaspoon cumin

1 can (16-oz.) baked beans

1 can (15-oz.) black beans,
drained, rinsed

1 can (15-oz.) garbanzo beans,
drained

1 can (11-oz.) vacuum-packed
whole kernel corn, drained

toppings

4 to 8 oz. shredded Monterey
Jack cheese (1 to 2 cups)

1 to 1½ cups dairy sour cream

Crushed red pepper flakes,
if desired

1. Heat oven to 375°F. In large skillet, brown sausage with onion, bell peppers and garlic over medium-high heat until sausage is cooked and vegetables are crisp-tender; drain. Stir in ketchup, chili powder, cilantro and cumin; mix well. In 13x9-inch (3-quart) baking dish, combine baked beans, black beans, garbanzo beans and corn; mix well. Spoon sausage mixture over beans. Do not stir.

2. Bake at 375°F for 25 to 30 minutes or until bubbly and thoroughly heated. Remove from oven; stir well. Serve with cheese, sour cream and crushed red pepper flakes.

Nutrition Information Per Serving: Calories 470 • Total Fat 25g • Sodium 1080mg • Total Carbohydrate 46g • Protein 22g.

spinach-prosciutto-roasted pepper calzone

SERVINGS: 6

JEN RILEY ✳ WEST ROXBURY, MASSACHUSETTS

2 cans (8-oz. each) refrigerated
crescent dinner rolls

1 package (9-oz.) frozen
spinach in a pouch, thawed,
squeezed to drain

8 oz. thinly sliced provolone
cheese

2 large red bell peppers,
roasted, quartered, or 1 jar
(12-oz.) roasted red bell
peppers, drained, quartered

4 oz. thinly sliced prosciutto

2 tablespoons purchased pesto

1 egg yolk

1 tablespoon water

1. Heat oven to 350°F. Grease large cookie sheet. Unroll both cans of dough into 2 long rectangles. Place dough rectangles with long sides together on greased cookie sheet, forming 15x10-inch rectangle. Press edges and perforations to seal.

2. Place spinach lengthwise in 4-inch-wide strip down center of dough to within ½ inch of each end. Top with half of the cheese, the roasted peppers and prosciutto. Spread pesto over prosciutto. Top with remaining cheese. Bring long sides of dough up over filling, overlapping 1 inch; press edges and ends to seal.

3. In small bowl, combine egg yolk and water; beat well. Brush over top of dough. Bake at 350°F for 25 to 35 minutes or until golden brown. Cut into crosswise slices.

Nutrition Information Per Serving: Calories 520 • Total Fat 34g • Sodium 1630mg • Total Carbohydrate 34g • Protein 20g.

bow tie pasta and peas

bow tie pasta and peas

READY TO SERVE: 40 MINUTES
SERVINGS: 4

3 cups uncooked bow tie pasta (6 ounces)
1½ cups frozen baby sweet peas
1 cup prepared Alfredo sauce
½ cup real bacon pieces

1. Fill large saucepan (4-quarts) about half full with water. Heat the water over medium-high heat until boiling.

2. Add pasta to water and return to boil. Cook 6 minutes.

3. Add the peas to the boiling water; return to boil. Boil the pasta and peas for 4 minutes, stirring occasionally; drain. Return the pasta and peas to the saucepan.

4. Stir the Alfredo sauce and bacon pieces into the pasta.

5. Heat the pasta mixture over low heat, stirring occasionally, until heated throughout.

Nutrition Information Per Serving: Calories 450 • Total Fat 25g • Sodium 460mg • Total Carbohydrate 44g • Sugars 5g • Protein 16g. Dietary Exchanges: 1 Vegetable • 1 High-Fat Meat • 3 Fat.

pork cutlets with southwestern sauce

READY TO SERVE: 40 MINUTES
SERVINGS: 4

1 cup uncooked regular long-grain rice
2 cups water
1 lb. pork cutlets
1 tablespoon oil
1 can (14.5- or 16-oz.) whole tomatoes, undrained, cut up
1 can (8-oz.) tomato sauce
1 can (4.5-oz.) chopped green chiles
½ teaspoon salt
¼ teaspoon onion powder
¼ teaspoon cumin
¼ cup raisins
1 package (1-lb.) frozen mixed vegetables

1. Cook rice in water as directed on package.

2. Meanwhile, if necessary, cut pork into 4 serving-sized pieces. Heat oil in large skillet over medium-high heat until hot. Add pork; cook until lightly browned on both sides.

3. Reduce heat to medium. Stir in tomatoes, tomato sauce, chiles, salt, onion powder and cumin; cook 5 minutes.

4. Add raisins and frozen vegetables. Bring to a boil. Reduce heat to low; cover and simmer 15 to 20 minutes or until vegetables and pork are tender; stirring occasionally. Serve over rice.

Nutrition Information Per Serving: Calories 580 • Total Fat 16g • Saturated Fat 5g • Cholesterol 80mg • Sodium 1370mg • Total Carbohydrate 76g • Dietary Fiber 7g • Sugars 13g • Protein 32g. Dietary Exchanges: 4 Starch • 3 Vegetable • 2½ Medium-Fat Meat.

BUILD A MEMORABLE MEAL

For a one-dish wonder, give these tangy pork cutlets and long-grain rice a try. And if you want to round out the meal, consider adding one of these appealing partners to your supper-time lineup:

* Cornbread or cornbread twists

* Spinach salad with fresh tomatoes and bits of cooked bacon

* Sticks of Cheddar or Colby-Jack cheese

* Refried beans

* Steamed cauliflower

* Applesauce or a cup of mixed fruit

* Frosted glasses of lemonade or limeade

* Wedges of watermelon, cantaloupe, honeydew melon or pineapple

* Tapioca or vanilla pudding

honey-glazed pork chops

READY TO SERVE: 25 MINUTES
SERVINGS: 4

* super fast

glaze

- 2 tablespoons ketchup
- 2 tablespoons honey
- 2 tablespoons white wine vinegar
- 1 teaspoon dried thyme leaves
- ½ teaspoon ground mustard
- 2 garlic cloves, minced, or ¼ teaspoon garlic powder

pork chops

- 1 teaspoon paprika
- ½ teaspoon peppered seasoned salt
- 4 bone-in pork loin chops (6- to 7-oz. each)

1. Heat gas or charcoal grill. In small microwavable bowl, combine all glaze ingredients; mix well. Microwave on High for 30 seconds. Stir; set aside.

2. In small bowl, combine paprika and peppered seasoned salt. Sprinkle both sides of pork chops with paprika mixture; rub into surface of pork.

3. When grill is heated, place pork on gas grill over medium heat or on charcoal grill 4 to 6 inches from medium coals. Cook covered 12 to 15 minutes or until pork is slightly pink when cut near bone, turning twice, and brushing glaze on each side during last 5 minutes of cooking time. Discard any remaining glaze.

Nutrition Information Per Serving: Calories 230 • Total Fat 10g • Saturated Fat 4g • Cholesterol 85mg • Sodium 140mg • Total Carbohydrate 3g • Dietary Fiber 0g • Sugars 2g • Protein 31g. Dietary Exchange: 4½ Lean Meat.

glazed apples and canadian bacon

READY TO SERVE: 25 MINUTES
SERVINGS: 8

* super fast

- ½ cup firmly packed brown sugar
- ⅛ teaspoon pepper
- 1 tablespoon lemon juice
- 2 large red and/or green cooking apples, cored, each cut into 16 wedges
- 1 lb. sliced Canadian bacon

1. In large skillet, combine brown sugar, pepper and lemon juice; mix well. Cook and stir over medium heat until brown sugar is melted. Add apples; cook 5 to 6 minutes or until tender, stirring occasionally. With slotted spoon, place apples on serving platter.

2. Add Canadian bacon to same skillet; cook 1 to 2 minutes or until hot, turning once. Arrange on platter with apples. Spoon any remaining liquid in skillet over apples and Canadian bacon.

Nutrition Information Per Serving: Calories 180 • Total Fat 4g • Saturated Fat 1g • Cholesterol 30mg • Sodium 810mg • Total Carbohydrate 23g • Dietary Fiber 1g • Sugars 21g • Protein 12g. Dietary Exchanges: 1½ Fruit • 1½ Lean Meat OR 1½ Carbohydrate • 1½ Lean Meat.

au gratin potatoes and ham

PREP TIME: 15 MINUTES
READY TO SERVE: 9 HOURS 15 MINUTES
SERVINGS: 7

* slow cooked

- 6 cups sliced peeled potatoes (6 medium)
- 1 medium onion, coarsely chopped
- 1½ cups cubed cooked ham
- 4 oz. shredded American cheese (1 cup)
- 1 can (10¾-oz.) condensed cream of mushroom soup
- ½ cup milk
- ¼ to ½ teaspoon dried thyme leaves

1. In 3½ or 4-qt. slow cooker, layer half each of the potatoes, onion, ham and cheese; repeat layers. In small bowl, combine soup, milk and thyme; pour over top.

2. Cover; cook on High setting for 1 hour. Reduce heat to Low setting; cook for 6 to 8 hours or until potatoes are tender.

Nutrition Information Per Serving: Calories 370 • Total Fat 10g • Saturated Fat 5g • Cholesterol 30mg • Sodium 990mg • Total Carbohydrate 54g • Dietary Fiber 9g • Sugars 4g • Protein 15g. Dietary Exchanges: 3½ Starch • 1 Lean Meat • 1 Fat OR 3½ Carbohydrate • 1 Lean Meat • 1 Fat.

honey-glazed pork chops

ham and eggs frittata biscuits

ham and eggs frittata biscuits

SERVINGS: 8

SANDY BRADLEY ✻ BOLINGBROOK, ILLINOIS

Pillsbury Bake-Off

- 1 can (16.3-oz.) large refrigerated buttermilk biscuits
- 3 eggs
- 1¼ to 1½ teaspoons dried Italian seasoning
- ½ cup diced cooked ham
- 4 oz. shredded 6-cheese Italian blend (1 cup)
- ¼ cup roasted red bell peppers (from a jar), drained, chopped
- ½ cup diced seeded Italian plum tomatoes
- 2 tablespoons thinly sliced fresh basil leaves
- Fresh basil sprigs
- Cherry tomatoes

1. Heat oven to 375°F. Spray large cookie sheet with nonstick cooking spray. Separate dough into 8 biscuits. Place 3 inches apart on sprayed cookie sheet. Press out each biscuit to form 4-inch round with ¼-inch-high rim around outside edge.

2. Beat 1 of the eggs in small bowl. Brush over tops and sides of biscuits. Sprinkle with 1 teaspoon of the Italian seasoning.

3. In another small bowl, combine remaining 2 eggs and remaining ¼ to ½ teaspoon Italian seasoning; beat well. Spoon evenly into indentations in each biscuit. Top with ham, ½ cup of the cheese, roasted peppers, tomatoes, sliced basil and remaining ½ cup cheese.

4. Bake at 375°F for 15 to 20 minutes or until biscuits are golden brown and eggs are set. Garnish with basil sprigs and cherry tomatoes.

Nutrition Information Per Serving: Calories 290 • Total Fat 15g • Sodium 870mg • Total Carbohydrate 26g • Protein 12g.

southern-style barbecued ribs

PREP TIME: 30 MINUTES
READY TO SERVE: 1 HOUR
SERVINGS: 4

sauce

- ½ cup chopped onions
- ¼ cup cider vinegar
- ¼ cup lemon juice
- 2 tablespoons margarine or butter
- 1 tablespoon sugar
- ½ to 1 teaspoon coarse ground black pepper
- ½ teaspoon dry mustard
- 1½ teaspoons Worcestershire sauce
- ½ teaspoon Liquid Smoke, if desired

ribs

- 1 lb. boneless pork country-style ribs
- 1 quart water (4 cups)
- 1 cup vinegar
- 1 teaspoon crushed red pepper flakes

1. In medium saucepan, combine all sauce ingredients; bring to a boil over medium heat. Boil 10 to 12 minutes or until slightly thickened, stirring occasionally.

2. Meanwhile, place ribs in large saucepan; add water, 1 cup vinegar and red pepper flakes. Bring to a boil over medium-high heat. Reduce heat; cover and simmer 30 minutes. Drain.

3. Heat grill. When ready to grill, brush ribs with sauce. Place on gas grill over medium heat or on charcoal grill 4 to 6 inches from medium coals. Cook 10 to 20 minutes or until ribs are browned and tender, turning and brushing with sauce once. Heat remaining sauce to a boil and serve with ribs.

Nutrition Information Per Serving: Calories 380 • Total Fat 28g • Saturated Fat 9g • Cholesterol 80mg • Sodium 400mg • Total Carbohydrate 11g • Dietary Fiber 1g • Sugars 4g • Protein 20g. **Dietary Exchanges:** ½ Starch • 2½ High-Fat Meat • 1½ Fat OR ½ Carbohydrate • 2½ High-Fat Meat • 1½ Fat.

ENTICING ALTERNATIVE FOR BUSY COOKS

If you'd like to sample these finger-licking ribs, but just don't have time to make them, start the preparation a day early, and finish the job in your broiler the next night. After you've drained the ribs in Step 2, refrigerate the meat and sauce for up to 24 hours. To broil the ribs, place them on a broiler pan. Broil them 4 to 6 inches from the heat, using the times above as a guide. Turn the ribs and brush them with the sauce once during broiling.

fish & seafood

crispy fish-asian pasta salad ✳ p. 229

salmon cakes ✳ p. 227

shrimp marinara with angel hair pasta ✳ p. 233

fish fillets primavera ✳ p. 237

lemon butter catfish fillets * p. 240

seaside shortcakes

READY TO SERVE: 30 MINUTES
SERVINGS: 5

1   can (10.2-oz.) large
    refrigerated buttermilk
    biscuits (5 biscuits)
½   cup dry white wine
1   jar (16-oz.) Alfredo sauce
1   container (8-oz.) cream
    cheese with chives and onion
1   cup frozen small sweet peas
½   lb. shelled deveined cooked
    medium shrimp
1   can (6-oz.) crabmeat, drained
2   oz. shredded Cheddar
    cheese (½ cup)
¼   cup chopped fresh chives

1. Heat oven to 375°F. Bake biscuits as directed on can.

2. Meanwhile, cook wine in large skillet over high heat for 3 to 5 minutes or until slightly reduced. Reduce heat to medium. Add Alfredo sauce, cream cheese, peas, shrimp and crabmeat; mix well. Cook 8 to 10 minutes or until sauce is smooth and peas are tender, stirring occasionally.

3. Split warm biscuits; place bottom halves on serving plates. Spoon half of seafood mixture over biscuits. Cover with top halves of biscuits. Top with remaining seafood mixture. Sprinkle with cheese and chives.

Nutrition Information Per Serving: Calories 650 • Total Fat 44g • Saturated Fat 22g • Cholesterol 225mg • Sodium 1660mg • Total Carbohydrate 33g • Dietary Fiber 2g • Sugars 8g • Protein 29g. Dietary Exchanges: 2 Starch • 3½ Lean Meat • 6½ Fat OR 2 Carbohydrate • 3½ Lean Meat • 6½ Fat.

shrimp and scallop kabobs

READY TO SERVE: 20 MINUTES
SERVINGS: 6

* super fast

2 tablespoons butter, melted

½ teaspoon grated lemon peel

2 tablespoons fresh lemon juice

½ teaspoon dried marjoram leaves

¼ teaspoon salt

2 garlic cloves, minced

¾ lb. shelled deveined uncooked large shrimp, tails left on

1 lb. uncooked fresh sea scallops

1. Heat grill. In medium bowl, combine butter, lemon peel, lemon juice, marjoram, salt and garlic; mix well. Add shrimp and scallops; toss to coat. Alternately thread shrimp and scallops onto six 12- to 14-inch metal skewers. Reserve butter mixture.

2. When ready to grill, place kabobs on gas grill over medium heat or on charcoal grill 4 to 6 inches from medium coals; brush shrimp and scallops with butter mixture. Cook 6 to 8 minutes or until shrimp turn pink and scallops turn opaque, turning and brushing frequently with butter mixture. Discard any remaining butter mixture.

Nutrition Information Per Serving: Calories 110 • Total Fat 2g • Saturated Fat 1g • Cholesterol 110mg • Sodium 250mg • Total Carbohydrate 2g • Dietary Fiber 0g • Sugars 0g • Protein 21g. **Dietary Exchange:** 3 Very Lean Meat.

fish and vegetable stir-fry

PREP TIME: 30 MINUTES
SERVINGS: 4

⅔ cup uncooked regular long-grain white rice

1⅓ cups water

¼ cup water

2 tablespoons lite soy sauce

2 teaspoons cornstarch

¼ teaspoon ginger

⅛ to ¼ teaspoon pepper

⅛ teaspoon red pepper flakes

1 garlic clove, minced

1 lb. cod or haddock fillets, cut into 1½-inch squares

2 tablespoons water

1 package (1-lb.) frozen broccoli florets, carrots and water chestnuts

1. Cook rice in 1⅓ cups water as directed on package.

2. Meanwhile, in a small bowl, combine ¼ cup water, soy sauce, cornstarch, ginger pepper, red pepper flakes and garlic; blend well. Set aside.

3. Spray large nonstick skillet or wok with nonstick cooking spray. Heat over high heat until hot. Add cod; cook and stir for 2 to 4 minutes or until fish is opaque and flakes easily with a fork. Remove from skillet; cover and keep warm.

4. Remove skillet from heat; spray with nonstick cooking spray. Add 2 tablespoons water and frozen vegetables; cover and cook 6 to 7 minutes or until vegetables are crisp-tender.

5. Stir cornstarch mixture until smooth. Add to skillet; cook and stir until thickened. Return fish to skillet; toss gently to heat thoroughly. Serve over rice.

Nutrition Information Per Serving: Calories 230 • Total Fat 1g • Saturated 0g • Cholesterol 50mg • Sodium 430mg • Total Carbohydrate 31g • Dietary Fiber 3g • Sugars 3g • Protein 25g. Dietary Exchanges: 1½ Starch • 1 Vegetable • 2½ Very Lean Meat OR 1½ Carbohydrate • 1 Vegetable • 2½ Very Lean Meat.

warm italian shrimp salad

READY TO SERVE: 15 MINUTES
SERVINGS: 4

* super fast

3 cups uncooked rotini pasta (8 oz.)

½ lb. cooked peeled deveined medium shrimp, thawed if frozen, tail shells removed

2 large tomatoes or 6 roma (plum) tomatoes, chopped (about 2 cups)

¼ cup chopped fresh basil

¼ cup shredded Parmesan cheese (1 oz.)

2 tablespoons chopped ripe olives

¼ teaspoon garlic powder

⅛ teaspoon salt

Dash pepper

3 tablespoons red wine vinegar

2 tablespoons olive or canola oil

1. Cook pasta as directed on package. Place shrimp in colander or strainer; rinse briefly with cold water. Let stand in colander until pasta is cooked. To drain pasta, pour over shrimp in colander.

2. Meanwhile, in large bowl, mix remaining ingredients.

3. Gently stir cooked pasta and shrimp into tomato mixture. Serve immediately.

Nutrition Information Per Serving: Calories 380 • Total Fat 11g • Saturated Fat 2.5g • Trans Fat 0g • Cholesterol 115mg • Sodium 580mg • Total Carbohydrate 50g • Dietary Fiber 5g • Sugars 3g • Protein 23g. Dietary Exchanges: 3 Starch • 1 Vegetable • 1½ Very Lean Meat • 1½ Fat.

salmon cakes

READY TO SERVE: 30 MINUTES
SERVINGS: 4

¾ cup unseasoned dry bread crumbs

¼ cup finely chopped celery

¼ cup finely chopped onion

¼ cup nonfat sour cream

1 tablespoon Dijon mustard

1 egg white, beaten

1 can (14¾-oz.) salmon, drained, skin and large bones removed, flaked

1 can (4.5-oz.) chopped green chiles, drained

1. In large bowl, combine all ingredients; mix well. Cover; refrigerate 10 minutes or until slightly firm.

2. Shape mixture into 4 patties, about ¾-inch thick.

3. Spray 12-inch nonstick skillet with nonstick cooking spray. Heat over medium-high heat until hot. Add patties; cook 6 to 8 minutes or until golden brown, turning once. If desired, serve with additional nonfat sour cream.

Nutrition Information Per Serving: Calories 240 • Total Fat 8g • Saturated Fat 2g • Cholesterol 35mg • Sodium 870mg • Total Carbohydrate 18g • Dietary Fiber 2g • Sugars 2g • Protein 23g. Dietary Exchanges: 1 Starch • 3 Very Lean Meat • 1 Fat OR 1 Carbohydrate • 3 Very Lean Meat • 1 Fat.

crispy fish-asian pasta salad

baked breaded walleye

READY TO SERVE: 30 MINUTES
SERVINGS: 4

1 lb. walleye fillets or other lean white fish

2 egg whites

¼ cup skim milk

¼ cup all-purpose flour

½ cup unseasoned dry bread crumbs

¼ teaspoon pepper

¼ teaspoon paprika

1. Place 1 oven rack in center rack position; heat oven to 500°F. Line cookie sheet with foil; spray with nonstick cooking spray. Remove skin from walleye fillets; cut into 8 equal pieces, cutting diagonally if necessary for uniform size.

2. In shallow bowl, combine egg whites and milk; beat well. Place flour and bread crumbs on separate dinner-sized plates. Add pepper to flour; mix well. Add paprika to bread crumbs; mix well.

3. Dip fish in flour mixture, coating thoroughly. Dip floured fish in egg white mixture; dip in bread crumbs mixture, coating thoroughly. Place on sprayed foil-lined cookie sheet.

4. Place cookie sheet on center oven rack; bake at 500°F for 10 minutes.

5. Reduce oven temperature to 450°F. Remove cookie sheet from oven; carefully turn fish over. Return to oven; bake an additional 5 minutes or until fish flakes easily with fork. If desired, sprinkle with salt and pepper before serving.

Nutrition Information Per Serving: Calories 190 • Calories from Fat 20 • Total Fat 2g • Saturated Fat 0g • Cholesteral 100mg • Sodium 190mg • Total Carbohydrate 16g • Dietary Fiber 1g • Sugars 1g • Protein 27g. Dietary Exchanges: 1 Starch • 3 Very Lean Meat OR 1 Carbohydrate • 3 Very Lean Meat.

crispy fish-asian pasta salad

READY TO SERVE: 25 MINUTES
SERVINGS: 4

✳ super fast

salad

2½ cups uncooked farfalle (bow-tie) pasta (6 oz.)

1 cup frozen sugar snap peas (from 1-lb. bag)

12 frozen breaded fish sticks

2 cups coleslaw blend (from 16-oz. bag)

½ medium red bell pepper, chopped (½ cup)

4 cups torn iceberg and romaine lettuce blend (from 11-oz. bag)

dressing

⅓ cup mayonnaise or salad dressing

⅓ cup Asian vinaigrette or vinegar and oil vinaigrette

1. Cook pasta as directed on package, adding sugar snap peas during last 3 minutes of cooking time. Drain; rinse with cold water to cool. Drain well.

2. Meanwhile, cook fish sticks as directed on package. Carefully cut each fish stick into 3 or 4 pieces.

3. In large bowl, combine dressing ingredients; mix well. Add cooked pasta and sugar snap peas, coleslaw blend and bell pepper; stir to coat. Add fish sticks; stir gently to mix. Arrange lettuce blend on individual serving plates. Spoon salad onto lettuce.

Nutrition Information Per Serving: Calories 510 • Total Fat 24g • Saturated Fat 4g • Cholesterol 25mg • Sodium 840mg • Total Carbohydrate 58g • Dietary Fiber 4g • Sugars 14g • Protein 15g. Dietary Exchanges: 3½ Starch • 1 Vegetable • ½ Medium-Fat Meat • 4 Fat.

RAPID REPLACEMENTS

Even if your family is not particularly fond of fish, you can still take advantage this delicious, time-saving recipe by making an easy adjustment. Simply prepare the salad by substituting the frozen fish sticks with a 10-ounce package of frozen, breaded chicken breast chunks.

Just cook the chicken as directed on the package, and use it in place of the fish. And while the recipe calls for farfalle pasta, feel free to use 6 ounces of whatever pasta you have on hand. Shell pasta and wagon wheels make this no-fuss favorite a fun meal that kids are sure to ask for time and again.

easy breaded fish fillets

READY TO SERVE: 20 MINUTES
SERVINGS: 4

* super fast

Nonstick cooking spray

¾ cup crushed seasoned croutons

¼ cup grated Parmesan cheese

2 teaspoons dried parsley flakes

¼ teaspoon paprika

1 egg

1 tablespoon water

1 tablespoon lemon juice

1 lb. fish fillets (¼ to ½ inch thick)

1. Heat oven to 350°F. Spray 15x10x1-inch baking pan with nonstick cooking spray. In shallow bowl, combine croutons, Parmesan cheese, parsley flakes and paprika; blend well. In another shallow bowl, combine egg, water and lemon juice; beat well.

2. Cut fish fillets into serving-sized pieces. Dip in egg mixture; coat with crouton mixture. (Tuck thin ends of fish under to form pieces of uniform thickness.) Place fish in sprayed pan. Spray fish with cooking spray for about 5 seconds.

3. Bake at 350°F for 10 to 15 minutes or until fish flakes easily with fork.

Nutrition Information Per Serving: Calories 250 • Total Fat 9g • Saturated Fat 3g • Cholesterol 110mg • Sodium 460mg • Total Carbohydrate 14g • Dietary Fiber 1g • Sugars 1g • Protein 27g. Dietary Exchanges: 1 Starch • 3½ Very Lean Meat • 1 Fat OR 1 Carbohydrate • 3½ Very Lean Meat • 1 Fat.

creamy shrimp and broccoli rotini

READY TO SERVE: 30 MINUTES
SERVINGS: 4

2 cups uncooked rotini (spiral pasta) (6 oz.)

2 cups small broccoli florets

¼ lb. shelled deveined uncooked medium shrimp, tails removed

1 container (6.5-oz.) light garlic and herbs soft spreadable cheese (about 1 cup)

2 tablespoons milk

½ teaspoon salt

1. In large saucepan, cook rotini to desired doneness as directed on package, adding broccoli and shrimp during last 2 to 4 minutes of cooking time. Cook until broccoli is tender and shrimp turn pink. Drain; return to saucepan.

2. Add cheese, milk and salt to cooked rotini, broccoli and shrimp; toss gently to coat.

Nutrition Information Per Serving: Calories 320 • Total Fat 9g • Saturated Fat 5g • Cholesterol 100mg • Sodium 710mg • Total Carbohydrate 37g • Dietary Fiber 2g • Sugars 4g • Protein 22g. Dietary Exchanges: 2 Starch • 1 Vegetable • 2 Very Lean Meat • 1½ Fat OR 2 Carbohydrate • 1 Vegetable • 2 Very Lean Meat • 1½ Fat.

stir-fried lemon-garlic shrimp

READY TO SERVE: 25 MINUTES
SERVINGS: 4

* super fast

1 tablespoon olive or vegetable oil

2 garlic cloves, minced, or ¼ teaspoon garlic powder

1 lb. uncooked peeled deveined medium shrimp, tails removed

⅓ cup stir-fry sauce

4 medium green onions, sliced (¼ cup)

2 teaspoons honey

1 teaspoon grated lemon peel

1 tablespoon lemon juice

1. In 10-inch nonstick skillet, heat oil over high heat until hot. Add garlic and shrimp; cook and stir 2 to 3 minutes or until shrimp are pink and firm.

2. Add all remaining ingredients; toss to mix. Cook 1 to 2 minutes or until sauce is of desired consistency.

Nutrition Information Per Serving: Calories 140 • Total Fat 4g • Saturated Fat 1g • Cholesterol 160mg • Sodium 890mg • Total Carbohydrate 8g • Dietary Fiber 0g • Sugars 4g • Protein 19g. Dietary Exchanges: 2½ Very Lean Meat • ½ Fat • ½ Other Carbohydrate.

fiesta flounder fillets

SERVINGS: 6

DENISE LAPNOW ✳ BRIDGEWATER, NEW JERSEY

4 oz. shredded Colby-
    Monterey Jack cheese blend
    or shredded Cheddar cheese
    (1 cup)

½ cup unseasoned dry bread
    crumbs

2 cans (6-oz. each) crabmeat,
    drained, flaked

1 can (4.5-oz.) chopped green
    chiles

2 teaspoons taco seasoning
    mix (from 1.25-oz. pkg.)

2 eggs

2 lb. flounder fillets (6 pieces)

2 teaspoons lemon juice

1 jar (16-oz.) chunky-style
    salsa

¼ cup water

1 tablespoon unseasoned dry
    bread crumbs

1. Heat oven to 400°F. In large bowl, combine cheese, ½ cup bread crumbs, crabmeat, 3 tablespoons of the chiles, taco seasoning mix and eggs; mix well. Sprinkle each flounder fillet with lemon juice. Spread crabmeat mixture over each fillet. Roll up each. Place in ungreased 12x8-inch (2-quart) glass baking dish.

2. In small bowl, combine salsa and water; mix well. Spoon over rolled fish. Sprinkle with remaining chiles and 1 tablespoon bread crumbs. If desired, sprinkle with additional cheese.

3. Bake at 400°F for 20 to 30 minutes or until fish flakes easily with fork.

Nutrition Information Per Serving: Calories 350 • Total Fat 11g • Sodium 1220mg • Total Carbohydrate 16g • Protein 47g.

shrimp marinara with angel hair pasta

shrimp marinara with angel hair pasta

READY TO SERVE: 20 MINUTES
SERVINGS: 4

*super fast

1 pkg. (9-oz.) refrigerated angel hair pasta (capellini)

1 tablespoon olive or vegetable oil

1 lb. shelled deveined uncooked medium shrimp

2 garlic cloves, minced

1 container (15-oz.) refrigerated marinara sauce

1 tablespoon lime juice

1 tablespoon vodka, if desired

1/8 teaspoon crushed red pepper flakes

1. Cook pasta to desired doneness as directed on package. Drain; cover to keep warm.

2. Meanwhile, heat oil in large skillet over medium-high heat until hot. Add shrimp and garlic; cook and stir 2 to 3 minutes or until shrimp just begin to turn pink.

3. Stir in all remaining ingredients. Simmer 3 to 5 minutes or until mixture is thoroughly heated. Serve over pasta.

Nutrition Information Per Serving: Calories 370 • Total Fat 9g • Saturated Fat 1g • Cholesterol 210mg • Sodium 610mg • Total Carbohydrate 43g • Dietary Fiber 4g • Sugars 7g • Protein 26g. Dietary Exchanges: 3 Starch • 2½ Very Lean Meat • 1 Fat OR 3 Carbohydrate • 2½ Very Lean Meat • 1 Fat.

lemon butter flounder fillets

READY TO SERVE: 20 MINUTES
SERVINGS: 4

*super fast

1 lb. flounder fillets

1 cup water

2 teaspoons cornstarch

½ teaspoon chicken-flavor instant bouillon

Dash pepper

2 tablespoons all-natural butter-flavor granules

1 teaspoon grated lemon peel

1 tablespoon chopped fresh chives

1. Line 15x10x1-inch baking pan with foil; spray foil with nonstick cooking spray. Pat flounder fillets dry with paper towels; place on sprayed foil-lined pan.

2. Broil 4 to 6 inches from heat for 6 to 8 minutes or until fish flakes easily with fork, turning once.

3. Meanwhile, in small saucepan, combine water, cornstarch, bouillon and pepper; blend well. Cook and stir over medium heat until bubbly and thickened. Reduce heat to low; stir in butter-flavor granules and lemon peel. Remove from heat; stir in chives. Serve sauce over fish.

Nutrition Information Per Serving: Calories 140 • Total Fat 2g • Saturated 1g • Cholesterol 80mg • Sodium 510mg • Total Carbohydrate 3g • Dietary Fiber 0g • Sugars 0g • Protein 28g. Dietary Exchange: 4 Very Lean Meat.

italian roasted salmon

READY TO SERVE: 30 MINUTES
SERVINGS: 4

¼ cup purchased Italian salad dressing

2 tablespoons chopped fresh parsley

½ teaspoon dried basil leaves

1 tablespoon lemon juice

1 (1-lb.) salmon fillet

Lemon slices

1. Heat oven to 425°F. Line shallow baking pan with foil. Spray foil with nonstick cooking spray. In shallow dish, combine salad dressing, parsley, basil and lemon juice; mix well.

2. Place salmon, skin side down, in sprayed foil-lined pan. Spoon about half of salad dressing mixture over salmon.

3. Bake at 425°F for 15 to 20 minutes or until fish flakes easily with fork, spooning remaining salad dressing mixture over fish once or twice during baking. Serve fish with lemon slices.

Nutrition Information Per Serving: Calories 225 • Total Fat 13g • Saturated Fat 2g • Cholesterol 80mg • Sodium 200mg • Total Carbohydrate 2g • Dietary Fiber 0g • Sugars 2g • Protein 25g. Dietary Exchanges: 3½ Lean Meat • ½ Fat.

tangy scallops with chinese noodles

READY TO SERVE: 30 MINUTES
SERVINGS: 4

- 8 oz. fresh Chinese noodles (from 16-oz. pkg.) or 8 oz. uncooked vermicelli
- 1 cup chicken broth
- ⅓ cup dry sherry
- ¼ cup oyster sauce
- 2 tablespoons cornstarch
- 2 tablespoons honey
- 1 tablespoon soy sauce
- ⅛ to ¼ teaspoon crushed red pepper flakes
- ¾ lb. scallops, cut in half if large, rinsed and drained
- 2 tablespoons water
- 2 packages (9-oz. each) fresh stir-fry vegetables (broccoli, green cabbage, carrots and snow pea pods) (7 cups)

1. Cut noodles into 4-inch pieces. Cook noodles as directed on package. Drain; cover to keep warm.

2. Meanwhile, in small bowl, combine broth, sherry, oyster sauce, cornstarch, honey, soy sauce and red pepper flakes; blend well. Add scallops; stir until coated. Set aside.

3. In large skillet or wok, combine water and vegetables. Cover; cook over medium-high heat for 5 to 7 minutes or until crisp-tender.

4. Add scallop mixture; cook and stir 1 to 2 minutes or until scallops are opaque and sauce is bubbly and thickened. Stir in cooked noodles; mix well. Cook until thoroughly heated.

Nutrition Information Per Serving: Calories 390 • Total Fat 2g • Saturated 0g • Cholesterol 30mg • Sodium 1520mg • Total Carbohydrate 69g • Dietary Fiber 5g • Sugars 16g • Protein 23g. Dietary Exchanges: 2 Starch • 2 Fruit • 1½ Vegetable • 2 Very Lean Meat OR 4 Carbohydrate • 1½ Vegetable • 2 Very Lean Meat.

shrimp and mango salad

READY TO SERVE: 25 MINUTES
SERVINGS: 4

✱ super fast

dressing
- ⅓ cup frozen concentrated limeade mix, thawed
- 2 tablespoons orange marmalade
- 2 tablespoons vegetable oil

salad
- 1 lb. cooked peeled deveined medium shrimp, tails removed
- 1½ cups cubed unpeeled seedless cucumber
- ½ medium red bell pepper, chopped (½ cup)
- 2 ripe medium mangoes, peeled, seeds removed and chopped
- 1 fresh jalapeño chile, seeded, finely chopped
- 4 cups mixed baby salad greens
- ¼ cup chopped macadamia nuts or almonds, toasted, if desired

1. In medium bowl, combine dressing ingredients; blend well. Add shrimp, cucumber, bell pepper, mangoes and chile; toss to coat.

2. Arrange salad greens on individual serving plates. Spoon shrimp mixture onto salad greens. Sprinkle with nuts.

Nutrition Information Per Serving: Calories 390 • Total Fat 15g • Saturated Fat 2g • Cholesterol 220mg • Sodium 270mg • Total Carbohydrate 38g • Dietary Fiber 4g • Sugars 30g • Protein 26g. Dietary Exchanges: 1 Fruit • 1 Vegetable • 3½ Very Lean Meat • 2½ Fat • 1 Other Carbohydrate.

PRODUCE POINTERS

Mangoes are available year round in most large grocery stores, but the lip-smacking fruit is at its peak in May and June. Because mangoes vary in color, you can't always rely on the fruit's skin to determine how ripe it is.

When buying mangoes for Shrimp and Mango Salad, look for those with a fruity aroma at the stem end. The flesh of a ripe mango will usually give way slightly when gently squeezed. If fresh mangoes aren't available, pick up a jar of sliced mangoes, often found in the refrigerated produce section of most large grocery stores.

If you're not sure your family will enjoy mangoes, you can also prepare the salad with peaches. Simply replace the mangoes with two large, fresh peaches that are particularly ripe, or toss together the salad using four canned peach halves instead.

crispy oven-baked fish

READY TO SERVE: 30 MINUTES
SERVINGS: 2

1 egg or 1 egg white

1 teaspoon water

⅓ cup Italian-style dry bread crumbs

½ teaspoon lemon-pepper seasoning

¼ teaspoon garlic salt

2 catfish or tilapia fillets (3 to 4 oz. each)

Cooking spray

4 lemon wedges

1. Heat oven to 400°F. Line cookie sheet with foil; generously spray foil with cooking spray. In shallow bowl or dish, beat egg and water with wire whisk until well blended. In another shallow bowl or dish, mix bread crumbs, lemon-pepper seasoning and garlic salt.

2. Dip fish into egg mixture; coat with bread crumb mixture. Place on cookie sheet. Spray fish with cooking spray.

3. Bake 10 minutes. Turn fillets; bake 5 to 10 minutes longer or until fish flakes easily with fork. Place fillets on serving platter; garnish with lemon wedges.

Nutrition Information Per Serving: Calories 280 • Total Fat 12g • Saturated Fat 2.5g • Trans Fat 0g • Cholesterol 190mg • Sodium 460mg • Total Carbohydrate 15g • Dietary Fiber 0g • Sugars 2g • Protein 29g. Dietary Exchanges: 1 Starch • 4 Lean Meat.

zesty fish stick tacos

fish fillets primavera

READY TO SERVE: 30 MINUTES
SERVINGS: 4

3 tablespoons margarine or butter

4 (4- to 5-oz. each) orange roughy fillets

1 tablespoon lemon juice

Dash salt and pepper

1 garlic clove, minced

1½ cups fresh broccoli florets

1 cup fresh cauliflower florets

1 cup julienne-cut (2x⅛x⅛-inch) carrots

1 cup sliced fresh mushrooms or 1 jar (2.5-oz.) sliced mushrooms, drained

½ cup diagonally sliced celery

¼ teaspoon salt

¼ teaspoon dried basil leaves

¼ cup grated Parmesan cheese

1. Heat oven to 450°F. In oven, melt 2 tablespoons of the margarine in 13x9-inch (3-quart) glass baking dish. Place fish in melted margarine; turn to coat. Sprinkle with lemon juice, salt and pepper. Bake at 450°F for 5 minutes. Remove from oven.

2. While fish is baking, in large skillet, melt remaining 1 tablespoon margarine over medium-high heat. Add garlic; cook until lightly browned. Add all remaining ingredients except the Parmesan cheese; cook and stir 5 to 6 minutes or until the vegetables are crisp-tender.

3. Spoon hot vegetables in center of baking dish, moving fish to ends of dish. Sprinkle with Parmesan cheese. Return to oven; bake an additional 3 to 5 minutes or until fish flakes easily with fork.

Nutrition Information Per Serving: Calories 240 • Total Fat 12g • Saturated Fat 3g • Cholesterol 35mg • Sodium 510mg • Total Carbohydrate 8g • Dietary Fiber 3g • Sugars 3g • Protein 26g. Dietary Exchanges: 1 Vegetable • 3½ Very Lean Meat • 2 Fat.

zesty fish stick tacos

READY TO SERVE: 30 MINUTES
SERVINGS: 6 (2 TACOS EACH)

24 frozen fish sticks

¾ cup mayonnaise

2 tablespoons taco seasoning mix

1 medium tomato

1½ cups chopped lettuce

1 box (10.5-oz.) flour tortillas for soft tacos and fajitas (12 tortillas)

Taco sauce, if desired

1. Prepare the fish sticks as directed on the box.

2. Meanwhile, in a medium bowl, combine the mayonnaise and taco seasoning mix.

3. Dice the tomato.

4. Stack the tortillas on a microwave-safe plate and cover with microwavable plastic wrap. Microwave the tortillas on High 1 minute.

5. When the fish sticks are done, cut each into 4 pieces.

6. Divide the mayonnaise mixture evenly onto the tortillas. Top 1 side of each tortilla with 8 fish stick pieces, a little of the lettuce and some of the tomato. Fold the side of each tortilla without the toppings over the top. Serve with taco sauce.

Nutrition Information Per Serving: Calories 570 • Total Fat 36g • Sodium 810mg • Total Carbohydrate 48g • Sugars 7g • Protein 14g. Dietary Exchanges: 3 Starch • 6 Fat.

EASY IDEAS

If you don't have any tortillas in the house, consider making Zesty Fish Stick Sandwiches. Just use hamburger buns or even last night's dinner rolls instead of the flour tortillas.

And remember to keep the two-ingredient, seasoned mayonnaise in mind the next time you want to add easy flair to any sandwich. It's great with deli meats or even on hamburgers.

pesto shrimp and pasta

READY TO SERVE: 20 MINUTES
SERVINGS: 4

2 cups uncooked rotini pasta (6 oz.)

2 cups frozen broccoli florets, carrots and cauliflower (from 1-lb. bag)

8 oz. cooked peeled deveined small or medium shrimp, tails removed

1 container (7-oz.) refrigerated basil pesto (¾ cup)

¼ cup shredded Parmesan cheese (1 oz.)

1. In 2½- to 3-quart saucepan, cook rotini as directed on package, adding vegetables during last 5 minutes of cooking time. Drain; return to saucepan.

2. Add shrimp and pesto; toss gently to coat. Sprinkle with cheese.

Nutrition Information Per Serving: Calories 530 • Total Fat 30g • Saturated Fat 7g • Cholesterol 125mg • Sodium 880mg • Total Carbohydrate 39g • Dietary Fiber 4g • Sugars 2g • Protein 26g. Dietary Exchanges: 2 Starch • 1 Vegetable • 2½ Very Lean Meat • 6 Fat.

sweet-and-sour fillets

READY TO SERVE: 30 MINUTES
SERVINGS: 4

1 tablespoon oil

8 oz. fresh snow pea pods, trimmed (2 cups)

1 cup coarsely chopped red bell pepper

1 cup purchased sweet-and-sour or duck sauce

1½ teaspoons grated lemon peel

1 lb. orange roughy, sole or flounder fillets

1. Heat oil in large skillet over medium-high heat until hot. Add pea pods and bell pepper; cook and stir 4 to 6 minutes or until vegetables are crisp-tender. Arrange vegetables on serving platter; cover to keep warm.

2. In same skillet, combine sweet-and-sour sauce and 1 teaspoon of the lemon peel. Reduce heat to medium; cook and stir 1 to 2 minutes or until sauce is bubbly.

3. Arrange orange roughy fillets in sauce, spooning sauce over each fillet. Cover; cook 5 to 7 minutes or until fish flakes easily with fork.

4. To serve, carefully arrange fillets over warm vegetables on platter. Spoon sauce from skillet over fillets and vegetables. Sprinkle with remaining ½ teaspoon lemon peel.

Nutrition Information Per Serving: Calories 210 • Total Fat 4g • Saturated Fat 0g • Cholesterol 25mg • Sodium 450mg • Total Carbohydrate 24g • Dietary Fiber 2g • Sugars 18g • Protein 19g. Dietary Exchanges: 1½ Fruit • 1 Vegetable • 2½ Very Lean Meat • ½ Fat OR 1½ Carbohydrate • 1 Vegetable • 2½ Very Lean Meat • ½ Fat.

tuna noodle skillet

READY TO SERVE: 20 MINUTES
SERVINGS: 4

8 oz. mini lasagna noodles (mafalda) (3½ cups)

1 cup chopped celery

2 tablespoons water

½ cup nonfat sour cream

½ cup purchased fat-free ranch salad dressing

1 can (12-oz.) water-packed solid white tuna, drained, flaked

1 jar (7.25-oz.) roasted red bell peppers, drained, chopped

1. Cook noodles to desired doneness as directed on package. Drain.

2. Meanwhile, in a 12-inch nonstick skillet, combine celery and water. Cover; cook over medium heat for 2 to 3 minutes or until celery is crisp-tender.

3. Add cooked noodles, sour cream, salad dressing, tuna and roasted peppers; mix well. Cook about 5 minutes or until thoroughly heated, stirring frequently.

Nutrition Information Per Serving: Calories 370 • Total Fat 2g • Saturated Fat 0g • Cholesterol 20mg • Sodium 630mg • Total Carbohydrate 60g • Dietary Fiber 3g • Sugars 10g • Protein 28g. Dietary Exchanges: 4 Starch • 2 Very Lean Meat OR 4 Carbohydrate • 2 Very Lean Meat.

sweet-and-sour fillets

lemon butter catfish fillets

READY TO SERVE: 20 MINUTES
SERVINGS: 4

* super fast

1 lb. catfish fillets

1 cup water

2 teaspoons cornstarch

½ teaspoon chicken bouillon granules

Dash pepper

2 tablespoons all-natural butter-flavor granules

1 teaspoon grated lemon peel

1 tablespoon chopped fresh chives

1. Set oven control to broil. Line 15x10-inch pan with sides with foil; spray foil with cooking spray. Pat catfish fillets dry with paper towels; place in pan.

2. Broil 4 to 6 inches from heat 8 to 10 minutes, turning once, until fish flakes easily with fork.

3. Meanwhile, in 1-quart saucepan, mix water, cornstarch, bouillon and pepper until smooth. Cook over medium heat, stirring frequently, until bubbly and thickened. Reduce heat to low; stir in butter-flavor granules and lemon peel. Remove from heat; stir in chives. Serve sauce over fish.

Nutrition Information Per Serving: Calories 170 • Total Fat 7g • Saturated Fat 1.5g • Trans Fat 0g • Cholesterol 85mg • Sodium 440mg • Total Carbohydrate 3g • Dietary Fiber 0g • Sugars 0g • Protein 23g. Dietary Exchange: 3 Lean Meat.

southern-style shrimp and rice

READY TO SERVE: 45 MINUTES
SERVINGS: 4

⅔ cup uncooked regular long-grain rice

1⅓ cups water

6 slices bacon

2 green bell peppers, cut into 1-inch pieces

2 medium onions, cut into eighths

¼ teaspoon pepper

¼ teaspoon hot pepper sauce

1 can (14½-oz.) whole tomatoes, undrained, cut up

1 can (6-oz.) tomato paste

1 lb. shelled, deveined, cooked medium shrimp

1. Cook rice in water as directed on package.

2. Meanwhile, cook bacon in large skillet until crisp. Remove bacon from skillet; drain on paper towels. Set aside.

3. Reserve 2 tablespoons drippings in skillet. Add bell peppers and onions; cook and stir until tender.

4. Stir in cooked rice, pepper, hot pepper sauce, tomatoes and tomato paste. Cover; simmer 15 minutes, stirring occasionally.

5. Crumble bacon. Add bacon and shrimp to skillet mixture; cook until thoroughly heated.

Nutrition Information Per Serving: Calories 410 • Total Fat 13g • Saturated 5g • Cholesterol 235mg • Sodium 900mg • Total Carbohydrate 42g • Dietary Fiber 5g • Sugars 7g • Protein 32g. Dietary Exchanges: 2 Starch • 2 Vegetable • 3 Very Lean Meat • 2 Fat OR 2 Carbohydrate • 2 Vegetable • 3 Very Lean Meat • 2 Fat.

linguine with seafood sauce

READY TO SERVE: 20 MINUTES
SERVINGS: 8

* super fast

12 oz. uncooked linguine

4 tablespoons margarine or butter

4 green onions, sliced

1 garlic clove, minced

1 package (12-oz.) frozen shelled deveined uncooked medium shrimp, thawed, drained and tails removed

1 can (6½-oz.) minced clams, undrained

1 cup chicken broth

½ cup dry white wine

2 tablespoons lemon juice

¼ cup chopped fresh parsley

1 teaspoon dried basil leaves

1 teaspoon dried oregano leaves

¼ teaspoon pepper

2 tablespoons cold water

2 tablespoons cornstarch

¼ cup sour cream

1. Cook the linguine to desired doneness as directed on package. Drain; cover to keep warm.

2. Meanwhile, melt 2 tablespoons of the margarine in large skillet over medium heat. Add onions and garlic; cook and stir until onions are tender. Stir in shrimp, clams, broth, wine, lemon juice, parsley, basil, oregano and pepper. Bring to a boil. Reduce heat to low; simmer 5 minutes or until shrimp turn pink.

3. In small bowl, combine water and cornstarch; blend well. Gradually stir into seafood mixture. Cook until mixture boils and thickens, stirring constantly.

4. In large bowl, combine cooked linguine, sour cream and remaining 2 tablespoons margarine; toss to coat. Serve seafood sauce over linguine.

Nutrition Information Per Serving: Calories 280 • Total Fat 10g • Saturated Fat 3g • Cholesterol 105mg • Sodium 300mg • Total Carbohydrate 34g • Dietary Fiber 2g • Sugars 2g • Protein 14g. Dietary Exchanges: 2½ Starch • 1 Very Lean Meat • 1½ Fat OR 2½ Carbohydrate • 1 Very Lean Meat • 1½ Fat.

SENSATIONAL SEAFOOD SUPPER

For an easy dinnertime delight, serve Linguine with Seafood Sauce alongside a tomato salad and store-bought whole grain rolls. While waiting for the pasta water to boil, cut a few large tomatoes and set them in a bowl. Top the tomato wedges with balsamic vinaigrette, cover and set in the refrigerator until serving. Put the rolls in a warm oven just before you make the seafood sauce.

mixed seafood grill

READY TO SERVE: 20 MINUTES
SERVINGS: 6

2 tablespoons butter, melted

1 teaspoon lemon-pepper seasoning

½ teaspoon fennel seed, crushed

¼ teaspoon salt

1 lb. halibut, cut into 1¼- to 1½-inch pieces

12 shelled deveined uncooked large shrimp, tails left on (about 1 lb.)

1. Heat grill. In large bowl, combine butter, lemon-pepper seasoning, fennel seed and salt; mix well. Add halibut and shrimp; toss to coat. Place in grill basket.

2. When ready to grill, place basket on gas grill over medium-high heat or on charcoal grill 4 to 6 inches from medium-high coals. Cook 5 to 10 minutes or until fish flakes easily with fork and shrimp turn pink, turning once or twice.

Nutrition Information Per Serving: Calories 160 • Total Fat 6g • Saturated Fat 3g • Cholesterol 140mg • Sodium 380mg • Total Carbohydrate 0g • Dietary Fiber 0g • Sugars 0g • Protein 27g. Dietary Exchanges: 4 Very Lean Meat • ½ Fat.

NO-STRESS SUPPER PLAN

It's a snap to round out menus that feature Mixed Seafood Grill. Earlier in the day, stop by the grocery store and pick up a bunch of fresh broccoli, blueberries, cream and bran muffins.

While the grill heats up, cut the fish and crush the fennel. After you set the fish on the grill, saute the broccoli spears on the stovetop in a little butter. Toss the hot, cooked broccoli with Parmesan cheese before serving. Set the muffins in a basket and dinner is ready. The blueberries and cream make a perfect dessert.

sole fillets with broccoli stuffing

READY TO SERVE: 1 HOUR
SERVINGS: 4

stuffing

1 package (7-oz.) seasoned cube-style stuffing mix (4 cups)

¼ cup margarine or butter

Water

1 package (9-oz.) frozen cut broccoli in a pouch, thawed, drained

fillets

1 lb. sole or flounder fillets

1 tablespoon margarine or butter, melted

2 teaspoons, lemon juice

½ teaspoon onion powder

Paprika

1. Heat oven to 375°F. Lightly grease a 12x8-inch (2-quart) baking dish. Prepare stuffing mix as directed on package using ¼ cup margarine and water. Stir in broccoli. Spoon evenly into greased baking dish. Place fillets evenly over stuffing mixture.

2. In a small bowl, combine 1 tablespoon margarine, lemon juice and onion powder. Brush over fish. Sprinkle with paprika. Cover with foil.

3. Bake at 375°F for 30 minutes. Uncover; bake an additional 10 minutes or until fish flakes easily with a fork.

Nutrition Information Per Serving: Calories 440 • Total Fat 17g • Saturated 3g • Cholesterol 60mg • Sodium 1060mg • Total Carbohydrate 42g • Dietary Fiber 5g • Sugars 3g • Protein 29g. Dietary Exchanges: 2½ Starch • 1 Vegetable • 3 Very Lean Meat • 2½ Fat OR 2½ Carbohydrate • 1 Vegetable • 3 Very Lean Meat • 2½ Fat.

CUTTING KITCHEN TIME

To quickly thaw the broccoli called for in Sole Fillets with Broccoli Stuffing, remove the broccoli from the pouch. Place it in a colander or strainer and rinse with warm water until thawed; drain well. You can also cut a small slit in the center of the pouch; microwave on High for 2 to 3 minutes or until thawed. Remove the broccoli from the pouch; drain well.

mixed seafood grill

speedy sides

herbed wild-rice pilaf * p. 264

almond baby carrots * p. 247

breadstick focaccia * p. 274

marinated roasted vegetable antipasto * p. 251

honey-mustard marinated vegetables ✳ p. 273

almond baby carrots

almond baby carrots

READY TO SERVE: 15 MINUTES
SERVINGS: 6

* super fast

1 package (16-oz.) fresh baby carrots
2 tablespoons slivered almonds
2 tablespoons butter
2 tablespoons amaretto
Dash salt
1 tablespoon chopped fresh parsley

1. In 1½-quart microwave-safe casserole, combine carrots and ¼ cup water; cover. Microwave on High for 7 to 10 minutes or until tender, stirring once halfway through cooking. Drain.

2. Meanwhile, cook almonds in medium saucepan over medium heat for 3 to 5 minutes or until toasted, stirring frequently.

3. Add butter, amaretto, salt and cooked carrots to saucepan; mix well. Cook 2 to 3 minutes or until most of liquid is evaporated, stirring occasionally. Sprinkle with parsley.

Nutrition Information Per Serving: Calories 90 • Total Fat 5g • Saturated Fat 3g • Cholesterol 10mg • Sodium 75mg • Total Carbohydrate 10g • Dietary Fiber 2g • Sugars 6g • Protein 1g. Dietary Exchanges: 1 Vegetable • 1 Fat.

crisp-coated mushrooms

READY TO SERVE: 25 MINUTES
SERVINGS: 20 MUSHROOMS

* super fast

¼ cup refrigerated or frozen fat-free egg product, thawed, or 1 egg
½ teaspoon onion salt
8 to 10 drops hot pepper sauce, if desired
¼ cup all-purpose flour
¾ cup crushed Melba round snacks (about 18 snacks)
1 package (8-oz.) fresh whole mushrooms
Olive oil nonstick cooking spray, if desired

1. Heat oven to 450°F. Line 15x10x1-inch baking pan with foil.

2. In small bowl, combine egg product, onion salt and hot pepper sauce; blend well. Place flour in resealable food storage plastic bag or another small bowl. Place snack crumbs on sheet of waxed paper or in another small bowl.

3. Brush mushrooms or wipe clean with damp cloth. Place mushrooms in bag with flour; shake to coat. For each mushroom, shake off excess flour. Dip each in egg product mixture; coat well with snack crumbs. Place in foil-lined pan. For crispier mushrooms, spray all sides of mushrooms with nonstick cooking spray.

4. Bake at 450°F for 8 to 12 minutes or until hot and crisp.

Nutrition Information Per Serving: Calories 20 • Total Fat 0g • Saturated Fat 0g • Cholesterol 0mg • Sodium 75mg • Total Carbohydrate 4g • Dietary Fiber 0g • Sugars 0g • Protein 1g. Dietary Exchange: Free.

apple and grape salad

READY TO SERVE: 25 MINUTES
SERVINGS: 4

* super fast

½ teaspoon lemon juice
⅓ cup mayonnaise or salad dressing
1 medium apple, cubed (1 cup)
½ cup halved grapes
¼ cup chopped celery
2 tablespoons chopped walnuts

1. In medium bowl, blend lemon juice and mayonnaise. Add remaining ingredients; stir gently to coat.

2. Serve immediately, or cover and refrigerate until serving time.

Nutrition Information Per Serving: Calories 190 • Total Fat 17g • Saturated Fat 2g • Cholesterol 10mg • Sodium 110mg • Total Carbohydrate 9g • Dietary Fiber 1g • Sugars 8g • Protein 1g. Dietary Exchanges: ½ Fruit • 3½ Fat.

five-layer salad

1 package (5-oz.) mixed salad greens

1 medium cucumber, peeled, seeded and coarsely chopped

½ cup three-cheese ranch salad dressing

¼ cup cooked real bacon pieces (from 2.5-oz. pkg.)

½ cup finely shredded Cheddar and Monterey Jack cheese blend (2 oz.)

1. On large serving platter or in large bowl, layer all ingredients.

2. To serve, spoon from platter or toss.

Nutrition Information Per Serving: Calories 225 • Total Fat 20g • Saturated Fat 6g • Cholesterol 25mg • Sodium 480mg • Total Carbohydrate 4g • Dietary Fiber 1g • Sugars 4g • Protein 7g. Dietary Exchanges: 1 Vegetable • ½ High-Fat Meat • 3 Fat.

easy vegetable bulgur salad

SERVINGS: 12

ANNETTE ERBECK ✳ MASON, OHIO

1 cup uncooked bulgur (cracked wheat)

2 cups boiling water

1 package (1-lb.) frozen broccoli, cauliflower and carrots

½ cup chopped fresh parsley

¼ cup sliced green onions

½ to 1 cup purchased Italian salad dressing

1. In medium bowl, combine bulgur and boiling water. Let stand 1 hour. Drain well. To thaw vegetables, place in colander under cold running water for 6 minutes. Drain well.

2. In large bowl, combine softened bulgur, thawed vegetables, parsley, green onions and Italian dressing; blend well. Cover; refrigerate 1 to 2 hours to blend flavors if desired. Store in refrigerator.

Nutrition Information Per Serving: Calories 160 • Total Fat 10g • Sodium 170mg • Total Carbohydrate 15g • Protein 2g.

festive coleslaw with citrus vinaigrette

1 package (16-oz.) coleslaw blend

½ medium green bell pepper, cut into small thin strips

½ medium red bell pepper, cut into small thin strips

⅓ cup sugar

¼ cup orange juice

2 tablespoons lemon juice

½ teaspoon salt

½ teaspoon onion powder

½ teaspoon dry mustard

⅓ cup oil

1. In large bowl, combine coleslaw blend and bell peppers.

2. In medium bowl, combine all remaining ingredients except oil; mix well with wire whisk. Gradually beat in oil until well combined. Pour dressing over salad; mix well.

Nutrition Information Per Serving: Calories 150 • Total Fat 12g • Saturated Fat 2g • Cholesterol 0mg • Sodium 105mg • Total Carbohydrate 9g • Dietary Fiber 1g • Sugars 7g • Protein 1g. Dietary Exchanges: 2½ Fat • ½ Other Carbohydrate.

DO-AHEAD OPTIONS

Perfect for simple family suppers as well as weekend entertaining, the coleslaw can be prepared ahead of time when you know your night will be particularly busy. For instance, you can mix up the vinaigrette a day early. You can also combine the cabbage and bell peppers, refrigerating the mixture for up to 2 hours before serving. If you like coleslaw less crisp, prepare the recipe a few hours in advance, cover it and store it the refrigerator.

cranberry upside-down muffins

PREP TIME: 15 MINUTES
READY TO SERVE: 35 MINUTES
SERVINGS: 12 MUFFINS

¾ cup whole-berry cranberry sauce

¼ cup firmly packed brown sugar

2 cups all-purpose flour

2 tablespoons sugar

3 teaspoons baking powder

½ teaspoon salt

1 cup skim milk

¼ cup vegetable oil

1 teaspoon grated orange peel

2 egg whites

1. Heat oven to 400°F. Place wire rack over sheet of waxed paper. Spray 12 medium muffin cups with nonstick cooking spray. Spoon 1 tablespoon cranberry sauce into each muffin cup. Top each with 1 teaspoon brown sugar.

2. In large bowl, combine flour, sugar, baking powder and salt; mix well. In small bowl, combine milk, oil, orange peel and egg whites; blend well. Add to flour mixture all at once; stir just until dry ingredients are moistened. Divide batter evenly over cranberries and brown sugar in muffin cups.

3. Bake at 400°F for 14 to 18 minutes or until toothpick inserted in center comes out clean. Cool in pan for 1 minute. Run knife around edges of cups to loosen. Invert muffins onto wire rack over waxed paper; remove pan. Cool 5 minutes. Serve warm.

Nutrition Information Per Serving: Calories 180 • Total Fat 5g • Saturated Fat 0g • Cholesterol 0mg • Sodium 250mg • Total Carbohydrate 31g • Dietary Fiber 0g • Sugars 14g • Protein 3g. Dietary Exchanges: 1 Starch • 1 Fat • 1 Other Carbohydrate.

marinated roasted vegetable antipasto

cheddar twisters

PREP TIME: 10 MINUTES
READY TO SERVE: 35 MINUTES
SERVINGS: 8

2 cans (8-oz. each) refrigerated crescent dinner rolls

1½ cups finely shredded sharp Cheddar cheese (6 oz.)

¼ cup chopped green onions (4 medium)

1 egg

1 teaspoon water

2 teaspoons sesame seeds

½ teaspoon garlic salt with parsley blend (from 4.8-oz. jar)

1. Heat oven to 375°F. Lightly grease large cookie sheet with shortening or cooking spray. Unroll both cans of the dough. Separate into 8 rectangles; firmly press perforations to seal.

2. In small bowl, mix cheese and onions. Spoon scant ¼ cup cheese mixture in 1-inch-wide strip lengthwise down center of each rectangle to within ¼ inch of each end. Fold dough in half lengthwise to form long strip; firmly press edges to seal. Twist each strip 4 or 5 times; bring ends together to form ring and pinch to seal. Place on cookie sheet.

3. In another small bowl, beat egg and water until well blended; brush over dough. Sprinkle with sesame seeds and garlic salt blend.

4. Bake 15 to 20 minutes or until golden brown. Immediately remove from cookie sheet; cool 5 minutes. Serve warm.

Nutrition Information Per Serving: Calories 310 • Total Fat 20g • Saturated Fat 9g; Trans Fat 3g • Cholesterol 50mg • Sodium 640mg • Total Carbohydrate 23g • Dietary Fiber 0g • Sugars 5g • Protein 10g. Dietary Exchanges: 1½ Starch • 1 High-Fat Meat • 2 Fat.

marinated roasted vegetable antipasto

PREP TIME: 45 MINUTES
READY TO SERVE: 1 HOUR 45 MINUTES
SERVINGS: 12

* plan ahead

roasted vegetables

½ large onion, cut into ⅜-inch-thick wedges

4 tablespoons extra-virgin olive oil

½ small eggplant (cut lengthwise)

1 small red bell pepper

1 small yellow bell pepper

4 oz. portobello mushrooms, cut into ⅜-inch-thick slices

marinade

¼ cup white wine or chicken broth

2 tablespoons balsamic vinegar

1 teaspoon dried basil leaves

½ teaspoon dried oregano leaves

½ teaspoon salt

¼ teaspoon pepper

2 garlic cloves, minced

1. Heat oven to 400°F. Arrange onion wedges in ungreased 15x10x1-inch baking pan. Drizzle with 1 tablespoon of the oil. Bake at 400°F for 5 minutes.

2. Meanwhile, cut eggplant half crosswise into ⅜-inch-thick slices. Cut top and bottom from red and yellow bell peppers; reserve for another use. Remove seeds and membranes from bell peppers. Cut into 2x1-inch strips.

3. Remove onion from oven. Arrange eggplant, bell peppers and mushrooms in pan. Drizzle with remaining 3 tablespoons oil.

4. Return to oven; bake an additional 10 minutes. Turn vegetables; bake an additional 5 to 10 minutes or until vegetables are crisp-tender.

5. In medium bowl, combine all marinade ingredients; mix well. Add roasted vegetables; toss to coat. Cover; refrigerate 1 hour or until cool.

6. To serve, drain vegetables; arrange on serving platter. Discard marinade.

Nutrition Information Per Serving: Calories 50 • Total Fat 5g • Saturated Fat 1g • Cholesterol 0mg • Sodium 25mg • Total Carbohydrate 2g • Dietary Fiber 1g • Sugars 1g • Protein 0g. Dietary Exchange: 1 Fat.

CUTTING FAT AND TIME

Oven roasting brings out the fabulous sweetness of onion, eggplant, peppers and mushrooms, making this dish a surefire hit with everyone at your table. If you're watching your gang's fat intake, you can shave a few fat grams from the recipe by omitting the extra-virgin olive oil and lightly spritzing the vegetables with nonfat cooking spray. You can also cut down on your time in the kitchen by preparing the veggies a day early and storing them in the refrigerator.

---

vegetarian fried rice

PREP TIME: 45 MINUTES
SERVINGS: 3

1½ cups uncooked instant brown rice
1½ cups water
½ cup sliced fresh mushrooms
½ cup shredded carrot
¼ cup sliced green onion
¼ cup chopped green bell pepper
¼ teaspoon ginger
1 garlic clove, minced
2 tablespoons lite soy sauce
2 eggs, beaten
⅛ teaspoon pepper
¾ cup frozen sweet peas, thawed, drained

1. Cook rice in water as directed on package.

2. Meanwhile, spray large nonstick skillet or wok with nonstick cooking spray. Heat over medium heat until hot. Add mushrooms, carrot, green onions, bell pepper, ginger and garlic; cook and stir 1 minute.

3. Reduce heat to low. Stir in cooked rice and soy sauce; cook 5 minutes, stirring occasionally.

4. Push rice mixture to side of skillet; add eggs and pepper to other side. Cook over low heat for 3 to 4 minutes, stirring constantly until eggs are cooked.

5. Add peas to rice and egg mixture; stir gently to combine. Cook until thoroughly heated. If desired, serve with additional soy sauce.

Nutrition Information Per Serving: Calories 350 • Total Fat 6g • Saturated 1g • Cholesterol 140mg • Sodium 540mg • Total Carbohydrate 61g • Dietary Fiber 6g • Sugars 3g • Protein 13g. Dietary Exchanges: 4 Starch • ½ Vegetable • ½ Fat OR 4 Carbohydrate • ½ Vegetable • ½ Fat.

easy egg rolls

PREP TIME: 45 MINUTES
SERVINGS: 8

1 teaspoon cornstarch
4 teaspoons soy sauce
½ teaspoon sesame oil
1 tablespoon oil
4 cups purchased coleslaw blend
1 cup fresh bean sprouts
2 tablespoons sliced green onions
½ teaspoon grated gingerroot
½ cup shredded cooked chicken
Oil for deep frying
8 egg roll skins (from 1-lb. pkg.)

1. In small bowl, combine cornstarch, soy sauce and sesame oil; blend well. Set aside.

2. Heat 1 tablespoon oil in large skillet or wok over medium-high heat until hot. Add coleslaw blend, bean sprouts, green onions and gingerroot; cook and stir 3 to 4 minutes or until tender. Add chicken and cornstarch mixture; cook and stir 1 to 2 minutes or until mixture is thoroughly coated. Remove from skillet; cool to room temperature.

3. In deep fryer, heavy saucepan or wok, heat 3 to 4 inches of oil to 375°F.

4. Meanwhile, place 1 egg roll skin on work surface with 1 corner facing you. (Cover remaining skins with damp paper towel to prevent drying out.) Place ¼ cup coleslaw mixture slightly below center of egg roll skin. Fold corner of egg roll skin closest to filling over filling, tucking point under. Fold in and overlap right and left corners. Wet remaining corner with water; gently roll egg roll toward remaining corner and press to seal. (Cover filled egg roll with damp paper towel to prevent drying out.) Repeat with remaining egg roll skins and coleslaw mixture.

5. Fry egg rolls, a few at a time, in hot oil (375°F) for 4 to 6 minutes or until golden brown, turning once. Drain on paper towels.

Nutrition Information Per Serving: Calories 240 • Total Fat 14g • Saturated Fat 2g • Cholesterol 10mg • Sodium 370mg • Total Carbohydrate 22g • Dietary Fiber 1g • Sugars 3g • Protein 7g. Dietary Exchanges: 1 Starch • 1 Vegetable • 3 Fat OR 1 Carbohydrate • 1 Vegetable • 3 Fat.

easy egg rolls

cabbage salad with crunchy noodles

SERVINGS: 16

BIRDIE CASEMENT ✳ DENVER, COLORADO

salad

- 4½ cups shredded red or green cabbage (1 medium head)
- 5 green onions, thinly sliced (including tops)
- 1 can (11-oz.) vacuum-packed whole kernel corn, drained
- 1½ cups frozen sweet peas (from 1-lb. pkg.), cooked, drained
- 1 jar (4.5-oz.) sliced mushrooms, undrained

dressing

- 1 package (3-oz.) instant Oriental noodles with chicken-flavor seasoning packet
- ¼ cup tarragon vinegar
- ¼ cup oil
- 3 tablespoons sugar
- ½ teaspoon pepper
- ½ cup slivered almonds, toasted
- 2 tablespoons sesame seeds, toasted

1. In large bowl, combine all salad ingredients. In small bowl, combine contents of seasoning packet from noodles, vinegar, oil, sugar and pepper; blend well. Pour dressing over salad ingredients; toss to coat. Refrigerate 2 hours to chill if desired.

2. Break noodles into ¾-inch pieces. Before serving, stir noodles, almonds and sesame seeds into salad mixture. Store in refrigerator.

Nutrition Information Per Serving: Calories 130 • Total Fat 7g • Sodium 210mg • Total Carbohydrate 14g • Protein 3g.

ADDING FLAVOR IN A HURRY

The ingredients called for in the salad are available year-round, so you can prepare the colorful side dish as often as you like. Best of all, toasting the almonds and sesame seeds brings out an earthy flavor you're sure to enjoy time and again.

To toast the almonds, spread the nuts on a cookie sheet and bake them at 375°F for 5 to 6 minutes or until they turn a light golden brown, stirring occasionally. You can also spread them in a microwave-safe pie pan and microwave on High for 6 to 7 minutes or until light golden brown, stirring frequently.

To toast the sesame seeds, simply spread the seeds in a medium skillet. Stir the seeds over medium heat for 8 to 10 minutes or until they turn golden brown. You can also spread them in a layer in a baking pan. Bake the seeds at 375°F for 5 to 7 minutes or until light golden brown.

---

winter fruit salad

PREP TIME: 15 MINUTES
SERVINGS: 12

* super fast

- 2 cups cubed unpeeled red apples (2 medium)
- 2 cups cubed unpeeled pears (2 medium)
- ¾ cup chopped dates
- 1 tablespoon fresh lemon juice
- 2 medium bananas, sliced
- ⅓ cup light mayonnaise or salad dressing
- 2 tablespoons honey
- ½ teaspoon grated lemon peel
- ⅛ teaspoon allspice

1. In large bowl, combine apples, pears, dates and lemon juice; mix well. Add bananas; stir gently to mix.

2. In small bowl, combine all remaining ingredients; blend well. Add to salad; stir gently to coat. If desired, serve in lettuce-lined bowl.

Nutrition Information Per Serving: Calories 125 • Total Fat 3g • Saturated Fat 0g • Cholesterol 5mg • Sodium 40mg • Total Carbohydrate 24g • Dietary Fiber 2g • Sugars 19g • Protein 1g. Dietary Exchanges: 1 Fruit • ½ Fat • ½ Other Carbohydrate.

three-cheese crescent pinwheels

PREP TIME: 30 MINUTES
SERVINGS: 8

- 2 oz. crumbled blue cheese (½ cup)
- 1 oz. shredded hot pepper Monterey Jack cheese (¼ cup)
- 2 tablespoons cream cheese, softened
- 1 tablespoon mayonnaise
- 1 can (8-oz.) refrigerated crescent dinner rolls
- 2 teaspoons chopped fresh parsley

1. Heat oven to 375°F. Lightly spray cookie sheet with nonstick cooking spray. In small bowl, combine all cheeses and mayonnaise; mix until well blended and soft.

2. Unroll dough into 2 long rectangles; press perforations to seal. Spread cheese mixture evenly over rectangles. Starting at short sides, roll up each; pinch edges to seal. Cut each roll into 8 slices. Place cut side down on sprayed cookie sheet. Sprinkle each with parsley.

3. Bake at 375°F for 12 to 15 minutes or until golden brown. Immediately remove from cookie sheet; cool 3 minutes. Serve warm.

Nutrition Information Per Serving: Calories 165 • Total Fat 10g • Saturated Fat 4g • Cholesterol 15mg • Sodium 480mg • Total Carbohydrate 14g • Dietary Fiber 0g • Sugars 4g • Protein 5g. Dietary Exchanges: 1 Starch • ½ High-Fat Meat • 1 Fat.

honeydew melon-orange salad

PREP TIME: 25 MINUTES
SERVINGS: 4

* super fast

- 1 tablespoon lime juice
- 1 tablespoon honey
- ¼ teaspoon grated lime peel, if desired
- 3 cups cubed honeydew melon
- 1 can (11-oz.) mandarin orange segments, well drained

1. In medium bowl, combine lime juice, honey and lime peel; mix well.

2. Add melon and oranges; toss lightly. Serve immediately or refrigerate until serving time.

Nutrition Information Per Serving: Calories 110 • Total Fat 0g • Saturated Fat 0g • Cholesterol 0mg • Sodium 20mg • Total Carbohydrate 28g • Dietary Fiber 1g • Sugars 23g • Protein 1g. Dietary Exchange: 2 Fruit.

herb vegetable couscous

PREP TIME: 15 MINUTES
SERVINGS: 6

* super fast

1 cup chicken broth

⅔ cup frozen early June peas

⅛ teaspoon salt

⅛ teaspoon pepper

1 teaspoon chopped fresh thyme or ¼ teaspoon dried thyme leaves

1 garlic clove, minced

¾ cup uncooked couscous

1 medium tomato, seeded, chopped

1. In medium saucepan, combine broth, peas, salt, pepper, thyme and garlic. Bring to a boil.

2. Remove saucepan from heat; stir in couscous and tomato. Cover; let stand 5 minutes. Fluff with fork before serving.

Nutrition Information Per Serving: Calories 100 • Total Fat 0g, Saturated 0g • Cholesterol 0mg • Sodium 200mg • Total Carbohydrate 21g • Dietary Fiber 2g • Sugars 1g • Protein 5g. Dietary Exchange: 1½ Starch OR 1½ Carbohydrate.

peas with dill

PREP TIME: 25 MINUTES
SERVINGS: 4

* super fast

1 teaspoon butter or margarine

¼ cup chopped onion

1 package (16-oz.) frozen sweet peas

2 tablespoons diced roasted red pepper or pimiento, drained

1 teaspoon dried dill

1. In medium nonstick skillet, melt butter over low heat. Add onion; cook and stir until tender.

2. Stir in remaining ingredients; cook 8 to 10 minutes or until thoroughly heated.

Nutrition Information Per Serving: Calories 80 • Total Fat 1g • Saturated Fat 0g • Cholesterol 0mg • Sodium 100mg • Total Carbohydrate 16g • Dietary Fiber 6g • Sugars 6g • Protein 5g. Dietary Exchange: 1 Starch.

pepper biscuit pull-apart

SERVINGS: 10 BISCUITS
JULIE ANN ROBASSE * BIG LAKE, MINNESOTA

¼ teaspoon garlic powder

¼ teaspoon salt, if desired

¼ teaspoon dried basil leaves, crushed

¼ teaspoon dried oregano leaves, crushed

1 can (12-oz.) refrigerated flaky biscuits

4½ teaspoons olive oil

¼ cup chopped green bell pepper

¼ cup chopped red bell pepper

1 oz. shredded mozzarella cheese (¼ cup)

2 tablespoons grated Romano or Parmesan cheese

1. Heat oven to 400°F. In small bowl, combine garlic powder, salt, basil and oregano; blend well. Set aside.

2. Separate dough into 10 biscuits. Place 1 biscuit in center of ungreased cookie sheet. Arrange remaining biscuits in circle, edges slightly overlapping, around center biscuit. Gently press out to 10-inch circle. Brush with olive oil; top with bell peppers and cheeses. Sprinkle garlic powder mixture over top. Bake at 400°F for 12 to 15 minutes or until golden brown. To serve, pull apart warm biscuits.

Nutrition Information Per Serving: Calories 130 • Total Fat 7g • Sodium 450mg • Total Carbohydrate 14g • Protein 3g.

pepper biscuit pull-apart

tex-mex baked beans

PREP TIME: 10 MINUTES
READY TO SERVE: 4 HOURS 10 MINUTES
SERVINGS: 14

* slow cooked

2 cans (15.5-oz. each) great northern beans, drained, rinsed

2 cans (15-oz. each) black beans, drained, rinsed

1 can (8-oz.) tomato sauce

1 can (4.5-oz.) chopped green chiles

¾ cup barbecue sauce

¾ cup chunky-style salsa

¼ cup firmly packed brown sugar

1. In 3½- or 4-quart slow cooker, combine all ingredients; mix well.

2. Cover; cook on Low setting for at least 4 hours.

Nutrition Information Per Serving: Calories 130 • Total Fat 1g • Saturated Fat 0g • Cholesterol 0mg • Sodium 550mg • Total Carbohydrate 24g • Dietary Fiber 6g • Sugars 6g • Protein 6g. Dietary Exchanges: 1 Starch • ½ Fruit • ½ Very Lean Meat OR 1½ Carbohydrate • ½ Very Lean Meat.

TAKE IT TO GO

These zesty baked beans make a crowd-pleasing contribution to picnics, backyard barbecues and other covered-dish events. Best of all, you can bring the beans in the same slow cooker used to prepare them. When you're ready to leave the house, wrap the slow cooker in a towel to keep the beans warm on the drive. Place the slow cooker in a box to keep it standing flat in the car. Attach rubber bands around the handles and lid to secure the lid.

broccoli with walnut-garlic butter

PREP TIME: 10 MINUTES
SERVINGS: 6

✳ super fast

1 package (14-oz.) frozen broccoli florets
1 tablespoon butter
1 garlic clove, minced
¼ cup walnut pieces

1. Cook broccoli as directed on package. Drain.

2. Meanwhile, melt butter in small saucepan over low heat. Add garlic; cook until butter is lightly browned, stirring constantly. Stir in walnuts.

3. Pour walnut mixture over cooked broccoli; toss gently to coat.

Nutrition Information Per Serving: Calories 75 • Total Fat 5g • Saturated Fat 2g • Cholesterol 5mg • Sodium 25mg • Total Carbohydrate 4g • Dietary Fiber 2g • Sugars 1g • Protein 3g. Dietary Exchanges: 1 Vegetable • 1 Fat.

grilled pesto french bread

PREP TIME: 25 MINUTES
SERVINGS: 4

✳ super fast

¼ cup butter or margarine, softened
1 package (3-oz.) cream cheese, softened
½ cup basil pesto
1 loaf (1-lb.) French bread, halved crosswise, split lengthwise

1. Heat gas or charcoal grill. In small bowl, mix butter, cream cheese and pesto.

2. When grill is heated, place bread pieces, cut sides down, on gas grill over medium heat or on charcoal grill 4 to 6 inches from medium coals. Cook covered 1 to 2 minutes or until lightly brown.

3. Turn bread pieces over; spread pesto mixture evenly on cut sides of bread. Cook covered 3 to 4 minutes or until heated. Cut bread into 2-inch sections.

Nutrition Information Per Serving: Calories 160 • Total Fat 10g • Saturated Fat 4g • Cholesterol 15mg • Sodium 270mg • Total Carbohydrate 15g • Dietary Fiber 0g • Sugars 0g • Protein 4g. Dietary Exchanges: 1 Starch • 2 Fat.

italian mixed salad

PREP TIME: 15 MINUTES
SERVINGS: 4

✳ super fast

4 cups bite-size pieces romaine lettuce
1 jar (6-oz.) marinated quartered artichoke hearts, drained
1 jar (6-oz.) whole mushrooms, drained
2 Italian plum tomatoes, cut into small wedges
½ small cucumber, halved lengthwise, seeded and sliced
¼ cup olive oil
2 tablespoons red wine vinegar

1. In large bowl, combine all ingredients except oil and vinegar; toss to mix.

2. Drizzle salad with oil and vinegar; toss gently to coat.

Nutrition Information Per Serving: Calories 180 • Total Fat 15g • Saturated Fat 2g • Cholesterol 0mg • Sodium 320mg • Total Carbohydrate 10g • Dietary Fiber 5g • Sugars 4g • Protein 4g. Dietary Exchanges: 2 Vegetable • 3 Fat.

CUSTOMIZING MADE SIMPLE

To give the salad a slightly different flavor, try using ¼ cup of your favorite Italian salad dressing instead of the olive oil and red wine vinegar called for in the recipe. For fun, toss in a few slices of packaged pepperoni, chopped banana pepper rings or a few rings of red onion.

If cheese is big with your family, mix in some bite-sized cubes of mozzarella or top the salad with a little bit of shredded Parmesan.

carrot zucchini muffins

PREP TIME: 10 MINUTES
READY TO SERVE: 35 MINUTES
SERVINGS: 12 MUFFINS

2 cups all-purpose flour

1 cup rolled oats

¾ cup firmly packed brown sugar

3 teaspoons baking powder

½ teaspoon cinnamon

¼ teaspoon salt

⅔ cup skim milk

3 tablespoons oil

2 egg whites

1 cup finely shredded carrots

½ cup shredded unpeeled zucchini (1 small)

1. Heat oven to 400°F. Spray 12 muffin cups with nonstick cooking spray, or line muffin cups with paper baking cups and spray paper cups with nonstick cooking spray.

2. In large bowl, combine flour, oats, brown sugar, baking powder, cinnamon and salt; mix well.

3. In small bowl, combine milk, oil and egg whites; blend well. Add to dry ingredients all at once; stir just until dry ingredients are moistened. Stir in carrots and zucchini just until blended. Spoon batter evenly into sprayed muffin cups.

4. Bake at 400°F for 16 to 21 minutes or until muffins are golden brown and toothpick inserted in center comes out clean. Immediately remove from pan. Serve warm.

Nutrition Information Per Serving: Calories 200 • Total Fat 4g • Saturated 1g • Cholesterol 0mg • Sodium 150mg • Total Carbohydrate 36g • Dietary Fiber 2g • Sugars 15g • Protein 4g. **Dietary Exchanges:** 2 Starch • 1 Fat OR 2 Carbohydrate • 1 Fat.

potato corn bake

SERVINGS: 6

MARION BEDIENT ✳ CAMERON, WISCONSIN

½ lb. bacon, cut into ¾-inch pieces

½ cup finely chopped green bell pepper

⅓ cup finely chopped onion

1 can (15-oz.) cream-style corn

2 cups milk

3 tablespoons margarine or butter

¾ teaspoon salt, if desired

⅛ teaspoon pepper

2 cups mashed potato flakes

½ cup dairy sour cream

¼ cup grated Parmesan cheese

2 tablespoons finely chopped green onion tops, if desired

1. Heat oven to 375°F. Grease 11x7-inch or 9-inch square pan. Cook bacon in large saucepan until crisp. Drain, reserving 1 tablespoon bacon drippings. Set bacon aside. Return 1 tablespoon bacon drippings to saucepan. Add bell pepper and onion to drippings. Cook over medium heat until tender.

2. Stir in corn, milk, margarine, salt and pepper; cook over medium heat until mixture is hot and bubbly. Remove from heat; stir in potato flakes and sour cream until well blended.

3. Spoon mixture into greased pan. Top the casserole with bacon, Parmesan cheese and green onions.

4. Bake at 375°F for 20 to 25 minutes or until thoroughly heated.

Nutrition Information Per Serving: Calories 360 • Total Fat 21g • Sodium 860mg • Total Carbohydrate 33g • Protein 11g.

MAKE-AHEAD EASE

Potato Corn Bake is a hearty and comforting side dish whether you are serving it with grilled chicken or featuring it alongside broiled steaks. It's easy enough for workweek suppers and impressive enough for weeknight entertaining. You can get a head start on dinner preparations by assembling the casserole up to 4 hours before baking it.

Simply remove the dish from the refrigerator, and bake the casserole at 375°F for 25 to 30 minutes or until it is heated through.

potato corn bake

mozzarella and pesto
crescent tarts

basil sugar snap peas with mushrooms

PREP TIME: 15 MINUTES
SERVINGS: 5

* super fast

1 tablespoon olive oil

1 cup sliced fresh mushrooms

1 garlic clove, minced

3 cups frozen sugar snap peas

½ cup halved cherry tomatoes

2 teaspoons chopped fresh basil or ½ teaspoon dried basil leaves

1 tablespoon grated Parmesan cheese

1. Heat oil in medium nonstick saucepan over medium heat until hot. Add mushrooms and garlic; cook until tender, stirring occasionally. Remove from saucepan; cover to keep warm.

2. Add ⅓ cup water to same saucepan; bring to a boil. Add sugar snap peas; return to a boil. Stir; reduce heat. Cover; simmer 2½ to 4½ minutes or until crisp-tender.

3. Drain sugar snap peas; return to saucepan. Stir in mushroom mixture, tomatoes and basil. Spoon into serving bowl; sprinkle with cheese.

Nutrition Information Per Serving: Calories 70 • Total Fat 3g • Saturated 1g • Cholesterol 0mg • Sodium 25mg • Total Carbohydrate 8g • Dietary Fiber 3g • Sugars 3g • Protein 3g. Dietary Exchanges: 1 Vegetable • 1 Fat.

mozzarella and pesto crescent tarts

PREP TIME: 20 MINUTES
READY TO SERVE: 35 MINUTES
SERVINGS: 16 SLICES

1 can (8-oz.) refrigerated crescent dinner rolls

2 tablespoons purchased pesto

2 medium tomatoes, seeded, sliced

1 small red onion, thinly sliced

1 to 2 teaspoons chopped fresh rosemary or ½ teaspoon dried rosemary leaves

2 oz. diced fresh mozzarella cheese or shredded mozzarella cheese (½ cup)

1 oz. shredded fresh Parmesan cheese (¼ cup)

1. Heat oven to 425°F. Unroll dough into 2 long rectangles. Place 3 inches apart on ungreased cookie sheet. Firmly press perforations to seal. Press to form two 10x3-inch strips, forming rim around edge of dough.

2. Spread each strip with 1 tablespoon pesto. Top each with tomatoes, onion and rosemary. Sprinkle each with mozzarella and Parmesan cheese.

3. Bake at 425°F for 10 to 14 minutes or until edges are golden brown and cheese is melted. Cut each into crosswise slices. Serve warm or cool.

Nutrition Information Per Serving: Calories 90 • Total Fat 5g • Saturated Fat 1g • Cholesterol 3mg • Sodium 170mg • Total Carbohydrate 7g • Dietary Fiber 0g • Sugars 2g • Protein 3g. Dietary Exchanges: ½ Starch • 1 Fat OR ½ Carbohydrate • 1 Fat.

easy baked onion rings

SERVINGS: 8 ROLLS

KEVIN KOORS ***** LAFAYETTE, INDIANA

⅓ cup chopped onion

2 tablespoons margarine or butter, melted

1 tablespoon grated Parmesan cheese

½ teaspoon poppy seeds

¼ teaspoon chili powder

¼ teaspoon garlic powder

⅛ teaspoon pepper

1 can (8-oz.) refrigerated crescent dinner rolls

¼ cup seasoned dry bread crumbs

¼ teaspoon chili powder

1 egg, beaten

1. Heat oven to 375°F. In small bowl, combine onion, margarine, Parmesan cheese, poppy seeds, ¼ teaspoon chili powder, garlic powder and pepper; mix well. Separate dough into 4 rectangles; firmly press perforations to seal. Cut each rectangle lengthwise into 2 strips, forming 8 strips. Spoon about 2 teaspoons onion mixture down center of each strip. Bring long sides of dough together over filling; firmly pinch edges to seal. Twist each filled dough strip; form into a ring. Pinch ends of strips together to seal.

2. In small bowl, combine bread crumbs and ¼ teaspoon chili powder. Dip tops and sides of rings in beaten egg and then in bread crumb mixture. Place crumb side up on ungreased cookie sheet. Bake at 375°F for 10 to 15 minutes or until deep golden brown. Serve warm.

Nutrition Information Per Serving: Calories 150 • Total Fat 9g • Sodium 330mg • Total Carbohydrate 14g • Protein 3g.

herbed wild rice pilaf

PREP TIME: 10 MINUTES
READY TO SERVE: 5 HOURS 10 MINUTES
SERVINGS: 12

＊ slow cooked

1½ cups uncooked wild rice
½ cup sliced green onions
1 jar (4.5-oz.) sliced mushrooms, drained
1 garlic clove, minced
¾ teaspoon salt
1 can (14-oz.) chicken broth
2 cups water
½ cup dried cherries
¾ teaspoon dried thyme leaves
¼ teaspoon nutmeg
2 tablespoons chopped fresh parsley

1. Spray 4- to 6-quart slow cooker with nonstick cooking spray. Rinse rice with cold water; drain. In sprayed slow cooker, combine rice, onions, mushrooms, garlic, salt, broth and water; stir gently to mix.

2. Cover; cook on High setting for 3 to 4 hours.

3. About 1 hour before serving, stir cherries, thyme and nutmeg into rice mixture. Reduce heat setting to Low; cover and cook an additional 30 to 60 minutes or until rice is opened and tender. Stir parsley into rice pilaf before serving.

Nutrition Information Per Serving: Calories 110 • Total Fat 1g • Saturated Fat 0g • Cholesterol 0mg • Sodium 180mg • Total Carbohydrate 21g • Dietary Fiber 2g • Sugars 4g • Protein 4g. Dietary Exchanges: 1 Starch • ½ Fruit OR 1½ Carbohydrate.

vegetable-rice pilaf

PREP TIME: 10 MINUTES
READY TO SERVE: 2 HOURS 10 MINUTES
SERVINGS: 12

＊ slow cooked

1 can (14-oz.) chicken broth with roasted garlic
⅔ cup water
1½ cups uncooked converted long-grain white rice
1 tablespoon olive oil
1¼ cups frozen cut green beans
½ cup sliced carrot
2 green onions, sliced
½ teaspoon salt
¼ teaspoon lemon-pepper seasoning

1. In 4-cup microwave-safe measuring cup, combine broth and water. Microwave on High for 4 to 5 minutes or until steaming hot.

2. Meanwhile, spray 4- to 6-quart slow cooker with nonstick cooking spray. Combine rice and oil in sprayed slow cooker; mix well. Add all remaining ingredients and hot broth mixture.

3. Cover; cook on High setting for 1½ to 2 hours.

Nutrition Information Per Serving: Calories 110 • Total Fat 2g • Saturated Fat 0g • Cholesterol 0mg • Sodium 120mg • Total Carbohydrate 21g • Dietary Fiber 1g • Sugars 1g • Protein 2g. Dietary Exchange: 1½ Starch OR 2½ Carbohydrate.

chili cheese bread

READY TO SERVE: 15 MINUTES
SERVINGS: 4

＊ super fast

¼ cup light chives and onion cream cheese spread (from 8-oz. container)
2 tablespoons chopped green chiles (from 4.5-oz. can), drained
½ loaf French bread (16-in. long), halved lengthwise
½ cup reduced-fat shredded Cheddar and Monterey Jack cheese blend (2 oz.)

1. In small bowl, combine cream cheese and chiles.

2. Place bread halves, cut sides up, on broiler pan. Broil 4 to 6 inches from heat for 1 to 2 minutes or until light golden brown.

3. Top with cream cheese mixture and shredded cheese. Broil additional 2 minutes or until cheese is melted. Cut each bread half into 4 pieces.

Nutrition Information Per Serving: Calories 115 • Total Fat 4g • Saturated Fat 2g • Cholesterol 10mg • Sodium 270mg • Total Carbohydrate 15g • Dietary Fiber 0g • Sugars 1g • Protein 5g. Dietary Exchanges: 1 Starch • 1 Fat.

herbed wild rice pilaf

vegetable-rice pilaf

alfredo green bean casserole

PREP TIME: 10 MINUTES
READY TO SERVE: 4 HOURS 10 MINUTES
SERVINGS: 10

✴ slow cooked

- 1 package (28-oz.) frozen cut green beans
- 1 can (8-oz.) sliced water chestnuts, drained
- ½ cup roasted red bell pepper strips (from a jar)
- ¼ teaspoon salt
- 1 container (10-oz.) refrigerated Alfredo sauce
- 1 can (2.8-oz.) French-fried onions

1. In 4- to 6-quart slow cooker, combine all ingredients except onions. Stir in half of the onions.

2. Cover; cook on High setting for 3 to 4 hours, stirring after 1 to 1½ hours.

3. About 5 minutes before serving, in small skillet, heat remaining half of onions over medium-high heat for 2 to 3 minutes or until hot, stirring frequently. Stir bean mixture; sprinkle with onions.

Nutrition Information Per Serving: Calories 180 • Total Fat 14g • Saturated Fat 7g • Cholesterol 30mg • Sodium 260mg • Total Carbohydrate 13g • Dietary Fiber 3g • Sugars 3g • Protein 4g. Dietary Exchanges: 2½ Vegetable • 2½ Fat.

BAKE UP SOME BUTTERY BISCUITS

These green beans are terrific with chicken, turkey and ham. If they appear on your menu, consider whipping up some Garlic and Herb Biscuits. The no-fuss bites perfectly round out the favor of the beans.

Start by separating 1 can (16.3-oz.) of large refrigerated buttermilk biscuits into 8 biscuits. Brush the top and sides of each biscuit with a little butter or margarine that you have melted in the microwave.

Coat the biscuits with some seasoned bread crumbs. If you're out of seasoned bread crumbs, season plain crumbs with some garlic powder. Bake the biscuits as directed on the can, and you'll have an incredible dinner addition that's bound to become a staple in your home.

garden risotto

READY TO SERVE: 30 MINUTES
SERVINGS: 3

- 1 tablespoon olive oil
- ¼ cup chopped green onions
- ¼ cup chopped red bell pepper
- 1 cup uncooked short-grain Arborio rice, rinsed
- 1 can (14½-oz.) ready-to-serve vegetable broth
- ¾ cup water
- 1 cup chopped fresh broccoli
- ½ cup shredded carrot
- 1 teaspoon dried thyme leaves
- 2 tablespoons shredded fresh Parmesan cheese

1. In a large nonstick saucepan or Dutch oven, heat oil over medium heat until hot. Add green onions and bell pepper; cook 2 minutes or until tender, stirring occasionally. Add rice; cook and stir 2 minutes.

2. Add broth and water; bring to a boil. Reduce heat to medium-low; cover and cook 10 minutes.

3. Stir in broccoli and carrot; simmer an additional 5 to 10 minutes. Remove from the heat; stir in thyme. Cover; let stand 3 minutes. Sprinkle with cheese.

Nutrition Information Per Serving: Calories 260 • Total Fat 7g • Saturated Fat 1g • Cholesterol 3mg • Sodium 700mg • Total Carbohydrate 43g • Dietary Fiber 2g • Sugars 4g • Protein 36g. Dietary Exchanges: 2½ Starch • 1 Vegetable • 1 Fat OR 2½ Carbohydrate • 1 Vegetable • 1 Fat.

biscuit mini focaccia

SERVINGS: 10

LINDA J. GREESON ✳ SPRING VALLEY, CALIFORNIA

½ cup fresh basil leaves

¼ cup fresh thyme sprigs

2 garlic cloves, chopped

¼ teaspoon salt, if desired
   Dash pepper

¼ cup olive oil or vegetable oil

1 can (12-oz.) refrigerated
   flaky biscuits

¼ cup pine nuts

⅓ cup grated Parmesan cheese

TURN BACK TIME

When you are really racing against the clock, grab a jar of prepared pesto. Use 1 cup of the pesto in place of the basil, thyme, garlic, salt, pepper and oil called for in the recipe. And if you don't have any pine nuts on hand, save a trip to the store by replacing them with slivered almonds or sunflower kernels.

1. Heat oven to 400°F. In blender container or food processor bowl with metal blade, combine basil, thyme, garlic, salt, pepper and oil. Cover; blend until finely chopped, scraping down sides of container, if necessary.

2. Separate dough into 10 biscuits. On ungreased cookie sheets, press or roll each biscuit to a 3-inch circle. Make several indentations with fingers in tops of biscuits. Spread about 1 teaspoon basil mixture evenly over each biscuit. Sprinkle each biscuit evenly with 1 teaspoon pine nuts; press gently. Sprinkle with cheese.

3. Bake at 400°F for 10 to 12 minutes or until biscuits are golden brown. Serve warm.

Nutrition Information Per Serving: Calories 180 • Total Fat 12g • Sodium 470mg • Total Carbohydrate 15g • Protein 4g.

red grapefruit tossed salad

READY TO SERVE: 25 MINUTES
SERVINGS: 4

✳ super fast

dressing

¼ cup sour cream

2 tablespoons frozen grapefruit juice concentrate, thawed

1 tablespoon brown sugar

salad

3 cups mixed salad greens

1 large red, pink or white grapefruit, peeled, sectioned

¼ large sweet onion, thinly sliced, separated into rings (Walla Walla, Maui or Texas Sweet)

1. In medium bowl, combine all dressing ingredients; blend well.

2. Add all salad ingredients; toss gently.

Nutrition Information Per Serving: Calories 90 • Total Fat 3g • Saturated Fat 2g • Cholesterol 10mg • Sodium 20mg • Total Carbohydrate 15g • Dietary Fiber 2g • Sugars 12g • Protein 2g. Dietary Exchanges: ½ Fruit • 1 Vegetable • ½ Fat.

cheddar-chive drop biscuits

orange-glazed carrots and sugar snap peas

READY TO SERVE: 25 MINUTES
SERVINGS: 4

* super fast

1 cup water

2 cups baby-cut carrots

1 cup frozen sugar snap peas
(from 1-lb. bag)

2 tablespoons orange
marmalade

¼ teaspoon salt

Dash pepper

1. In 2-quart saucepan, heat water to boiling. Add carrots; return to boiling. Reduce heat to low; cover and simmer 8 to 10 minutes or until carrots are tender, adding sugar snap peas during last 5 minutes of cooking time. Drain; return to saucepan.

2. Stir in marmalade, salt and pepper. Cook and stir over medium heat until marmalade is melted and vegetables are glazed.

Nutrition Information Per Serving: Calories 45 • Total Fat 0g • Saturated Fat 0g • Cholesterol 0mg • Sodium 115mg • Total Carbohydrate 10g • Dietary Fiber 2g • Sugars 6g • Protein 1g. Dietary Exchange: ½ Starch.

SIMPLY VERSATILE SIDE DISH

If your family loves peas and carrots, try this orange-flavored veggie using 1 cup of frozen peas for the sugar snap peas instead. The side dish is wonderful with everything from burgers to chicken breasts. Just try it with the Apple-Honey-Mustard Chicken found on page 170 of this book.

cheddar-chive drop biscuits

PREP TIME: 15 MINUTES
READY TO SERVE: 30 MINUTES
SERVINGS: 18 BISCUITS

2 cups all-purpose flour

3 teaspoons baking powder

1 teaspoon salt

½ cup shortening

1¼ cups plain yogurt

1 cup shredded Cheddar
cheese (4 oz.)

¼ cup chopped fresh chives

1. Heat oven to 450°F. Grease large cookie sheet with shortening or cooking spray. In large bowl, mix flour, baking powder and salt. With pastry blender or fork, cut in shortening until mixture resembles coarse crumbs. Stir in yogurt, cheese and chives just until moistened.

2. Drop dough by generous tablespoonfuls onto cookie sheet.

3. Bake 9 to 12 minutes or until light golden brown. Serve warm.

Nutrition Information Per Serving: Calories 140 • Total Fat 8g • Saturated Fat 3g • Trans Fat 1g • Cholesterol 10mg • Sodium 260mg • Total Carbohydrate 12g • Dietary Fiber 0g • Sugars 1g • Protein 4g. Dietary Exchanges: 1 Starch • 1½ Fat.

crispy onion biscuits

READY TO SERVE: 30 MINUTES
SERVINGS: 6 BISCUITS

6 frozen buttermilk biscuits
(from 25-oz. pkg.)

1 egg white, beaten

⅓ cup French-fried onions
(from 2.8-oz. can), crushed

1. Heat oven to 375°F. Place frozen biscuits on ungreased cookie sheet, sides touching. Brush tops with beaten egg white. Top each with onions.

2. Bake at 375°F for 20 to 24 minutes or until golden brown. Serve warm.

Nutrition Information Per Serving: Calories 210 • Total Fat 11g • Saturated Fat 3g • Cholesterol 0mg • Sodium 620mg • Total Carbohydrate 23g • Dietary Fiber 0g • Sugars 3g • Protein 5g. Dietary Exchanges: 1½ Starch • 2 Fat.

parmesan-garlic butter green beans

READY TO SERVE: 15 MINUTES
SERVINGS: 6

* super fast

1 package (14-oz.) frozen whole green beans

2 tablespoons butter

1 small garlic clove, minced

1 tablespoon grated Parmesan cheese

1. Cook green beans as directed on package. Drain.

2. Meanwhile, melt butter in small saucepan over medium-low heat. Add garlic; cook 2 to 3 minutes or until garlic is tender, stirring frequently.

3. Pour garlic butter over cooked green beans; stir to coat. Sprinkle with cheese; toss gently.

Nutrition Information Per Serving: Calories 55 • Total Fat 4g • Saturated Fat 3g • Cholesterol 10mg • Sodium 50mg • Total Carbohydrate 4g • Dietary Fiber 1g • Sugars 2g • Protein 1g. Dietary Exchanges: 1 Vegetable • 1 Fat.

romaine-broccoli salad with strawberries

READY TO SERVE: 25 MINUTES
SERVINGS: 4

* super fast

4 cups torn romaine lettuce

2 cups broccoli-coleslaw blend (from 16-oz. pkg.)

1 cup fresh strawberries, quartered

2 thin slices red onion, quartered

⅓ cup raspberry vinaigrette salad dressing

1. In large serving bowl, combine all ingredients except salad dressing; toss to mix.

2. Pour dressing over salad; toss to coat.

Nutrition Information Per Serving: Calories 75 • Total Fat 5g • Saturated Fat 1g • Cholesterol 0mg • Sodium 40mg • Total Carbohydrate 6g • Dietary Fiber 2g • Sugars 5g • Protein 2g. Dietary Exchanges: 1 Vegetable • 1 Fat.

hot 'n spicy sautéed mushrooms

SERVINGS: 6

GLADYS RANDALL ***** HOUSTON, TEXAS

½ cup margarine or butter

½ cup chopped green bell pepper

½ cup chopped red bell pepper

¼ cup sliced green onions

2 garlic cloves, minced

3 jars (6-oz. each) sliced mushrooms, drained

¼ cup sherry

½ teaspoon Creole or Cajun seasoning

¼ teaspoon ground red pepper (cayenne)

¼ teaspoon pepper

1. Melt margarine in large skillet. Add bell peppers, green onions and garlic; cook and stir over medium heat until tender.

2. Stir in mushrooms, sherry, Creole seasoning, ground red pepper and pepper. Simmer for 2 to 3 minutes or until thoroughly heated, stirring occasionally.

Nutrition Information Per Serving: Calories 180 • Total Fat 15g • Sodium 660mg • Total Carbohydrate 6g • Protein 3g.

JAZZ UP WEEKNIGHT MEALS

Seasoned with red pepper, minced garlic and Creole seasoning, this zesty side dish will add a bit of spicy heat to any meal. The mushrooms, peppers and onions make it an ideal addition to grilled sirloin steaks or savory pork chops. You can even spoon the mixture over the meat for a great presentation that doesn't take any additional time. Add some freshly baked breadsticks to your menu, and you will have a memorable meal in moments.

parmesan-garlic butter green beans

honey-mustard marinated vegetables

savory nutty crescents

READY TO SERVE: 25 MINUTES
SERVINGS: 8 ROLLS

* super fast

2 tablespoons butter, softened

1 teaspoon dried sage leaves

1 can (8-oz.) refrigerated crescent dinner rolls

¼ cup chopped pecans

1. Heat oven to 375°F. In small bowl, combine butter and sage; mix well.

2. Separate dough into 8 triangles. Reserve 1 tablespoon butter mixture for topping. Spread remaining mixture evenly on triangles. Sprinkle each with pecans.

3. Roll up, starting at shortest side of each triangle, rolling to opposite point. Place on ungreased cookie sheet; curve each into crescent shape. Spread reserved butter mixture over tops of rolls.

4. Bake at 375°F for 11 to 13 minutes or until golden brown. Serve warm.

Nutrition Information Per Serving: Calories 155 • Total Fat 10g • Saturated Fat 3g • Cholesterol 10mg • Sodium 360mg • Total Carbohydrate 14g • Dietary Fiber 0g • Sugars 4g • Protein 2g. Dietary Exchanges: 1 Starch • 2 Fat.

honey-mustard marinated vegetables

PREP TIME: 30 MINUTES
READY TO SERVE: 1 HOUR
SERVINGS: 8

* plan ahead

½ lb. fresh whole green beans

1½ cups fresh baby carrots

1½ cups fresh cauliflower florets

⅓ cup purchased fat-free honey mustard salad dressing

¼ teaspoon dried dill weed

⅛ teaspoon salt

1 cup fresh small whole mushrooms

1 red bell pepper, cut lengthwise into thin strips

Lettuce leaves

1. Bring about 5 cups water to a boil in large saucepan. Add green beans; cook 3 minutes. Add carrots and cauliflower. Return to a boil; boil 2 to 3 minutes or just until blanched. Drain; rinse with cold water to cool.

2. In small bowl, combine salad dressing, dill and salt; blend well.

3. In large nonmetal bowl, combine blanched vegetables, mushrooms and bell pepper. Add dressing mixture; toss to coat. Cover; refrigerate at least 30 minutes or until serving time.

Nutrition Information Per Serving: Calories 45 • Total Fat 0g • Saturated Fat 0g • Cholesterol 0mg • Sodium 170mg • Total Carbohydrate 10g • Dietary Fiber 3g • Sugars 5g • Protein 1g. Dietary Exchanges: ½ Fruit • 1 Vegetable OR ½ Carbohydrate • 1 Vegetable.

easy scalloped corn

PREP TIME: 15 MINUTES
READY TO SERVE: 3 HOURS 15 MINUTES
SERVINGS: 8

* slow cooked

⅔ cup all-purpose flour

¼ cup margarine or butter, melted

1 carton (8-oz.) refrigerated or frozen fat-free egg product, thawed (1 cup)

¾ cup evaporated milk

2 teaspoons sugar

1 teaspoon salt

⅛ teaspoon pepper

1 can (14.75-oz.) cream-style corn

1 can (15.25-oz.) whole kernel corn, drained

1. Spray 2- to 4-quart slow cooker with nonstick cooking spray. In large bowl, combine all ingredients except whole kernel corn; mix well. Stir in whole kernel corn. Pour into sprayed slow cooker.

2. Cover; cook on High setting for 2 to 3 hours.

Nutrition Information Per Serving: Calories 220 • Total Fat 8g • Saturated Fat 2g • Cholesterol 5mg • Sodium 670mg • Total Carbohydrate 32g • Dietary Fiber 3g • Sugars 7g • Protein 8g. Dietary Exchanges: 2 Starch • ½ Fat OR 2 Carbohydrate • ½ Fat.

tarragon green peas

READY TO SERVE: 15 MINUTES
SERVINGS: 6

* super fast

1 package (1-lb.) frozen sweet peas

3 tablespoons butter

2 green onions, sliced

1/8 teaspoon dried tarragon leaves

1. Cook peas as directed on package. Drain.

2. Meanwhile, melt butter in small saucepan over medium heat. Add onions; cook 2 to 3 minutes or until onions are tender, stirring occasionally. Stir in tarragon.

3. Pour onion-butter mixture over cooked peas; stir to coat.

Nutrition Information Per Serving: Calories 110 • Total Fat 6g • Saturated Fat 4g • Cholesterol 15mg • Sodium 95mg • Total Carbohydrate 10g • Dietary Fiber 3g • Sugars 4g • Protein 4g. Dietary Exchanges: 1/2 Starch • 1 1/2 Fat.

breadstick focaccia

PREP TIME: 15 MINUTES
READY TO SERVE: 40 MINUTES
SERVINGS: 6

1 can (11-oz.) refrigerated breadsticks (12 breadsticks)

1 teaspoon olive oil

2 teaspoons chopped fresh rosemary

1/2 teaspoon coarse salt

1 tablespoon slivered pitted ripe olives

6 thin red bell pepper strips

1. Heat oven to 375°F. Unroll dough; separate into 12 strips. Starting at center of ungreased cookie sheet, coil strips loosely into a spiral, pinching ends together securely as strips are added. Press down very firmly on tops of dough strips to form 1/2-inch-thick round of dough.

2. Drizzle olive oil over dough. Sprinkle with rosemary, salt and olives. Arrange bell pepper strips in spoke-fashion on top.

3. Bake 20 to 25 minutes or until edges are deep golden brown. Cut into wedges; serve the bread warm.

Nutrition Information Per Serving: Calories 150 • Total Fat 3.5g • Saturated Fat .5g • Cholesterol 0mg • Sodium 580mg • Total Carbohydrate 25g • Dietary Fiber 0g • Sugars 3g • Protein 4g. Dietary Exchanges: 1 1/2 Starch • 1/2 Fat.

savory red beans and rice

PREP TIME: 15 MINUTES
READY TO SERVE: 5 HOURS 35 MINUTES
SERVINGS: 16

* slow cooked

1 package (16-oz.) dried kidney beans, sorted, rinsed (2 1/2 cups)

1 large green bell pepper, chopped (1 1/2 cups)

1 cup chopped onions

2 garlic cloves, minced

7 cups water

1 1/2 teaspoons salt

1/4 teaspoon pepper

2 cups uncooked instant rice

Hot pepper sauce, if desired

1. In 3 1/2- to 6-quart slow cooker, combine all ingredients except rice and hot pepper sauce; mix well.

2. Cover; cook on High setting for 4 to 5 hours.

3. Stir rice into bean mixture. Cover; cook on High setting an additional 15 to 20 minutes or until rice is tender. Serve beans and rice with hot pepper sauce.

Nutrition Information Per Serving: Calories 125 • Total Fat 0g • Saturated Fat 0g • Cholesterol 0mg • Sodium 220mg • Total Carbohydrate 29g • Dietary Fiber 5g • Sugars 1g • Protein 7g. Dietary Exchanges: 2 Starch • 2 Vegetable OR 2 Carbohydrate • 2 Vegetable.

MAKING A MEATLESS MEAL

For some, meatless menus are a way of life and for others meat-free dinners merely mix up recipe fatigue. Regardless of how often you prepare meatless items, you can easily turn red beans and rice into a main course. Simply add some shredded cheese and salsa and wrap the satisfying mixture in flour tortillas. Topped with enchilada sauce, it's a zesty no-stress, meatless meal.

breadstick focaccia

stovetop specialties

taco-topped potatoes ✳ p. 280

chicken ravioli marinara ✳ p. 279

smoked turkey quesadillas ✳ p. 302

skillet nacho chili ✳ p. 300

chicken lo mein * p. 307

chicken ravioli marinara

chicken ravioli marinara

READY TO SERVE: 20 MINUTES
SERVINGS: 6

* super fast

1 package (25-oz.) frozen chicken or cheese-filled ravioli

3 to 4 small zucchini, halved lengthwise, sliced

1 jar (26-oz.) marinara or spaghetti sauce

1. Cook ravioli to desired doneness as directed on package. Drain; arrange on serving platter or return to saucepan. Cover to keep warm.

2. Meanwhile, in large saucepan, combine zucchini and marinara sauce; cook and stir over medium-high heat for 6 to 7 minutes or until zucchini is crisp-tender and sauce is thoroughly heated.

3. Spoon zucchini mixture over cooked ravioli, or add zucchini mixture to ravioli and toss gently. If desired, garnish with grated fresh Romano or Parmesan cheese.

Nutrition Information Per Serving: Calories 320 • Total Fat 9g • Saturated Fat 2g • Cholesterol 15mg • Sodium 680mg • Total Carbohydrate 47g • Dietary Fiber 5g • Sugars 12g • Protein 12g. Dietary Exchanges: 3 Starch • 1 Lean Meat • 1 Fat OR 3 Carbohydrate • 1 Lean Meat • 1 Fat.

harvest skillet supper

READY TO SERVE: 25 MINUTES
SERVINGS: 4

* super fast

2 teaspoons oil

¾ lb. pork tenderloin, cut into ¼-inch slices

¾ cup apple juice

2 tablespoons Dijon mustard

2 teaspoons cornstarch

2 teaspoons brown sugar

Dash salt

Dash pepper

1 sweet potato, peeled, cut into ¼-inch slices (2 cups)

1 apple, cut into 16 wedges

½ cup coarsely chopped green bell pepper

1. Heat oil in large nonstick skillet over medium-high heat until hot. Add pork; cook until no longer pink and browned on each side. Remove pork from skillet; cover to keep warm. Drain drippings from skillet.

2. In small bowl, combine apple juice, mustard, cornstarch, brown sugar, salt and pepper; blend well. Add cornstarch mixture and sweet potato to skillet. Cover; cook over medium heat for 10 to 15 minutes or until sweet potato is crisp-tender, stirring occasionally.

3. Stir in apple, bell pepper and pork. Cover; cook an additional 5 minutes or until bell pepper is crisp-tender, stirring occasionally. If desired, serve with hot cooked rice sprinkled with chopped fresh parsley.

Nutrition Information Per Serving: Calories 250 • Total Fat 9g • Saturated Fat 2g • Cholesterol 45mg • Sodium 260mg • Total Carbohydrate 24g • Dietary Fiber 2g • Sugars 14g • Protein 18g. Dietary Exchanges: 1 Starch • ½ Fruit • 2 Lean Meat • ½ Fat OR 1½ Carbohydrate • 2 Lean Meat • ½ Fat.

skillet ham steak

READY TO SERVE: 20 MINUTES
SERVINGS: 4

* super fast

2 tablespoons frozen orange juice concentrate

2 tablespoons brown sugar

¼ teaspoon allspice

¾ lb. fully cooked center-cut ham steak (¾-inch thick)

1. In small bowl, combine orange juice concentrate, brown sugar and allspice; blend well.

2. Spray large nonstick skillet with nonstick cooking spray. Heat over medium-high heat until hot. Place ham in skillet; cook 4 minutes. Turn ham; brush with orange juice mixture. Cook an additional 4 to 6 minutes or until thoroughly heated.

Nutrition Information Per Serving: Calories 140 • Total Fat 4g • Saturated Fat 1g • Cholesterol 40mg • Sodium 1080mg • Total Carbohydrate 10g • Dietary Fiber 0g • Sugars 10g • Protein 17g. Dietary Exchanges: ½ Fruit • 2½ Lean Meat • ½ Fat OR ½ Carbohydrate • 2½ Lean Meat • ½ Fat.

taco-topped potatoes

READY TO SERVE: 25 MINUTES
SERVINGS: 4

* super fast

4 medium baking potatoes

1 container (18-oz.) refrigerated taco sauce with seasoned ground beef

½ cup shredded Cheddar cheese (2 oz.)

1 medium Italian plum tomato, chopped (⅓ cup)

2 medium green onions, sliced (2 tablespoons)

1. Pierce potatoes with fork. Arrange in spoke pattern on microwave-safe paper towel in microwave. Microwave on High for 12 to 14 minutes or until tender, turning potatoes and rearranging halfway through cooking. Cool 3 minutes.

2. Meanwhile, heat taco sauce with seasoned ground beef as directed on container.

3. To serve, place potatoes on individual serving plates. Cut potatoes in half lengthwise; mash slightly with fork. Spoon about ½ cup ground beef mixture over each potato. Top with cheese, tomato and onions.

Nutrition Information Per Serving: Calories 340 • Total Fat 17g • Saturated Fat 8g • Cholesterol 50mg • Sodium 770mg • Total Carbohydrate 35g • Dietary Fiber 2g • Sugars 7g • Protein 21g. Dietary Exchanges: 2 Starch • 1 Vegetable • 2 Medium-Fat Meat.

shrimp scampi

READY TO SERVE: 20 MINUTES
SERVINGS: 4

* super fast

8 oz. uncooked fettuccine

2 tablespoons margarine or butter

1 tablespoon olive or vegetable oil

4 garlic cloves, minced

1 lb. shelled deveined uncooked medium shrimp

¼ cup chopped fresh parsley

2 teaspoons grated lemon peel

¼ teaspoon salt

¼ teaspoon pepper

⅓ cup dry white wine or chicken broth

1. Cook fettuccine to desired doneness as directed on package. Drain; cover to keep warm.

2. Meanwhile, melt margarine with oil in medium skillet over medium heat. Add garlic; cook and stir 1 minute. Add shrimp; cook and stir 1 minute.

3. Add all remaining ingredients; cook and stir 1 to 2 minutes or until shrimp turn pink. Serve over fettuccine.

Nutrition Information Per Serving: Calories 390 • Total Fat 12g • Saturated Fat 2g • Cholesterol 215mg • Sodium 400mg • Total Carbohydrate 42g • Dietary Fiber 2g • Sugars 2g • Protein 26g. Dietary Exchanges: 3 Starch • 2½ Very Lean Meat • 1½ Fat OR 3 Carbohydrate • 2½ Very Lean Meat • 1½ Fat.

pan-fried steaks with mustard sauce

READY TO SERVE: 20 MINUTES
SERVINGS: 4

* super fast

4 beef tenderloin steaks (4-oz. each and 1-inch thick)

2 teaspoons coarsely ground black pepper

2 garlic cloves, minced

⅓ cup dry red wine

⅓ cup beef broth

1 tablespoon country-style Dijon mustard

1. Coat both sides of steaks with pepper. Spray medium nonstick skillet with nonstick cooking spray. Heat over medium-high heat until hot. Add steaks; cook 6 to 12 minutes or until of desired doneness, turning once.

2. Add garlic; cook and stir 1 minute or until golden brown. Add wine and broth; boil 1 minute. Remove steaks from skillet; cover to keep warm. With wire whisk, stir in mustard until sauce is well blended. Serve sauce over steaks.

Nutrition Information Per Serving: Calories 160 • Total Fat 8g • Saturated Fat 3g • Cholesterol 50mg • Sodium 200mg • Total Carbohydrate 2g • Dietary Fiber 0g • Sugars 0g • Protein 18g. Dietary Exchanges: 2½ Lean Meat • ½ Fat.

taco-topped potatoes

easy italian skillet

easy italian skillet

READY TO SERVE: 20 MINUTES
SERVINGS: 4

* super fast

1 package (1-lb.) frozen pasta, broccoli, corn and carrots in a garlic seasoned sauce

1 can (15.5- or 15-oz.) pinto or kidney beans, drained

1 can (14.5-oz.) diced tomatoes, undrained

1 teaspoon dried Italian seasoning

2 oz. shredded mozzarella cheese (½ cup)

1. In large skillet, combine all ingredients except cheese. Bring to a boil. Reduce heat; simmer 8 to 10 minutes or until vegetables and pasta are tender, stirring occasionally.

2. Remove skillet from heat. Sprinkle with cheese. Cover; let stand until cheese is melted.

Nutrition Information Per Serving: Calories 310 • Total Fat 9g • Saturated Fat 4g • Cholesterol 15mg • Sodium 830mg • Total Carbohydrate 43g • Dietary Fiber 7g • Sugars 7g • Protein 13g. Dietary Exchanges: 2½ Starch • 1 Vegetable • ½ Very Lean Meat • 1½ Fat OR 2½ Carbohydrate • 1 Vegetable • ½ Very Lean Meat • 1½ Fat.

skillet pizza potatoes

READY TO SERVE: 30 MINUTES
SERVINGS: 5

1 lb. bulk Italian pork sausage

½ cup pepperoni slices (about 3 oz.)

1 jar (14-oz.) pizza sauce

½ cup water

1 package (28-oz.) frozen potatoes O'Brien with onions and peppers

4 oz. shredded Italian cheese blend (1 cup)

1. Brown sausage in Dutch oven or 12-inch nonstick skillet over medium-high heat until no longer pink, stirring frequently. Add pepperoni; cook 2 minutes. Drain.

2. Add pizza sauce and water; mix well. Add potatoes; stir to mix. Reduce heat to medium; cover and cook 10 to 15 minutes or until potatoes are tender, stirring occasionally.

3. Sprinkle with cheese. Remove from heat; cover and let stand 5 minutes or until cheese is melted.

Nutrition Information Per Serving: Calories 540 • Total Fat 33g • Saturated Fat 13g • Cholesterol 80mg • Sodium 1710mg • Total Carbohydrate 35g • Dietary Fiber 4g • Sugars 7g • Protein 26g. Dietary Exchanges: 2 Starch • ½ Fruit • 3 High-Fat Meat • 1½ Fat OR 2½ Carbohydrate • 3 High-Fat Meat • 1½ Fat.

salad bar vegetable stir-fry

READY TO SERVE: 30 MINUTES
SERVINGS: 4

⅔ cup uncooked regular long-grain white rice

1⅓ cups water

1 tablespoon sesame oil

8 cups assorted cut-up fresh vegetables from salad bar

3 tablespoons water

½ cup purchased stir-fry sauce

¼ cup nuts or shelled sunflower seeds from salad bar, if desired

1. Cook rice in 1⅓ cups water as directed on package.

2. Meanwhile, heat oil in large skillet or wok over medium-high heat until hot. Add only the firm vegetables; cook and stir 4 minutes.

3. Add the medium-firm vegetables; cook and stir 1 minute. Add 3 tablespoons water. Reduce heat to medium; cover and cook 2 to 3 minutes or until all vegetables are crisp-tender, stirring occasionally.

4. Add stir-fry sauce and the tender vegetables; cook and stir until thoroughly heated. Sprinkle with nuts. Serve over rice.

Nutrition Information Per Serving: Calories 410 • Total Fat 9g • Saturated Fat 1g • Cholesterol 0mg • Sodium 1090mg • Total Carbohydrate 71g • Dietary Fiber 7g • Sugars 11g • Protein 12g. Dietary Exchanges: 4 Starch • 2 Vegetable • 1 Fat OR 4 Carbohydrate • 2 Vegetable • 1 Fat.

penne with zucchini and ricotta

READY TO SERVE: 30 MINUTES
SERVINGS: 6

1 package (16-oz.) uncooked penne (tube-shaped pasta)
1 tablespoon olive or vegetable oil
2 garlic cloves, minced
1 lb. small zucchini, sliced (3½ cups)
1 cup ricotta cheese
1 cup half-and-half
½ teaspoon salt
½ cup finely sliced fresh basil
2⅔ oz. shredded fresh Parmesan cheese (⅔ cup)

1. Cook penne to desired doneness as directed on package. Drain; cover to keep warm.

2. Meanwhile, heat oil in 12-inch nonstick skillet over medium-high heat until hot. Add garlic and zucchini; cook and stir 3 to 4 minutes or until zucchini is tender.

3. In small bowl, combine ricotta cheese, half-and-half and salt; stir until well blended. Add to zucchini mixture; cook and stir until hot.

4. In large serving bowl, combine cooked penne, zucchini mixture and basil; toss gently to mix. Sprinkle with Parmesan cheese.

Nutrition Information Per Serving: Calories 460 • Total Fat 14g • Saturated Fat 7g • Cholesterol 35mg • Sodium 440mg • Total Carbohydrate 63g • Dietary Fiber 3g • Sugars 6g • Protein 21g. Dietary Exchanges: 4 Starch • 1 Medium-Fat Meat • 1½ Fat OR 4 Carbohydrate • 1 Medium-Fat Meat • 1½ Fat.

ramen skillet supper

READY TO SERVE: 30 MINUTES
SERVINGS: 4

1 lb. lean ground beef
2½ cups water
2 packages (3-oz. each) oriental-flavor ramen noodle soup mix
½ cup purchased stir-fry sauce
3 cups frozen broccoli florets, carrots and cauliflower

1. Brown ground beef in large skillet over medium-high heat until thoroughly cooked, stirring frequently. Drain.

2. Add water, contents of 1 of the soup mix seasoning packets, stir-fry sauce and frozen vegetables; mix well. (Discard remaining seasoning packet or reserve for a later use.) Bring to a boil. Reduce heat to medium-low; cover and cook 5 minutes or until vegetables are tender, stirring occasionally.

3. Break up ramen noodles; add to skillet. Cover; cook 5 to 8 minutes or until sauce is of desired consistency, stirring occasionally and separating noodles as they soften.

Nutrition Information Per Serving: Calories 460 • Total Fat 23g • Saturated Fat 10g • Cholesterol 70mg • Sodium 2000mg • Total Carbohydrate 35g • Dietary Fiber 3g • Sugars 5g • Protein 27g. Dietary Exchanges: 2 Starch • 1 Vegetable • 2 Lean Meat • 3 Fat OR 2 Carbohydrate • 1 Vegetable • 2 Lean Meat • 3 Fat.

herb-seasoned chicken breasts

READY TO SERVE: 20 MINUTES
SERVINGS: 4

* super fast

4 boneless skinless chicken breasts (1 lb.)
1 teaspoon Italian seasoning
½ teaspoon garlic-pepper blend
½ teaspoon paprika
¼ teaspoon salt
¼ cup chicken broth
1 package (8 oz.) sliced fresh mushrooms (3 cups)

1. Sprinkle both sides of chicken with Italian seasoning, garlic-pepper blend, paprika and salt.

2. Heat 10-inch nonstick skillet over medium heat. Add chicken; cook 3 minutes. Turn chicken; reduce heat to medium-low. Stir in broth and mushrooms. Cover; cook 4 to 7 minutes or until juice of chicken is no longer pink when center of thickest part is cut (170°F).

Nutrition Information Per Serving: Calories 150 • Total Fat 4g • Saturated Fat 1g • Trans Fat 0g • Cholesterol 70mg • Sodium 280mg • Total Carbohydrate 3g • Dietary Fiber 0g • Sugars 0g • Protein 27g. Dietary Exchanges: 1 Vegetable • 3½ Very Lean Meat.

penne with zucchini and ricotta

lemon-basil skillet chicken with rice

READY TO SERVE: 10 MINUTES
SERVINGS: 4

* super fast

4 boneless skinless chicken breasts (1 lb.)

Paprika

1½ cups hot water

1½ cups uncooked instant white rice

2 tablespoons butter or margarine

1 tablespoon lemon juice

1 teaspoon dried basil leaves

¼ teaspoon salt

1. Heat 10-inch nonstick skillet over high heat. Sprinkle both sides of chicken breasts with paprika; add to hot skillet. Immediately reduce heat to medium-high; cover and cook 4 minutes.

2. Meanwhile, in 2-quart saucepan, place hot water; cover tightly. Heat to boiling. Stir in rice; remove from heat. Let stand 5 minutes.

3. Turn chicken; cover and cook 4 to 5 minutes longer or until juice of chicken is no longer pink when center of thickest part is cut (170°F). Remove chicken from skillet; place on serving platter. Cover to keep warm.

4. In same hot skillet, mix butter, lemon juice, basil and salt. If necessary, return to heat to melt butter.

5. Place rice on serving platter; arrange chicken over rice. Spoon butter mixture over chicken.

Nutrition Information Per Serving: Calories 340 • Total Fat 10g • Saturated Fat 4g • Trans Fat 0g • Cholesterol 85mg • Sodium 250mg • Total Carbohydrate 35g • Dietary Fiber 0g • Sugars 0g • Protein 28g. **Dietary Exchanges:** 2 Starch • 3 Very Lean Meat • 1½ Fat.

fast and easy jambalaya

READY TO SERVE: 40 MINUTES
SERVINGS: 6

1 cup uncooked regular long-grain white rice

2 cups water

1/2 teaspoon lemon-pepper seasoning

1/2 teaspoon garlic powder

5 boneless skinless chicken breast halves, cut into 1/2-inch pieces

3 tablespoons oil

1 cup chopped onions

3/4 lb. smoked Polish or kielbasa sausage, cut into 1/2-inch slices

1 jar (16-oz.) picante sauce

1 can (14 1/2-oz.) Italian-style stewed tomatoes, undrained

1 1/4 cups frozen sweet peas

1. Cook rice in water as directed on package.

2. Meanwhile, sprinkle lemon-pepper seasoning and garlic powder over chicken pieces. Heat oil in large skillet or 3-quart saucepan over medium-high heat until hot. Add chicken; cook 5 minutes or until no longer pink, stirring frequently.

3. Add onions and sausage; cook an additional 5 minutes, stirring occasionally. Stir in picante sauce and tomatoes. Reduce heat to medium; cook 12 minutes. Add peas; cook an additional 5 to 7 minutes or until peas are tender. Serve over rice.

Nutrition Information Per Serving: Calories 510 • Total Fat 25 • Saturated 7g • Cholesterol 95mg • Sodium 1430mg • Total Carbohydrate 37g • Dietary Fiber 4g • Sugars 6g • Protein 33g. Dietary Exchanges: 2 Starch • 1 Vegetable • 3 1/2 Lean Meat • 3 Fat OR 2 Carbohydrate • 1 Vegetable • 3 1/2 Lean Meat • 3 Fat.

PASS THE PEAS, PLEASE!

Frozen peas are a staple in stovetop cooking, as demonstrated with Fast and Easy Jambalaya. Another variety popular with skillet dishes is the sugar snap pea. This type involves sweet peas and edible pods of thick, crunchy flesh. After you snap off the stem end and peel the strings from the sides, toss sugar snap peas into stir-fries or other Asian dishes. The pea pods are also terrific in green salads and even mixed into creamy chicken and tuna salads.

beef dinner nachos

READY TO SERVE: 15 MINUTES
SERVINGS: 6

* super fast

1/2 lb. extra-lean (at least 90%) ground beef

1 can (15- or 15.5-oz.) pinto beans, drained, rinsed

1 package (1.25-oz.) 40%-less-sodium taco seasoning mix

1/3 cup water

3 1/2 cups reduced-fat nacho cheese tortilla chips (3 oz.)

1/2 cup shredded reduced-fat Colby-Monterey Jack cheese blend (2 oz.)

1 medium tomato, chopped (3/4 cup)

1 cup shredded leaf lettuce

1/2 cup fat-free sour cream

2 tablespoons chopped fresh cilantro

1. In 10-inch nonstick skillet, cook ground beef over medium-high heat, stirring frequently, until brown; drain. Stir in beans, taco seasoning mix and water. Heat to boiling. Reduce heat to medium-low; simmer uncovered 1 to 2 minutes or until water is absorbed.

2. Arrange tortilla chips evenly on individual plates. Spoon beef mixture evenly over chips. Top with cheese, tomato, lettuce, sour cream and cilantro.

Nutrition Information Per Serving: Calories 240 • Total Fat 5g • Saturated Fat 2 1/2g • Trans Fat 0g • Cholesterol 30mg • Sodium 560mg • Total Carbohydrate 36g • Dietary Fiber 6g • Sugars 2g • Protein 17g. Dietary Exchanges: 2 1/2 Starch • 1 1/2 Very Lean Meat • 1/2 Fat.

DRESSING UP THE DISH

Beef Dinner Nachos are sure to be a hit whenever they grace your supper table. Jazz them up a bit by topping them with some chopped or sliced olives or even a few spicy peppers if you'd like. A little salsa goes a long way in adding flavor and flair to Southwestern dishes, so feel free to add your favorite variety, too. Diced green onions, a dollop or two of guacamole and chopped roasted red pepper are effortless ways to bring a splash of color to the weeknight meal.

easy tex-mex hash

READY TO SERVE: 30 MINUTES
SERVINGS: 4

1 lb. lean ground beef

1 tablespoon oil

3 cups frozen potatoes O'Brien with onions and peppers (from 24-oz. pkg.)

1 cup chunky-style salsa

2 teaspoons chili powder, if desired

4 oz. shredded Colby-Monterey Jack cheese blend (1 cup)

1. Brown ground beef in large nonstick skillet until thoroughly cooked, stirring frequently. Remove ground beef from skillet; cover to keep warm. Discard drippings.

2. In same skillet, heat oil over medium heat until hot. Add potatoes; cook and stir 8 to 10 minutes or until browned.

3. Stir in salsa, chili powder and cooked ground beef. Cook 5 to 8 minutes or until thoroughly heated, stirring occasionally.

4. Sprinkle with cheese. Cover; cook 2 to 4 minutes or until cheese is melted.

Nutrition Information Per Serving: Calories 440 • Total Fat 27g • Saturated Fat 12g • Cholesterol 95mg • Sodium 730mg • Total Carbohydrate 20g • Dietary Fiber 2g • Sugars 3g • Protein 28g. Dietary Exchanges: 1½ Starch • 3½ Medium-Fat Meat • 1½ Fat OR 1½ Carbohydrate • 3½ Medium-Fat Meat • 1½ Fat.

cheesy noodle skillet supper

READY TO SERVE: 25 MINUTES
SERVINGS: 4

* super fast

1 lb. ground turkey

½ cup chopped onion

1 jar (14-oz.) spaghetti sauce

1 can (10¾-oz.) condensed Cheddar cheese soup

1 cup water

3 oz. uncooked dumpling egg noodles (2 cups)

1 jar (4½-oz.) sliced mushrooms, drained

4 oz. shredded Cheddar cheese (1 cup)

1. In a large skillet, brown ground turkey with onion. Drain. Add spaghetti sauce and soup; mix well. Stir in water. Bring to a boil. Reduce heat to medium; cover and cook 8 to 10 minutes or until noodles are tender stirring occasionally.

2. Uncover; stir in mushrooms. Cook uncovered for 2 to 4 minutes or until sauce is of desired consistency, stirring occasionally. Sprinkle with cheese; cover and cook 1 to 2 minutes or until cheese is melted.

Nutrition Information Per Serving: Calories 550 • Total Fat 29g • Saturated 13g • Cholesterol 150mg • Sodium 1340mg • Total Carbohydrate 33g • Dietary Fiber 4g • Sugars 3g • Protein 39g. Dietary Exchanges: 2 Starch • 4½ Medium-Fat Meat • 1 Fat OR 2 Carbohydrate • 4½ Medium-Fat Meat • 1 Fat.

turkey and penne pasta

READY TO SERVE: 25 MINUTES
SERVINGS: 4

* super fast

8 oz. uncooked penne pasta (2 cups)

½ lb. lean ground turkey

2 garlic cloves

½ teaspoon dried Italian seasoning

¼ teaspoon fennel seed, crushed, if desired

2 cups no-fat extra-chunky spaghetti sauce

¼ teaspoon sugar

2 oz. finely shredded or shredded mozzarella cheese (½ cup)

1. Cook penne to desired doneness as directed on package. Drain; cover to keep warm.

2. Meanwhile, spray large nonstick skillet or Dutch oven with nonstick cooking spray. Add turkey, garlic, Italian seasoning and fennel; cook over medium-high heat for 3 to 5 minutes or until turkey is no longer pink.

3. Stir in spaghetti sauce and sugar. Bring to a boil. Reduce heat; cover and simmer 10 minutes to blend flavors. Serve sauce over penne. Sprinkle with mozzarella cheese.

Nutrition Information Per Serving: Calories 380 • Total Fat 8g • Saturated Fat 3g • Cholesterol 50mg • Sodium 520mg • Total Carbohydrate 53g • Dietary Fiber 2g • Sugars 11g • Protein 23g. Dietary Exchanges: 3 Starch • ½ Fruit • 1 Very Lean Meat • 1 Fat OR 3½ Carbohydrate • 2 Very Lean Meat • 1 Fat.

honey mustard-glazed pork chops

READY TO SERVE: 15 MINUTES
SERVINGS: 4

* super fast

⅓ cup honey

2 tablespoons prepared
yellow mustard

⅛ teaspoon ground cloves

½ teaspoon onion salt

¼ teaspoon pepper

4 boneless pork loin chops,
¾-inch thick (1 lb.)

Orange slices, if desired

1. In small bowl, mix honey, mustard and cloves. Sprinkle onion salt and pepper over pork chops.

2. Heat 10-inch nonstick skillet over medium-high heat. Add pork chops; cook 3 minutes. Turn pork. Reduce heat to medium-low; pour honey mixture over pork chops. Cover; cook 5 to 8 minutes longer or until pork is slightly pink in center and thermometer inserted in center of pork reads 160°F. If desired, garnish with orange slices.

Nutrition Information Per Serving: Calories 310 • Total Fat 13g • Saturated Fat 4.5g • Cholesterol 70mg • Sodium 330mg • Total Carbohydrate 24g • Dietary Fiber 0g • Sugars 24g • Protein 23g. **Dietary Exchanges:** 1½ Other Carbohydrate • 3½ Lean Meat • ½ Fat.

chili-cheese hash browns

READY TO SERVE: 25 MINUTES
SERVINGS: 4

* super fast

1 package (12-oz.) frozen chili or 1 can (15-oz.) chili

4 frozen rectangular hash-brown potato patties (from 27-oz. box)

Oil for frying

½ cup finely shredded Cheddar cheese (2 oz.)

½ cup chunky-style salsa

1 tablespoon chopped fresh cilantro, if desired

1. Heat chili as directed on package or can. Fry potato patties in oil as directed on package.

2. To serve, place potato patties on individual serving plates. Top each serving with chili. Sprinkle each with cheese. Top with salsa and cilantro.

Nutrition Information Per Serving: Calories 340 • Total Fat 22g • Saturated Fat 6g • Cholesterol 30mg • Sodium 600mg • Total Carbohydrate 25g • Dietary Fiber 4g • Sugars 4g • Protein 11g. Dietary Exchanges: 1½ Starch • 1 Medium-Fat Meat • 3 Fat.

GIVE CILANTRO A TRY

Also known as fresh coriander or Chinese parsley, cilantro lends its distinctive flavor to dishes with Chinese, Indian, Mexican and Southwestern inspiration. It resembles a more delicate version of fresh parsley but has a brighter, almost citrusy flavor. It's a great herb for those who need to set dinner on the table quick. Not only does it add a bright spark of color to whatever foods it's mixed with, but it punches up flavor without much effort. Try it with a trusted recipe that calls for fresh parsley. Simply replace part of the parsley with cilantro and you'll have a new spin on an old favorite.

---

rio grande beef salad

READY TO SERVE: 25 MINUTES
SERVINGS: 4

* super fast

6½ oz. uncooked wagon wheel pasta (2 cups)

¼ cup chopped onion

1 garlic clove, minced

1 tablespoon oil

1 can (10-oz.) diced tomatoes and green chiles, undrained

½ teaspoon dried oregano leaves

¼ teaspoon cumin

½ lb. deli-sliced cooked roast beef, chopped (1½ cups)

1 package (9-oz.) frozen corn in a pouch, cooked, drained

1 medium tomato, chopped

½ cup chopped green bell pepper

1 tablespoon chopped fresh cilantro

1. Cook pasta to desired doneness as directed on package.

2. Meanwhile, in small nonstick saucepan, cook onion and garlic in oil until tender. Stir in tomatoes, oregano and cumin. Bring to a boil over medium-high heat. Boil 4 minutes or until slightly thickened, stirring frequently to prevent sticking. Remove from heat.

3. Drain pasta; rinse with cold water. Drain well. In large bowl, combine cooked pasta, roast beef, corn, chopped tomato, bell pepper and cilantro; mix gently.

4. Add tomato mixture; toss gently until well mixed. Serve immediately, or cover and refrigerate until serving time. If desired, serve on lettuce-lined plates and garnish with tortilla chips and additional cilantro.

Nutrition Information Per Serving: Calories 400 • Total Fat 9g • Saturated Fat 2g • Cholesterol 55mg • Sodium 800mg • Total Carbohydrate 52g • Dietary Fiber 4g • Sugars 7g • Protein 27g. Dietary Exchanges: 3 Starch • 1 Vegetable • 2 Lean Meat • ½ Fat OR 3 Carbohydrate • 1 Vegetable • 2 Lean Meat • ½ Fat.

sausage and potato skillet sizzle

READY TO SERVE: 25 MINUTES
SERVINGS: 4

* super fast

1 tablespoon butter or margarine

1 cup frozen bell pepper and onion stir-fry (from 1-lb. bag)

1 bag (1-lb. 4-oz.) refrigerated new potato wedges

¼ teaspoon pepper

6 oz. cooked, smoked turkey kielbasa or Polish sausage, cut into ¼-inch slices

1½ cups frozen broccoli florets (from 14-oz. bag)

1½ cups frozen cauliflower florets (from 1-lb. bag)

½ cup shredded Cheddar and American cheese blend (2 oz.)

1. In 10-inch nonstick skillet, melt butter over medium heat. Add bell pepper and onion stir-fry, potatoes and pepper; cook 10 minutes, stirring occasionally.

2. Add kielbasa, broccoli and cauliflower; mix well. Cover; cook 8 to 10 minutes or until vegetables are tender, stirring occasionally. Remove from heat. Sprinkle with cheese; cover and let stand 1 to 2 minutes or until cheese is melted.

Nutrition Information Per Serving: Calories 290 • Total Fat 12g • Saturated Fat 6g • Cholesterol 45mg • Sodium 960mg • Total Carbohydrate 32g • Dietary Fiber 6g • Sugars 3g • Protein 14g. Dietary Exchanges: 1½ Starch • 1 Vegetable • 1 Medium-Fat Meat • 1½ Fat.

SELECTING STOVETOP COOKWARE

Stovetop meals turn combinations of everyday ingredients into scrumptious blends of mouth-watering flavors and comforting textures. Most skillet dishes offer unbeatable time-savings for today's family cooks as well as easy cleanup. If you're in the market for a new skillet, consider the following options:

* CAST IRON. For a virtually indestructible skillet, consider cast iron. The more you use it, the more the iron is seasoned, so you can add less fat to recipes. The skillet browns food nicely and heats items evenly for years. The skillets are perfect for use on the stovetop as well as inside the oven, but keep in mind that cast iron isn't recommended for tomato dishes. The acid in the tomatoes will often react with the iron to create a metallic flavor.

* ALUMINUM. Skillets and saucepans made of aluminum conduct heat very well. Heavy aluminum pots perform better, and anodized aluminum has a coating that won't react to acids in food.

* STAINLESS STEEL. These skillets don't conduct heat as well as others and food tends to stick unless the skillets feature nonstick surfaces.

---

cabbage and bratwurst

PREP TIME: 25 MINUTES
READY TO SERVE: 1 HOUR 10 MINUTES
SERVINGS: 8

4 slices bacon, cut into 1-in. pieces

2 medium onions, thinly sliced

2 garlic cloves, minced

2 cups thickly sliced carrots

1 medium head cabbage or savor cabbage (about 2 lb.), cut into 1-in. chunks

2 whole cloves

1 bay leaf

1 to 1½ lb. cooked bratwurst, cut into 2-in. pieces

1 cup beef broth

½ cup dry white wine, water or beef broth

Dash salt and pepper

1. In 12-in. skillet or Dutch oven, cook bacon, onions and garlic over medium heat until bacon is crisp, stirring occasionally. Stir in carrots and cabbage.

2. Tie cloves and bay leaf in piece of cheesecloth or, if desired, place in tea ball. Add to cabbage mixture. Add bratwurst; partially cover with cabbage mixture. Pour broth and wine over cabbage mixture. Bring to a boil. Reduce heat; cover and simmer 30 to 45 minutes or until vegetables are tender.

3. Remove spices. Stir in salt and pepper. If desired, serve with German-style or Dijon mustard and dark bread.

Nutrition Information Per Serving: Calories 390 • Total Fat 29g • Saturated Fat 10g • Cholesterol 60mg • Sodium 770mg • Total Carbohydrate 14g • Dietary Fiber 4g • Sugars 8g • Protein 17g. Dietary Exchanges: 2 Vegetable • 2 High-Fat Meat • 3 Fat.

chicken and vegetable skillet supper

READY TO SERVE: 40 MINUTES
SERVINGS: 4

2 tablespoons oil

2 lb. cut-up frying chicken, skin removed

2 small onions, thinly sliced

2 teaspoons chicken-flavor instant bouillon

1 teaspoon dried tarragon leaves

1½ cups hot water

1 package (1-lb.) frozen broccoli florets, carrots and cauliflower

¼ cup hot water

2 tablespoons cornstarch

1. Heat oil in a large skillet over medium heat until hot. Add chicken and onions; cook until chicken is browned on all sides.

2. Meanwhile, in a small bowl, combine bouillon, tarragon and 1½ cups hot water; mix well. Add bouillon mixture to chicken; bring to a boil. Reduce heat to low; cover and simmer 15 to 20 minutes or until chicken is fork-tender and juices run clear.

3. Add frozen vegetables to chicken; cook 4 to 6 minutes or until vegetables are crisp-tender.

4. Meanwhile, in a small bowl, combine ¼ cup water and cornstarch; blend well. Add to liquid in skillet; cook and stir until bubbly and thickened.

Nutrition Information Per Serving: Calories 260 • Total Fat 13g • Saturated Fat 2g • Cholesterol 65mg • Sodium 590mg • Total Carbohydrate 12g • Dietary Fiber 3g • Sugars 4g • Protein 24g. Dietary Exchanges: ½ Starch • 1 Vegetable • 3 Lean Meat • ½ Fat OR ½ Carbohydrate • 1 Vegetable • 3 Lean Meat • ½ Fat.

skillet ham and penne pasta

READY TO SERVE: 30 MINUTES
SERVINGS: 4

8 oz. uncooked penne pasta (about 2½ cups)

1 tablespoon margarine or butter

1 cup frozen whole kernel corn

½ cup sliced green onions

6 oz. cooked ham, cut into 1½x¼x¼-inch julienne strips (1 cup)

1 medium zucchini, cut into 1½x¼x¼-inch julienne strips

4 Italian plum tomatoes, quartered, sliced (2 cups)

¼ teaspoon salt

⅛ teaspoon freshly ground black pepper

½ cup half-and-half

1 oz. shredded fresh Parmesan cheese (¼ cup)

1. Cook penne to desired doneness as directed on package. Drain; cover to keep warm.

2. Meanwhile, melt margarine in 12-inch nonstick skillet over medium-high heat. Add corn, onions, ham and zucchini; cook and stir 4 to 6 minutes or until vegetables are crisp-tender.

3. Add cooked penne and all remaining ingredients except cheese. Reduce heat to medium; cook and stir 3 to 5 minutes or until thoroughly heated. Stir in cheese.

Nutrition Information Per Serving: Calories 420 • Total Fat 12g • Saturated Fat 5g • Cholesterol 35mg • Sodium 920mg • Total Carbohydrate 56g • Dietary Fiber 4g • Sugars 8g • Protein 21g. Dietary Exchanges: 3½ Starch • 1 Vegetable • 1½ Very Lean Meat • 1½ Fat OR 3½ Carbohydrate • 1 Vegetable • 1½ Very Lean Meat • 1½ Fat.

THREE-ITEM MENU IN MOMENTS

For a sensational menu timed right for weeknights, swing by the grocery store and purchase orange sorbet and vanilla ice cream from the freezer section and pick up a package of refrigerated dinner rolls.

Allow the frosty treats to soften by leaving the containers out on your kitchen counter. Meanwhile, put the water on the stove for the pasta and preheat the oven for the dinner rolls as directed on the package. While you're waiting for the water to boil, slice the green onions, ham, zucchini and tomatoes. As this mixture simmers on the stove, bake the dinner rolls per the package directions.

Put a scoop of softened orange sorbet into each of four dessert dishes, then add a scoop of vanilla ice cream to each dish. Swirl the scoops together; cover and store in the freezer until dessert time. Prepare the main course as directed, remove the rolls from the oven and you have a complete dinner in no time!

skillet ham and penne pasta

tomato and cheese pasta skillet

tomato and cheese pasta skillet

READY TO SERVE: 30 MINUTES
SERVINGS: 4

1   can (15-oz.) Italian-style tomato sauce

1¾   cups water

1   package (7-oz.) small pasta shells (2 cups)

2   tablespoons finely chopped onion

¾   cup shredded mozzarella cheese (3 oz.)

1. In an 8-inch skillet, mix tomato sauce, water, pasta and onion. Heat to boiling. Reduce heat to medium-low; cover and simmer 12 minutes, stirring occasionally.

2. Sprinkle cheese over top. Cover; cook 1 minute longer or until cheese is melted.

Nutrition Information Per Serving: Calories 360 • Total Fat 9g • Saturated Fat 3.5g • Trans Fat 0g • Cholesterol 10mg • Sodium 640mg • Total Carbohydrate 60g • Dietary Fiber 4g • Sugars 9g • Protein 13g. Dietary Exchanges: 4 Starch • 1 Fat.

lemon-ginger chicken

READY TO SERVE: 20 MINUTES
SERVINGS: 4

* super fast

4   boneless skinless chicken breast halves

2   teaspoons ginger

⅓   cup water

½   teaspoon grated lemon peel

3   tablespoons lemon juice

3   tablespoons honey

2   tablespoons orange juice

2   teaspoons cornstarch

1. Rub chicken breast halves with ginger. Spray large nonstick skillet with nonstick cooking spray. Heat over medium-high heat until hot. Add chicken; cover and cook 8 to 12 minutes or until chicken is fork-tender and juices run clear, turning once.

2. Meanwhile, in small microwave-safe bowl, combine all remaining ingredients; blend well. Microwave on High for 1½ to 2 minutes or until sauce has thickened.

3. To serve, spoon sauce over chicken. If desired, serve with lemon slices and green onions.

Nutrition Information Per Serving: Calories 200 • Total Fat 3g • Saturated Fat 1g • Cholesterol 75mg • Sodium 65mg • Total Carbohydrate 17g • Dietary Fiber 0g • Sugars 14g • Protein 27g. Dietary Exchanges: 1 Fruit • 4 Very Lean Meat OR 1 Carbohydrate • 4 Very Lean Meat.

delaware crab cakes

READY TO SERVE: 20 MINUTES
SERVINGS: 4

* super fast

½   cup unseasoned dry bread crumbs

¼   cup chopped green onions

¼   cup nonfat plain yogurt

1   tablespoon chopped fresh dill

1   teaspoon dry mustard

¼ to ½   teaspoon pepper

1   tablespoon lemon juice

1   egg, beaten

1   package (8-oz.) frozen imitation crabmeat (surimi), thawed, finely chopped, or 1 can (6-oz.) crabmeat drained, flaked

1   teaspoon oil

1. In large bowl, combine all ingredients except oil; mix well. Shape mixture into 16 patties, about 1½-inches thick.

2. Heat oil in large nonstick skillet over medium heat until hot. Add patties; cook 6 to 8 minutes or until golden brown, turning once. If desired, serve with seafood cocktail sauce.

Nutrition Information Per Serving: Calories 150 • Total Fat 4g • Saturated Fat 1g • Cholesterol 65mg • Sodium 620mg • Total Carbohydrate 18g • Dietary Fiber 1g • Sugars 6g • Protein 11g. Dietary Exchanges: 1 Starch • 1 Very Lean Meat • ½ Fat OR 1 Carbohydrate • 1 Very Lean Meat • ½ Fat.

hamburger divan skillet

6 oz. uncooked spaghetti, broken into 2-inch pieces (1½ cups)

3 cups frozen cut broccoli (from 1-lb. bag)

1½ lb. lean (at least 80%) ground beef

1 container (10-oz.) refrigerated Alfredo pasta sauce

⅓ cup half-and-half

1 package (3-oz.) cream cheese, cut into cubes

1 jar (6-oz.) sliced mushrooms, drained

1 cup shredded Cheddar cheese (4 oz.)

1. Cook spaghetti as directed on package, adding broccoli during last minute of cooking time. Drain; return to saucepan. Cover to keep warm.

2. Meanwhile, in 10-inch skillet, cook ground beef over medium-high heat for 5 to 7 minutes or until thoroughly cooked, stirring frequently. Drain. Reduce heat to medium.

3. Stir in pasta sauce, half-and-half, cream cheese and mushrooms. Cook an additional 2 to 3 minutes or until cream cheese is melted and mixture is thoroughly heated, stirring frequently.

4. Stir in cooked spaghetti and broccoli; cook an additional minute until broccoli is hot. Sprinkle with Cheddar cheese.

Nutrition Information Per Serving: Calories 675 • Total Fat 45g • Saturated Fat 24g • Cholesterol 150mg • Sodium 660mg • Total Carbohydrate 31g • Dietary Fiber 3g • Sugars 4g • Protein 37g. Dietary Exchanges: 2 Starch • 1 Vegetable • 4 Medium-Fat Meat • 5 Fat.

mexican fried rice

SERVINGS: 4

KATIE COOK * STAFFORD, VIRGINIA

1 cup uncooked jasmine rice

1½ cups water

1 egg

1 tablespoon garlic-flavored olive oil or olive oil

1 lb. fresh chicken tenders

½ cup chopped onion

2 garlic cloves, minced

1 can (15-oz.) black beans, drained

1 can (11-oz.) vacuum-packed whole kernel corn with red and green peppers

1 jar (7-oz.) sliced roasted red bell peppers, drained

1 jar (8-oz.) taco sauce

¼ cup chopped green onion

¼ cup chopped fresh cilantro

1. Cook rice in water as directed on package. Meanwhile, spray 12-inch skillet with nonstick cooking spray. Heat over medium heat until hot. Beat egg in small bowl. Add egg to skillet; cook 1 minute or until firm but still moist, stirring frequently. Remove from pan; cover to keep warm.

2. Heat oil in same skillet over medium heat until hot. Add chicken, onion and garlic; cook 4 to 6 minutes or until chicken is no longer pink in center, stirring frequently. Add beans, corn and roasted peppers; mix well. Cook 1 minute or until thoroughly heated, stirring constantly and breaking up chicken and roasted peppers as mixture cooks.

3. Add cooked egg and rice; cook and stir 1 minute. Stir in taco sauce; cook 2 minutes or until thoroughly heated, stirring occasionally. Stir in green onions. Spoon mixture onto serving platter. Garnish with cilantro.

Nutrition Information Per Serving: Calories 550 • Total Fat 10g • Sodium 1080mg • Total Carbohydrate 76g • Protein 38g.

EASY ALTERNATIVES

Mexican Fried Rice is a fast and fun take on classic Chinese fried rice. If garlic-flavored olive oil isn't something you have on hand, you can add ¼ teaspoon of garlic powder to regular olive oil. Similarly, 1 pound of boneless, skinless chicken breasts can be substituted for the pound of fresh chicken tenders that the recipe calls for. Just cut each breast lengthwise into 1-inch strips before proceeding with the dish.

pan-roasted halibut over rotini

READY TO SERVE: 15 MINUTES
SERVINGS: 4

* super fast

2²⁄₃ cups uncooked rainbow rotini pasta (8 oz.)

4 halibut fillets, skin removed (4 oz. each and ½- to ¾-inch thick)

1 teaspoon seasoned salt

½ teaspoon coarse ground black pepper

1. Cook pasta as directed on package. Drain; cover to keep warm.

2. Meanwhile, sprinkle both sides of halibut with salt and pepper. Heat 10-inch nonstick skillet over high heat. Immediately place fish in skillet; cook 1 minute or until golden brown.

3. Turn fish; reduce heat to medium. Add ⅓ cup water; cover and cook 5 to 8 minutes or until fish flakes easily with fork. Serve fish over pasta.

Nutrition Information Per Serving: Calories 310 • Total Fat 2.5g • Saturated Fat 0g • Trans Fat 0g • Cholesterol 60mg • Sodium 660mg • Total Carbohydrate 45g • Dietary Fiber 3g • Sugars 0g • Protein 29g. Dietary Exchanges: 3 Starch • 3 Very Lean Meat.

tex-mex pasta

SERVINGS: 6

KAREN WETCH ✳ SANTA ROSA, CALIFORNIA

8 oz. uncooked penne pasta

1 lb. bulk Italian turkey sausage

1 medium onion, chopped

1 medium red bell pepper, chopped

1 small zucchini, chopped

2 cups frozen whole kernel corn (from 1-lb. pkg.)

1 cup chunky-style salsa

1 can (14.5-oz.) diced tomatoes, undrained

¾ teaspoon dried oregano leaves

6 oz. reduced-fat shredded Cheddar cheese (1½ cups)

½ cup fresh cilantro, chopped

1. Cook penne to desired doneness as directed on package. Drain; cover to keep warm.

2. Meanwhile, spray large nonstick skillet or wok with nonstick cooking spray. Heat over medium-high heat until hot. Add sausage; cook 5 minutes or until no longer pink and thoroughly cooked, stirring frequently. Drain.

3. Add onion, bell pepper, zucchini, corn, salsa, tomatoes and oregano; mix well. Bring to a boil. Cook 5 minutes, stirring occasionally.

4. Reserve ½ cup cheese and 2 tablespoons cilantro. Add remaining 1 cup cheese and cilantro to mixture in skillet; mix well. Add cooked penne; toss to mix.

5. Spoon mixture onto serving platter. Garnish with reserved cheese and cilantro.

Nutrition Information Per Serving: Calories 440 • Total Fat 15g • Total Carbohydrate 49g • Sodium 1140mg • Protein 28g.

winter chicken stew

READY TO SERVE: 30 MINUTES
SERVINGS: 4

1 teaspoon onion powder

1 lb. fresh chicken breast tenders, cut in half crosswise

3 medium Yukon gold or russet potatoes, cut into 1-inch cubes (about 3½ cups)

1 cup fresh baby carrots

1 package (8-oz.) fresh whole mushrooms, halved

1 can (14½-oz.) ready-to-serve fat-free chicken broth with ⅓ less sodium

1 tablespoon tomato paste

½ teaspoon salt

½ teaspoon dried thyme leaves

¼ cup water

2 tablespoons cornstarch

1. Sprinkle onion powder evenly over chicken; toss to coat. Spray nonstick Dutch oven with nonstick cooking spray. Heat over medium-high heat until hot. Add chicken; cook until browned.

2. Add all remaining ingredients except water and cornstarch. Bring to a boil. Reduce heat to low; cover and simmer 15 minutes or until vegetables are tender and chicken is no longer pink in center.

3. In small bowl, combine water and cornstarch; blend well. Add to chicken mixture; mix well. Bring to a boil. Cook and stir until thickened.

Nutrition Information Per Serving: Calories 300 • Total Fat 3g • Saturated Fat 1g • Trans Fat 0g • Cholesterol 65mg • Sodium 620mg • Total Carbohydrate 38g • Dietary Fiber 4g • Sugars 4g • Protein 30g. Dietary Exchanges: 2½ Starch • 3 Very Lean Meat OR 2½ Carbohydrate • 3 Very Lean Meat.

elbow macaroni and beef

READY TO SERVE: 25 MINUTES
SERVINGS: 8

8 cups water

6 oz. uncooked elbow macaroni (1½ cups)

1 package (1-lb.) frozen broccoli florets, carrots and cauliflower

1 lb. ground beef

1 jar (14-oz.) spaghetti sauce

4 slices American cheese, halved diagonally

1. Bring water to a boil in Dutch oven or large saucepan. Add macaroni and vegetables; cook 8 to 10 minutes or until macaroni and vegetables are tender. Drain.

2. Meanwhile, in 12-in. skillet, brown ground beef over medium-high heat until thoroughly cooked. Drain.

3. Reduce heat to low. Add spaghetti sauce and cooked macaroni and vegetables; mix well. Place cheese around edge of skillet with longest side of each triangle touching skillet. Cover; let stand 1 to 2 minutes or until cheese is melted.

Nutrition Information Per Serving: Calories 280 • Total Fat 14g • Saturated Fat 6g • Cholesterol 45mg • Sodium 410mg • Total Carbohydrate 23g • Dietary Fiber 3g • Sugars 2g • Protein 16g. Dietary Exchanges: 1½ Starch • 1½ Medium-Fat Meat • 1 Fat OR 1½ Carbohydrate • 1½ Medium-Fat Meat • 1 Fat.

spicy ham and cheese pasta

READY TO SERVE: 30 MINUTES
SERVINGS: 4

1 package (10-oz.) frozen cut broccoli with cheese-flavored sauce in a pouch

7 oz. uncooked medium shell pasta (about 2 cups)

1 teaspoon oil

¼ teaspoon crushed red pepper flakes

1 medium red bell pepper, chopped

6 oz. cooked ham, cut into thin strips (1 cup)

1. Bring large saucepan of water to a boil. Add unopened pouch of broccoli with cheese-flavored sauce; cook 5 minutes. Add pasta to water; return to a boil. Cook an additional 10 to 11 minutes or until pasta is tender. Drain.

2. Meanwhile, in medium nonstick skillet, heat oil and red pepper flakes over medium-high heat until hot. Add bell pepper and ham; cook and stir 3 to 4 minutes or until bell pepper is crisp-tender.

3. Return cooked pasta to large saucepan. Open broccoli pouch; add to pasta. Add ham mixture; toss gently to mix.

Nutrition Information Per Serving: Calories 300 • Total Fat 6g • Saturated Fat 2g • Cholesterol 25mg • Sodium 970mg • Total Carbohydrate 44g • Dietary Fiber 3g • Sugars 6g • Protein 17g. Dietary Exchanges: 3 Starch • 1 Lean Meat OR 3 Carbohydrate • 1 Lean Meat.

skillet nacho chili

READY TO SERVE: 40 MINUTES
SERVINGS: 4

½ cup chopped onion

1 pound lean (at least 80% lean) ground beef

1 can (19-oz.) ready-to-serve hearty tomato soup

1 can (15-oz.) spicy chili beans, undrained

1 can (4.5-oz.) chopped green chiles

1 cup frozen whole kernel corn

1 bag (4-oz.) shredded Cheddar cheese (1 cup)

2 cups corn chips

1. In an extra-large (12-inch) nonstick skillet, combine the onion and ground beef. Cook over medium-high heat for 5 to 7 minutes or until the beef is cooked through.

2. Stir in the soup, chili beans, green chiles and corn into the skillet. Cook over medium-high heat until simmering. Reduce heat to medium. Cook another 8 to 10 minutes or until the sauce thickens, stirring occasionally.

3. Divide the chili among 4 bowls. Sprinkle each serving with cheese. Serve with chips.

Nutrition Information Per Serving: Calories 600 • Total Fat 32g • Sodium 1750mg • Total Carbohydrate 45g • Sugars 10g • Protein 37g. Dietary Exchanges: 3 Starch • 4 Lean Meat • 3 Fat.

skillet nacho chili

smoked turkey quesadillas

SERVINGS: 4

DEAN PHILIPP ✳ PORTLAND, OREGON

1 ripe avocado, pitted, peeled

4 oz. cream cheese or
⅓-less-fat cream cheese
(Neufchâtel), softened

½ teaspoon cumin

¼ teaspoon garlic powder

¼ teaspoon salt

⅛ teaspoon pepper

½ cup julienne-cut oil-packed
sun-dried tomatoes, drained

1 can (4.5-oz.) chopped green
chiles, drained

4 oz. shredded hot pepper
Monterey Jack or Monterey
Jack cheese (1 cup)

1 package (11.5-oz.) flour
tortillas for burritos (8
tortillas)

8 slices smoked turkey breast
(1½-oz.)

4 oz. shredded
Cheddar cheese (1 cup)

2 tablespoons butter or
margarine

4 ripe olive slices, if desired

1. Mash avocado in medium bowl. Add cream cheese, cumin, garlic powder, salt and pepper; blend well. Stir in tomatoes and chiles.

2. Sprinkle ¾ cup of the Monterey Jack cheese on 4 of the tortillas. Top each with turkey slice. Spread avocado mixture over turkey. Top with remaining turkey slices. Sprinkle with ¾ cup of the Cheddar cheese. Top with remaining tortillas.

3. Melt ½ tablespoon of the butter in 12-inch skillet over medium heat. Add 1 quesadilla; cook 2 to 4 minutes or until golden brown, turning once. Repeat with remaining butter and quesadillas. Garnish with remaining Monterey Jack and Cheddar cheese. Top each quesadilla with olive slice.

Nutrition Information Per Serving: Calories 825 • Total Fat 51g • Sodium 2190mg • Total Carbohydrate 57g • Protein 40g.

A CROWD-PLEASER FOR ALL OCCASIONS

A quesadilla is a flour tortilla folded in half over a savory filling and fried to a golden brown. Some recipes sandwich the fillings between two flour tortillas and others bake the quesadillas to a crispy perfection in the oven.

Some versions, such as Smoked Turkey Quesadillas are hearty enough to be served as a quick, weeknight main course. They are also well received as a savory snack, perfect for watching the big game on TV or for casual movie nights at home. Lots of folks slice up several quesadillas for use as party appetizer, too.

peppery pan-roasted halibut

READY TO SERVE: 20 MINUTES
SERVINGS: 2

❋ super fast

- 2 halibut fillets, skin removed (4-oz. each and ½- to ¾-inch thick)
- ½ teaspoon seasoned salt
- ¼ teaspoon coarsely ground black pepper
- 3 tablespoons water

SKINNING A FILLET

You'll likely find halibut fillets at the supermarket with the skins already removed. If you are using fresh fish you caught yourself, remove the skin with a sharp, flexible knife.

Position the fillet's tail end closest to you. Starting at the tail end, make a small 45° angle cut in the meat to, but not through, the skin.

Using that cut as a starting point, insert knife and angle it flat against the skin. Hold the skin taut with one hand and slide the knife along the skin, separating the skin from the flesh. As you push the knife away from you, pull the skin toward you.

1. Sprinkle both sides of halibut with salt and pepper.

2. Spray medium nonstick skillet with nonstick cooking spray. Heat over high heat until very hot. Immediately place fish in skillet; cook 1 minute or until golden brown.

3. Turn fish; reduce heat to medium. Add 3 tablespoons water; cover and cook 5 to 8 minutes or until fish flakes easily with fork.

Nutrition Information Per Serving: Calories 120 • Total Fat 3g • Saturated Fat 0g • Cholesterol 35mg • Sodium 440mg • Total Carbohydrate 0g • Dietary Fiber 0g • Sugars 0g • Protein 24g. Dietary Exchange: 3½ Very Lean Meat.

turkey tortellini divan

READY TO SERVE: 20 MINUTES
SERVINGS: 4

❋ super fast

- 1 can (14½-oz.) ready-to-serve chicken broth
- 2 tablespoons all-purpose flour
- 1 package (9-oz.) frozen cut broccoli in a pouch
- 1 package (9-oz.) refrigerated cheese-filled tortellini
- 2 cups cubed smoked turkey breast (from deli)
- ½ cup sour cream

1. In small bowl, combine ¼ cup of the broth and the flour; blend until smooth. Set aside.

2. In medium saucepan, bring remaining broth to a boil over medium-high heat. Add broccoli; return to a boil. Stir in tortellini. Cook 3 to 5 minutes or until broccoli and tortellini are tender.

3. Stir in turkey. Add flour mixture; cook an additional 2 to 3 minutes, stirring constantly. Reduce heat to medium-low; stir in sour cream. Cook and stir until thoroughly heated.

Nutrition Information Per Serving: Calories 370 • Total Fat 13g • Saturated Fat 6g • Cholesterol 70mg • Sodium 1290mg • Total Carbohydrate 38g • Dietary Fiber 3g • Sugars 3g • Protein 25g. Dietary Exchanges: 2½ Starch • 2½ Lean Meat • 1 Fat OR 2½ Carbohydrate • 2½ Lean Meat • 1 Fat.

taco turkey medallions

READY TO SERVE: 25 MINUTES
SERVINGS: 4

* **super fast**

1 package (1.25-oz.) taco seasoning mix

2 tablespoons all-purpose flour

1 lb. fresh turkey breast tenderloins, cut crosswise into ½-inch slices

1 tablespoon olive or vegetable oil

1 cup chunky-style salsa

2 tablespoons honey

2 tablespoons chopped fresh cilantro, if desired

1. In large resealable food storage plastic bag, combine taco seasoning mix and flour; mix well. Add turkey slices; seal bag and shake to coat.

2. Heat oil in 10-inch nonstick skillet over medium-high heat until hot. Add turkey; cook until brown on both sides.

3. Add salsa, honey and any remaining coating mixture; mix well. Reduce heat to medium-low; cover and simmer 5 to 10 minutes or until turkey is no longer pink in center, stirring occasionally. Sprinkle with cilantro.

Nutrition Information Per Serving: Calories 250 • Total Fat 5g • Saturated Fat 1g • Cholesterol 75mg • Sodium 1320mg • Total Carbohydrate 21g • Dietary Fiber 1g • Sugars 11g • Protein 29g. Dietary Exchanges: ½ Starch • 4 Very Lean Meat • 1 Other Carbohydrate.

DELICIOUS ADDITIONS

While the medallions simmer, cook instant white rice to serve alongside the entree. It complements the turkey perfectly as it soaks up the tangy sauce. You can also open a can of corn with red peppers, pour it in a bowl and zap it in the microwave for a time-saving side. For dessert, consider bakery-bought chocolate brownies or toss together a combination of kiwifruit and red grapes. Drain a can of mandarin oranges and gently stir in the wedges.

tortellini with tomato sauce

READY TO SERVE: 20 MINUTES
SERVINGS: 4

* **super fast**

1½ teaspoons olive oil

1 medium onion, chopped

1 can (10½-oz.) condensed beef consommé

1 can (8-oz.) no-salt-added tomato sauce

2 teaspoons brown sugar

½ teaspoon dried Italian seasoning

¼ teaspoon garlic powder

1 package (9-oz.) refrigerated cheese-filled tortellini

½ medium green bell pepper, chopped

1½ cups chopped seeded tomatoes

1. Heat oil in large nonstick skillet over medium heat until hot. Add onion; cook 2 minutes. Stir in consommé, tomato sauce, brown sugar, Italian seasoning and garlic powder. Bring to a boil. Cook over medium heat for 2 minutes.

2. Add tortellini and bell pepper; simmer 5 minutes, stirring occasionally. Add tomatoes; cook an additional 3 minutes or until thoroughly heated.

Nutrition Information Per Serving: Calories 320 • Total Fat 9g • Saturated 3g • Cholesterol 35mg • Sodium 650mg • Total Carbohydrate 44g • Dietary Fiber 5g • Sugars 10g • Protein 15g. Dietary Exchanges: 2½ Starch • 1 Vegetable • 1 High-Fat Meat OR 2½ Carbohydrate • 1 Vegetable • 1 High-Fat Meat.

PRODUCE POINTERS

The way you store your tomatoes can actually affect their taste and texture. It is not a good idea to try to ripen picked tomatoes in the refrigerator or on a window ledge in the sun. Place them in a cool spot out of the sunlight or in a closed paper bag instead. Enjoy the tomatoes once they are ripe or refrigerate them for a few days so they don't spoil.

golden rice and chicken pilaf

READY TO SERVE: 30 MINUTES
SERVINGS: 4

2 teaspoons oil

1 lb. fresh chicken tenders

½ cup chopped onion

1 cup uncooked regular long-grain white rice

½ cup shredded carrot

¼ cup golden raisins

1 teaspoon curry powder

1 teaspoon coriander

¼ teaspoon salt

1 can (14½-oz.) ready-to-serve chicken broth

½ cup water

¼ cup slivered almonds, toasted if desired

1. Heat oil in large nonstick skillet over medium-high heat until hot. Add chicken and onion; cook 5 minutes or until chicken is browned and onion is tender, stirring occasionally.

2. Add all remaining ingredients except almonds; mix well. Bring to a boil. Reduce heat to medium-low; cover and cook 15 to 20 minutes or until chicken is no longer pink, rice is tender and liquid is absorbed.

3. Top each serving with almonds.

Nutrition Information Per Serving: Calories 410 • Total Fat 10g • Saturated Fat 2g • Cholesterol 65mg • Sodium 530mg • Total Carbohydrate 49g • Dietary Fiber 3g • Sugars 8g • Protein 32g. Dietary Exchanges: 3 Starch • ½ Fruit • 3 Very Lean Meat • 1 Fat OR 3½ Carbohydrate • 3 Very Lean Meat • 1 Fat.

chicken lo mein

glazed mandarin chicken

✳ **super fast**

- 1 cup water
- 1 cup uncooked instant white rice
- ½ cup frozen sweet peas
- ¼ cup barbecue sauce
- ¼ cup frozen orange juice concentrate, thawed
- ¼ teaspoon salt
- 3 boneless skinless chicken breast halves, cut into 1-inch pieces
- 1 tablespoon oil
- ¼ cup water

1. In medium saucepan, bring 1 cup water to a boil. Add rice and peas; return to a boil. Cover; remove from heat. Set aside.

2. In medium bowl, combine barbecue sauce, orange juice concentrate and salt; blend well. Add chicken; stir to coat thoroughly.

3. Heat oil in large nonstick skillet over high heat for 1 minute. Add chicken; cook and stir about 4 minutes or until chicken is no longer pink. Remove skillet from heat. Remove chicken from skillet; set aside.

4. Add ¼ cup water to skillet. Cook and stir over high heat, scraping sides and bottom of skillet to remove cooked-on marinade. Cook about 30 seconds or until slightly thickened. Return chicken to skillet; toss to coat. Cook 1 minute or until chicken is glazed.

5. Serve over rice.

Nutrition Information Per Serving: Calories 270 • Total Fat 6g • Saturated Fat 1g • Cholesterol 55mg • Sodium 340mg • Total Carbohydrate 31g • Dietary Fiber 1g • Sugars 6g • Protein 23g. Dietary Exchanges: 2 Starch • 2 Very Lean Meat • 1 Fat OR 2 Carbohydrate • 2 Very Lean Meat • 1 Fat.

chicken lo mein

- 1 tablespoon oil
- 2 boneless skinless chicken breast halves, cut into thin bite-sized strips
- 1 garlic clove, minced
- ¼ teaspoon ginger
- ½ cup water
- 2 tablespoons soy sauce
- 1 can (10½-oz.) condensed chicken broth
- 4 oz. uncooked angel hair pasta (capellini), broken into thirds
- 1 package (1-lb.) frozen broccoli florets, carrots and water chestnuts

1. Heat oil in large skillet or wok over medium-high heat until hot. Add chicken and garlic; cook and stir 4 to 5 minutes or until chicken is no longer pink in center.

2. Add ginger, water, soy sauce and broth. Bring to a boil. Stir in pasta. Add frozen vegetables; stir gently. Return to a boil. Reduce heat to medium-low; cover and simmer 5 to 8 minutes or until pasta and vegetables are tender, stirring occasionally.

Nutrition Information Per Serving: Calories 280 • Total Fat 7g • Saturated Fat 1g • Cholesterol 35mg • Sodium 1050mg • Total Carbohydrate 30g • Dietary Fiber 3g • Sugars 4g • Protein 23g. Dietary Exchanges: 1½ Starch • 1 Vegetable • 2½ Very Lean Meat • 1 Fat OR 1½ Carbohydrate • 1 Vegetable • 2½ Very Lean Meat • 1 Fat.

SUPER DINNER IN A SNAP

Crescent dinner rolls and rice pudding are delightful ways to round out Chicken Lo Mein. Start by preheating the oven per the directions on the package of rolls. Next, cut up the chicken and mince the garlic for the lo mein. Assemble all of the ingredients for the entree before heating the skillet. Bake the crescent rolls while the chicken cooks. At dessert time, sprinkle each serving of rice pudding with a dash of cinnamon and top with raisins.

cajun black beans with sausage and corn

READY TO SERVE: 20 MINUTES
SERVINGS: 4

* super fast

1. Heat oil in large skillet over medium-high heat until hot. Add garlic; cook and stir 1 minute. Add bell pepper and onion stir-fry; cook and stir 2 to 3 minutes or until crisp-tender.

2. Add corn, kielbasa, salt, pepper blend and thyme; mix well. Cook 3 to 5 minutes or until corn is tender, stirring occasionally.

3. Add tomatoes and beans; cook 3 to 5 minutes or until thoroughly heated, stirring occasionally.

Nutrition Information Per Serving: Calories 390 • Total Fat 23g • Saturated Fat 7g • Cholesterol 40mg • Sodium 1110mg • Total Carbohydrate 30g • Dietary Fiber 7g • Sugars 5g • Protein 15g. Dietary Exchanges: 2 Starch • 1½ High-Fat Meat • 2 Fat OR 2 Carbohydrate • 1½ High-Fat Meat • 2 Fat.

2 tablespoons oil

2 garlic cloves, minced

1 cup frozen bell pepper and onion stir-fry

1½ cups frozen whole kernel corn

½ lb. cooked kielbasa or Polish sausage, coarsely chopped

½ teaspoon salt

¼ teaspoon black and red pepper blend

½ teaspoon dried thyme leaves

1½ cups chopped fresh tomatoes

1 can (15-oz.) black beans, drained, rinsed

ADD A BIT OF SPICE...AND THEN SOME

This dish lands on the mild side of Cajun cuisine. If you like a main course with more fiery overtones, shake in a few drops of hot pepper sauce or a bit of cayenne pepper. If some family members like a spicy meal even though others don't, simply set the bottle of hot pepper sauce on the table.

Don't be afraid to get creative with the dish. Chop any leftover chicken or pork and stir it into the entree. You can also mix in a can of mushrooms if you'd like or toss in a handful of frozen peas. You can also substitute the black beans with whatever 15-ounce can of beans you might have hand. Instant rice makes a tasty accompaniment to the Cajun specialty. For extra flavor, try cooking the rice in chicken broth instead of water. Just remember to set the broth on the stove to boil before you begin preparing the entree.

spicy chinese chicken tacos

READY TO SERVE: 20 MINUTES
SERVINGS: 6 (2 TACOS EACH)

* super fast

1 box (4.6-oz.) taco shells (12 shells)

3 boneless skinless chicken breasts (¾ lb.), cut into thin bite-size strips

1 teaspoon grated gingerroot

1 small clove garlic, minced

2 tablespoons soy sauce

1 tablespoon honey

1 large green onion, sliced

½ teaspoon crushed red pepper

1½ cups shredded iceberg lettuce

1. If desired, heat taco shells as directed on box.

2. Heat large nonstick skillet over medium-high heat. Add chicken, gingerroot and garlic; cook 3 to 5 minutes, stirring frequently, until lightly browned.

3. Stir in soy sauce, honey, onion and red pepper to coat. Reduce heat to low; cover and cook 5 minutes, stirring occasionally, until chicken is no longer pink in center.

4. To serve, place scant ¼ cup chicken mixture in each taco shell. Top each with lettuce. Serve immediately.

Nutrition Information Per Serving: Calories 180 • Total Fat 7g • Saturated Fat 1g • Cholesterol 35mg • Sodium 260mg • Total Carbohydrate 18g • Dietary Fiber 2g • Sugars 4g • Protein 14g. Dietary Exchanges: 1 Starch • 1½ Very Lean Meat • 1 Fat.

spicy chinese chicken tacos

fancy dipped strawberries ✳ p. 314

oatmeal-raisin cookies ✳ p. 318

peanutty rice cake rounds ✳ p. 338

toaster apple sundaes ✳ p. 321

chocolate-dipped peanut butter fingers ✳ p. 329

strawberry-kiwi parfait

strawberry-kiwi parfait

READY TO SERVE: 10 MINUTES
SERVINGS: 5

＊ super fast

1 small kiwifruit

1 container (6-oz.) strawberry-mango low-fat yogurt

½ cup Honey NutClusters® cereal

1. Peel the kiwifruit and cut it into small pieces.

2. Spoon half of the yogurt into a drinking glass.

3. Top the yogurt with half of the kiwifruit and half of the cereal.

4. Repeat with remaining yogurt, kiwifruit and cereal.

Nutrition Information Per Serving: Calories 330 • Total Fat 3.5g • Sodium 230mg • Total Carbohydrate 67g • Sugars 44g • Protein 10g. Dietary Exchanges: 1 Fruit • 2 Other Carbohydrate • 1 Low-Fat Milk.

cheese-topped pumpkin muffins

READY TO SERVE: 30 MINUTES
SERVINGS: 1 DOZEN

1¾ cups all-purpose flour

½ cup sugar

3 teaspoons baking powder

1 teaspoon pumpkin pie spice

¼ teaspoon salt

¾ cup canned pumpkin

½ cup skim milk

¼ cup oil

2 egg whites

4 oz. fat-free cream cheese (from 8-oz. pkg.), cut into 12 cubes

2 tablespoons brown sugar

1. Heat oven to 400°F. Spray 12 muffin cups with nonstick cooking spray, or line muffin cups with paper baking cups and spray paper cups with nonstick cooking spray.

2. In large bowl, combine flour, sugar, baking powder, pumpkin pie spice and salt; mix well.

3. In small bowl, combine pumpkin, milk, oil and egg whites; blend well. Add to dry ingredients all at once; stir just until dry ingredients are moistened. Spoon batter evenly into sprayed muffin cups. Press 1 cube cream cheese into center of each muffin. Top each with ½ teaspoon brown sugar.

4. Bake at 400°F for 14 to 18 minutes or until toothpick inserted near center, but not into cream cheese, comes out clean. Immediately remove from pan. Serve warm. Store in refrigerator.

Nutrition Information Per Serving: Calories 170 • Total Fat 5g • Saturated Fat 1g • Cholesterol 0mg • Sodium 200mg • Total Carbohydrate 27g • Dietary Fiber 1g • Sugars 12g • Protein 4g. Dietary Exchanges: 1½ Starch • 1 Fat OR 1½ Carbohydrate • 1 Fat.

caramel chocolate crunch bars

PREP TIME: 15 MINUTES
READY TO SERVE: 45 MINUTES
SERVINGS: 16 BARS

＊ plan ahead

⅓ cup firmly packed brown sugar

¼ cup margarine or butter, softened

½ cup all-purpose flour

½ cup quick-cooking rolled oats

½ cup Grape-Nuts® cereal

¼ cup caramel ice cream topping

¼ cup miniature chocolate chips

1. Heat oven to 425°F. Line an 8-inch square pan with foil; spray the foil with nonstick cooking spray.

2. In a medium bowl, combine brown sugar and margarine; blend well. Add flour, oats and cereal to sugar mixture; mix well. Press in bottom of sprayed foil-lined pan. Drizzle caramel topping to within ½ inch of edges.

3. Bake at 425°F for 10 minutes or until edges are light golden brown. Immediately sprinkle bars with chocolate chips; let stand 1 to 2 minutes to melt. Spread melted chips evenly over bars; cool 5 minutes. Remove bars from pan by carefully lifting foil. Cool in freezer for 15 minutes. Cut into bars.

Nutrition Information Per Serving: Calories 110 • Total Fat 4g • Saturated Fat 1 g • Cholesterol 0mg • Sodium 80mg • Total Carbohydrate 17g • Dietary Fiber 1g • Sugars 9g • Protein 2g. Dietary Exchanges: 1 Starch • 1 Fat OR 1 Carbohydrate • 1 Fat.

fancy dipped strawberries

READY TO SERVE: 45 MINUTES
SERVINGS: 40 STRAWBERRIES

toppings

Miniature semisweet chocolate chips

Chopped nuts

Colored sugars and candy sprinkles

Grated chocolate

Shredded coconut

dipped berries

1 quart fresh whole strawberries with stems (4 cups)

1 cup vanilla ready-to-spread frosting

1. Cover a cookie sheet with waxed paper. Decide what toppings you want to put on the strawberries. Put some of each of the toppings in a different custard cup.

2. Rinse and pat dry strawberries.

3. In a microwave-safe bowl, heat the frosting on High 15 to 20 seconds, until it is melted; stirring the frosting once.

4. Dip the bottom of a strawberry halfway into the melted frosting. Immediately dip the strawberry into one of the toppings. Put the strawberries on the cookie sheets. Put the cookie sheet in the refrigerator for 5 minutes or until the frosting on the strawberries has hardened.

Nutrition Information Per Serving: Calories 50 • Total Fat 2g • Sodium 0mg • Total Carbohydrate 8g • Sugars 8g • Protein 0g. Dietary Exchanges: ½ Fruit • ½ Fat.

saucy center chocolate cakes

PREP TIME: 20 MINUTES
READY TO SERVE: 40 MINUTES
SERVINGS: 7

½ cup butter

8 oz. semisweet baking chocolate, chopped

4 eggs

2 tablespoons hazelnut coffee drink syrup

½ cup granulated sugar

2 tablespoons all-purpose flour

Powdered sugar

1. Heat oven to 400°F. Generously grease 7 (6-oz.) custard cups with shortening; lightly flour. In 2-quart saucepan, melt butter and chocolate over low heat, stirring frequently, until smooth; set aside.

2. In medium bowl, beat eggs and syrup with electric mixer on high speed until foamy. Gradually beat in granulated sugar. Beat on high speed 2 minutes or until light and thickened, scraping bowl occasionally. On low speed, beat in flour and chocolate mixture just until blended, scraping bowl occasionally. Divide batter evenly among custard cups, filling each about ¾ full. Place cups on cookie sheet.

3. Bake 11 to 15 minutes or until cakes have formed top crust, but are still soft in center. Cool 5 minutes. Place individual dessert plate over each custard cup; turn plate and cup over. Remove cup. Sift powdered sugar over cakes; serve warm.

Nutrition Information Per Serving: Calories 420 • Total Fat 26g • Saturated Fat 13g • Trans Fat 1g • Cholesterol 155mg • Sodium 125mg • Total Carbohydrate 41g • Dietary Fiber 2g • Sugars 37g • Protein 5g. Dietary Exchanges: 1 Starch • 2 Other Carbohydrate • 5 Fat.

strawberry-banana yogurt smoothie

READY TO SERVE: 10 MINUTES
SERVINGS: 5

* super fast

3 cups fresh strawberries or individually frozen strawberries, slightly thawed

3 medium ripe bananas, cut up

1½ cups milk

3 containers (8-oz. each) low-fat strawberry yogurt

1. In blender container, place 1½ cups strawberries, half of the banana pieces, ¾ cup milk and 1½ containers of yogurt. Cover; blend at medium speed 30 to 60 seconds or until smooth.

2. Repeat with remaining ingredients. Serve immediately.

Nutrition Information Per Serving: Calories 270 • Total Fat 3.5g • Saturated Fat 2g • Cholesterol 11mg • Sodium 120mg • Total Carbohydrate 53g • Dietary Fiber 4g • Sugars 34g • Protein 10g. Dietary Exchanges: 2 Fruit • 1 Low-Fat Milk.

fancy dipped strawberries

black forest cherry cake

black forest cherry cake

PREP TIME: 25 MINUTES
READY TO SERVE: 55 MINUTES
SERVINGS: 12

cake

- 1 box (1-lb. 2.25-oz.) devil's food cake mix with pudding
- 2 tablespoons all-purpose flour
- 1¾ cups water
- 3 eggs

filling and topping

- 1 can (21-oz.) cherry or cherry-cranberry pie filling
- ¾ teaspoon almond extract
- 1 container (8-oz.) frozen reduced-fat whipped topping, thawed

  Maraschino or candied cherries and chocolate curls, if desired

1. Heat oven to 350°F. Grease 15x10x1-inch pan with shortening or cooking spray. Line with foil, extending foil over short sides of pan; grease foil. In large bowl, beat cake mix, flour, water and eggs with electric mixer on low speed until moistened, scraping bowl occasionally. Beat on high speed 2 minutes, scraping bowl occasionally. Spread batter evenly in pan.

2. Bake 18 to 20 minutes or until cake springs back when touched lightly in center. Remove cake from pan by lifting foil; place on wire rack. Cool completely, about 15 minutes.

3. Meanwhile, in small bowl, mix pie filling and ½ teaspoon of the almond extract.

4. Cut cooled cake in half crosswise to make 2 (10x7-inch) layers; remove foil. Place one cake layer on serving platter or tray; spread pie filling mixture over top. Top with remaining cake layer.

5. Stir remaining ¼ teaspoon almond extract into whipped topping. Spread mixture over sides and top of cake. Serve immediately, or loosely cover and refrigerate until serving time. If desired, garnish each serving with maraschino or candied cherry and chocolate curls. Store in refrigerator.

Nutrition Information Per Serving: Calories 290 • Total Fat 7g • Saturated Fat 4g • Trans Fat 0g • Cholesterol 55mg • Sodium 360mg • Total Carbohydrate 53g • Dietary Fiber 2g • Sugars 35g • Protein 5g. Dietary Exchanges: 1½ Starch • 2 Other Carbohydrate • 1 Fat.

banana roll-ups

READY TO SERVE: 10 MINUTES
SERVINGS: 4

* super fast

- 3 tablespoons peanut butter
- 2 flour tortillas (7- to 8- inch)
- 2 tablespoons hot fudge ice cream topping
- 2 bananas
- 2 teaspoons toasted wheat germ, if desired
- 1 pint chocolate or vanilla ice cream (2 cups)

  Additional hot fudge ice cream topping, if desired

1. Spread peanut butter on tortillas. Carefully spread ice cream topping over peanut butter.

2. Place banana in center of each tortilla. (If bananas are very curved, make 2 cuts at intervals on inside edge to make them lay straight.) Sprinkle each with wheat germ. Roll up tortillas; cut each into 1-inch pieces.

3. Arrange roll-ups on 4 dessert plates; top with ½ cup ice cream and ice cream topping.

Nutrition Information Per Serving: Calories 350 • Total Fat 16g • Saturated Fat 7g • Cholesterol 30mg • Sodium 220mg • Total Carbohydrate 47g • Dietary Fiber 3g • Sugars 25g • Protein 8g. Dietary Exchanges: 2 Starch • 1 Fruit • 3 Fat.

brownie macaroons

SERVINGS: 2 DOZEN

RONALD GRASGREEN * SUGARLAND, TEXAS

- 1 package (15.5-oz.) fudge brownie mix with chocolate chunks
- 2 cups coconut
- 2 tablespoons water
- 1 tablespoon oil
- 1 egg

1. Heat oven to 350°F. Lightly grease cookie sheets or line with parchment paper. In large bowl, combine all ingredients; beat 50 strokes with spoon. Shape dough into 1½-inch balls. Place 3 inches apart on greased cookie sheet; flatten slightly.

2. Bake at 350°F for 12 to 15 minutes or until edges are set. (Centers will be soft.) Remove from cookie sheets.

Nutrition Information Per Serving: Calories 120 • Total Fat 5g • Sodium 75mg • Total Carbohydrate 18g • Protein 1g.

oatmeal-raisin cookies

READY TO SERVE: 45 MINUTES
SERVINGS: 3½ DOZEN

- ¾ cup granulated sugar
- ¼ cup packed brown sugar
- ½ cup butter or margarine, softened
- ½ teaspoon vanilla
- 1 egg
- ¾ cup all-purpose flour
- ½ teaspoon baking soda
- ½ teaspoon ground cinnamon
- ¼ teaspoon salt
- 1½ cups quick-cooking oats
- ½ cup raisins
- ½ cup chopped nuts

1. Heat oven to 375°F. Grease cookie sheets with shortening or cooking spray. In large bowl, beat granulated sugar, brown sugar and butter with electric mixer on medium speed until light and fluffy, scraping bowl occasionally. Beat in vanilla and egg until well blended. On low speed, beat in flour, baking soda, cinnamon and salt until well combined, scraping bowl occasionally. Stir in oats, raisins and nuts.

2. Drop dough by rounded teaspoonfuls 2 inches apart onto cookie sheets.

3. Bake 7 to 10 minutes or until edges are light golden brown. Cool 1 minute; remove from cookie sheets.

Nutrition Information Per Serving: Calories 80 • Total Fat 3.5g • Saturated Fat 1.5g • Trans Fat 0g • Cholesterol 10mg • Sodium 45mg • Total Carbohydrate 10g • Dietary Fiber 0g • Sugars 6g • Protein 1g. Dietary Exchanges: ½ Other Carbohydrate • 1 Fat.

crescent caramel swirl

SERVINGS: 12

LOIS ANN GROVES ✳ SAN ANTONIO, TEXAS

- ½ cup butter (do not use margarine)
- ½ cup chopped nuts
- ¾ cup firmly packed brown sugar
- 1 tablespoon water
- 2 cans (8-oz. each) refrigerated crescent dinner rolls

1. Heat oven to 350°F. Melt butter in small saucepan. Coat bottom and sides of 12-cup Bundt pan with 2 tablespoons of the melted butter; sprinkle pan with 3 tablespoons of the nuts. Add remaining nuts, brown sugar and water to remaining 6 tablespoons melted butter. Bring to a boil, stirring occasionally. Boil 1 minute, stirring constantly.

2. Remove dough from cans; do not unroll. Cut each roll into 4 slices (for total of 16 slices). Arrange 8 slices, cut side down, in nut-lined pan; separate layers of each pinwheel slightly. Spoon half of brown sugar mixture over dough. Place remaining dough slices alternately over bottom layer. Spoon remaining brown sugar mixture over slices.

3. Bake at 350°F for 23 to 33 minutes or until deep golden brown. Cool 3 minutes. Invert onto serving platter or waxed paper.

Nutrition Information Per Serving: Calories 280 • Total Fat 18g • Sodium 400mg • Total Carbohydrate 29g • Protein 3g.

MUST-TRY MASTERPIECE

It's hard to believe that a dessert as decadent as Crescent Caramel Swirl starts with only five kitchen staples and doesn't require hours of work. And as if the cake isn't impressive enough, you can even dress up individual slices of the no-fuss sweet without much effort. Keep the following in mind when you really want to surprise your family with a weeknight treat:

✳ If you baked the cake ahead of time, warm slices in the microwave.

✳ Drizzle a little caramel ice cream topping over each piece.

✳ Serve slices of the cake alongside scoops of vanilla ice cream.

✳ Sprinkle servings with cinnamon.

oatmeal-raisin cookies

toaster apple sundaes

strawberry-rhubarb shortcakes

READY TO SERVE: 30 MINUTES
SERVINGS: 8

topping

4	cups fresh or frozen sliced rhubarb
½	cup sugar
2	tablespoons grated orange peel
1	pint fresh strawberries, sliced (2 cups)

shortcakes

1¾	cups all-purpose flour
1	tablespoon sugar
3	teaspoons baking powder
¼	cup margarine or butter, cut into pieces
1	cup skim milk

1. In medium saucepan, combine rhubarb, ½ cup sugar and orange peel; mix well. Cook over medium heat for 8 to 10 minutes or until rhubarb is tender, stirring occasionally. Cool slightly. Stir in strawberries.

2. Heat oven to 450°F. Spray cookie sheet with nonstick cooking spray. In medium bowl, combine flour, 1 tablespoon sugar and baking powder; mix well. Using pastry blender or fork, cut in margarine until mixture resembles coarse crumbs. Add milk; stir just until all dry ingredients are moistened. Drop dough by about ¼ cupfuls onto sprayed cookie sheet; flatten slightly.

3. Bake at 450°F for 9 to 12 minutes or until light golden brown. Immediately remove from cookie sheet. Split shortcakes; place 2 halves on each individual dessert plate. Spoon about ⅓ cup topping over each shortcake.

Nutrition Information Per Serving: Calories 250 • Total Fat 6g • Saturated Fat 1g • Cholesterol 0mg • Sodium 270mg • Total Carbohydrate 43g • Dietary Fiber 3g • Sugars 19g • Protein 5g. Dietary Exchanges: 1 Starch • 2 Fruit • 1 Fat OR 3 Carbohydrate • 1 Fat.

pineapple caramel sundae

READY TO SERVE: 25 MINUTES
SERVINGS: 8

* super fast

1	can (20-oz.) pineapple slices in unsweetened juice, drained
½	cup packed light brown sugar
1	quart vanilla frozen yogurt or ice cream (4 cups)
½	cup caramel ice cream topping
1	cup coarsely chopped toasted almonds, if desired

1. On ungreased cookie sheet, place pineapple slices. Sprinkle ¼ cup of the brown sugar evenly over pineapple. Broil 3 inches from heat about 4 minutes or until lightly brown. Turn pineapple over; sprinkle with remaining ¼ cup brown sugar. Broil an additional 4 minutes. Cool.

2. To serve, place pineapple on dessert plates or in bowls. Top each with scoop of frozen yogurt. Drizzle each with caramel topping; sprinkle with almonds.

Nutrition Information Per Serving: Calories 250 • Total Fat 1g • Saturated Fat 1g • Cholesterol 5mg • Sodium 135mg • Total Carbohydrate 56g • Dietary Fiber 1g • Sugars 50g • Protein 5g. Dietary Exchanges: 1 Starch • 3 Other Carbohydrate.

toaster apple sundaes

READY TO SERVE: 15 MINUTES
SERVINGS: 4

* super fast

4	toaster strudel frozen brown sugar cinnamon pastries
1	cup apple pie filling
2	cups vanilla ice cream

1. Toast the pastries per the package directions.

2. While the pastries are in the toaster, pour the apple pie filling into a microwave-safe bowl. Microwave on High for 1 minute or until the pie filling is heated through.

3. Put each of the pastries on a serving plate. Top each with the hot apple pie filling. Put a scoop of ice cream on top of each pastry.

4. Cut off a corner of the icing packet from the pastries package. Drizzle the icing over each pastry.

Nutrition Information Per Serving: Calories 410 • Total Fat 15g • Sodium 240mg • Total Carbohydrate 66g • Sugars 41g • Protein 5g. Dietary Exchanges: 1 Starch • 3½ Other Carbohydrate • 3 Fat.

crunchy biscuit bites

READY TO SERVE: 20 MINUTES
SERVINGS: 32 BISCUIT BITES

＊ super fast

2 tablespoons sugar

½ teaspoon ground cinnamon

1 can (10.2-oz.) large refrigerated buttermilk homestyle biscuits

2 tablespoons butter or margarine

¾ cup finely crushed Cinnamon Toast Crunch® cereal

1. Heat the oven to 400°F. Spray a cookie sheet with cooking spray.

2. Combine the sugar and cinnamon in a large bowl.

3. Separate the dough into 5 biscuits. Use kitchen scissors to cut each biscuit into 6 equal wedges. Put the biscuit wedges in the bowl with the sugar and cinnamon.

4. In a microwave-safe bowl, heat the butter on High 20 to 30 seconds, until it is melted.

5. Drizzle the butter over the dough wedges in the bowl. Stir the dough wedges to cover with butter.

6. Put some cereal in a resealable food storage plastic bag and seal. Use a rolling pin to crush the cereal. Add cereal to the bag until you can measure out ¾ cup. Add the crushed cereal to the bowl. Gently stir until the dough wedges are covered with as much cereal as possible.

7. Place the biscuit wedges in rows on cookie sheet. Make sure their sides do not touch.

8. Bake the dough wedges for 13 minutes or until golden brown. Serve warm.

Nutrition Information Per Serving: Calories 70 • Total Fat 4g • Sodium 95mg • Total Carbohydrate 9g • Sugars 4g • Protein 0g. Dietary Exchange: Free.

mini fruit pizzas

PREP TIME: 25 MINUTES
READY TO SERVE: 40 MINUTES
SERVINGS: 20 COOKIES

1 package (18-oz.) refrigerated ready-to-bake sugar cookies (20 cookies)

1 package (8-oz.) cream cheese, softened

2 tablespoons frozen limeade concentrate

½ cup powdered sugar

10 fresh strawberries, quartered

1 kiwifruit, peeled, cut in half lengthwise and cut into 10 slices

½ cup fresh blueberries

½ cup fresh raspberries

1. Bake cookies as directed on package. Cool completely, about 10 minutes.

2. Meanwhile, in medium bowl, beat cream cheese, limeade concentrate and powdered sugar with electric mixer on medium speed until smooth.

3. Spread each cooled cookie with 1 tablespoon cream cheese mixture. Arrange fruit on top of each. Serve immediately, or cover and refrigerate up to 2 hours before serving.

Nutrition Information Per Serving: Calories 170 • Total Fat 9g • Saturated Fat 3.5g • Trans Fat 1.5g • Cholesterol 20mg • Sodium 100mg • Total Carbohydrate 21g • Dietary Fiber 0g • Sugars 13g • Protein 2g. Dietary Exchanges: 1½ Other Carbohydrate • 2 Fat.

STORAGE SMARTS

When selecting fresh berries for the fruit pizzas, remember that individual varieties have their own peak seasons. In general, you should feel confident if you select berries that are plump and not bruised.

Strawberries may be stored in a paper towel-lined, moisture-proof container in the refrigerator for 2 to 3 days. Blueberries refrigerate well in the containers they're packed in for up to a week. Raspberries can be refrigerated for 3 days if they are spread in a single layer on a paper towel-lined cookie sheet and covered with additional paper towels.

crunchy biscuit bites

creamy applesauce dunk

creamy applesauce dunk

READY TO SERVE: 10 MINUTES
SERVINGS: 2

* super fast

dunk

½ cup applesauce

2 tablespoons vanilla low-fat yogurt

⅛ teaspoon ground cinnamon

dunkers

Animal crackers

Chocolate graham crackers

Rainbow-colored vanilla wafers

Sweetened miniature shredded wheat cereal

1. In a small bowl, combine the applesauce, yogurt and cinnamon; mix well.

2. Serve dip with your choice of dunkers.

Nutrition Information Per Serving: Calories 170 • Total Fat 4g • Sodium 115mg • Total Carbohydrate 33g • Sugars 21g • Protein 2g. Dietary Exchanges: 1 Starch • 1 Other Carbohydrate.

spiced walnut brittle

PREP TIME: 15 MINUTES
READY TO SERVE: 45 MINUTES
SERVINGS: 20 PIECES

* plan ahead

1 cup sugar

½ cup light corn syrup

1 cup coarsely chopped walnuts

½ teaspoon cinnamon

1 teaspoon butter

1 teaspoon vanilla

1 teaspoon baking soda

1. Butter cookie sheet. In 8-cup microwavable measuring cup or medium microwavable bowl, combine sugar and corn syrup; mix well. Microwave on High for 4 minutes. Stir; microwave on High for an additional 3 to 5 minutes or until mixture turns light brown.

2. Add walnuts, cinnamon, butter and vanilla; blend well. Microwave on High for 1 minute.

3. Add baking soda; stir until light and foamy. Pour onto buttered cookie sheet. Cool 30 minutes or until firm. Break brittle into 2-inch pieces. Store in tightly covered container.

Nutrition Information Per Serving: Calories 110 • Total Fat 4g • Saturated Fat 0g • Cholesterol 0mg • Sodium 75mg • Total Carbohydrate 17g • Dietary Fiber 0g • Sugars 13g • Protein 1g. Dietary Exchanges: 1 Fat • 1 Other Carbohydrate • 1 Carbohydrate Choice.

maple oat chewies

SERVINGS: 5 DOZEN

KITTY CAHILL * ST. PAUL, MINNESOTA

1 cup sugar

1 cup firmly packed brown sugar

1 cup margarine or butter, softened

1 tablespoon molasses

2 teaspoons maple extract

2 eggs

1¾ cups all-purpose flour

2 teaspoons baking powder

1 teaspoon cinnamon

½ teaspoon salt

2 cups rolled oats

2 cups crisp rice cereal

1. Heat oven to 350°F. Grease cookie sheets. In large bowl, beat sugar, brown sugar and margarine until light and fluffy. Add molasses, maple extract and eggs; blend well. Add flour, baking powder, cinnamon and salt; beat at medium speed until well blended. Stir in rolled oats and cereal. Drop by heaping teaspoonfuls 2 inches apart onto greased cookie sheets.

2. Bake at 350°F for 8 to 12 minutes or until light golden brown. Cool 2 minutes; remove from cookie sheets.

Nutrition Information Per Serving: Calories 80 • Total Fat 3g • Sodium 80mg • Total Carbohydrate 13g • Protein 1g.

quick 'n chewy crescent bars

SERVINGS: 4 DOZEN

ISABELLE COLLINS ✷ ELK RIVER, MINNESOTA

- ½ cup all-purpose flour
- 1 cup coconut
- ¾ cup firmly packed brown sugar
- ½ cup chopped pecans
- ¼ cup margarine or butter
- 1 can (8-oz.) refrigerated crescent dinner rolls
- 1 can (14-oz.) sweetened condensed milk (not evaporated)

COCONUT CLUE

A bag of shredded coconut may be stored in the refrigerator for up to 3 weeks. If you don't think you will use the coconut during that time frame, however, you can simply set the bag in a resealable, freezer-proof storage bag, press out as much air as possible and seal the bag. Freeze the coconut for up to 6 months. Coconut that has become dry can be rehydrated with milk.

1. Heat oven to 400°F. In medium bowl, combine flour, coconut, brown sugar and pecans. Using pastry blender or fork, cut in margarine until mixture resembles coarse crumbs. Set aside.

2. Unroll dough into 2 long rectangles. Place in ungreased 15x10x1-inch baking pan; gently press dough to cover bottom of pan. Firmly press perforations to seal. Pour condensed milk evenly over dough to within ½ inch of edges. Sprinkle coconut mixture over condensed milk; press in lightly.

3. Bake at 400°F for 12 to 15 minutes or until deep golden brown. Cool. Cut into bars.

Nutrition Information Per Serving: Calories 80 • Total Fat 4g • Sodium 60mg • Total Carbohydrate 12g • Protein 1g.

banana snack cake

PREP TIME: 10 MINUTES
READY TO SERVE: 45 MINUTES
SERVINGS: 16

- 1 cup sugar
- 1 cup butter or margarine, softened
- 2 eggs
- ½ cup buttermilk
- 1 cup mashed ripe bananas (2 medium)
- 1 teaspoon vanilla
- 2 cups all-purpose flour
- 1 cup quick-cooking oats
- 1½ teaspoons baking soda
- ½ teaspoon salt
- 1 cup semisweet chocolate chips (6 oz.)
- ½ cup chopped nuts

1. Heat oven to 350°F. Grease 13x9-inch pan with shortening or cooking spray. In large bowl, mix sugar, butter and eggs with spoon until combined. Stir in buttermilk, bananas and vanilla until well blended.

2. Stir in flour, oats, baking soda and salt until well combined. Fold in chocolate chips. Spread batter evenly in pan. Sprinkle nuts evenly over top.

3. Bake at 350°F for 30 to 35 minutes or until toothpick inserted in center comes out clean. Serve warm or cool.

Nutrition Information Per Serving: Calories 340 • Total Fat 18g • Saturated Fat 8g • Trans Fat 0.5g • Cholesterol 55mg • Sodium 290mg • Total Carbohydrate 39g • Dietary Fiber 2g • Sugars 20g • Protein 5g. Dietary Exchanges: 1½ Starch • 1 Other Carbohydrate • 3½ Fat.

quick apple cranberry pear muffins

SERVINGS: 18

JOYCE L. BOWMAN ✷ RALEIGH, NORTH CAROLINA

1 package apple cinnamon bread mix

¾ cup buttermilk

3 tablespoons oil

1 egg

1 cup fresh or frozen cranberries, thawed

¾ cup coarsely chopped walnuts

1 large firm pear, peeled, cut into ½-inch pieces

1. Heat oven to 400°F. Line with paper baking cups or grease 18 muffin cups. In large bowl, combine quick bread mix, buttermilk, oil and egg. Stir 50 to 75 strokes with spoon until mix is moistened. Stir in cranberries, walnuts and pear. Spoon batter into paper-lined muffin cups. (Cups will be full.)

2. Bake at 400°F for 18 to 25 minutes or until golden brown. Serve warm or cool.

Nutrition Information Per Serving: Calories 170 • Total Fat 7g • Sodium 125mg • Total Carbohydrate 24g • Protein 3g.

chocolate-dipped peanut butter fingers

chocolate-dipped peanut butter fingers

PREP TIME: 35 MINUTES
READY TO SERVE: 1 HOUR
SERVINGS: 32 COOKIES

* plan ahead

1 roll (18-oz.) refrigerated peanut butter cookies

⅓ cup all-purpose flour

8 oz. sweet baking chocolate, broken into squares

1 tablespoon vegetable oil

Finely chopped peanuts and/or multicolored candy sprinkles

1. Heat oven to 375°F. In large bowl, break up cookie dough. Stir or knead in flour until well blended.

2. Divide dough into 32 equal pieces. Shape each into 2½-inch-long log; place 2 inches apart on ungreased cookie sheets. With knife, make 3 shallow (about ¼-inch-deep) cuts lengthwise in each log.

3. Bake 6 to 8 minutes or until golden brown. Immediately remove from cookie sheets; place on wire racks. Cool completely, about 15 minutes.

4. In microwavable measuring cup, microwave chocolate and oil on High 30 to 60 seconds, stirring every 15 seconds, until smooth. Dip ⅓ of each cookie into chocolate, allowing excess to drip off. Dip into peanuts; return to wire racks. Let stand until chocolate is set before storing.

Nutrition Information Per Serving: Calories 130 • Total Fat 7g • Saturated Fat 2.5g • Trans Fat 0g • Cholesterol 0mg • Sodium 80mg • Total Carbohydrate 15g • Dietary Fiber 0g • Sugars 9g • Protein 2g. Dietary Exchanges: 1 Other Carbohydrate • 1½ Fat.

tangy crescent nut tart

SERVINGS: 12

DEBI WOLF * SALEM, OREGON

1 can (8-oz.) refrigerated crescent dinner rolls

1 cup sugar

¼ cup all-purpose flour

2 to 3 teaspoons grated lemon peel

3 to 4 tablespoons lemon juice

1 teaspoon vanilla

4 eggs

1 cup coconut

1 cup finely chopped hazelnuts (filberts) or walnuts

1 to 2 tablespoons powdered sugar

1. Heat oven to 350°F. Lightly grease 10-inch tart pan with removable bottom. Separate dough into 8 triangles. Place in greased pan; press in bottom and up sides to form crust. Seal perforations. Bake at 350°F for 5 minutes. Cool 5 minutes; gently press sides of warm crust to top of pan.

2. In large bowl, combine sugar, flour, lemon peel, lemon juice, vanilla and eggs; beat 3 minutes at medium speed. Stir in coconut and hazelnuts. Pour filling into partially baked crust.

3. Bake at 350°F for an additional 25 to 30 minutes or until filling is set and crust is golden brown. Cool completely. Sprinkle with powdered sugar. Store in refrigerator.

Nutrition Information Per Serving: Calories 230 • Total Fat 14g • Sodium 180mg • Total Carbohydrate 23g • Protein 5g.

orange-pineapple twister

READY TO SERVE: 10 MINUTES
SERVINGS: 4

* super fast

2 cans (20-oz. each) pineapple chunks in unsweetened juice, chilled, drained

1 pint orange sherbet (2 cups)

½ cup skim milk

1. In blender container or food processor bowl with metal blade, blend pineapple until smooth.

2. Spoon sherbet into container; add milk. Cover; blend until smooth. Serve immediately.

Nutrition Information Per Serving: Calories 300 • Total Fat 2g • Saturated Fat 1g • Cholesterol 5mg • Sodium 55mg • Total Carbohydrate 68g • Dietary Fiber 3g • Sugars 58g • Protein 3g. Dietary Exchanges: 1 Starch • 2 Fruit • 1½ Other Carbohydrate.

frosty choco-banana snacks

READY TO SERVE: 1 HOUR 30 MINUTES
SERVINGS: 5

✳ plan ahead

2   medium bananas

1   teaspoon multicolored
    candy sprinkles

⅓   cup semisweet
    chocolate chips

⅓   cup milk chocolate
    ready-to-spread frosting

1. Cut each banana into 5 chunks.

2. Put the banana chunks, cut side down, on waxed paper-lined plate. Stick a toothpick into each banana chunk. Put the plate in the freezer for about 20 minutes or until the banana chunks are hard.

3. Set the chocolate chips in a small microwavable bowl; microwave on High for 60 to 90 seconds or until melted. Stir until smooth.

4. Add frosting to melted chips; blend well. Microwave the chocolate mixture on High for 15 to 20 seconds or until well combined.

5. Remove the banana chunks from the freezer. Dip each into the chocolate mixture. Spoon some chocolate onto the sides of each chunk. Sprinkle the banana chunks with candy sprinkles. Set bananas on large waxed paper-lined plate.

6. Return the dipped banana chunks to the freezer for 1 hour or until the chocolate and bananas are hard. Serve frozen.

Nutrition Information Per Serving: Calories 190 • Total Fat 8g • Sodium 0mg • Total Carbohydrate 30g • Sugars 23g • Protein 1g. Dietary Exchanges: 1 Fruit • 1 Other Carbohydrate.

KIDS IN THE KITCHEN

Frosty Choco-Banana Snacks are a great treat that children can help prepare. There's no cooking or baking, involved, the directions are simple and the final product is sure to be enjoyed by little and big appetites alike.

Let your tiny helpers get creative by sprinkling the bananas with items other than candy sprinkles. Consider using finely chopped peanuts, shredded coconut, mini candy-coated chocolates or toffee bits.

---

peanutty chocolate candy cookies

READY TO SERVE: 45 MINUTES
SERVINGS: 3 DOZEN

1   box (1-lb. 2.25-oz.)
    chocolate fudge cake mix
    with pudding

½   cup butter or margarine,
    softened

2   eggs

1   bag (14-oz.) candy-coated
    peanut butter pieces

1   cup coarsely chopped salted
    peanuts

1. Heat oven to 350°F. Grease cookie sheets with shortening or cooking spray. In large bowl, beat cake mix, butter and eggs with electric mixer on low speed just until moistened. With spoon, stir in peanut butter pieces and peanuts.

2. Drop dough by rounded tablespoonfuls 2 inches apart onto cookie sheets.

3. Bake 7 to 10 minutes or until edges are set and tops appear dry. Cool 2 minutes; remove from cookie sheets.

Nutrition Information Per Serving: Calories 160 • Total Fat 8g • Saturated Fat 2.5g • Trans Fat 0g • Cholesterol 20mg • Sodium 170mg • Total Carbohydrate 19g • Dietary Fiber 1g • Sugars 13g • Protein 4g. Dietary Exchanges: 1 Starch • 1½ Fat.

peanutty chocolate candy cookies

so-easy sugar cookies

so-easy sugar cookies

SERVINGS: 4 DOZEN

KATHRYN BLACKBURN ✳ NATIONAL PARK, NEW JERSEY

¾ cup sugar

⅓ cup margarine or butter, softened, or shortening

⅓ cup oil

1 tablespoon milk

1 to 2 teaspoons almond extract

1 egg

1½ cups all-purpose flour

1½ teaspoons baking powder

¼ teaspoon salt

1 tablespoon sugar

1. Heat oven to 375°F. In large bowl, beat ¾ cup sugar, margarine, oil, milk, almond extract and egg until light and fluffy. Stir in flour, baking powder and salt; blend well. Spread evenly in ungreased 15x10x1-inch baking pan; sprinkle with 1 tablespoon sugar.

2. Bake at 375°F for 10 to 12 minutes or until light golden brown. Cool 5 minutes. Cut into bars.

Nutrition Information Per Serving: Calories 50 • Total Fat 3g • Sodium 35mg • Total Carbohydrate 6g • Protein 1g.

cherry-chocolate chip cookies

READY TO SERVE: 45 MINUTES
SERVINGS: 20 COOKIES

1 roll (18-oz.) refrigerated oatmeal chocolate chip cookies

¼ cup chopped maraschino cherries, well drained

1 tablespoon all-purpose flour

2 cups Wheaties® cereal, coarsely crushed

1. Heat oven to 350°F. In large bowl, break up cookie dough. Pat cherries dry with paper towels. Stir or knead cherries and flour into dough until well mixed.

2. Drop dough by heaping teaspoonfuls into cereal crumbs; coat well, pressing cereal into dough. Shape into balls; place 2 inches apart on ungreased cookie sheets.

3. Bake 12 to 15 minutes or until golden brown. Immediately remove from cookie sheets.

Nutrition Information Per Serving: Calories 130 • Total Fat 6g • Saturated Fat 2g • Trans Fat 0g • Cholesterol 0mg • Sodium 110mg • Total Carbohydrate 19g • Dietary Fiber 0g • Sugars 10g • Protein 1g. Dietary Exchanges: 1½ Other Carbohydrate • 1 Fat.

double-chocolate chunk cupcakes

PREP TIME: 15 MINUTES
READY TO SERVE: 40 MINUTES
SERVINGS: 1½ DOZEN

2 cups all-purpose flour

½ cup packed brown sugar

¼ cup unsweetened baking cocoa

1 teaspoon baking soda

¼ teaspoon salt

1 cup buttermilk

½ cup butter or margarine, melted

½ teaspoon almond extract

1 egg

½ cup white vanilla baking chips or 3 oz. chopped white chocolate baking bar

½ cup milk chocolate chips

¼ cup chopped slivered almonds

1. Heat oven to 375°F. Line 18 regular-size muffin cups with paper baking cups or grease cups with shortening or cooking spray. In large bowl, mix flour, brown sugar, cocoa, baking soda and salt. Beat in buttermilk, butter, almond extract and egg with electric mixer on medium speed just until dry ingredients are moistened, scraping bowl occasionally.

2. Gently stir in vanilla baking chips, milk chocolate chips and almonds. Divide batter evenly among muffin cups, filling each three-quarters full.

3. Bake 15 to 20 minutes or until toothpick inserted in center comes out clean. Cool 3 minutes; remove from muffin cups. Serve warm or cool.

Nutrition Information Per Serving: Calories 200 • Total Fat 10g • Saturated Fat 4.5g • Trans Fat 0g • Cholesterol 25mg • Sodium 170mg • Total Carbohydrate 24g • Dietary Fiber 1g • Sugars 12g • Protein 3g. Dietary Exchanges: 1 Starch • ½ Other Carbohydrate • 2 Fat.

s'mores nachos

READY TO SERVE: 10 MINUTES
SERVINGS: 4

1. Break each graham cracker into 4 pieces. Put the pieces in a 9-inch pie pan. (Don't use a glass pan as it could break under the broiler.)

2. Sprinkle the chocolate chips and the marshmallows over the graham crackers.

3. Put the pan under the broiler about 6 inches from the heat. Broil for 30 to 60 seconds, until the marshmallows turn puffy and light brown.

Nutrition Information Per Serving: Calories 340 • Total Fat 12g • Sodium 190mg • Total Carbohydrate 55g • Sugars 40g • Protein 4g. Dietary Exchanges: 1 Starch • 2½ Other Carbohydrate • 2 Fat.

8 graham cracker rectangles
¾ cup milk chocolate chips
1½ cups miniature marshmallows

baked apples with granola

READY TO SERVE: 15 MINUTES
SERVINGS: 2

* super fast

1 large crisp apple
1 tablespoon raisins or sweetened dried cranberries
1 tablespoon brown sugar
2 teaspoons butter or margarine
½ cup granola

1. Cut the apple in half and scoop out the seeds and core. Discard the seeds and core, and put an apple half in each of two microwavable bowls.

2. Sprinkle the raisins and brown sugar equally over each of the apple halves. Put 1 teaspoon of butter on top of each apple half. Cover each bowl with plastic wrap, leaving a little of the bowl uncovered.

3. Microwave each apple half on High for 2½ to 3 minutes or until the apple is soft. Carefully remove the plastic wrap. Sprinkle the granola over each apple half.

Nutrition Information Per Serving: Calories 230 • Total Fat 5g • Sodium 90mg • Total Carbohydrate 46g • Sugars 31g • Protein 2g. Dietary Exchange: 1 Fat.

brown sugar shortbread puffs

READY TO SERVE: 1 HOUR
SERVINGS: 4 DOZEN PUFFS

1 cup packed brown sugar
1¼ cups butter, softened
1 teaspoon vanilla
1 egg yolk
2¼ cups all-purpose flour

1. Heat oven to 350°F. In large bowl, beat brown sugar and butter with electric mixer on medium speed until light and fluffy, scraping bowl occasionally. Beat in vanilla and egg yolk until blended. On low speed, beat in flour until mixture forms a smooth dough.

2. Drop dough by rounded teaspoonfuls 2 inches apart onto ungreased cookie sheets.

3. Bake at 350°F for 10 to 15 minutes or until light golden brown and set. Immediately remove from cookie sheets.

Nutrition Information Per Serving: Calories 80 • Total Fat 5g • Saturated Fat 2.5g • Trans Fat 0g • Cholesterol 15mg • Sodium 35mg • Total Carbohydrate 9g • Dietary Fiber 0g • Sugars 4g • Protein 0g. Dietary Exchanges: ½ Other Carbohydrate • 1 Fat.

baked apples with granola

cookie ice cream-a-rounds

apricot pecan biscuit pull-apart

SERVINGS: 12

THELMA ZIEAMMERMANN * NEWTON, KANSAS

- ¾ cup chopped pecans
- ⅔ cup firmly packed brown sugar
- ½ cup chopped dried apricots
- ½ cup butter, melted
- ½ cup dairy sour cream
- 1 teaspoon maple flavor
- 2 cans (12-oz. each) refrigerated buttermilk flaky biscuits

1. Heat oven to 350°F. Grease 12-cup Bundt pan or one-piece 10-inch tube pan. In large bowl, combine all ingredients except biscuits; mix well.

2. Separate dough into 10 biscuits. Cut each biscuit into 4 pieces; place in bowl with pecan mixture. Toss gently to coat. Spoon biscuit mixture into greased pan.

3. Bake at 350°F for 30 to 40 minutes or until deep golden brown. Immediately invert onto serving plate; cool 10 minutes. Serve warm.

Nutrition Information Per Serving: Calories 380 • Total Fat 22g • Sodium 690mg • Total Carbohydrate 41g • Protein 5g.

coffee shop cookies

PREP TIME: 20 MINUTES
READY TO SERVE: 40 MINUTES
SERVINGS: 9 COOKIES

＊plan ahead

- 1 roll (18-oz.) refrigerated sugar cookies
- ⅓ cup packed brown sugar
- 1 teaspoon vanilla
- ¾ cup old-fashioned oats
- ½ cup butterscotch chips
- 2 milk chocolate candy bars (1.55-oz. each), unwrapped, chopped

1. Heat oven to 350°F. Grease 1 large or 2 small cookie sheets with shortening or cooking spray. In large bowl, break up cookie dough. Stir or knead in brown sugar and vanilla until well mixed. Stir or knead in oats, butterscotch chips and chocolate (dough will be stiff).

2. Drop dough by rounded ¼ cupfuls 2 inches apart onto cookie sheets. Flatten each with fingers to ½-inch thickness.

3. Bake 13 to 18 minutes or until cookies are slightly puffed and edges are golden brown. Cool 1 minute; remove from cookie sheets.

Nutrition Information Per Serving: Calories 400 • Total Fat 17g • Saturated Fat 7g • Trans Fat 2.5g • Cholesterol 20mg • Sodium 170mg • Total Carbohydrate 58g • Dietary Fiber 2g • Sugars 37g • Protein 4g. Dietary Exchanges: 1 Starch • 3 Other Carbohydrate • 3 Fat.

cookie ice cream-a-rounds

PREP TIME: 1 HOUR
READY TO SERVE: 4 HOURS
SERVINGS: 9

＊plan ahead

- 1 roll (18-oz.) refrigerated chocolate chip cookies
- ½ cup miniature semisweet chocolate chips or candy sprinkles
- 2¼ cups any flavor ice cream, slightly softened

1. Heat oven to 350°F. Shape cookie dough into 18 balls; place 3 inches apart on ungreased cookie sheets.

2. Bake 10 to 15 minutes or until light golden brown. Cool 1 minute; remove from cookie sheets. Cool completely, about 15 minutes.

3. Meanwhile, cut nine 12x9-inch sheets of plastic wrap or waxed paper. Place chocolate chips in small shallow bowl.

4. For each sandwich, spoon about ¼ cup ice cream onto bottom of 1 cooled cookie. Top with second cookie, bottom side down; press together gently. Roll outer edge of ice cream in chocolate chips. Quickly wrap each sandwich in plastic wrap. Freeze until firm, about 3 hours (for longer storage, place wrapped sandwiches in resealable freezer plastic bag). Let stand 10 minutes before serving.

Nutrition Information Per Serving: Calories 400 • Total Fat 21g • Saturated Fat 8g • Trans Fat 2g • Cholesterol 25mg • Sodium 210mg • Total Carbohydrate 48g • Dietary Fiber 2g • Sugars 31g • Protein 4g. Dietary Exchanges: 1½ Starch • 1½ Other Carbohydrate • 4 Fat.

peanutty rice cake rounds

READY TO SERVE: 20 MINUTES
SERVINGS: 6

* super fast

¼ cup creamy or crunchy
 peanut butter

1 teaspoon honey

3 fresh whole strawberries

24 miniature rice cakes

1. In a small bowl, combine the peanut butter and honey until smooth.

2. Rinse the strawberries and pat dry. Remove the stems and cut each strawberry into 4 round slices.

3. Spread the peanut butter mixture over the rice cakes. Put 1 slice of strawberry on top of 12 of the rice cakes. Take the other 12 rice cakes and stack them, peanut butter side down, on top of the strawberries.

Nutrition Information Per Serving: Calories 100 • Total Fat 6g • Sodium 75mg • Total Carbohydrate 10g • Sugars 2g • Protein 3g. Dietary Exchange: Free.

caramelized apple sundaes

READY TO SERVE: 20 MINUTES
SERVINGS: 4

* super fast

2 medium Granny Smith apples

2 tablespoons butter
 or margarine

½ cup packed brown sugar

¼ cup sweetened dried
 cranberries, if desired

⅛ teaspoon ground cinnamon

¼ cup apple juice

1 pint frozen vanilla yogurt
 or ice cream (2 cups)

1. Peel and core apples. Cut into thin slices; cut each slice in half crosswise. In medium skillet, melt butter over medium heat. Add apples; cook 2 minutes, stirring frequently.

2. Add brown sugar, cranberries, cinnamon and apple juice; cook 6 to 8 minutes or until apples are tender and sauce is desired consistency, stirring occasionally.

3. To serve, spoon frozen yogurt into individual dessert dishes. Spoon apple mixture over frozen yogurt.

Nutrition Information Per Serving: Calories 300 • Total Fat 7g • Saturated Fat 4g • Cholesterol 20mg • Sodium 105mg • Total Carbohydrate 57g • Dietary Fiber 2g • Sugars 51g • Protein 4g. Dietary Exchanges: 1 Starch • 1 Fat • 3 Other Carbohydrate.

coconut lemon crescent bars

SERVINGS: 3 DOZEN

MARILYN BLANKSCHIEN * CLINTONVILLE, WISCONSIN

crust
1 can (8-oz.) refrigerated
 crescent dinner rolls

filling
1 cup sugar

1 cup flaked coconut

2 tablespoons all-purpose flour

½ teaspoon baking powder

½ teaspoon grated lemon peel

¼ teaspoon salt

2 tablespoons lemon juice

2 tablespoons margarine or
 butter, melted

2 eggs, slightly beaten

1. Heat oven to 375°F. Unroll dough into 2 long rectangles. Place in ungreased 13x9-inch pan; press over bottom and ½ inch up sides to form crust. Firmly press perforations to seal. Bake at 375°F for 5 minutes.

2. Meanwhile, in medium bowl, combine all filling ingredients; mix well. Pour over partially baked crust. Return to oven; bake an additional 12 to 17 minutes or until light golden brown. Cool completely. Cut into bars.

Nutrition Information Per Serving: Calories 70 • Total Fat 3g • Sodium 80mg • Total Carbohydrate 9g • Protein 1g.

peanutty rice cake rounds

cinnamon twisties

coconut pecan brownies

SERVINGS: 2 DOZEN

ODDNY CERISANO ✳ HOUSTON, TEXAS

1 package (1 lb. 3.5-oz.) fudge brownie mix

½ cup water

½ cup oil

1 egg

1 can (15-oz.) coconut pecan frosting

1 cup dairy sour cream

½ cup chopped pecans

½ cup miniature semi-sweet chocolate chips

1. Heat oven to 350°F. Grease bottom only of 13x9-inch pan. In large bowl, combine brownie mix, water, oil and egg. Beat 50 strokes by hand. Add pecan frosting and sour cream; mix well. Spread batter in greased pan. Sprinkle pecans and chocolate chips evenly over top.

2. Bake at 350°F for 42 to 52 minutes or until toothpick inserted in center comes out clean. Cool completely. Cut into bars.

Nutrition Information Per Serving: Calories 290 • Total Fat 17g • Sodium 100mg • Total Carbohydrate 31g • Protein 2g.

cinnamon twisties

READY TO SERVE: 30 MINUTES
SERVINGS: 6 (4 TWISTIES EACH)

1 can (8-oz.) refrigerated crescent dinner rolls

1 tablespoon butter or margarine

2 teaspoons cinnamon-sugar blend

1. Heat the oven to 375°F.

2. Lightly spray a cookie sheet with cooking spray. Unroll the dough and seal the perforations. Press into a 12x7-inch rectangle.

3. In a small microwavable bowl, heat the butter on High 5 to 10 seconds until it is melted. Brush the dough with the butter.

4. Sprinkle the cinnamon-sugar blend evenly over the butter on the dough. Using a pizza cutter, cut the dough crosswise into 12 strips that are 7 inches long and 1 inch wide. Next, cut the strips in half crosswise, so they are 3½ inches long. You should now have 24 strips. Twist each strip and put it on a cookie sheet.

5. Bake the strips for 8 to 10 minutes or until golden brown. Remove the cinnamon twisties to a wire rack. Cool for at least 5 minutes before serving.

Nutrition Information Per Serving: Calories 150 • Total Fat 7g • Sodium 470mg • Total Carbohydrate 19g • Sugars 7g • Protein 3g. Dietary Exchange: 1 Starch.

strawberry-rhubarb sundaes

READY TO SERVE: 20 MINUTES
SERVINGS: 6

✳ super fast

2 cups sliced fresh or frozen rhubarb

½ cup sugar

¼ cup water

1 package (10-oz.) frozen strawberries in syrup

6 individual sponge cake cups

1½ pints vanilla frozen yogurt or ice cream (3 cups)

1. In medium saucepan, combine rhubarb, sugar and water; mix well. Bring to a boil. Reduce heat to medium-low; simmer 5 minutes, stirring occasionally.

2. Add strawberries; cook and stir 1 to 2 minutes or until berries are thawed.

3. To serve, place sponge cake cups on individual dessert plates or dish. Place ½ cup frozen yogurt in each cake cup. Spoon about ⅓ cup warm strawberry-rhubarb sauce over each.

Nutrition Information Per Serving: Calories 290 • Total Fat 2g • Saturated Fat 1g • Cholesterol 45mg • Sodium 70mg • Total Carbohydrate 61g • Dietary Fiber 2g • Sugars 52g • Protein 6g. Dietary Exchanges: 1 Skim Milk • 3½ Other Carbohydrate.

peanut butter fudge-topped chippers

READY TO SERVE: 45 MINUTES
SERVINGS: 20 COOKIES

½ cup peanut butter chips

½ cup chocolate whipped
   ready-to-spread frosting

1 package (18-oz.)
   refrigerated ready-to-bake
   chocolate chip cookie
   dough (20 cookies)

1. Heat oven to 350°F.

2. Pour peanut butter chips into a small saucepan. Heat the chips over low heat, stirring regularly until melted. Remove the saucepan from the heat.

3. Stir the frosting into the melted chips. Cool the peanut butter mixture in the saucepan about 10 minutes or until cool enough to handle.

4. Set the cookie dough chunks 2 inches apart on an ungreased cookie sheet. Bake the cookies for 10 to 14 minutes or until golden brown.

5. While the cookies are baking, shape the peanut butter mixture into 20 balls, each about 1 inch around.

6. As soon as the cookies are done, press 1 peanut butter ball into the center of each hot cookie. Let the cookies cool 2 minutes on the sheet before removing.

Nutrition Information Per Serving: Calories 180 • Total Fat 8g • Sodium 110mg • Total Carbohydrate 23g • Sugars 14g • Protein 3g. Dietary Exchanges: 1 Starch • ½ Other Carbohydrate • 1½ Fat.

double-decker malts

READY TO SERVE: 50 MINUTES
SERVINGS: 4

1 pint vanilla ice cream (2 cups)

1 pint chocolate ice cream
   (2 cups)

½ cup malted milk balls

½ cup milk

2 tablespoons malted milk
   powder

   Refrigerated whipped
   cream topping from an
   aerosol can

HAVE IT YOUR WAY

You don't have to use the vanilla and chocolate ice cream flavors called for in this recipe. Feel free to use whatever variety you and your gang enjoy the most. In fact, while you are at it, why not do a little experimenting and try the malts with your favorite candy, too?

1. Put both containers of ice cream in the refrigerator for 30 minutes to soften up the ice cream.

2. Pour the malted milk balls into a plastic bag. Break the milk balls into small pieces with a rolling pin.

3. In a blender, combine the vanilla ice cream and ¼ cup of milk. Blend until the mixture is smooth. Divide the mixture between 4 glasses.

4. Measure out 1 tablespoon smashed malted milk balls. Sprinkle the top of the ice cream mixture with 1 tablespoon of the malted milk balls. Set the glasses in the freezer.

5. In a blender, combine the chocolate ice cream, ¼ cup of milk and malted milk powder. Blend until the mixture is smooth.

6. Take the 4 malts out of the freezer. Spoon the chocolate malt mixture evenly over the malted milk balls in the glasses. Top each serving with about 2 tablespoons whipped cream topping. Sprinkle remaining malted milk balls over each malt.

Nutrition Information Per Serving: Calories 380 • Total Fat 19g • Sodium 160mg • Total Carbohydrate 47g • Protein 7g. Dietary Exchanges: 3 Starch • 3 Fat.

double-decker malts

General Recipe Index